The
Lost Child of
Philomena Lee

A Mother, Her Son and a Fifty-Year Search

MARTIN SIXSMITH

MACMILLAN

First published 2009 by Macmillan
an imprint of Pan Macmillan Ltd
Pan Macmillan, 20 New Wharf Road, London N1 9RR
Basingstoke and Oxford
Associated companies throughout the world
www.panmacmillan.com

ISBN 978-0-230-74427-1

5 7 9 8 6 4

A CIP catalogue record for this book is available from
the British Library.

Typeset by Ellipsis Books Limited, Glasgow
Printed and bound in the UK by CPI Mackays, Chatham ME5 8TD

Acknowledgements

I wish to thank the many people who spoke to me in recorded interviews or over a pint of Guinness and furnished the memories, information and documents that made this book possible. Their stories are the stuff of the pages that follow. I am also grateful to Conor O'Clery, Don Murray, Besty Vriend, Stephen Taylor, Mary Sixsmith, Brian Walsh, Tobias Hoheisel, Jane Libberton, John Cooney and Kit Grover for their generous help with my research and their attentive reading of the text.

Contents

Prologue *1*

PART ONE *3*

PART TWO *95*

PART THREE *195*

PART FOUR *311*

Epilogue *439*

Prologue

The New Year of 2004 had come in. It was getting late and I was thinking of leaving – the party was flat and I was tired – but someone tapped my shoulder. The stranger was about forty-five and a little tipsy. She told me she was married to the brother of a mutual friend, but she wasn't planning to remain so much longer. I smiled politely. She put her hand on my arm and said she had something that might interest me.

'You're a journalist, aren't you?'

'I used to be.'

'You can find things out, can't you?'

'It depends what they are.'

'You have to meet my friend. She has a puzzle she needs you to solve.'

I was intrigued enough to meet the friend in the cafe of the British Library – a financial administrator in her late thirties, smartly dressed with sharp blue eyes and jet-black hair. A family mystery was troubling her. Her mother, Philomena, had drunk too much sherry that Christmas and had broken down in tears. She'd had a secret to tell her family, a secret she'd kept for fifty years . . .

Do we all yearn to be detectives? The conversation in the British Library was the start of a search that lasted five years and led me from London to Ireland and on to the United States. Old photographs, letters and diaries now litter my desk – the hurried, anxious scrawl of an eager housewife, tearful signatures on sad documents and the image of a lost little boy in a blue jumper clutching a toy plane made of tin . . .

Everything that follows is true, or reconstructed to the best of my ability. There were clues to be found and no shortage of evidence. Some of the actors in the story kept diaries or left detailed correspondence; several are still alive and agreed to speak with me; others had confided their version of events to friends. Gaps have been filled, characters extrapolated and incidents surmised. But that's what detective work is all about, isn't it?

PART ONE

ONE

Saturday 5 July 1952;
Sean Ross Abbey, Roscrea, County Tipperary, Ireland

Sister Annunciata cursed the electric. Whenever there was thunder and lightning it flickered so desperate it was worse than the old paraffin lamps. And tonight they needed all the light they could get.

She was trying to run but her feet were catching in her habit and her hands were shaking. Hot water slopped from the enamel bowl onto the stone flags of the darkened corridor. It was all right for the others: all they had to do was pray to the Virgin, but Sister Annunciata was expected to do something practical: the girl was dying and no one had a clue how to save her.

In the makeshift surgery above the chapel, she knelt by the patient and whispered encouragement. The girl responded with a half-smile and something mumbled, incomprehensible. A lightning flash lit up the room. Annunciata pulled up the covers to shield the girl from the blood on the sheets.

Annunciata was barely older than her patient. Both of them were from the country; both from the depths of Limerick. But she was the birth sister and people were expecting her to do something.

In the chapel below, she could hear Mother Barbara gathering the girls, ordering them to pray for the Magdalene upstairs – a sinner like them, who was dying. The disembodied voices sounded distant and harsh. Annunciata squeezed the girl's hand and told her to take no notice. She lifted the patient's white linen gown and wiped her legs with the warm water. The baby was visible now, but it was the child's back she could see, not the head. She had heard about breech births; another hour and she knew mother and baby would both be dead. The fever was setting in.

The patient was flushed, her speech reduced to quick, stumbling phrases: 'Don't let them put him in the ground . . . It's dark down there . . . It's cold down there.' Her blue eyes were wide with panic, her jet-black hair stark against the white pillow.

Sister Annunciata bent down and wiped the girl's brow.

The girl had no idea what was happening to her. She'd had no visitors since she arrived, and that was nearly two months ago. Her father and brother had put her in the nuns' care, and now the nuns were going to let her die.

Annunciata thanked God that it wasn't herself lying there, but she was a practical girl, from a farming family. She gripped the baby's flesh. It was warm and alive. Mother Barbara said sinners deserved no painkillers, and the girl was screaming, screaming for her baby: 'Don't let them bury him . . . They're burying him in the convent . . .'

With her strong fingers – and then with the hard steel forceps – Annunciata pushed and twisted the tiny body. It moved, reluctantly, loath to abandon the sensuous warmth. A gush of pale red liquid spilled onto the white sheet. Annunciata had found the baby's head. Now she was pulling it steadily forward, dragging a new life into God's world.

Sister Annunciata was twenty-three. She had been Annunciata for five years. Before that she had been Mary Kelly, one of the Limerick Kellys, one of seven.

The night the priest came he had sat for a drink and commiserated with old Mr Kelly on the ill luck that had denied him sons. After the third whiskey, he had leaned forward and said quietly, 'Now, Tom. I know you love the girls. And what better could you be doing for them than look after their futures. Surely, Tom, you can spare one of them for God?'

Five years later, here she was – Sister Annunciata, spared for God.

*

For the next few days whenever Annunciata was with the little one she nursed him as if he were her own. It was she who had delivered him, saved him, launched him into the light. He had been christened Anthony at her suggestion and she felt they had a special bond. When he cried, she comforted him; when he was hungry, she longed to feed him.

The boy's mother was called Marcella by the nuns – in here no one was allowed to use their real name. Abandoned by her family, she clung to Annunciata. In turn, Annunciata gave Marcella comfort, reassuring her that she did not condemn her like the other nuns did. Defying the decree of silence, they would find quiet corners in which to exchange the secrets of their past lives. Cupping her hands round Marcella's ear, Annunciata whispered, 'Tell me about the man. Tell me what it was like . . .'

Marcella giggled, but Annunciata leaned in closer, desperate to understand.

'Go on . . . What was he like? Was he handsome?'

Marcella smiled. The few hours she'd spent with John McInerney now seemed like a flash of light in a benighted life. Since her arrival at the abbey she had treasured them, dreamt of them, endlessly reliving the memory of his embrace.

'He was the handsomest man I ever saw. He was tall and dark . . . and his eyes were so gentle and kind. He told me he worked for the Limerick post office.'

With a little encouragement from Annunciata, Marcella told her all about the night her baby was made – when she had still been free and happy, when she had still been Philomena Lee.

The evening had been warm; the lights of the Limerick Carnival, the music from the ceilidh and the smells of candy floss and toffee apples had given it the thrilling feel of adventure. Philomena had locked eyes with the tall young man from the post office who laughed with her and gave her a shot at his beer glass. They had looked at each other with a mixture of wariness and excitement. And then . . . and then . . .

TWO

7 July 1952;
Dublin, Ireland

The summer storms that had hindered Sister Annunciata on the night she delivered little Anthony hadn't been confined to Roscrea. The Irish Republic was modernizing its power systems and in the Dublin suburb of Glasnevin fallen cables meant Joe Coram awoke on Monday morning to a darkened house. A half-hour later, his wife Maire laughed to find him in the gloom, eating a breakfast of untoasted bread and cold tea. Joe laughed too. He was young and strong, still in love with his job, with his wife, his house, with the world in general. He gave Maire a hug, thinking how pretty she looked.

'I'll be late home tonight, Maire – assuming the trams're running. I've this blasted working group on Church–state relations' – he ignored her rolled eyes – 'and it's no secret things are a bit sticky right now.'

Luckily, the trams were OK and Joe Coram got to the office no bother. Within ten minutes, he was beginning to wish he hadn't. His secretary was off sick and a note on his desk informed him that the minister wished to see him *at once*.

Frank Aiken, the Free State's minister for external affairs, was in a foul mood and the whole of Iveagh House was holding its breath. Aiken was a stubborn man who bore a grudge conscientiously – he still had not forgiven former comrades who supported the Treaty back in 1921.

Joe knew what the fuss was about – he ran the department's

policy on passport and visa issues, so he'd been involved in the Russell–Kavanagh affair ever since the story first surfaced six months earlier. In the antechamber of the minister's office, a young private secretary gave Joe the briefest of briefings: 'It's the bloody Jane Russell thing coming back to bite us. Now the foreign papers have got a hold of it. I'd show you the telegram, but Frank has it in with him. You'd better be on your toes.'

Frank Aiken was on his fifth cigarette of the morning when Joe tapped and entered. The desk in front of him was the usual jumble of departmental documents, newspapers and discarded Manila envelopes, and Aiken looked almost comically livid – Joe briefly imagined fumes rising from his bald pate. Barely lifting his eyes from the copy of the *Irish Times* he was scanning, the minister held out the official telegram.

'What's this supposed to mean, Coram? Where have they got all this from? What are we going to do about it, man?'

Joe read it. It was the overnight bulletin from the boys in the Bonn embassy and its first agenda point was a translation of an article in a West German newspaper, a downmarket scandal sheet called *Acht Uhr Blatt*. There was little doubt why the embassy had decided Frank Aiken needed to see it: the headline was 1,000 CHILDREN DISAPPEAR FROM IRELAND.

The paper had unearthed the full story of the Jane Russell affair. It described how the childless Hollywood actress had flown to Ireland to try to adopt a young Irish boy; it gave all the details of her agreement with Michael and Florrie Kavanagh from Galway to take baby Tommy off their hands; suggested that large amounts of money were involved in the deal; and – worst of all – included a frighteningly accurate description of how the Irish legation in London had issued the child a passport to fly to New York with no questions asked. This, said the article, was proof of the Irish government's policy of condoning the export and sale of Irish children: 'Ireland has today become a sort of hunting ground for foreign millionaires who believe they can acquire children to suit their whims in just the same way as they would get valuable pedigree animals. In the last few months hundreds of children have left Ireland, without any official organization being in a position to make any enquiries as to their future habitat.'

Aiken wiped his brow.

'Right', he said. 'What I need from you, Coram, is a thorough brief – no details withheld, however embarrassing. I want every bit of information, every bit of bad practice and every bit of evidence about the archbishop and the Church's malarkey. Is that clear? And I want it by Friday. Off you go!'

The evening's meeting on Church–state relations was fraught. Joe was stuck taking minutes until well after eight o'clock. Most of the cabinet members were there – even Eamon de Valera, the Taoiseach, turned up for a good part of it – and the discussion had become increasingly heated. By the time Joe got back to Glasnevin Maire had made the dinner, seen it go cold and scraped the congealed mess into the bin.

'There's your dinner, Joe Coram.' She laughed. 'Blame it on de Valera or whoever you want to, but there's no remedy for it – you'll have to be happy with the old bread and dripping tonight!'

Joe laughed too and put his arm round Maire's waist. 'I'd live on bread alone and think I was a king so long as I had you, dear,' he said. 'And I'm sorry for your trouble with dinner. Once Frank and Dev got going about the Church and the nuns and the passports, there was no stopping them. I've twenty-five pages of notes that I've to decipher for Wednesday, and then Frank wants a briefing paper on the whole shenanigan, going right back to the Mother and Child fiasco, by the end of the week. I tell you, there'll be a few more late nights before the month is out, Maire dear, and a few more dinners in the bin, no doubt.'

Maire made as if to clout him round the back of the head, but paused mid-swipe and gave him a kiss on the cheek.

'Did you see the *Evening Mail* tonight?' she asked, remembering the mental note she'd made to show him the article about Jane Russell and the allegations from the German press. 'You see people like her in the cinema and you think they must have life easy, don't you? Then you find out she's got her own sorrows just like the rest of us.'

Joe picked up the paper lying on the kitchen table.

'I saw it right enough. Frank made us send out for a copy from the stall in Merrion Street. And Jane Russell's not the only one: we've been handing out passports for these babies like there's no tomorrow. Off to America they go and no one knows what becomes of them.'

Maire looked at her husband and saw he was thinking the same thing she was: they'd been married for three years now and the family were starting to ask questions.

'Never mind Jane Russell,' she said, kissing the back of his neck. 'It's us who need a baby, Joe Coram. So finish that feast you're eating and come and give me a hand to do something about it!'

THREE

11 July 1952;
Roscrea

Affairs of state did not trouble the inhabitants of the convent of Sean Ross Abbey a mile outside the Tipperary town of Roscrea. And neither nuns nor sinners got to see the posters for *His Kind of Girl* starring Jane Russell and Robert Mitchum on the walls of the Roscrea cinema. Neither nuns nor sinners read the newspapers, and Mother Barbara kept the solitary wireless set safely under lock and key. The long days in the laundries, the long nights in the dormitory were filled with thoughts of God, or thoughts of the life that had gone before.

The mother superior was not a woman to be kept waiting. It was 9 a.m. and she had already been to Mass, eaten her frugal breakfast and spent a trying half-hour untangling some unnecessary and potentially embarrassing entries in the abbey's double-entry accounts book. She was looking at the wall clock of her office and tutting when the door knocked and Sister Annunciata rushed in, out of breath and apologizing for turning up late – she so dreaded these weekly meetings that she seemed always to be late for them.

'I'm so sorry, Reverend Mother; it's been a terrible tizzy this morning. We've had three girls in labour overnight – one of them took over seven hours – and there've been five new admissions and—'

Mother Barbara motioned her to be quiet.

'Come in and sit down, Sister. Then you can tell me about it in good time and good order. Do the births first. What is the total for the week?'

'Well, including the three from last night,' Annunciata said, 'I make it seven in total. That's including a breech birth I did last Saturday and—'

'Thank you, Sister. I don't need the details. Any stillbirths to report?'

Mother Barbara was making notes as she spoke, and she looked up to check Annunciata was following her questions properly.

'No, Reverend Mother, thanks be to God. But that breech birth, the girl's in a lot of pain, what with all the tearing, and I'm wondering if I could have the key to the cabinet and give her some painkillers, or get the doctor to stitch her up . . .' She trailed off uncertainly.

Mother Barbara looked at her and smiled.

'Annunciata, I'm sure you're not listening to me, are you? How many times have I told you that pain is the punishment for sin? These girls are sinners: they must pay for what they've done. Now, I don't have all morning. How many admissions in total, and how many departures?'

Annunciata gave her the figures and Mother Barbara entered them in the ledger. After a moment's calculation she raised her head and said, 'One hundred and fifty-two, unless I'm very much mistaken. We have 152 souls lost to God. And very lucky they are to have us to care for them, I would say.'

Annunciata made as if to reply, but Mother Barbara was no longer listening.

'Very well, child. Send me the new arrivals this morning. And I'll see the new mothers this afternoon. Can any of them pay, would you say?'

Sister Annunciata looked doubtful. A hundred pounds was a fierce amount of money.

Mother Barbara saw twelve girls that day. As each girl told her story, she sat patiently with hands clasped before her. She did not think of herself as a cruel woman – the Church enjoined her to charity and the work she did fulfilled that obligation – but she was immensely sure of the boundaries between good and evil, and to her mind the greatest evil without doubt was love of the flesh.

The girls who came to see her stuttered and blushed with the shame of their sins – and Mother Barbara encouraged them to recount those sins in as much detail as they could remember. One after another she heard their stories – the thirty-year-old Dublin shop assistant who fell for the charms of the Englishman who had promised her wealth and marriage but gone back to his wife in Liverpool; the red-headed Cork girl engaged to a car mechanic who disowned her when she fell pregnant; and the mentally retarded teenager from Kerry who cried the whole time and had no idea what had happened to her or why she was here. She listened to the farmer's daughter whose father had always slept in the same bed with her, and to the schoolgirl who had been raped by three cousins at a wedding. And she asked the same, mechanical question she had posed to generations of young women who came to her for help: 'Tell me, girl, was the five minutes of pleasure worth all this?'

Philomena – Marcella, as she was now – was called to Mother Barbara late in the afternoon. It was six days since she had given birth and the breech delivery had left her torn and sore, but her lying-in was over and the rules said she should be back on her feet. She was made to wait in the corridor outside the superioress's office with the other new mothers. The convent banned the girls from talking, but they chivvied each other along with little smiles and grimaces of understanding.

Philomena answered the mother superior's questions in a voice strangled by fear. Asked for her name, she replied, 'Marcella,' but Mother Barbara looked at her with an expression of derision.

'Not your house name, girl; your real name!'

'Philomena, Reverend Mother. Philomena Lee.'

'Place and date of birth?'

'Newcastle West, Reverend Mother, County Limerick. On the twenty-fourth of March 1933.'

'So you were eighteen when you sinned. You were old enough to know better.'

Philomena hardly knew she had sinned at all, but she nodded her head.

'Parents?'

'My mammy's dead, Reverend Mother. From the TB. When I was six. And Daddy's a butcher.'

'So what happened to you children? Did your father keep you?'

'No, Reverend Mother. Mammy left six of us and he couldn't keep us all. So he put me and Kaye and Mary into the convent school, and he kept Ralph and Jack and little Pat at home with him.'

'And what school did you go to, girl?'

'The Sisters of Mercy, Reverend Mother. Mount St Vincent in Limerick City. We were boarders and we only ever got home for two weeks in the summer. We were there twelve years and we never went home for Christmas or Easter, and Daddy and Jack only came a couple of times. It was lonely, Reverend Mother—'

Mother Barbara waved irritably at the black-haired girl in front of her.

'That's enough of that. What happened after you left the sisters?'

'Sure I went to live with my auntie.'

Philomena's voice was barely audible, her sad eyes lowered to the floor.

'And what is her name?'

'Kitty Madden, Reverend Mother, Mammy's sister in Limerick City.'

'How long were you living with your Aunt Madden?'

Philomena frowned and looked up at the ceiling as she tried to muster the facts of her short life.

'Well, I was living with her for about – I left the school in May last year . . . And my auntie's children were all gone away and she wanted me there to help her. And I met him – John – at the carnival in October, so . . .'

But Mother Barbara wasn't interested in this yet.

'Your aunt, girl. What work does she do? Is she rich?'

'Well, I think she is not, Reverend Mother. She works for the nuns at St Mary's. She got me a job there – dusting around, cleaning, that kind of thing . . .'

Mother Barbara, having decided there was little use pursuing financial enquiries, returned to her favourite subject.

'And yet, with all her connections to the Church, your aunt failed to prevent you falling into sin. How can that be? Are you such a wilful sinner that you set out to deceive those who care for your spiritual welfare?'

Philomena blanched and swallowed.

'Oh no, Reverend Mother! I never did set out to sin—'

'So why did you deceive your aunt, then?'

'I did not, indeed. My auntie saw me going off to the carnival – she was with a friend of hers, and she said, "Off you go" – and off I went and . . . and then . . . the thing happened.'

Mother Barbara snorted.

'What do you mean, "the thing", girl? You had no shame when you sinned, so you must have no shame in telling me of it now!'

Philomena thought back to the night at the fair and tried to find a way to make Mother Barbara understand, but her voice caught in her throat.

'He . . . he was handsome, Reverend Mother, and he was nice to me . . .'

'You mean you led him into sin. And did you let him put his hands on you?'

Philomena hesitated again and replied quietly, 'Yes, Reverend Mother, I did.'

Mother Barbara's face darkened, her voice softened.

'And did you enjoy that? Did you enjoy your sin?'

Philomena's eyes were brimming with tears and her words sounded to her as if they came from a great, lonely distance.

'Yes, Reverend Mother.'

'And did you take your knickers off, girl? Tell me that.'

Philomena began to weep.

'Oh, Reverend Mother. Nobody told me about all this. Nobody ever told us about babies. The sisters never told us anything . . .'

Mother Barbara was in a sudden fury.

'Don't dare to blame the sisters!' she shouted. '*You* are the cause of this shame. Your own indecency and your own carnal incontinence!'

Philomena let out a sob. 'But it's not fair!' she wailed. 'Why is my mammy dead and gone? Why does no one care for us? No one puts an arm round us. No one gives us a hug . . .'

Mother Barbara glared at her in disgust.

'Silence, girl! What happened when you returned from the carnival?'

Philomena drew the back of her hand across her eyes and sniffed sharply. She could remember that night easily enough . . .

She had come home well after midnight but found her aunt awake and waiting for her, full of suspicion and reproach. At first she'd laughed and told her aunt not to fuss. Told her nothing had happened: she'd just had a night out with the other girls. But her aunt smelt the beer on her breath and saw the flush in her cheeks. Her questions were insistent, stiffened by retribution if she didn't tell the truth.

In the end, she told.

Yes, she'd met a boy – he was lovely, tall, handsome – but her aunt didn't want to hear. 'And what did you do together? What did you get up to?'

'Nothing, Auntie. He held my hand. He's the finest man in all the world. He'll be waiting for me on Friday on the corner of—'

Her aunt gave her a slap.

'He can wait all he likes, but you're not going out to meet some boy, not while you're living under my roof!'

The girl had felt the pain on her cheek and the tears in her eyes.

'What do you mean, Auntie? I've promised him I'll be there. I love him . . .'

But Auntie was through with love. It had been many years since love had lighted her life and if she had anything to do with it, it was not going to light her niece's.

Philomena was sent to her room and told to stay there until her stupid thoughts had left her, until the stupid boy from the post office had come and waited . . . waited and left.

It was anguish to be locked in her room when she knew the boy was waiting for her.

After ten days, she gave in.

She told her aunt she would never stay out late again; never talk to people outside the girls from her school; above all, never seek to find the boy.

For the next few weeks she had brooded over plots for running away and finding him, but her aunt was watchful. She knew the passions that stirred in a young girl's breast and she made sure her niece stayed at home.

●Then the baby had started to show, and Philomena's surprise and remorse had done nothing to appease her aunt's fury. The Church had told her kissing a man was sinful, but no one told her that was the way babies were made.

'And what did your aunt do?' Mother Barbara broke in.

Philomena shook herself from the memories of those terrible weeks.

'Well, Reverend Mother, she rang my brother Jack and my dad. And I think she wanted to marry my dad too, because he was on his own and she was on her own. But Da wasn't having any of it. Then she got me up to the doctor's in Limerick and he said I had to go to Roscrea. So I came here two months ago. I left school last year, so I was only a year out of freedom.'

Mother Barbara waved her hand.

'What did your father say? I see he hasn't come to visit you here.'

The question was deliberately hurtful; Philomena bit her lip.

'My da was sad for me, Reverend Mother, I'm sure he was. But he couldn't tell anyone about me, not even the family. Kaye and Mary think I've gone away to England. And now I miss my mammy and I miss being at home . . .'

The utter loneliness of all the hundreds of girls in that place, and others like it across Ireland, was etched on Philomena's face. Sent away for a sin they barely knew they had committed, they were in many cases mere children subjected to cruel, adult punishment.

Mother Barbara noted the girl's story in her ledger and brought the interview to a close.

'Now, Marcella, you must go back to the dormitory. This is not a holiday home and we expect you to work hard. You must stay here and pay for your sins. The only way out is the hundred pounds. Do you think your family will pay the hundred pounds?'

Philomena looked blankly at the mother superior.

'I do not know, Reverend Mother. But if my da has not paid any money, then I think it means he does not have it.'

FOUR

Roscrea

In the weeks that followed Anthony's birth, Philomena began to see the true face of life in Sean Ross Abbey and it was not a happy one.

Like the majority of Ireland's homes for unmarried mothers, it was attached to a much older convent. When it was taken over by the Sisters of the Sacred Hearts of Jesus and Mary in 1931, Sean Ross occupied an imposing Georgian mansion with extensive lawns and a walled garden. The remains of a medieval monastery still stood in the grounds and a small, neat graveyard contained the last resting place of a handful of nuns; the mothers and babies who died here were buried in unmarked graves in an adjacent field tended by no one.

Next to the convent – but to all intents a separate universe – was another, darker building, all harsh lines and plain grey concrete. The Church's vision of where sinful women should dwell did not extend to considerations of comfort or beauty. At its heart were the dormitories, one for expectant mothers, one for the newly delivered, and further rooms for those whose children were being raised in the adjoining nurseries.

Like her fellows, Philomena was destined to progress through these dormitories, one among scores of girls billeted for three years on iron-framed single beds ranged under long cream-painted walls, starched white spreads on their mattresses and statues of Our Lady above their heads. A square window at each end of the room was placed high in the wall; even when the sun shone bright, the place remained in shadow.

The girls gave up their own clothes on the day they arrived at Sean Ross Abbey. For the rest of their time there they wore coarse denim uniforms, loose and smock-like to disguise the swollen stomachs that were the shameful manifestation of their sin. They were given heavy wooden clogs that cut their feet. Their hair was cropped to avoid nits and their heads covered with crocheted skullcaps. Philomena had worn her black hair in a dramatic side parting with the ends curled under her delicate shapely chin, but now it was cut short and spiky like everyone else's.

The girls were forbidden to talk among themselves and told not to reveal their real identities or even where they came from. Their lives here were cloaked in secrecy, loneliness and shame. They had, as everyone said, been 'put away' to spare their families and society. Few if any received visits from relatives; the fathers of their babies never came.

The dormitories sprang into life each morning at six when lay staff flicked on the lights and shouted the girls out of bed. Those who did not respond found the blankets ripped off them and strong hands shaking their shoulders. They were taken to the nursery to tend their babies and then to eight o'clock Mass, a hundred silent waifs, pregnant or newly delivered, shuffling down darkened corridors to the convent chapel. Each morning one or more would faint during Communion, something regarded as deliberate insubordination deserving punishment.

After Mass the girls were set to work. They were assigned to one of three jobs: preparing meals in the convent kitchen, looking after the babies and young children in the nurseries or working in the abbey's laundries. The kitchens were the most sought after – the work was hard and the hours long, but the girls could supplement their meagre rations by filching scraps. The girls who worked in the nurseries were supervised by nursing sisters in their long white robes and by lay staff the sisters employed. They worked day and night, washing and changing the babies and making sure they were fed by their mothers. To save on baby food the nuns insisted mothers should breast-feed for at least a year, and usually longer.

The laundries were the least popular assignment – and the one Philomena was chosen for. Every day after Mass she would walk with the other laundry girls to the hot, dark rooms where vats of water boiled on coke fires and weary, sweating women brought piles of sheets, nuns' habits and inmates' uniforms to be thrown into the bubbling water. For hours at a time they stirred the steaming vats with wooden poles and worked the wet linen with hands that became raw and covered in sores.

The sisters took in laundry from the town of Roscrea and surrounding villages, hospitals and state boarding schools. Few of those who sent their washing to Sean Ross could have imagined the hellish conditions in which it was done. The nuns told the girls their scrubbing, wringing and ironing symbolized the cleansing of the moral stain on their souls, but they were also profitable for the convent: the Church may have been saving souls, but it was not averse to making money.

The morning shift in the laundry lasted until a short lunch break, when the mothers were allowed to see their children. Another shift followed and evenings were spent in cleaning and chores around the building. The hour after dinner was set aside for knitting and sewing. The girls had to make the clothes their children wore, and many became accomplished seamstresses. There were no radios or books, but the girls were allowed to sit in the nursery with their babies or in the day room with those who were already toddlers. It was this hour – the time they looked forward to most – which brought the girls close to their children and established the bond that would haunt mother and child for the rest of their lives. To allow such love to blossom seemed crueller even than taking the babies away at birth.

FIVE

Dublin

While Philomena Lee was toiling in the laundries of Sean Ross Abbey, the Irish government was waking up to a problem it had long tried to ignore.

In that interminably hot summer of 1952, Anthony Lee was just one baby among hosts of others in the Republic's mother-and-baby homes, which for the most part were bursting at the seams. When Joe Coram researched the figures to give to his minister, he calculated that more than 4,000 illegitimate children from all corners of the country were in the care of the Church and there was little prospect of the number going down.

Frank Aiken was not relishing the battle that lay ahead. The morning after the Jane Russell story, he had acted – belatedly – to protect his department's interests. He told the Dáil that newspaper reports 'were not correct in stating that the passport was granted to enable the child to be adopted in the United States' – he knew this to be misleading, but there was nothing else for it. Miss Russell, he said, had told the consulate she was merely taking little Tommy with her for a three-month holiday. But at the same time he dictated an urgent telegram to all Irish legations and embassies, instructing them to refer to the department all future passport applications for children under the age of eighteen. 'The whole business regarding the recent granting of a passport to an infant brought to the United

States by an American film actress,' the telegram concluded, 'received a great amount of undesirable publicity. The reason for this instruction is that we wish to ensure an Irish passport will not again be issued in such circumstances.'

The following morning Joe Coram settled down to write the policy briefing Aiken had demanded from him. He was conscious of the issues at stake and the sensitivities of those involved: the government had allowed the Catholic Church free rein in handling the nation's illegitimate children, partly because it was ill equipped to deal with the problem itself and partly because Eamon de Valera depended heavily on the support of the archbishop of Dublin, John Charles McQuaid. But Joe still had some of his youthful idealism and his briefing was a chance to get the minister to do something about a national scandal.

'There is a market for children in the USA,' Joe wrote:

And among certain Americans Ireland enjoys quite a reputation as a place where one can get children for adoption without much difficulty.

We have seen over the past few years the emergence of a veritable trade in babies heading west over the Atlantic. There is nothing to stop anyone coming into this country and taking away children for adoption.

The situation in large part stems from the stance of the Roman Catholic Hierarchy. As you know, the Government has been trying to enact an Adoption Bill to introduce state control over adoption policy. But its efforts have foundered on the opposition of the Hierarchy, who regard the Church's mother-and-baby homes as a convenient way to make the problem – and the woman – disappear.

The Church's financial stake is substantial. The nuns receive payment from the adopting parents, particularly those from the USA, and few checks are made on the suitability of the homes they are sent to. The Jane Russell case is the tip of a rather large iceberg.

One check that is always made by the Church authorities is on the religious standing of the adopting family. These are the relevant passages from Archbishop McQuaid's directive:

'The following are the conditions required by His Grace the Archbishop before he allows the adoption of a Catholic child by an American or other foreign family:
1. *The prospective adopting parents must have a written recommendation from the Director of Catholic Charities in the diocese in which they live . . . and from the Priest of their parish.*
2. *The prospective adopting parents must submit medical certificates stating . . . that they are not deliberately shirking natural parenthood.*
3. *The prospective adopting parents must swear an affidavit to rear the adopted child as a Catholic, and to educate the adopted child during the whole of its schooling in Catholic schools.'*

You will note there is no check on the adopters' suitability to have the child; the only criterion is religious fidelity. And yet the DoEA has accepted the McQuaid rules as 'very satisfactory' and we issue passports to each and every child the Archbishop tells us to. The DoEA has no control; we lack the most basic information, and the Government has been unwilling to confront the Hierarchy on the matter.

We are now seeing a rampant trade in the buying and selling of Irish babies and although we have kept it relatively secret so far, it would be hard to defend were the full extent of it to be made public.

SIX

Roscrea

Young Anthony Lee suffered no lasting damage from the mauling he had taken at the hands of Sister Annunciata. The swollen purple bruises on his head were the only souvenirs of his savage birth. The doctor who called three days later laughed and called him 'a sugar-bun loaf baby'. Anthony was left with a strikingly high forehead – a legacy of the forceps, but a portent too of the ferocious intelligence that would mark him out in life and ultimately help decide his destiny.

His first acquaintance with life was not unhappy. As his mother sweated under the burdens of guilt and steaming laundry, Anthony was surrounded by a universe unexpectedly tender in its treatment of him.

Even in the convent of Sean Ross Abbey, where the sisters communed with a demanding deity and fallen women laboured to expiate their sins, where frustration, regret and cruelty abounded in equal measures, Anthony luxuriated in tenderness and feminine affection. The sunshine of the nursery and the convent garden lit his world; the long high ceilings of the children's dormitory provided its reassuring boundaries. Two rows of cribs – tall and narrow for the newborns, wider and sturdier for the older ones – ran the length of his universe. Nuns in white habits walked among them, brushing the side of his cot with the soft rustle of cloth impregnated with incense.

One wall of the children's nursery was floor-to-ceiling windows overlooking the convent grounds, so light poured in from early morning. In the exceptionally bright days of July and August 1952 the French windows were opened and the baby cribs wheeled onto the concrete flags of the terrace, sunlight and fresh air the best protection against TB and rickets. Later, when winter came, the windows would be sealed with adhesive tape and the odour of mild disinfectant would permeate the room. The smells of long-boiled vegetables drifted in from the communal cookhouse that prepared food for nuns and sinners alike.

The girls were never permitted to leave the abbey and were allowed into the convent grounds only when pressed into gardening duties. Pregnant or otherwise, they scrubbed the floors of the abbey, washed windows and dusted and polished daily. Those who worked on stringing rosaries were given a minimum of sixty decades to complete every day. The taut wire of the beads wore a groove in their fingers that would stay with them for life.

After the initial lying-in period, babies were taken away to the children's nursery. But from shared flesh and nine months' intimacy there stems a mother–child intuition, and whenever Anthony cried in the night nursery, Philomena, on the other side of the convent, woke.

Sister Annunciata was Philomena's comfort. They sang together in the choir. They poured the emotions they were forbidden to express into the sacred music. The joy of singing brought the two women close. In snatched quiet moments together, Philomena whispered her hopes for a future with John McInerney, the man she yearned to tell about the wonder of their child. She told Sister Annunciata how much she loved her son and Annunciata hugged her like a sister. In the evening, when the girls were allowed to be with their babies, Annunciata sat with her and played with Anthony. She loved the way she could make him laugh – a gurgling chortle that seemed out of all proportion to his tiny frame – by nuzzling her nose into the pink softness of his tummy. Philomena would lift him up in the air and kiss him on the cheek until he squealed with delight. When he fell asleep, they would take turns putting him into the cot and tucking the blanket round his shoulders. Then they sat and whispered about the day's events and the other girls in the convent. One evening Philomena told

Annunciata she had something to ask her, something that had been worrying her for a while.

'You know, Sister, the girl from Sligo – the fat one with the red hair – do you know what she told me? Well, she said we all must stay here in the abbey and none of us ever gets to keep our babies. Now that's nonsense isn't it, Sister? How can anyone ever take a baby from its mammy? And Anthony so beautiful and all, isn't he?'

Annunciata looked down and was silent: she had no idea how Philomena could be so naive.

Philomena tried to lighten the moment. 'He is beautiful, isn't he, Sister? And you love him too, sure you do.'

But Annunciata was not responding and Philomena felt a panic in the pit of her stomach.

'Sister, please tell me it's not true . . .'

SEVEN

Drumcondra

Joe Coram and Frank Aiken were still debating as the black Humber Hawk pulled out of the courtyard of Iveagh House and onto St Stephen's Green. The audience in Drumcondra had been granted somewhat unwillingly, Joe felt, but he was pleased Frank had insisted. Joe knew his boss was caught between Scylla and Charybdis on this one, and he was subtly trying to steer him onto his own preferred set of rocks.

'Our problem is we've let the Church do what they like for too long, Frank. The nuns think those babies are their own property and the poor girls have been so browbeaten into believing they are sinners that they do whatever the nuns say. Half the time, the mother superior packs the child off without even telling the mother. No consultation, no consent, no goodbyes. At least the Adoption Act would stop kids being sent abroad without the mother's written agreement. Not much, but it'd be a start.'

From his corner of the back seat, Frank Aiken said nothing. The car drove slowly along O'Connell Street and north towards Croke Park.

Joe continued to stoke his boss's anger: 'The state's complicit, Frank. We've just presumed the availability and suitability of the mother-and-baby homes as a means of solving the problem. But those homes operate outside our regulation. Public funds keep the system functioning, but the Church alone has authority over it and access to its revenues.'

Joe could see Aiken was nodding and decided to risk an argument he had previously considered too inflammatory.

'And to be frank, it has always suited us not to upset the hierarchy. It's cowardice at the root of the thing. If the politicians were to take on McQuaid, who knows what he would tell the priests to put in their sermons? If every priest from Cork to Donegal started preaching against the government, what would that do to its chances of re-election? De Valera knows it well enough – that's why he's thick as thieves with them. Whatever you say to McQuaid tonight, the system suits too many people. Every child sent to America is a donation more for the Church and a problem less for the state. Everyone's got a stake in keeping things the way they are.'

They were already in Drumcondra and pulling up the tree-lined drive to the archbishop's palace when Aiken finally grunted, 'So everyone's happy except us, is that it? Everyone wins except the poor old Department of External Affairs? And we get pilloried for issuing bloody passports? Well, we'll see about that.'

At five to seven – a full twenty-five minutes after the meeting was scheduled to begin – a stocky priest in a smartly pressed soutane opened the door to the antechamber.

'The archbishop will see you now, gentlemen. Follow me, please.'

Father Cecil Barrett, head of the Catholic Social Welfare Bureau and McQuaid's adviser on family policy, ushered them into the archbishop's study and motioned them to approach the silhouetted figure sitting behind a large mahogany desk in the corner of the dimly lit room. John Charles McQuaid looked up from the document he was studying and proffered his ring on the fourth finger of a languidly drooping left hand. Frank Aiken stepped forward and kissed it. Much to his own surprise, Joe Coram did likewise.

McQuaid in the flesh was slight of frame and remarkably diffident. When he rose to join them at the round baize-covered table, his visitors saw the stoop of his shoulders and the sallow skin of his emaciated cheeks. His fifty-seven years seemed to weigh on him. He had been archbishop for twelve years now and had consolidated his stranglehold on power by a skilful courting of the country's politicians. Eamon de Valera had fallen under his spell to the extent that McQuaid had been invited to vet the Irish constitution before it was made public: the 'special position of the Catholic Church in the Irish State', no divorce and no abortion, and the Church's 'special responsibility' for schools and hospitals were all provisions that came from McQuaid's pen.

In return, the hierarchy had supported de Valera through thick and thin. Frank Aiken knew there was nothing to be gained from attacking the archbishop.

'I thank you for receiving us, Your Grace,' he began. 'I know you are a busy man, but I believe we may have a shared interest in reviewing the recent unfortunate publicity regarding certain aspects of this country's adoption policy which is potentially detrimental to the standing of both Church and government . . .'

McQuaid raised an eyebrow.

'I can see, Minister, that the affair is detrimental to your department. I am not sure the standing of the Holy Church is any way diminished by the fact that the DoEA is criticized for its lack of . . . *circumspection*.'

Frank Aiken shifted on his seat and glanced at Joe Coram.

'Indeed, Your Grace. We have, as you say, been chastised. I am pleased to report that measures have been taken. Nonetheless, the fact that the Church is responsible for—'

McQuaid interrupted.

'Minister, if you will allow me. I believe the measures *I* have taken will go a long way towards resolving the problem you speak of. As soon as those unfortunate reports appeared I spoke privately to the Taoiseach and, following our conversation, the management of Shannon Airport and the chairman of the Pan Am airline were instructed to close down on any publicity regarding the transport of children to America. I am pleased to say that Father Barrett has received written confirmation that they will respect our request. I trust you agree this is a satisfactory outcome?'

Aiken grunted and was about to concur, but Joe Coram nudged his ankle.

'Your Grace,' Aiken said, 'that is welcome news. Preventing unhelpful press speculation is an important goal. But my department has concerns touching more than just, shall we say, the presentational aspects. As you know, this government has been negotiating to introduce legislation governing the way the adoption system itself is run. My department believes the case of the child Tommy Kavanagh highlights an inherent difficulty in the way children are placed – by the Church authorities – with adoptive parents abroad.'

McQuaid looked at him steadily and asked in an even, friendly tone, 'I do not suppose, Minister, that you are proposing changes to the Church's authority over adoption policy? It does not seem to me that the state, with its own lack of facilities for tackling the orphan problem, is in any position to take the responsibility on itself . . .'

Aiken seemed uncertain how to proceed. Joe Coram passed him a handwritten note. Frank scanned it and coughed.

'Your Grace. The scale of the orphan problem in our country is large and the efforts of the Catholic Church to cope with it are appreciated. Nonetheless, we believe in the second half of the twentieth century there may be some scope for dealing with this as a social rather than, shall we say, a moral issue. It seems to us there may no longer be such a pressing need for women who conceive out of wedlock to be cloistered away, and that some element of social support, a welfare programme backed by the state, may allow many of them to keep their child and bring it up in the community. Such a scheme has been introduced in England . . .'

The Archbishop smiled at his visitors as a parent may smile at an errant child.

'Minister, you underestimate both the size and the nature of the problem. Illegitimacy is in its very essence a moral issue, and the Church would fail in its duty to God if it allowed this to be overlooked. I take it you have read Father Barrett's book on the subject, which was published last month? Father Barrett . . .' The Archbishop motioned for his adviser to step forward. 'Do please present these gentlemen with a copy of your work.'

Cecil Barrett bowed his head slightly and handed Frank Aiken a slim volume with the words 'Adoption: the parent, the child, the home' in blue letters on a pink cover.

'If I may perhaps indicate the relevant passages . . .' Barrett leaned over and opened the book. 'You will see there is compelling evidence that women who allow themselves to produce such children are in the vast majority of cases grave sinners with severe moral problems. There is scientific data showing that the offspring of fallen women are fated to become rebels and to suffer from complexes analogous to those of certain invalids. This is scientific evidence. Such offspring are destined for suffering and often for failure. No material or social assistance, such as you propose, would be of any use to such people unless and until the rents in the mother's spiritual fabric have been repaired. Sinful mothers are unfit to have custody of their own children. Therefore it would be cruelty to both to leave them together.'

Frank Aiken was not a man who enjoyed being lectured. His response now was brisk.

'Gentlemen, I thank you for your exposition of the hierarchy's position. I would like to explain why I am reluctant to accept it. For a start, there is the financial side of the thing.'

Aiken shuffled through a bundle of papers and pulled out Joe's briefing.

'Your Grace. Here we are. Our figures show there are currently more than 4,000 children in Catholic mother-and-baby homes. When women go to the sisters, they sign away their baby and three years of their life. Are we agreed on that? After the baby is born, they stay there and work for the nuns – laundry work, labouring in the fields, commercial glasshouses, cooking and catering, producing rosary beads – and the Church keeps the profits.'

Aiken scanned the faces of the clerics.

'And that is in addition to what the state pays you for every single inmate. A sum which currently stands, I believe, at one pound per mother and two shillings and sixpence per child per week. Quite a nice source of income for the Church. Now, the only way a woman can avoid the three years of labour is if her family pay a hundred pounds directly to the mother superior, in which case I believe she can get out a week after the baby is born. But in either event the key provision is that *she cannot keep her baby*. Am I correct?'

McQuaid and Barrett made as if to interject, but Aiken was in full flow.

'And what happens to the babies after their mother is gone? I understand the sisters have sold thousands of them to Americans about whom we know nothing, who could be murdering the little things for all we know. And those left behind? Well, you've blocked the adoption legislation, so they go to our wonderful orphanages, or our lovely, caring industrial schools. And all of those are run by the Church, of course, so we carry on paying you! The state has no control over what the brothers and the sisters do to them – and they don't treat them with kid gloves, that's for sure. Half of them come out so damaged they spend the rest of their lives trying to recover from it . . . or they turn into thugs and criminals themselves.'

Frank Aiken was in his stride now and vaguely conscious he had gone farther than he intended. The archbishop was not a man to be crossed and Aiken was expecting a rebuke, but to his surprise McQuaid replied in a voice that trembled with emotion.

'Minister, I beg your pardon. You accuse me of putting our children in danger. This is not fair. I love these children, Minister. I *love* them.'

And with that he rose to his feet, gathered his silken robes and strode out of the room.

EIGHT

Roscrea

Anthony Lee was growing into the world. His mother doted on him and Sister Annunciata brought him surreptitious treats – little toys and rattles, sugar biscuits and rusks. The faces of those who leaned over his bed to tuck him up at night were friendly, and Anthony learned early on that he could be a powerful generator of affection. He responded to the love of others with smiles of his own; he found life an easy art. The suffering and cruelty that swirled through Sean Ross Abbey, the pretence, the anonymity, the cowed silence and frustrated anger meant nothing to him.

Philomena Lee found it less easy to make friends. Like all the girls there, her abiding feeling in a world full of silence and secrecy was one of loneliness. Now that she knew what lay ahead, now that Sister Annunciata had confirmed the inevitable separation, she grew even more attached to her son. In the evening she was loath to leave him; she pleaded with the nursing sisters and the lay staff to be given more time before he was taken away to the night nursery. Every parting became a rehearsal for the final parting.

One winter evening early in 1953 Philomena returned from the laundry to find Anthony gripped by colic: the spasms of pain were twisting his little body this way and that. She spent the knitting hour and her own dinner time walking him up and down the long corridor, trying to ease his distress, but her baby screamed inconsolably. She was young, with no experience of infantile disorders, and she panicked. She convinced herself Anthony was seriously sick. When the night sister came to take him from her, she told her how worried she was and asked if she could keep him overnight.

'Just this once, Sister. Just while he's sick. He needs me to be with him. He'll never sleep if I'm not there, and I'll never sleep if I don't have him.'

But the sister told her not to be so stupid.

'It's not for you girls to say what happens to the children. They no more belong to you than the sun or the moon. Your job is to feed them and work your three years. Then we'll find them proper mothers who deserve to have children.'

Philomena listened with growing alarm. It appeared to her that Anthony – her world, her only joy – was in danger. She wrapped him in her arms and fled. Her heavy wooden clogs clattering on the flag-stones brought nuns and girls running as the sister caught up with her by the locked door at the end of the corridor. Both women were panting and Philomena was weeping, but the nun showed no pity. Taking Anthony from her, she laid him on the floor and beat Philomena with hard, practised fists. Philomena slumped to the ground, sobbing as the nun picked up her baby.

'Do that one more time and your next stop is the asylum,' the nun spat. 'You won't like it in there, take it from me; and you can be sure you'll *never* get out!'

The nun walked off. Philomena lay there until a tentative hand rubbed her shoulder and a gentle voice whispered in her ear. She could barely make out the girl's face, but she felt her arm around her. The girl lifted her from the floor and helped her to the mothers' dormitory, laid her on her bed and tucked up the blanket. She said her house name was Nancy and she would come in the morning to see how Philomena was doing.

Nancy was two years younger than Philomena, a quiet, stocky girl with a round face and dark eyes. She eased Philomena out of bed and supported her down to Mass; she took her arm as they walked over the courtyard to the laundries; and she helped her through a day's work made unbearable by the bruises that covered her body. In the evening they talked. Both of them were lonely and scared, both looking for a friend, and the drama of their meeting drew them close. They ignored the ban on real names, ignored the ban on speaking about the past and told each other everything. Nancy said she was really Margaret McDonald, that she came from Dublin and had a newborn daughter called Mary. She had concealed her pregnancy from her family, given birth in the Coombe Hospital and been put away in Sean Ross Abbey immediately after.

'And you know, Phil,' she said, 'no one has come to see me at all. Not a one since the day I came here. I know it's a terrible thing I've done and I know my da's ashamed of me, but sure I thought my mammy would come; I thought she'd come and see her lovely beautiful grand-babby . . .'

It was Philomena's turn to offer comfort.

'Now, Margaret, don't upset yourself,' she said, holding her friend's hand between hers. 'Our parents all have their own troubles and they can't be thinking of us all the time. We're grown up now: we've got the babies to prove it, sure we have.' Philomena smiled ruefully. 'So we've got to get on with it and not complain about things. You know how Mother Barbara hates moaners.'

Margaret nodded. She too had suffered at the hands of the mother superior.

'Sure you're right. I know that. But I miss my friends and I miss my brothers and sisters. And then I get to thinking how all alone we are in the world and sometimes I just get so unhappy I wish I could die . . .'

Margaret broke off with tears welling in her eyes. Philomena put her arm round her friend and pulled her close. She told her she was not alone; told her how everyone in that place felt the same loneliness and the same despair, however much they put a brave face on it. And she told her they both should count God's blessings: their children were fine and healthy and both of them the most beautiful babbies anyone ever had seen.

*

Margaret's little Mary was six months younger than Anthony, a striking baby with auburn hair and a small, finely chiselled face. Philomena admired her, and Margaret admired Anthony's dark good looks. They sat and knitted together most evenings – jumpers for Anthony, fluffy cardigans for Mary – and they placed their children side by side so that when they woke in their cots the first thing they saw was each other. As the little ones grew and began to crawl, they played on the same rug, bumping into each other and laughing delightedly at the touch of another tiny being. Anthony, slightly older and more advanced, taught Mary to crawl and play. There was affection between the babies, and they brought joy to their parents, but sorrow was never far away.

Young mothers would often come in from their day's work to find their baby's cot empty. Departures were rarely signalled in advance. In some cases the girl would act as if all was well and she was looking forward finally to being released from the convent; more frequently she would be overcome by the anguish of her bereavement, premature, irrevocable and brooking no appeal.

Philomena and Margaret shuddered every time a baby disappeared. But they also had a tale of hope, to which they clung with the desperation of the condemned. One girl had managed to 'escape' from Roscrea and her story had entered the mythology of the place. With the help of relatives she had found a job as a maid to a wealthy Dublin lady who agreed to accommodate both her and her child. The nuns had seemingly been pressured into letting her take the boy with her and she had been free for six months. Then, to the sorrow of those still in the abbey, she returned. The experiment had failed: the girl was sent back and two months later her baby disappeared like all the others. Despite its outcome, the story was cited as proof that there was after all a possibility they would keep their babies. Philomena and Margaret were frantically determined to do so.

NINE

Dublin

A week after the audience in Drumcondra, Frank Aiken came back from a meeting with the Taoiseach in a foul mood. When Joe asked how things had gone, he grunted and slammed his office door. It was an hour before he asked for Coram to be sent in.

'Well, that's it, lad. We're well and truly done for. Dev says he's not going against the archbishop, and if the Church wants to send our babies to the Sahara Desert, then they can just go ahead and do it. McQuaid's been on the phone telling him he doesn't want the Adoption Bill and Dev says we can try what we like, but he's not going to back us unless His Grace has a Pauline conversion on the road to Maynooth.'

Joe Coram had been expecting something similar, but even he was surprised by the vigorousness of de Valera's hand-washing.

'So did the Taoiseach say what we should do? Just go on issuing passports to any child McQuaid wants sent abroad?'

Aiken stood up and paced the room.

'That's the measure of it. I tried everything, but he keeps harking back to the bloody Mother and Baby Scheme and what that did to the last government.'

Three years earlier, a short-lived opposition government had attempted to introduce the Mother and Baby Bill, offering free medical treatment and advice for all expectant mothers. The then health minister, Noel Browne, had promoted the scheme on the grounds it would bring Ireland into line with other civilized nations. But Archbishop McQuaid had railed against it, saying it would encourage single mothers and illegitimate births, allow state interference in moral issues (the preserve of the Church) and 'usher socialism into Ireland by the back door'. The rhetoric had grown so heated and opposing positions so entrenched that the issue became a trial of strength between Church and state. McQuaid had denounced Browne's proposals as 'totalitarianism' and had written the Vatican that it was 'an attack on the Church under the guise of social reform'. Browne was summoned before an inquisitional court of bishops which read him a formal statement saying his scheme was contrary to Catholic social teaching. He had been forced to resign in April 1951 and the collapse of his scheme had brought down the government two months later.

In his resignation speech Taoiseach John Costello had acknowledged, 'As a Catholic, I obey my Church authorities and will continue to do so. All of us in the government . . . are bound to give obedience to the rulings of our Church and our hierarchy.'

Joe Coram had been a middle-ranking official in the Department of External Affairs at the time of the row. In December 1949 Browne had sent a formal note to the department, querying the lack of safeguards for the children being exported by the Church to America. 'There is no means of knowing,' he wrote, 'that those adopting are suitable persons . . . or if they may be persons already turned down as adopters in their own country.' He asked the DoEA for an assurance that 'the fate of children sent to the United States will be protected'.

Joe replied, promising to look into Browne's concerns, but found the subject blocked by senior DoEA officials. A departmental memo advised against replying to the minister 'until the Archbishop has arrived at his policy' adding, 'Our policy should be to keep out of this as much as possible.' Disappointed by the pusillanimity of his superiors and alarmed by the dangers Irish children were being exposed to, Joe had contacted Noel Browne privately to express his personal support and the two men had become friends.

'The hierarchy are the factual instrument of government on social and economic policies,' Browne had told Joe. 'Our prospects for the preservation of effective cabinet government and for badly needed reforms are utterly gone.' In a series of bitter conversations Browne had expressed his loathing for McQuaid and had shared his suspicions about one specific, 'unnatural' facet of the man's character. Joe had listened and absorbed everything the former minister told him. Now he was going to use this information to help his current boss avoid the same fate that had befallen Noel Browne.

Maire was horrified when she heard what Joe was contemplating. He told her one evening after a couple of sherries. The news pulled her up sharp.

'But why would you do it, Joe? Why would you pick a fight with the most powerful man in Dublin? And did you ever think what it means for us if you lose?'

Joe handed her the single typewritten page he had discussed that afternoon with Frank Aiken.

With growing alarm, Maire read the reported testimony of an unnamed boy recounting a meeting he claimed to have had with 'John the Bishop'. The boy told how John Charles McQuaid had invited him to a private room in a pub near the archbishop's palace, placed him on the sofa beside him and asked him how he was enjoying school.

'Slowly,' the statement went on, 'it became clear to the child that John the Bishop's roving hands and long fingers had intentions other than getting information about school.'

Maire was in a panic.

'Where did you get this from, Joe? How do you know it's even true?'

Joe said quietly, 'I don't know it's true. And it was Noel Browne who gave it to me. He's convinced McQuaid is a pederast.'

Maire's eyes opened wide.

'Noel Browne the TD? But everyone knows he hates McQuaid. Don't you think he's made it all up, Joe? It's a hell of gamble.'

Joe had run through the same arguments endlessly over the past few days and suspected Maire was right.

'All I can tell you is that Noel was sure the story's true. And all we're going to do is let the palace know we've got it . . .'

But Maire was beside herself with fear.

'McQuaid will deny it. And you've only Browne's word for it. You don't have the boy himself, do you?'

'Sure we don't. But McQuaid doesn't know that. If Browne's making it all up, McQuaid will throw the thing in the trash and that's an end of it. But if it's true, His Grace might start being a bit more helpful . . .'

Joe sent the note, and a week later Frank Aiken received a communication from the secretariat of Archbishop McQuaid that he should expect a visit from Father Cecil Barrett. Next morning Barrett came to see Aiken, and when he had gone the minister called Joe in to give him the news – McQuaid had consented to begin negotiations on the drafting of an adoption bill.

Joe ran to his office and locked the door. Relief and triumph welled up inside him. When he looked down, he saw his hands were trembling.

TEN

November 1954;
St Louis, Illinois

As he waited for his sister to arrive, Loras T. Lane was thinking about Ireland.

The Lanes had emigrated in the potato famine of the 1840s and like many Irish-American families they liked to think they remained connected to the old country. Loras had been born in Cascade, Iowa in October 1910, studied for law and business degrees and become a priest in 1937. He had spent a year in Rome, reading canon law, and been created a bishop in 1951.

That was three years ago now, but the archdiocese had no vacancies and he had been put into what he laughingly called the clerical reserve, an auxiliary bishop waiting for a post. In the meantime he was serving as president of Loras College in Dubuque, Iowa; this was a Catholic college named for its nineteenth-century founder Bishop Mathias Loras of Dubuque, but Loras Lane used to joke it had adopted the name to honour his presence there. Now, though, Bishop Lane was on a mission. He had arranged to spend a week in St Louis, staying at the bishop's residence on May Drive. He had made the trip down the icy Mississippi valley on a series of Greyhound buses. He had come to see his sister.

Marjorie Hess, née Lane, was married to a German-American, a urologist by the name of Michael 'Doc' Hess, and the couple had three fine sons and a colonial-style house outside St Louis. But Marge had written Loras a couple of letters recently and he'd got the impression something was making her mightily unhappy. They'd always been close. Marjorie had been born just fifteen months after he was and it seemed natural he should spend his life loving and protecting her. After he got her letters he had written and called repeatedly to ask what was wrong, but Marge had clammed up. The months passed and still Marge would not open up to him. Loras sensed the thing was becoming a barrier between them so he had come to St Louis.

Now as she entered the mahogany-panelled dusk of the bishop's parlour, Marge seemed small, vulnerable, in need of his help like all those years ago when they were kids. Bishop Loras turned up the electric dimmer switch a tad so he could see her eyes. She didn't want to talk, she said, but he knew she did. She was OK, she said, but he knew she wasn't. He asked her if it was a problem with the boys, but she said no. A problem with Doc? Marge hesitated and her brother asked again.

'Not exactly with Doc,' she said finally. 'Doc's a fine man and he loves us all. But, you know, Doc wants a baby girl and he ain't going to get one.'

Bishop Loras came and sat on the soft worn arm of the leather couch, leaned over his little sister and laid a hand on her shoulder. Marge looked up at him like she always had done and gave a little sob.

'It's me,' she said. 'I've let him down. We were trying for so many years, Loras. For a little girl. But it just never happened. Then after poor Timmy died of the spinal meningitis and all . . .'

Marge hesitated for a moment and blew her nose; the cruel unexpected death of their five-year-old son had hit the Hesses hard.

'After that I went to see the baby doctor. And he told me . . . Things have gone wrong. You know, inside . . .'

Dubuque, Iowa

Loras went back to Dubuque. He had found the meeting with his sister upsetting. And he was tormented by the knowledge that he could do nothing to help her. Back in college he asked God for guidance and help, but no solution appeared.

In early 1955 Loras travelled to Chicago for a conference with bishops from dioceses around the US. On the last day before the participants were due to return home, they gathered for breakfast in the restaurant of the Blackstone Hotel on Michigan Avenue. Bishop Lane was seated next to a monsignor from Washington DC who introduced himself as John O'Grady, secretary of the National Conference of Catholic Charities. Loras knew of O'Grady from his opposition a couple of years earlier to the McCarran–Walter Act, which aimed to restrict immigration quotas. They got chatting and, in the way of these things, swapped stories about their shared Irish heritage. Loras said he believed his own family had come from County Cork in the mid-nineteenth century, a story Monsignor O'Grady was able to trump with the revelation that he had himself been born in Ireland. He was, he said, from County Tipperary and had a sister who was still there, serving as a nun in a place called Roscrea.

ELEVEN

Dublin

There was speculation about Archbishop McQuaid's sudden change of mind, but Joe Coram just shrugged his shoulders and threw himself into drafting the Adoption Bill. He was named Department of External Affairs lead official for liaison with Health and Social Welfare Minister Jim Ryan and with Gerry Boland at the Justice Department. Joe's belief that they were engaged on a mission to save Ireland's children seemed to fire up those he worked with.

At first the project went well, and Cecil Barrett was assiduous in attending the drafting sessions. But as the bill took shape disagreements arose, not just over the detailed wording of the legislation but over its broad principles too. Barrett and McQuaid became increasingly assertive in defending what they saw as the Church's sine qua nons, the clauses demanded by God and, on His behalf, by the hierarchy. As the months went by and negotiations dragged on, Joe felt the long hours at the office putting a strain on his life with Maire. When she lamented his constant absence, he said, 'But think what we can achieve with this – proper protection for our children, an end to the baby trade. Sure it must be worth it, mustn't it?'

Maire nodded, but her reply had none of the old laughter in it. 'You're always talking about "our children", Joe. But what about *our* children? You and me. Will we never have them?'

*

Once he knew the Church was cooperating, Eamon de Valera had given his backing to the Adoption Bill and set a deadline to get it passed in the Dáil. The time limit made the job of managing the archbishop particularly sensitive. In a memo to Frank Aiken, Joe warned that Barrett and McQuaid were putting pressure on officials in all three departments, and the Department of Justice now seemed to be 'working day and night to bring their draft bill into line with the Bishops' new position'.

By the time the bill was published in December 1952, hopes of an early end to the transatlantic traffic in Irish babies had taken a battering. Conflicts and compromises had watered down its original intentions. To Joe Coram's great disappointment, the final text seemed almost to condone the continued export of children from mother-and-baby homes: '*Section 40, Subsection 1:* No person shall remove out of the State a child under seven years of age who is an Irish citizen or cause or permit such removal . . . *Subsection 2:* This shall not apply to the removal of an illegitimate child by or with the approval of the mother.' For his part, Archbishop McQuaid now did not see the legislation as a problem. When it came into force in 1953, he told the heads of the Catholic adoption agencies, including Mother Barbara at Sean Ross Abbey in Roscrea, that they need not worry about the Adoption Act because he had 'been over every single clause in it'. A memo from the Justice Department acknowledged that large sections of text were 'inserted in the Bill at the suggestion of the Episcopal Committee in a memorandum that was handed to the Minister for Justice by His Grace the Archbishop'.

The years slipped imperceptibly by and in January 1955 Joe Coram found himself serving his third government – de Valera had been voted out in the middle of 1954, taking Aiken with him; John Costello was back at the helm, though with no ministerial post for the disgraced Noel Browne. Joe was reaching the stage in a civil servant's career when he had seen a lot of things and, if he were honest, not much of it pleased him any more. He was becoming disillusioned with politics; he was starting to feel disillusioned with life. Maire no longer rushed to meet him at the front door; mealtimes were no longer the occasion for shared humour and understanding.

Tonight he had come home in a foul mood. Maire gave him the *Evening Mail* and Joe read the headline: FIFTY AMERICAN COUPLES BUY IRISH BABIES THROUGH INTERNATIONAL ADOPTION RING. The article quoted a 'senior police source' as saying that 'upwards of 100 illegitimate children have recently passed through bogus and other nursing homes in this country and in no case was the birth recorded. At least half of them, we are convinced, are now in the United States ... Americans are paying up to $2,000 to obtain children illegally in Dublin.'

Joe looked at Maire and smiled bitterly.

'Well, my dear, I don't know why in God's name they would want to go to all that bother when they can write to any mother superior, hand over a few punts and we'll issue them with passports for as many kiddies as they want. We've had the act for two years now and it's changed nothing.'

The Department of External Affairs was still inundated with requests from Church mother-and-baby homes for passports to send Irish children to the USA. Joe told his officials to investigate each one of them and rigorously apply the rules of the Adoption Act. Rita Kenny, head of the Passport Office, shared his views and the two of them had hoped the clause demanding that mothers give their written consent would slow down the exodus. But it was clear from the figures that the sisters were having little trouble getting the girls to sign.

Maire looked at her husband and saw the difference the years had wrought. He was no longer the naive enthusiast she had fallen for – she could see the disenchantment in his eyes. The absence of children sat heavy in their marriage. She felt Joe blamed her for not giving him the baby he wanted and thought that was terribly unfair and sad. But they had refrained from talking about it for so long – at first for fear of hurting the other, then from feelings of guilt and shame – that they had retreated into their own complex web of thoughts and suspicions. Each felt the other thought badly of them; each had built a tower of self-reproach that neither could now tear down.

TWELVE

June 1955;
Roscrea

For Philomena Lee the controversy over adoption legislation and the
set-to between Ireland's dual seats of power passed by unnoticed. She
and her young son were the prizes in the battle between Church and
state but no one bothered to tell Philomena anything had changed.
By 1955 she had been in Sean Ross Abbey for three years, friendless
and alone, unvisited by her family.

Anthony had grown into a sturdy toddler with his mother's blue
eyes and jet-black hair. He had learned how to fend for himself in
the melee of communal life and how to fight for food in the children's refectory. He discovered early on that his most potent weapon
was his smile. The nursing sisters would put their cheek close to his
and say, 'How about it, little man?' and Anthony would respond with
a beaming face and a warm, wet kiss that set them all laughing.

He was devoted to little Mary McDonald. So constantly were the
two of them together, so affectionate were they to each other that all
who saw them were convinced they were brother and sister. When
Mary hurt herself, Anthony would comfort her; when something
worried her, she would turn to him for help. He sat next to her at
mealtimes, shared his food with her and protected her from the bullies
who terrorized the nurseries. Philomena and Margaret laughed to see
them together and wept when they thought of what lay ahead.

*

Anthony was a week short of his third birthday when Mother Barbara decided the time had come to do something about him.

It was the height of summer and temperatures in the laundry rooms were close to unbearable. Philomena was nearing the end of her shift, looking forward to dinner and the knitting hour, and amid the hubbub of the room she didn't quite catch what the laundry supervisor was shouting.

'I said Sister Hildegarde wants you! Are you deaf, girl?'

Philomena blanched. She had seen Sister Hildegarde from a distance – austere, unapproachable, constantly preoccupied, always busy with papers and files. On occasions the girls would see her arriving and departing in a big black automobile. Everyone knew she dealt with the adoptions.

Philomena dried her hands and ran to the dormitory. She knew she mustn't keep the sister waiting, but she desperately wanted to speak to Margaret. She found her at work in the kitchens and grabbed her arm.

'Margaret, they've come for me. What'll I do? We said we wouldn't give the babbies away, didn't we? Will you back me up? Tell me what to do!'

Margaret McDonald gave a cry and threw her arms round her friend.

'Tell them no, Phil! Tell them you won't give him up. You stand firm and I'll do the same. Sure they can't make us give them away, can they?'

Neither girl knew the answer to the question – no one had told them anything about the adoption laws or their rights – and they sensed the hollowness of their bravado, but at the same time their words gave them strength.

'I'll do it then. I'll tell them they can't have him. And then you'll do the same. And if they won't let us keep our babbies, we'll take them and run away . . . We'll run away, won't we, Margaret?'

Philomena hadn't been in the mother superior's study since the week after she gave birth and the rush of memories from that humiliating encounter made her flush with shame. Sister Hildegarde had instructed her to stand and wait until she fetched Mother Barbara, and in the quiet of the study her heart was racing.

When the two nuns came in they were accompanied by a man Philomena had not seen before – tall, bald-headed, with a black moustache and wearing a black three-piece suit. Sister Hildegarde introduced him as Mr Houlihan from Birr, but he did not offer to shake Philomena's hand. The room was swimming before her eyes. She felt her courage draining away. If she did not say something now, the game would be up.

'I know what this is all about,' she heard herself saying. 'I know what you want and I don't agree. I want to keep my baby. I won't let you take him from me.'

Mother Barbara looked at her with an expression of disgust; Sister Hildegarde told her to be quiet. The proceedings had an air of inevitability about them, an ineluctable process that was grinding towards its dreadful conclusion. Philomena fell silent – she had spent her life doing what the nuns told her to do and a lifetime of submission is not easy to overcome.

Sister Hildegarde told her to take a seat, told her Mr Houlihan had some important information for her. The man in the dark suit and white shirt with tobacco stains at the cuffs began reading from a sheet of paper that he held up to the light of the window. Philomena tried to concentrate. The reading went on for a long time, but she understood little. The man's voice was low and monotonous. He seemed bored with what he was reading, as if he had read it a great many times before. Philomena heard the words, 'according to the provisions of the act'; she heard him mention oaths and signing. And she very clearly heard him say, 'You must therefore never seek to know what becomes of your child . . . or in any way try to find or contact him.'

Philomena made to object, but her voice was weak and shook with fear.

'Please, Sister. Please, Reverend Mother, you don't understand. I love my baby; I'm his mammy and I'm the only one who knows how to look after him. Don't take him away from me. He would be so *sad* without me . . .'

Sister Hildegarde took control of the situation. She was used to this sort of nonsense. 'Don't be silly, girl,' she said. 'Just get on with it. Your signature goes here by this cross. You've no choice in the matter, anyway. Sign the paper and you'll be able to leave.'

Philomena was young and frightened; she felt her determination flag under the weight of old habits.

I, Philomena Lee of Limerick, Ireland, aged 22 years make oath and say: –

That I am the mother of Anthony Lee who was born to me out of wedlock at Sean Ross Abbey, Roscrea, Co. Tipperary, Ireland, on 5th July 1952.

That I hereby relinquish full claim forever to my said child Anthony Lee and surrender the said child to Sister Barbara, Superioress of Sean Ross Abbey, Roscrea, Co. Tipperary, Ireland.

The purpose of this relinquishment is to enable Sister Barbara to make my child available for adoption to any person she considers fit and proper, inside or outside the state.

That I further undertake never to attempt to see, interfere with or make any claim to the said child at any future time.

Signed: *Philomena Lee*
Philomena Lee

Subscribed and sworn to by the said Philomena Lee as her free act and deed this 27th day of June 1955.

Signed: *Desmond A. Houlihan*

Notary Public during the pleasure of The Chief Justice for Ireland, Birr, Co. Offaly, Ireland.

5 July 1955

There were no toys and no treats for Anthony Lee's third birthday. Sister Annunciata had left Roscrea earlier in the year, transferred to the order's headquarters at Homerton in the East End of London, where her love and energy were now serving England's homeless. Without Annunciata's support and tormented by the document she had signed, Philomena was at her wits' end. On the morning of Anthony's birthday she stared at the bare table by his bed and the single hand-drawn birthday card she and Margaret had made between them, and she burst into tears. She cried the whole morning in the laundry and she cried at lunchtime in the nursery.

Anthony tried to comfort her. He ran into the field and came back with a bunch of daisies and dandelions. 'Don't cry, Mammy,' he said. 'It'll be all right. Don't cry, Mammy . . . please don't cry . . .'

Everyone said Anthony was a good boy, but there was something worrying about his goodness. He seemed always vigilant, always looking for signs of unhappiness in others and always rushing to comfort them. It was as if he felt that by doing so he was staving off some relentless looming disaster.

That evening Sister Hildegarde appeared at the knitting hour and told Margaret she too must come to see Mother Barbara. She cried and protested, but she too signed.

THIRTEEN

Dubuque

Bishop Loras hesitated before dialling the number. He was aware how sensitive this was, but he had thought the matter through and decided it was an opportunity too good to miss.

'Ferguson 521-4135.'

Loras smiled when he heard his sister's voice.

'Hi, Marge. It's the bishop.'

'Oh hi, Loras. I was just thinking of you . . .'

As Loras read out Monsignor O'Grady's letter, he struggled to gauge Marge's reaction.

'"The abbey has a mother-and-baby home attached to it,"' he read, '"and this has in the past been a good source of children for adoption in the US."'

Loras paused, but the line remained silent so he went on with O'Grady's proposal: '"Following our conversation I took the liberty of writing my sister in Roscrea and she has now replied as follows.

All our children are born out of wedlock of respectable parents and no child is given for adoption unless the background is excellent. We currently have several girls available, including one lovely child with a particularly good background. Her mother was a very superior type of girl from Dublin. She was a shopkeeper and lived at home with her people. The family are very respectable: they sent her and the child to us after she gave birth. It is because of the child's excellent background that we are anxious to get a good home for her. She is a very gentle, loveable girl, perfectly healthy, with auburn hair and dark eyes, and reflects the gentleness and culture of her mother."'

Loras paused again and waited for Marjorie to speak.

When she did not, he asked softly, 'Marge, are you there?'

He heard her swallow.'Yes, Loras, I'm here . . .'

O'Grady's letter spelt out the mechanics of the thing and said his sister in Roscrea was recommending an early decision 'as this is an opportunity that may not present itself again'. It also broached the question of money: 'There would of course be expenses involved and, although not strictly necessary, we do advise that prospective parents travel to meet their future child in Ireland before completing the transaction. While neither the NCCC nor Sean Ross Abbey charge any fees, it is customary for the adopting party to make a donation to the Sisters of the Sacred Hearts of Jesus and Mary, the size of which may be determined in consultation with the Superioress of the Order.'

FOURTEEN

Evening, Saturday 6 August 1955;
New York

Marjorie Hess was worried about flying and she was worried about arriving. She was missing Doc and the boys, and she was anxious about the task that lay in wait at her destination. To make matters worse, the weather had been atrocious and the short flight from St Louis was delayed two hours. By the time she landed at La Guardia, the last bus had gone and Marge had had to take a cab to the hotel. New York was a dangerous place, Doc had said, and the cab drivers were crooks. Doc didn't like spending money, so the eight-dollar fare made her feel guilty.

In the dingy hotel room Marge wondered why she had agreed to the whole idea. Loras and Mamma weren't due until tomorrow, so tonight she was on her own. To raise her spirits, she called room service and ordered coffee and cake. She unpacked her nightdress and freshened up. An Italian waiter knocked and brought her order. She looked through the grimy window at the crowds still on the street when everyone in St Louis would long be in bed. She couldn't sleep. She took out the brown leather travel diary she'd bought specially for her journey; it was a milestone trip and she wanted a record of it, but she couldn't think what to say. So she inscribed her name and address in a careful, studied hand – '*Mrs M. Hess, 810 Moundale, Ferguson 21, Mo.*' – then, with her brand new Parker Jotter ballpoint, she began:

August 6 1955: St Louis–New York; Trans World Airlines, TWA.

Airplane: Constellation.
Captain: R.C. Pinel. Stewardess: Fran McShane.
Weather: Horrible. Lightning and storms.
Two hours late to New York, but safe, which is all that matters.

Visions of the disaster avoided rekindled her anxiety. She thought maybe she should set down her emotions, her hopes and fears about the venture she was embarking on – maybe her diary would survive her? But Marge was not much given to emotional talk.

> *Sat next to a machinist from Brooklyn on flight from St Louis*
> *to New York. He talked constantly – all about California –*
> *3 hours of things I already know. Plane too late for bus to*
> *Hotel so took cab. Cost $4.50. Was hungry on arrival so had*
> *cake and coffee. Must not have agreed – net 3½ hours sleep.*
> *Lonesome – lonesome – lonesome. Wish Daddy and Boys with*
> *me. Feel so alone.*

Morning, Sunday 7 August 1955

Josephine Lane flew into New York with her son Loras in tow. She was coming up to seventy, but the world held no fear for her. She had raised a family in the days when horses and carts filled the roads of Dubuque County; she and Tom Lane had produced five healthy children – James, Leanor, Loras, Marjorie and John. After Tom died, Josephine had raised them alone.

The Lanes had named Loras for Dubuque's ancient bishop Mathias Loras and had always intended him for the Church – Josephine knew Tom would have been so proud to see him now; she cried when she thought about it.

But Marjorie had disappointed them. Beautiful, tall and slender with thick brown hair, she had fallen in love with an unsuitable man, a medical student from a German family with no money and fewer prospects. When Josephine forbade them to marry, Marjorie and her beau Michael Hess had jumped a ride to Iowa City and got married in a church where the priest knew nothing of the family's wishes. For their first years together, they lived in a rented apartment over a hardware store and the farmers paid Doc for his services in eggs and rabbits. The couple were reconciled with Josephine only after Tom died, and for the rest of their lives Marge and Doc Hess kept the secret of their elopement, leaving photographs and letters about it for their children to discover only when both of them were dead.

Marjorie Hess looked at herself in the full-length mirror of the hotel lobby. It was 6 a.m. and she had a quarter-hour to wait for the airport bus. The bright lighting showed off the red Maybelline lip gloss she had bought at Roshek's in Dubuque before leaving and her hair shone flat and sleek. She smoothed the crimplene of her pale shift dress and adjusted the cameo brooch at her collar. Marge was forty-three but good for her age – the Brooklyn machinist had told her she looked thirty-five, but she knew he was spinning a line – and she noted with relief that the sleepless night had not wiped the bloom from her face.

She was tired, though, and looking forward to meeting up with Loras and Mamma at Idlewild; at least the three of them could look after each other on the long journey ahead.

They were flying TWA to Europe. The purpose of the trip was the business in Ireland, of course, but the always energetic Josephine had extended their itinerary to take in sightseeing for three weeks in France, Germany and Italy. Marge made a resolution to write her diary every day.

August 7 1955.

Hot and humid. Loras and Mamma arrived Idlewild 11 a.m. Was so glad to see them. I'm so tired. Had tea and toast and wrote cards. Name called over loudspeaker and it

*was Daddy – so wonderful to hear voice and little
Stevie, too.*

On board now. Stewardess says 9 hours to Ireland – wow!

*Weather good. God with us. Going to sleep now. Loras
and Mother fine.*

Monday August 8 1955. Shannon 6.30 a.m.

Weather: Cloudy and cold. Not used to it.

*Passed over Newfoundland and it was so desolate. Arrived
Shannon and went thru customs into dining room for breakfast – eggs – toast – bacon. A little Irish boy showed up and
proceeded to call Loras His Lordship or 'Me Lord'. He had
car for us with right-hand drive.*

*Lots of ruined castles and all houses are stone. Each
area is divided with stone walls and hedges and everything
so green. Gas expensive – $1.50 a gallon. Very few cars –
all ride bicycles.*

*Reached Limerick at 9 o'clock and checked into hotel.
Loras out contacting the Bishop and inquiring of orphanages.
None here. Changed money. Driving on to Cork tomorrow.*

In a separate notebook with tear-out pages another hand – Loras's?
– has written:

*Mother Rosamund, Sacred Heart Convent, County Westmeath;
Sister Elizabeth, Father Abbey, Castle Pollard;
Sister Monica, St Patrick's Children's Home;
Daughters of Charity St Vincent de Paul, Navan Road, Dublin;
Sister Casimer, St Brigid's Orphanage, 46 Eccles Street, Dublin;
Sister Hildegarde, Sean Ross Abbey, Roscrea, County Tipperary.*

The names are in different inks, some in pencil. It is a hastily compiled
shopping list. The last entry is double-underlined.

Tuesday August 9 1955. Cork–Roscrea.

> *Beautiful country.*
> *Stopped at many orphanages but too many are just little babies.*
> *Visited castle and kissed Blarney Stone. It was quite a chore. Had to climb 125 steps and lay on back. All call Loras His Lordship. Coffee terrible and there is no hot water. All people travel by bike and you see no slacks or shorts here.*
> *At Roscrea now.*

FIFTEEN

9 August 1955;
Roscrea

Philomena and Margaret saw the woman in the floral-pattern dress enter the convent through the front door and nudged each other in admiration. She looked so suave and so elegant; her little pillbox hat sat at an unbelievably fashionable tilt and her shoes had heels that went on forever. Philomena whispered, 'Sure, she looks like a film star,' and Margaret giggled, 'Yeah, Jayne Mansfield, I'd say!' but Philomena had never heard of Jayne Mansfield so the conversation turned to the others in the party. Behind the film star came an older lady and a priest, or rather a bishop or cardinal of some sort – Sister Hildegarde and Mother Barbara were making such a fuss of him, calling him Your Excellency and tripping over themselves to be nice. The group paused to admire the entrance hall and the grand Georgian staircase, then swept out of the girls' view into the convent offices.

On the walk back to work – across the courtyard, past the old monastery ruins, down to the laundry block – Philomena and Margaret seized the opportunity to talk. They had spoken a lot in the last month since they had signed the papers, plotting how they would sneak into the night nursery and lift their children before climbing out the window at the back of the dormitory or breaking open the lock on the front door. More than once they had fixed the night on which they were going to run away, but always something had intervened – a saint's day that brought extra cohorts of nuns into the convent and made the corridors a dangerous place, a thunderstorm that turned the grounds into an impassable bog, or a nervous headache that put one of the girls out of action. Each time they would choose another day for their escape and begin planning all over again, but eventually the obstacles and the postponements grew so great that their dream had faltered.

Margaret was the first to voice their doubts.

'Where would you go if we get out of here, Phil?' she asked. 'Do you have somewhere? Because it'd be pretty hard for me. I can't go back to Dublin, that's for sure . . .'

Philomena nodded sadly.

'I know. My da's told everyone I went away to England, so I can't turn up in Newcastle West with Anthony. No one knows I ever even had a baby and that's the truth.'

Neither girl spoke as they mulled over what they had long known in their hearts: no one escaped from Sean Ross Abbey and no one got the better of the nuns. Ireland was no place for a mother without a husband and no place for a child without a father.

'But maybe the game's not up,' Margaret said eventually. 'It's been weeks since they made us sign those things and nothing's happened. Maybe there's no one looking for babbies nowadays. Maybe they'll come back and say we've to keep them after all . . .'

That evening in the knitting hour Sister Hildegarde came to see the girls in a state of high excitement. She was a sprightly woman in her early forties, short and wiry with sharp eyes and a brain that always seemed one jump ahead of you. Normally she was cold and reserved, but tonight she was allowing herself a show of unaccustomed emotion.

'Nancy – Margaret, I mean – Margaret McDonald, come to me over here, will you?'

Margaret looked up, puzzled by the unexpected summons, and handed little Mary to Philomena. Much to Margaret's surprise, Hildegarde kissed her on both cheeks.

'Margaret my girl, you should be proud,' Sister Hildegarde

began. 'Today we have been honoured by the presence in our midst of a bishop from America. And not just any bishop, I'll say. This one is a big bishop – the bishop of a place called Illinois. Now just imagine what sort of a lovely life your Mary will have in a place like that!'

Caught between the sister's gushing amiability and the import of her words, Margaret's reply was a confused stammer. 'What do you mean, Sister? Does the bishop want to see my daughter?'

'No, no, no, girl! Goodness, what a nincompoop you are. It's his sister, of course. The Bishop's sister is going to take your daughter to America!'

Watching from the other side of the room, Philomena saw her friend burst into tears and hurried over to comfort her as Sister Hildegarde swept out into the corridor.

The weeks that followed were hard for Margaret. Not only did she know her child would soon be taken from her, but she had the additional burden of knowing that Mary would be separated from Anthony, and she herself would be parted from her best friend.

Philomena did what she could to reassure her – she told her Mary would have a far better life in America than anything she could have expected in Ireland, and what firmer guarantee of her future happiness than having the sister of a big bishop to look after her?

In her brighter moments Margaret acknowledged the truth of Philomena's arguments, but at others she was disconsolate. She kept saying, 'We should have stood up to them; we should have refused!' The woman she had thought of as a Hollywood film star now appeared little better than a child thief.

The two of them spent the evenings watching the children playing together in the nursery and thinking their own, now diverging thoughts. Philomena squeezed her friend's hand and said, 'I know one young fellow who'll be heartbroken when Mary goes,' but in private she breathed a silent sigh of relief that her Anthony at least was not being taken from her.

10 August 1955

The letter was addressed to Sister Barbara personally, but she saw it was copied to the superioresses of Castlepollard in Westmeath, St Patrick's Home in Dublin, St Clare's in Stamullen and the Sacred Heart Adoption Society in Cork.

The head of the Angel Guardian Adoption Home in Brooklyn, New York was writing to warn all of them that the National Conference of US Catholic Charities was having difficulties meeting its obligations over the vetting of American couples seeking to adopt Irish children. The NCCC, she wrote, could no longer guarantee the bona fides of all those who applied to take children from Ireland; in particular, she warned, 'we have reason to believe that would-be American adopters who have already been rejected for serious reasons in the US are now turning directly to Irish adoption societies for their babies'.

Mother Barbara sought guidance from the archbishop's palace and was told to disregard the letter.

SIXTEEN

If Sister Hildegarde had found it hard to contain her excitement at the events of that afternoon in August, Marjorie Hess seems to have been somewhat more phlegmatic. The evening entry in her diary reads, *'Mother Barbara and Sister Hildegarde had Mary and gave me many other ch[ildren] to see.'*

But the following morning Marge and Loras went back to Sean Ross Abbey and made another visit to the children's nurseries. It was during the girls' working time, so none of the mothers was there. Mary recognized Marge from the previous day and did not run away as she usually did. She was two and a half years old and Sister Hildegarde had trained her to sing a song called 'Over the Mountains, Over the Sea' and to recite the Lord's Prayer for visitors. As Mary was singing, Anthony stood close by, prompting her when she forgot her lines; at the end, he gave her a hug and a kiss.

Marge laughed to see the fondness between them and asked Sister Hildegarde what the little fellow's name was, but Hildegarde said she had no idea. When Marge bent down to ask Anthony what he was called, he mistook her approach for an invitation to give her a kiss, which he did – with great aplomb – on her cheek.

Marge giggled and said, 'How delightful!'

Mary's song had been taught to her with a purpose in mind. The lyrics ran, 'I see the moon and the moon sees me; / God bless the moon and God bless me. / Over the mountains, over the sea; / That's where my heart is longing to be . . .'

Any American mom with a heart would find the appeal hard to resist.

On the way from the abbey back to their hotel Marge told Loras that she liked the look of young Mary McDonald. Loras said how pleased he was to hear her say so – he had been predisposed towards Mary ever since Monsignor O'Grady sent him the letter from his sister in Roscrea. 'And you know what, Marge? I think that lovely little colleen looks just the image of you when you were her age! If that's not an omen, then I don't know what is!'

Marge smiled – she knew Loras wanted her to go ahead and adopt Mary, and she knew he had her best interests in his heart.

'Why, Loras, that's some kind of miracle, is it not – you remembering how I looked when I was Mary's age? Because you would only have been three years old yourself!'

Brother and sister burst out laughing and the banter between them continued until they were nearly back at the hotel.

Late the following morning, after His Excellency Bishop Loras Lane had said Mass for the Sisters of the Sacred Hearts in the chapel of Sean Ross Abbey, Josephine Lane, Loras and Marjorie squeezed into the Ford Popular hire car that had so impressed the nuns of Roscrea and made room on the back seat for Mother Barbara, who was carrying a little girl on her lap. Mother Barbara was full of excitement. She spent most of the journey through the farming country of the Irish midlands, seventy miles along minor roads through impossibly green fields, saying the rosary and exhorting Mary McDonald to stop squirming on her knee.

At 2.30 p.m. the little party had an appointment with Rita Kenny, head of the Irish Passport Office, at 78 St Stephens Green in Dublin.

The meeting began cordially and 'the Bishop and his friends' were offered tea and biscuits. Rita Kenny made a fuss over young Mary, but she asked Mother Barbara a few pointed questions about the child's state of health, in particular about a nasty rash on her face.

Mother Barbara was reassuring and mentioned the many other children Roscrea had sent through the Passport Office.

'Sure, they were all healthy, were they not?' She smiled challengingly. 'So why would we be sending an unhealthy one to the sister of His Excellency?'

Rita Kenny looked dubious.

'She'll have to undergo a thorough medical examination before the US authorities will admit her, you know,' she said, her eyes never leaving Mother Barbara's.

'Yes, of course she will,' Marge cut in, hoping to defuse the tension that had arisen. 'Thank you, ma'am.'

Loras wrote down the details of the doctor accredited by the US embassy. But Mother Barbara was a forceful woman, accustomed to authority and keen to show the bishop who was in charge of things.

'I trust everything is in order now,' she said firmly, 'so would you please let us have the passport? His Excellency is a busy man and we need to get to the American embassy before it closes.'

Rita Kenny was a good Catholic and she respected the high offices of the Church as much as anyone, but she was also a state official and entitled to a little respect herself.

She stood up.

'Right, well, if you wouldn't mind waiting a few moments, I'm needing to consult with someone before I can take a decision. Excuse me, please.' And she left the room.

The little party waited for her in uncomfortable silence.

Ten minutes later Miss Kenny returned with a middle-aged man in a brown tweed jacket and dark green tie, stocky but not yet fat, with a reddish, freckled face and straw-coloured hair that stood up in a tangled thatch.

'Your Grace, Reverend Mother, ladies. This is Mr Joe Coram; he's in charge of our policy on adoptions.'

Bishop Lane made as if to stand, but Joe motioned him not to put himself out and came over to shake hands. It gave him time to weigh the fellow up: Loras was powerfully built with broad shoulders under his black cassock, a plump face and an easy smile that revealed the gap between his two front teeth. Joe couldn't help thinking how Irish he looked, how different from the pinched, ascetic features of John Charles McQuaid. And yet, if Joe were honest with himself, he would have acknowledged a squeak of pleasure in holding the whip hand over a bishop whose Church had made such a fuss about its uninfringeable right to dispose of Ireland's children. They may have been physical opposites, but when Joe looked at Bishop Lane he saw Archbishop McQuaid, and he was seized with an irrational, irresistible desire to do everything in his power to block this adoption.

In a speech he found unexpectedly satisfying, Joe explained how the Adoption Act had made the issue of children's passports much more complex. For a start, the Irish government now had to be certain the child's mother had indeed given up her rights and that the prospective adopters were good Catholics. He was about to go on to the further impediments, when Mother Barbara interrupted.

'Well now, young man, you need have no qualms on the first of those points. I have myself witnessed the mother's relinquishment of custody and I have all the papers you could possibly want. And as for the new parents being Catholics, don't you think the bishop knows his sister and brother-in-law well enough?'

Joe bit his lip and managed a strained smile.

'That all sounds grand, right enough. But rules are rules, you know, and we have to stick by them. What we'll also need, now I think of it, is a home study report from the National Conference of Catholic Charities in America. They'll need to come and visit you at home, Mrs Hess. We can't let young Mary have a passport until we get their report, I'm afraid. But with your contacts, Bishop, I'm sure that won't be a problem . . .'

As Joe spoke, Marge wrote down what he was saying on a spare page of her diary. No one had warned them about this home report; she would have to get Doc working on it while she was still in Europe.

'Oh, and one more thing,' Joe continued: 'you will of course need to go to the US embassy here in Dublin and get your own country's agreement to have little Mary on the territory of the United States.'

Loras wrote down the details in his notebook. He had the distinct impression the fellow was making things difficult for them, and he had no idea why he was doing it.

SEVENTEEN

Dublin;
European tour

At the end of a tiring day, Loras, Marge and their mother had checked into the Clarence Hotel on Wellington Quay, where in honour of the bishop they were given superior rooms overlooking the River Liffey.

Mother Barbara had taken Mary and gone off to stay with her married sister outside Dublin before going back to Roscrea. Marge and Loras told her they would return after their sightseeing trip round Europe, which they expected to last about three weeks. They still hoped to be able to take Mary back with them to the United States, although the timetable for completing the paperwork was now looking challenging. It was nearly midnight before Marge sat down to write her diary.

August 10 1955. Roscrea–Dublin.
Weather: Nice.

> *Loras said Mass at Roscrea and had nice breakfast. Mother Barbara left for Dublin with us (said Rosary on way). Dublin a very busy city – crowded. Visited Passport Office and found out about the Home Study thing. Called Doc and told him the news – hope he can do something about it.*

> *Arranged to go to Paris tomorrow night. Aer Lingus is our airways.*

> *Eggs here are terrible. Feeling lonesome.*

Joe Coram stayed late at his desk that evening writing a report for the new minister, Liam Cosgrave, explaining why he had not acceded to the passport request made by the American bishop's party. He was worried Bishop Lane might complain to McQuaid and McQuaid might complain to the minister; and he knew the Taoiseach would cave in at the first sign of pressure from the Church, so he wanted to get his side of things in first.

On the tram home Joe was looking forward to telling Maire how he had stood up to the 'big bishop' who had been in his office thinking he could bend the rules and whisk a little Irish girl off to America 'just like that'. But when he let himself in at the front door, he found the house in darkness. Maire was in bed and didn't respond to his discreet cough and little tug on the bedclothes.

Marjorie Hess could not get to sleep. She lay tossing and turning, endlessly going over a plan that had been hatching in her heart and would give her no rest. Marge's plan stemmed from an unforeseen sudden promise of love and happiness, but for the moment she knew it must remain a secret. In a long letter to Doc she told him the news about Mary and about the problem with the NCCC home visit, but she deliberately did not mention the idea that was ripening in her imagination.

CLARENCE HOTEL, DUBLIN.

Wednesday night (August 10, 1955).
(It's cold here – I go to bed with a sweater on.)

Dearest Doc, Jim, Tom, Stevie

There was so much I wanted to say to you last night but at $7.50 per 3 min, I thought I'd better write. Hearing your voice made me so darned lonesome that if I could get home, I would. I can see now why they say travel when you're young, because you can't enjoy it when you're older. I told Mother *and Loras I'd give anything to be home with you all, the 'paper and a good TV program. I haven't stopped since we got off the plane. A car met us and we've been looking at little girls ever since. The one whose picture I'm sending has a terrible haircut and clothes, but you notice her face is perfect – her name is Mary McDonald aged 2½. She can sing 'Over the Mountains Over the Sea' (doesn't know about Davy Crockett) and is very intelligent. Says Hail Mary and Our Father (the boys couldn't do that many prayers). Loras thinks she looks like me when I was her age. She has real rosy cheeks – in fact kind of a dermatitis. Loras thinks it's from the soap and towels they use here, but if papers go thru, I'll have her checked real good. Physically and mentally, she's perfect according to their medical reports. Mary's mother was born in Dublin, and also the father. The only thing here, they don't marry. The girl goes to an abbey and has to stay there and work until child adopted. Parents are both shopkeepers, as is almost everyone in Dublin, and of very good background – no wealth, but good honest people. The Sisters have been saving Mary for a priest's niece who has been ill. But they can't keep her any longer – we're actually lucky to get an older child because the family paid them to keep her, but then decided to give up the adoption. Sean Ross Abbey, Roscrea, County Tipperary, Ireland seems to send more to U.S. than any other. (What do you think?)*

About the Catholic Charities home visit, Bishop Helmsing can do it for you. Tell him Loras told him to. And get the power of attorney. Then send your baptismal record whenever you get it. There's nothing to do here so guess I'll go on – and come back here about September 1.

Write me.

I miss you all. Hope you do me.

PS – Doc, please send the papers. When you write, thank Mother Barbara and rest of nuns for being so nice. The passport people won't do anything until Catholic Charities sends Home Report – so be sure the house is straight and you are there . . .

I'm going to pray now and if everything doesn't turn out and I don't bring Mary home, then it must be that we should be content with our own three wonderful boys – you feel that way too – and all I can do is cut down on things. I want to pay back for my trip. I'll be thinking of you all and loving you.

Kisses to all. Mommy.

The Aer Lingus flight from Dublin to Paris was a rough one and Marge didn't have the strength to write her diary. The following morning Loras had been invited to say Mass in Notre Dame, and for the next two days the indefatigable Josephine led her children round the sights of the city. On Saturday, Marge wrote again to Doc.

Moderne Palace Hotel,
8bis Place de la Republique,
Paris, 11e.

August 13, 1955

Dearest Doc – Jim – Tom – Stevie,

By this time I suppose you have received Mary's picture and I am wondering what you think of her.

Mother Barbara is having her checked out as regards X-rays and eyes, etc. The American embassy have their own clinic and do a very thorough check.

If you have trouble with the Home Visit you should call Bishop Byrne or Archbishop Ritter. Tell them that Loras is with me and told you to contact them. Good luck. I'm so anxious to hear from you. I miss you all so – do you miss me?

I'm praying you make out all right with Catholic Charities.

Ireland was some country. Men never marry until 35 – the taxi cab man told me they like to have a bit of a fling first.
    Bye now and love and kisses to you all. Do you ever hear of homesickness?
    Hope you're all well,
    Mom.

After Paris they drove through Germany and south as far as Venice. Marge felt invigorated by the sunshine, the wine and the solicitous presence of her brother. The death of her son was retreating into the past; the promise of the future was taking shape. Now she was certain she must press on with the plan she had conceived in the nursery of Sean Ross Abbey.

Thursday 1 September 1955, Dublin

The first morning back in Ireland brought Marge down to earth. The weather was cold and wet and at the Clarence Hotel the superior rooms with river view were all occupied. Loras suggested they spend the morning catching up on lost sleep, but Marge pleaded with him to take her straight to Sean Ross Abbey and he said, 'Sure, why not?'

They were met at the convent gate by Sister Hildegarde, who offered them tea, but Marge said she wanted to go straight to the children's nursery. When they reached the glass doors, she asked them not to enter but to stay with her a while and watch the children at play. Taking Loras by the sleeve, she pointed out Mary McDonald in her white cotton dress and white socks and indicated the little boy she was playing with.

'Look at those two, Loras. Can you see how much they love each other? And did you see what happened when we were here last time? How that little guy acted when I went to take Mary's hand? Watch this . . .'

Marge walked over to Mary – who recognized her – and made

to pick her up. As soon as she did so, little Anthony Lee in his baggy dungarees and knitted pullover began waving and smiling up at the two of them.

Marge bent down close to him and said, 'Well, little man, how about it?' and he gave her a big kiss on the cheek.

EIGHTEEN

Roscrea; St Louis

Philomena cried when they told her the news.

This time Sister Hildegarde didn't even bother trying to convince her of her child's good fortune. She just said, 'Well, girl, it seems your son's off with the bishop too. We've a few problems with the paperwork, but I'd say he'll be on his way pretty soon.'

In her heart Philomena had known it would happen one day, but the pitiless way she was told about it was devastating. In tears, she ran to the nursery and fell on her knees before her little boy. Anthony smiled as usual to see her but quickly sensed something was wrong.

'Mammy, what is it? What's a matter? Why are you crying?'

Philomena wiped her face and clasped him in her arms,

'I love you, Anthony,' she said. 'I love you now and I always will. I'll never forget you, little man . . . never.'

Seeing his mother so upset, he too burst into tears.

'Please don't cry, Mammy,' he said, stroking her hair. 'Please don't cry . . .'

Philomena tried to comfort him, but she was too distraught. She thought it so unfair that the love and affection her child exuded and the tenderness he evoked in others should be the cause of her losing him forever. His heart was so big that he had kisses for everyone – and the kiss he had given to some stranger now seemed to count for more than the sacred bond he shared with his mother. The thought tormented her. Why should another woman have her child, her own flesh, the baby she had borne and loved and cherished?

When Philomena spoke to Margaret, she apologized for not appreciating the pain she had been going through; she understood it now, she said. She was numb and empty and it was Margaret's turn to console her. 'At least there's one good thing,' she said. 'At least Mary and Anthony will be together now.'

But nothing seemed to help. Philomena tortured herself with unanswerable questions. How could such a random, unplanned intersection of two people's lives have so many dreadful consequences? The American woman had come to get a *girl*! That was what Philomena found so unfair. She had come to get a girl, and now she was leaving with her boy. The whole world seemed to rest on arbitrary chance. If Anthony had not tugged at the American woman's sleeve or kissed her on the cheek that day, how different things could have been . . .

Marge Hess wrote her husband to explain what she had felt since she first visited Roscrea: she told him that she loved little Mary, but could not bring Mary without bringing Anthony too; told him how cruel it would be to separate two tiny children with such a strong and loving bond.

'I hope you will understand,' she wrote. 'The two of them have different mothers, but they are closer than any brother and sister. They love each other and I love them. As soon as I saw them together, I knew what I had to do. When I went to take Mary, Anthony was there waving and smiling and giving me kisses. I have thought about it the whole time we were travelling. Please say it is OK for us to take them both. I know we can work it out. The boys will be hurt, but we can make it up to them, can't we?'

Doc Hess said he did understand; said, yes, it was OK to bring Anthony as well as Mary. But he was a practical man and he knew it would mean a whole new set of paperwork. There was no way Marge was going to be able to bring the kids home with her this trip.

*

Marjorie, Loras and their mother took the 1.50 p.m. TWA flight from Shannon to New York on Thursday 8 September. As soon as Marge got home to St Louis, she set herself the task of getting her two new children stateside as quickly as humanly possible. She was constantly on the phone to Sister Hildegarde and Mother Barbara, urging them to speed things up, and the nuns were assiduous in sending written accounts of their efforts to help. Their letters made much of the difficulties they were tackling on Marge's behalf and contained hints about donations and gifts to the convent.

By late 1955 Sean Ross Abbey was sending scores of children to the United States and Sister Hildegarde was dealing with all the transactions. A memo circulated in the Department of External Affairs described her as 'one of the three most important people in the Irish adoption picture'; the other two were Father Cecil Barrett of Archbishop McQuaid's Catholic Social Welfare Bureau and Rita Kenny of the Irish Passport Office.

On 7 November 1955 Sister Hildegarde took Mary and Anthony on another trip to Dublin, where they were examined by the US embassy's accredited doctor, John Malone. He reported that Anthony was a 'well developed child, mentally alert, friendly and cooperative. His mental development has been normal, and I consider him above average intelligence,' although Malone added a postscript: 'On Neurological examination, all deep reflexes were diminished and I could not elicit the patellar reflexes. This is an isolated finding and I do not consider it to be significant.'

For some reason Sister Hildegarde and Mother Barbara were finding the Irish Passport Office impossible to deal with – it was almost as if they were deliberately trying to block this adoption. The latest letter from Rita Kenny was categorical: '*I received your letter in connection with the application of Mr and Mrs Hess for the adoption of baby Mary McDonald and Anthony Lee . . . There is no Home Study Report attached. I made it quite clear that no consideration could be given to the application until a report of a Home Study conducted by Catholic Charities in St Louis had been submitted.*'

The nuns were perplexed. They suspected the unpleasant man Mother Barbara had spoken to at the meeting in Dublin was deliberately making things difficult for the bishop's sister. This was turning out to be the most difficult adoption of all the hundreds they had carried out. Within an hour of receiving Rita Kenny's letter, Sister Hildegarde was back at her typewriter and this time she was fuming.

16th November 1955

Dear Mrs Hess,

I am dashing this letter away to you so that you can see for yourself what the Passport Office have to say. I am quite weary of it all. Are they trying to be difficult or do they not understand? We answered every letter of theirs on your children by return post and this was not done without an effort. I have more than I can cope with from now until after Christmas. If you can do anything, please try and do it for I had hoped to finish transportation of the children before the end of this month.

   Sincerely in the Sacred Hearts,
   Sr M. Hildegarde.

PS Reverend Mother is like a child waiting for your parcel to her. To date it has not arrived.

When she received Sister Hildegarde's letter, Marjorie Hess did what she always did in a crisis – she rang her brother. What then seems to have followed was an instructive demonstration of the relationship between Church and state in the exercise of Ireland's adoption policy. A telephone call from Bishop Loras Lane of Rockford to Archbishop Ritter of St Louis seems to have led to another telephone call, to Archbishop McQuaid of Dublin; that call led to another one, this time to Irish Minister of External Affairs Liam Cosgrave, which in turn led to instructions being issued to the Irish Passport Office that passports for Anthony Lee and Mary McDonald must be furnished at once.

The person at the end of all the calls was Joe Coram. He put the phone down with a sigh and called Rita Kenny to countersign the authorizations. He didn't regret the efforts he had expended on the dossier – he thought of it as a test case for hundreds, perhaps thousands of others – but as the tram home to Glasnevin carried him past the archbishop's palace he doffed his trilby and smiled bitterly.

NINETEEN

December 1955;
Roscrea

In the three and a half years since her arrival at Sean Ross Abbey Philomena had had no contact with her family. Neither her father nor her brothers and sisters had visited her, and the nuns would not pass on any letters. But after Sister Hildegarde told her Anthony was being taken to America, Philomena had been allowed to write home. Her own future once the child was gone now had to be decided and the nuns would need to speak to her father.

On 1 December 1955 Patrick Lee and his son Jack pulled off the Templemore to Roscrea road and rang the bell on the abbey gate. They had driven from Newcastle West in Latchford's bread van and were ready for a cup of tea. Patrick was fifty-three and still working as a butcher; Jack was twenty-four, unmarried, and delivering bread for the Newcastle baker. The nuns who ushered them inside were polite, but the unspoken implication that the visitors were tainted by the family's collective shame hung heavy.

Sister Hildegarde sat them down in the high-ceilinged Georgian parlour off the grand entrance hall (men were not permitted to penetrate any further) and returned ten minutes later with Philomena.

'Here we are now.' Hildegarde smiled sweetly. 'Here's your daughter, Mr Lee. Now I'd say you have a couple of weeks before the boy goes out of here, so I'll be off and leave you to talk about your daughter's future. I'm sure you have a lot to say to each other.'

But after the nun had gone the three of them sat in awkward silence. Philomena wanted so much to hug her father, to hear that he loved her and forgave her, but something held her back. She sensed her da wanted to hug her too, but he was finding it hard. Constrained by the guilt the Church had inculcated in him and by the knowledge of his daughter's suffering, he spoke about anything but the things that really mattered – about the weather, about the rival butcher who'd opened in town and about Jack's plans to get a job as a projectionist in the cinema on Maiden Street. Jack nodded and looked uncomfortable. Philomena was close to tears, trying desperately not to cry in front of her father.

It was Anthony's arrival that changed things.

Sister Hildegarde had agreed they could have him for half an hour. Within minutes the two men were bouncing him up and down on their knees and tickling him till he squealed with delight. Anthony had run straight to them as soon as he entered the room and handed them two bunches of wild flowers (which Margaret had provided). He let them kiss him on the cheek and showed them how brave he was by climbing up the ladder that leaned against the tall bookshelves. They laughed out loud at the little fellow's antics and encouraged him to dance and sing for them. Jack couldn't hide his admiration.

'He's a beauty, Phil, sure he is. He's got the Lee black hair and all.'

Her father smiled and nodded wordlessly, his eyes filling with tears.

Philomena was overwhelmed with pride to see her child so loved by her family, pained by the thought that their joy could not last, and tormented by the wild, impossible idea that perhaps they could find a way to keep him.

'So what do you think, Da?' she said hesitantly. 'The nuns want to send him off to America, you know . . .'

Her father said nothing, but Jack was muttering about some woman he'd heard of out in the country who'd had a child with no father and still refused to give him up.

'I'm right, amn't I, Da? Kitty McLaughlin kept her baby. So why don't we just pick this little fellow up right now and grab him and run off with him? You know, just run with him . . . and then, Phil, you can come home and look after him.'

Philomena's heart leapt – she pulled Anthony to her as if she were ready to leave at once – but no one picked the boy up and no one ran with him. The minute of euphoria collapsed into the sad, unassailable reality that Philomena would not be coming home and Anthony would not be coming with her. All three of them knew perfectly well it was impossible for a fallen woman to come back to Newcastle West, or any town in Ireland, without causing a desperate scandal. And anyway the council house on Connolly's Terrace was small and Patrick Lee had not the space for her to sleep or the means for her to eat. He looked at his boots and said, 'There's no way around it, Phil. I'm sorry, but you'll have to go away.'

Jack Lee cried as he left the abbey that day. He'd just been paid by Mr Latchford at the bakery and he had a week's wages – three pounds – in his pocket. As he was going out the door he nudged his sister and pressed the three rolled-up notes into her hand. Then he turned away to wipe his eyes and ran down the drive to catch up with his dad.

TWENTY

December, 1955;
St Louis, Dublin

'No patellar reflexes and deep reflexes all diminished. That's not good, Marge, not good. It could mean a damaged nervous system or even brain abnormality. The boy could be a defective, and we sure don't want that kind of thing in the family.'

Marge looked distressed.

'But, Doc, I saw him and he's not defective. He's a lovely little guy and completely normal. Let me see the doctor's report . . . Look, he says here it's probably just some kind of freak reading.'

But Doc Hess did not like to be contradicted. Marge sensed he was in categorical mode, stuck on the idea that the Irish boy was damaged goods, but twenty years of marriage had taught her how to handle her husband.

'OK, Doc. You're right. We don't want anything to upset our family. I just think maybe . . . Why don't we get a second opinion before we make a decision? I'm sure you can get someone to take a second look at Anthony, can't you?'

Doc thought for a moment.

'Well . . . I guess that's logical. But, whatever this examination reveals, we follow its conclusion. If it says the boy's a defective, we turn him down, OK?'

*

John Malone was a little surprised at the tone of Dr Hess's letter – he certainly hadn't meant to suggest serious abnormalities in the patient – but he agreed to have the boy tested again. On 2 December 1955 Anthony Lee was taken one more time to Dublin, to St Laurence's Hospital on North Brunswick Street. He followed with interest as the nurse swabbed down parts of his scalp and face and attached little sticky things (they were electrodes, but he didn't know that), then wired them up to some sort of box. For twenty minutes a man in a white coat shone lights in Anthony's eyes, made loud noises beside his head and asked him to close his eyes, look up, look down, look all around. Anthony frowned a little but didn't cry. He was a trusting child and didn't expect the world to play tricks on him. He didn't understand the game the grown-ups were playing, but it didn't hurt so he decided to play along. At the end of it all the nurse bent down and gave him a red lollipop. When she offered her cheek for a kiss, he gave her one and she laughed out loud.

The report of the electro-encephalographic examination of Master Anthony Lee was written up by the hospital's chief neurologist, Andrew MacDermott. It showed 'no focal or specifically epileptic signs and is probably within normal limits'.

The hospital sent the results to Dr Malone, who smiled at being proved right.

Dear Dr Hess,

I am sorry that my brief report caused you so much anxiety. Personally I was quite satisfied with the child's mental state, general physical health, and Neurological examination.

His muscle tone, power, co-ordination, gait and stance were all normal, as were his cranial nerves.

Re-examination with a Neurological colleague (2/12/55) was satisfactory, and on this occasion the patellar reflexes

were elicited. I enclose the Neurologist's report and I give him
100% clearance certificate.
  With kind regards.
  Sincerely,
  John P Malone, MD

Doc Hess quibbled over the neurologist's wording – *probably* within normal limits was not the same as *definitely* within normal limits – but Marge was insistent. 'I've seen the little fellow,' she said, 'and I give you *my* personal guarantee that he's normal, Doc. Please let him come, won't you?'

Doc agreed, somewhat grudgingly, that if Marge *guaranteed* it, then the boy could come.

Marge Hess phoned Mother Barbara and urged her to send the children over as quickly as she could. Mother Barbara was relieved – the folk at the Passport Office had made such a fuss over this case and she was eager to get them dispatched. Marge said there were seats available on the Pan Am flight out of Shannon the following Sunday and Mother Barbara told her to go ahead and make the booking.

Marge was so excited she almost forgot to mention the photographs, but she remembered just in time.

'Reverend Mother, one last thing! Please take some photos of the children so we can have a record of them before they leave the abbey. You can put the cost of the film on the tab and we'll settle everything together with the donation.'

As Mother Barbara hung up the telephone, she was already shuffling through the pile of documents in her in tray. She found the ones she needed and put them ready to post, one for Mary and one for Anthony.

I, Margaret Feeney, Known in Religion as Sister Barbara, Superioress of Sean Ross Abbey, Roscrea, County Tipperary, Ireland, make Oath and say:

  That the custody of Anthony Lee born out of wedlock to

Philomena Lee has been surrendered to me as Superioress of Sean Ross Abbey, Roscrea, as evidenced by her Affidavit which is hereto attached relinquishing full claim forever to the said child.

That as legal guardian I hereby relinquish all claim to Anthony Lee and surrender him to Dr Michael and Mrs Marjorie Hess, 810 Moundale Drive, Ferguson, Missouri, U.S.A. for legal adoption.

Subscribed and sworn to by the said Margaret Feeney.

TWENTY-ONE

December 1955;
Roscrea

When Sister Annunciata had left for England, Anthony's supply of presents had come to an abrupt end and for the past year he had had nothing to play with other than the few battered communal toys that lay forlornly in the corner of the day room. But thanks to her brother Jack, Philomena now had some money of her own and she was desperate to spend it on her son. As the girls were not allowed out of the abbey she had no access to the shops in Roscrea, but one evening after the children had gone to bed she waylaid a member of the convent's lay staff who was about to go home for the night.

Philomena offered to pay her five shillings if she would go to the general store on Castle Street and see what Mrs Frawley had in the way of toys. The woman demanded ten and Philomena handed them over.

The next morning was better than any Christmas. When the woman came back for the morning shift she had a large brown-paper parcel with her, which she unwrapped to reveal a tin bus painted in the colours of the Irish state bus company and a plane painted red and yellow with the inscription 'GE 270' on its wings. The toys were cheap and shoddy, but Philomena could scarcely wait until the evening hour to give them to her son. When he saw them, Anthony's eyes opened wide. Without a word, he took the bus and rolled it across the floor. Then he did the same with the plane and burst into peals of laughter: the toy had a friction drive that made it whirr and gather speed when he pushed it, and sparks flew from its nose and wings.

Philomena sat and watched as Anthony launched the thing from one corner of the play room to the other, chasing after it with shrieks of pleasure, repeating the operation time after time with mounting excitement. But then he suddenly seemed to remember himself. He placed the two toys by the wall, ran to his mammy and without a word gave her a tender hug and nuzzled his face into her lap.

18 December 1955

Nobody actually told Philomena and Margaret their children were leaving that weekend; it just filtered down through the convent grapevine. A few people had spotted Sister Hildegarde taking photographs of Mary and Anthony on the steps of the old house – a lovely one of them holding hands together and a shot of Anthony on his own, clasping his beloved plane to his chest – and the girls had put two and two together.

They had eaten their lunch on the Sunday afternoon and were clearing the refectory table when an older sister who had spoken kindly to them in the past came running through.

'Girls, quickly! Come over to the window, will you?'

The nun was panting from running up the stairs.

'It's your babbies, girls. Quick. Sister Hildegarde's taking them . . .'

Philomena and Margaret ran to the casement window overlooking the drive in front of the house. Below, a large black car was sitting with its engine running and rear doors open. In the back seat were two little figures and, on either side of them, Mother Barbara and Sister Hildegarde were squeezing themselves in, beaming and chatting as they always did on their days out.

Philomena yelled, 'Anthony! Look up here!' and Margaret banged on the window. But the noise of the engine seemed to blot out their voices and neither child responded. As the car pulled away, Philomena wailed, 'No! No! Not my babby. Don't let them take my babby!' and at that precise moment Anthony twisted in his seat and climbed up to peer through the rear windscreen. He was wearing the brown shorts and blue knitted sweater Philomena had made for him and in his hand he was clutching his tin plane.

LONDON

Present Day

The table in front of me is covered with photographs and documents: letters and diaries, interviews, old hotel bills, postcards and scribbled notes in fading handwriting; the poignant fragments of an unravelling mystery that has been with me since that first meeting in the New Year of 2004.

Most of the data was furnished willingly – Marge Hess's diary and her copious correspondence about the adoption of Anthony and Mary; interviews with the surviving participants in the drama and friends and relatives of those who are dead; all the source material on which the narrative of the preceding pages, and those to come, has been based. But getting to other documents has involved a battle against concealment, against the reticence of people and organizations with things to hide. The Church's love affair with secrecy, for instance, and its belief in the unabsolvable guilt of the Magdalenes meant house names stripped the girls of their identity and true lives were hidden behind obfuscation. The girls rarely knew who shared their Calvary with them; they knew only that Marcella was not Marcella, Augustine was not Augustine and Nancy was not Nancy.

As a foretaste of their preordained separation, the Church banned mothers at Roscrea from having photographs of their children. But brave Sister Annunciata smuggled in a Box Brownie. The snaps Annunciata took for Philomena to keep are lying on my desk today, the record of a time and place that might have stayed obscure – a lost toddler in a convent garden, a puzzled-looking boy staring at us through the grainy mist of years, trying to mount a tricycle, climbing on a step, cradling a toy plane as wide as his shoulders, always looking at the photographer with trust in his eyes. This last photo in particular has stayed with me. It is in black and white, of course, but I know that the plane is a red-and-yellow lithographed tin GE 270 Sparkling Space Rocket with friction drive and a ten-inch wing-span, and that it was made in Germany between 1955 and 1965 by a toy manufacturer called Technofix.

As she passes by my desk, my daughter looks over and asks who the child is.

'Just a boy,' I tell her, 'who grew up a long time ago and a long way from here.'

Another photograph, this time in a yellowing newspaper cutting from somewhere in the United States, shows the same toy plane clutched to the chest of a young boy in a duffel coat, flanked by a bewildered-looking little girl and a tall elegant woman.

My daughter glances at the two photos and spots it is the same boy in each.

'He looks nice,' she says.

How strange that a tin plane in two photographs from different sides of the ocean provides such an important clue, a link to bring us closer to Anthony after years of seeking, years of absence.

His first child's passport is on my desk. The little photo under the Irish state seal shows a serious three-year-old in a hand-knitted sweater decorated with large shamrocks, and on the opposite page, this information in English and Gaelic:

Anthony Lee

Passport issued: *Dublin, 22 November 1955*
Nationality: *Citizen of Ireland*
Profession: *None*
Place of Birth: *Co. Tipperary*

Date of Birth: *5-7-1952*
Residence: *Ireland*
Height: *3'2"*
Colour of Eyes: *Blue*
Colour of Hair: *Black*
Face: *Oval*
Special Peculiarities: *None*
Signature: *Bearer is unable to write.*

Saddest of all are the renunciation papers, the documents under which mothers were forced to give away their children. *Never to attempt to see or make any claim* to their own flesh – what a betrayal that must have seemed in the years they had ahead of them to dwell on the oath they had sworn. The decorative seals and dry formulae mask a human tragedy that was repeated all over Ireland hundreds, thousands of times.

The task I had been handed by the stranger in the British Library would involve challenging this vow of acquiescence. It would mean seeking to know what happened to Anthony Lee. And it would bring startling discoveries.

PART TWO

ONE

18–19 December 1955

The novelty of the expedition soon wore off. Curious and excited, Anthony and Mary had begun the trip in high spirits, but their chatter quickly dwindled to uneasy silence. Mother Barbara and Sister Hildegarde were in good humour, gossiping and laughing, occasionally dabbing the children's faces with a moist handkerchief or telling Anthony to sit up straight.

They found Niall O'Hanlon waiting where they'd told him to be, by the airport taxi rank, a tattered suitcase on the ground between his feet. He was Sister Teresa's nephew, twenty-four years old and delighted to get his airfare paid. His da's pub in County Mayo was losing money and the few pounds he'd earned delivering the post hadn't covered his keep. Niall had never seen a plane before, let alone flown in one, but he told himself he was fine: Uncle Patrick would meet him in Chicago and looking after a couple of youngsters would be no trouble at all. Sure he must be doing a good deed – if the nuns were sending them to America, then it was God's work.

'You must be Mr O'Hanlon.' Mother Barbara offered Niall a thin hand. She had enjoyed the car journey but now she wanted to get away.

'Anthony, Mary, this is Mr O'Hanlon. He'll be looking after you for the next few hours, until you meet your new family. Isn't that nice?'

Without waiting for a reply, she handed Niall a photograph of the man who would collect the children in Chicago: he was balding, clean-shaven and of medium height, with long arms and a trim physique; he had a little smile that Niall thought made him look smug.

'You can't keep the photo,' said Mother Barbara, taking it back, 'but Mr Hess will be easy to spot – he'll be wearing a red bow tie and standing by the arrivals board.'

Niall nodded. The reality of what he was about to embark upon was sinking in. He looked at Mary and Anthony cowering by the nuns' legs and caught his breath. He felt like a scared little boy himself.

'Right,' said Mother Barbara, after they had run over the details of the journey. She drew herself up to her full height, giving the children a fleeting look. 'We'd best be off. The taxi's costing us and we don't want to get back to Sean Ross too late.'

The nuns shook Niall's hand, thanked him and wished him well. In an unexpected gesture of tenderness, Mother Barbara stooped down to give Anthony a kiss on the cheek. But Anthony, with an unusual expression of defiance, turned his face away.

'Well,' she said sharply as she straightened up, 'I suppose that's all the thanks we can expect.'

It was a rough ten-hour flight to Boston and to Niall it felt much longer; the children wouldn't respond to his efforts to reassure them, but he noticed Anthony kept a tight hold of Mary's hand and stroked her arm soothingly. Shortly before touchdown, the hostess came round with breakfast. Mary pushed it away, but Anthony sliced up her bread and fed it to her with milk from a cup that he held to her lips.

Boston was in the grip of winter. Logan Airfield was covered in snow, and as they were escorted to the terminal the air felt sharp on their cheeks. Mary and Anthony, who had never seen snow, gaped in wonder. *Thank God for that*, thought Niall, trying not to laugh with relief as the children's faces lit up.

The immigration official who examined their passports and their Irish Quota visas asked Niall if he was the children's father. Niall shrugged his shoulders and shook his head.

The transfer flight to Chicago was smoother and the children managed a couple of hours' sleep. The hours they spent together gave Niall the uncomfortable feeling that he was responsible for them, that they were looking to him for protection. When he took them to the bathroom at the back of the plane, Anthony looked up at him.

'Thank you, sir,' he said in a thin, strangely dignified voice. 'My sister is scared now but I told her she mustn't be, because you are looking after us.'

Niall patted the boy's head and felt his unease deepen.

At Chicago Midway Airport, Niall gathered their belongings and picked Mary up to carry her down the aircraft steps. Through the layers of clothing, he could feel her trembling like a scared bird. Anthony looked at him with trusting eyes and took his hand as they walked across the tarmac.

Once Niall had collected his baggage – the children had none – he searched for the man in the red bow tie. He was standing where the nuns had said he would be, smoking a fat brown cigar bigger than Niall had ever seen. By misfortune, Marge had run to the ladies' room and Doc Hess was alone. The two men shook hands awkwardly and Niall tried to think what to say.

'Well, mister, here are the kids I've been told to give you,' he managed, weighing up the man in front of him. 'I hope you'll look after them – they're tired out and hungry too, because they've hardly eaten nor slept.'

Doc sucked on his cigar and bent down to smile at the children, but to his horror Mary screamed and burst into tears. Terrified by all she had been through, gripped by panic, she attached herself to Niall's leg and would not let go. Anthony too looked on the verge of tears, but it was clear he was doing his utmost to hold them back. It was only when Marge came running that Mary finally began to calm down, and by then Niall too was shaking and sobbing.

After the Irishman had gone, Marge bent down and wiped the

children's faces. She'd brought warm coats for them and was eager to get them wrapped up against the December chill. Doc said he wanted a group photograph to mark the occasion and he evidently knelt down to take it, because the lens is pointing up at Mary's troubled face: in her smart new coat with its velvet collar and her white bobbled woollen bonnet, her cheeks are still stained with tears, her mouth is open and her bewildered eyes stare warily into the camera. Anthony is frowning and his gaze is directed over Doc's head into the middle distance, trying to make out the nature of the place they have landed in; he is wearing a brand new duffel coat and in his hand is the tin plane from Roscrea.

The drive from Chicago to St Louis took almost seven hours. It was the Monday before Christmas so the freeways were busy and the snow sweeping in from the east slowed them to a crawl. In the back of Doc's Cadillac, Marge tried to keep her voice bright and cheery. She plied the children with the candy and toys she had bought for the journey, but they responded with uncomprehending stares. Thrust into an unknown world where bright lights burned, crowds jostled, voices boomed from airport tannoys and cars and planes filled the universe with noise and speed, the children wanted to go back to the convent – they had assumed they would be going back – but now Anthony was sensing a horrible permanence to their new situation.

Marge understood what they were going through but the day was not easy for her either. As she watched them sitting there, taciturn and unsmiling, everything seemed suddenly to be at risk. Her mind filled with nagging, panicked doubts. *Is this all a terrible mistake? What will Doc say now?*

She glanced at the rear-view mirror and saw her husband's eyes focused on the road. He seemed to be taking things OK, at least for the time being: he didn't complain about having to sit up front alone; didn't complain about the driving or the weather; just stared ahead and hummed along with the show tunes and light musicals he liked to listen to on the radio. Anthony and Mary were watching him with apprehensive curiosity. In the exclusively feminine world of the convent, men had been an exotic phenomenon and neither of them knew what to make of him. Doc's masculine features and flinty gaze appeared harsh and forbidding; this word 'father' they kept hearing was strange and incomprehensible.

Mary's lower lip was beginning to tremble, and Marge was frantic at the thought she might start bawling – Doc hated noise and she didn't want to upset him while he was driving. She poured some Fanta into a cup and offered it to Mary, who choked on the unexpected fizzing sweetness. With a shriek she threw down the beaker on the seat and Marge watched in horror as the liquid seeped into the Cadillac's immaculate beige upholstery in a bright slash of orange. Seeing Marge's expression, Anthony whipped his little handkerchief from his pocket and tried feverishly to clean up the mess, but it was too late.

'What the hell's going on back there? What are those children up to?' roared Doc, and with that Mary burst into ear-splitting, uncontrollable tears.

After the worst was over, a tense, silent calm descended on the car. All four of them – even little Mary – knew something bad had happened, something worse than just spilled Fanta, and no one really knew how to put it right.

TWO

Christmas 1955

Number 810 Moundale Drive was a single-storey ranch-style house set
in a wooded plot with a backyard sloping down from a crazy-paved
patio. Like those around it, the house had been built seven years earlier,
and the district was still establishing itself. Ferguson, Missouri was full
of similar subdivisions; the place lacked the good-neighbourly feel of
older St Louis suburbs, but the Hesses had friends in the homes around
them and their boys had good buddies to play with. That first evening
when they arrived from the airport, Anthony and Mary found the house
disconcertingly full of noise and activity – after the cold bare convent,
the place was overwhelming in its opulence, its hubbub and clutter.

Before they had left for the airport, Marge had got the Christmas
decorations under way. She had bought a tall Norwegian spruce from
Magruder's Garden Supplies and erected it in the corner of the family
room, telling the boys to help her with the tinsel and baubles and
electric fairy lights. The two older ones, James and Thomas, were
fourteen and thirteen – kind of old for getting excited about Christmas
trees – but little Stevie was only nine and had always been her most
diligent helper.

As they untangled the flex of the tree lights, Marge had started
to explain that this would be a very special Christmas with the arrival
of a new brother and sister. But something in Stevie's face suggested
he didn't share her enthusiasm, and she put an arm around him.

'Oh, honey,' she said, 'don't look so worried. The new guys aren't going to take your place. We still love you best in the whole world.'

'OK.' Stevie had nodded dubiously, but when Marge put the Christmas presents under the tree she had noticed that he went round very carefully and counted a couple of times which pile had the most parcels.

Marge had intended the tree, the lights, the decorations and the presents to make Mary and Anthony feel loved and wanted. She had been imagining the happiness in their faces when they discovered the festive scene in the family room. But when they arrived, thirty-six hours after leaving the convent in Roscrea, the children were in no state to enjoy anything. Mary cried incessantly and would not say what was wrong. She had not spoken at all since she got off the plane and showed no pleasure at the surprises Marge had prepared for her. Anthony appeared disoriented and unsure how to react. He seemed interested in the coloured lights and the tree, and also in the three boys: as Marge introduced them he managed a shy smile, but his eyes kept flicking back to Doc, who was snapping photographs and instructing the boys to pose 'with the new kids'. Their rowdiness became too much for Anthony: amid a chorus of shrieked observations and mocking questions ('D'you grow up in a church?' 'Hey, Mom, what's with his hair?' 'Say something in Irish!') he found himself close to tears and buried his face in Marge's skirt.

In Sean Ross Christmas had never been an occasion for overt celebration – there was no tree and certainly no decorations or fairy lights – so Mary and Anthony were mystified by the fuss of Christmas morning. They were woken early by the excited whooping of the boys, and shortly afterwards Marge came into their bedroom with mugs of cocoa.

'Merry Christmas!' She beamed at Anthony, putting the mugs on the bedside table and kissing his forehead. 'And a Merry Christmas to *you*, dear!' she repeated to Mary, who looked at Anthony nervously but allowed herself to be kissed on the cheek. Marge had bought Mary a pretty sailor dress and Anthony a white sweater and neat cord pants, and she fussed around the room laying out their outfits at the bottom of their beds. Mary and Anthony watched her in silence.

Marge spent the morning preparing the Christmas meal while the boys played noisy games, shouting and racing round the house. Anthony and Mary sat in the den, speaking to one another quietly in strange words no one could quite understand, and Doc marched from room to room, snapping photographs. Carols blared from the radio; Doc whistled a tuneless accompaniment; Stevie roared with pleasure at the sight of his pile of parcels, and James and Thomas bickered good-naturedly about who would get the best presents.

Anthony found the ruckus intimidating. He thought of the nuns and the familiar halls of the convent and wanted to cry. He took Mary by the hand and pulled her with him into the space between the sofa and Doc's vast armchair, looking out with large, melancholy eyes at his big, strong new brothers. Marge found them there and knelt down beside them with a parcel in each hand.

'I know things are a little scary right now, sweetheart,' she said to Anthony – Mary seemed happier when she wasn't being addressed directly – 'but you'll soon get used to us. Here, this one's for you, and this one's for your sister.' She placed the parcels in the children's hands and said a silent prayer: *Please God, let the presents go down well. Let something go right.*

Her prayer was answered. Having unwrapped his package with almost comical caution, Anthony seemed entranced by a pack of plastic toy soldiers and leaned over to encourage Mary to open her parcel. With her thumb in her mouth, she gave the sparkly paper a half-hearted tug and Anthony helped her along, crawling out of his hiding place to give himself more space. As Mary caught a glimpse of light pink satin, she wriggled out after him and ripped the paper open. A pretty blonde-haired doll stared at her with wide blue eyes and Mary beamed from ear to ear for the first time since their arrival. Marge felt a wave of euphoria and relief.

'You like that, huh? What d'you wanna call her? She's yours now.' She smiled. But her elation was short-lived.

'Hey,' called Stevie, suddenly paying attention to the little group by the armchair, 'are they Marine Corps soldiers? He got *Marine Corps* soldiers! How come *he* gets soldiers and he doesn't even belong here? How come—'

Marge grasped Stevie by both shoulders and looked at him intently.

'He's one of us now, Stevie. Please don't you talk to him that way.'

But when she let him go, Stevie ran out of the room yelling 'It's not *fair*!' and slammed the door behind him.

By the afternoon things were looking a little better. Anthony and Mary had eaten their lunch with surprising gusto and they seemed full, sleepy and content, sitting side by side on the sofa, surrounded by presents. Stevie played on the floor beside the tree, Thomas was reading his new book about steam engines and James was somehow eating a third slice of cake. Feeling the warmth from the sherry wash over her, Marge proposed a toast.

'Well, Doc,' she said, with her glass raised, 'I've had my Christmas present with these two beautiful children and I thank you for that. Jim and Tom and Stevie have had their gifts, and the little ones sure got plenty too. But I think you need a present, Doc, a very special one. I would like very much if we were to name our new son in your honour. Your name – Michael – is a beautiful one, an angel's name. And I think we should give it to our new boy.'

THREE

1955–6

In the days that followed, Anthony Lee was transformed seamlessly into Michael A. Hess. Marge and Doc decided he could keep Anthony as a middle name, but they stipulated that from now on everyone would call him Michael, or – if needs be – Mike.

The Hess boys said nothing, but there was jealousy, and it manifested itself in small ways. When Michael first saw the TV playing in the den, he had been both fascinated and alarmed. He had crawled round the back of the set to see where the little men and women on the screen were coming from and, unable to find an explanation, had become indignant and stamped his foot.

'Get that man out of that box!' he had shouted. 'Get him out right now!'

The boys had laughed uproariously. They told all their friends how their simple Irish 'brother' thought there were real people in the TV set. Michael had been puzzled and abashed by the boys' scorn, and began to keep away from them as much as he could. They had also noticed Mike's attachment to his stupid Irish tin plane. When he woke on New Year's morning, he looked for it everywhere – in the house, in the backyard, in the trash – but to his sorrow and dismay it was nowhere to be found.

*

New Year 1956 was a tough time for the Hess household. The new arrivals had upset the family's balance. Settled patterns were disrupted and unfamiliar emotions were stirring.

Doc, in particular, had been struggling. He tried to be open and welcoming, but the Irish children were changing the way things were done here: the bathroom rota was unrecognizable since they arrived; the little girl's crying woke him in the night and left him irritable in the morning; Marge was always running round after them and he wasn't getting his breakfast on time.

By the time Doc returned to work in early January, he was deeply worried about Mary. After his medical studies in Iowa City Doc had majored in urology, but he prided himself on keeping up to date on other branches of medicine, including the newer sciences of psychology and mental health. He had observed Mary's behaviour with what he believed was an expert's eye, and he didn't like what he saw. Ever since she had arrived in America, the girl had not addressed a single word to anyone other than her brother, and even when she spoke to him it was in that strange gibberish that no one else could understand.

Doc had told Marge of his concerns on several occasions, but she'd insisted Mary was just a shy little chick intimidated by the sudden change in her life and taking time to get used to things. Doc wasn't buying it. He had always said he didn't want this experiment of Marge's to saddle the family with a long-term burden and knew it was best to nip the problem in the bud. The first morning back in his office, Doc had dictated a letter to his secretary expressing his concern and addressed it to Sister Hildegarde.

A couple of days later Doc received a letter from Bill King, the Hess family lawyer, which heightened his sense of urgency. Custody petitions were due to be filed; the children would be officially declared under the Alien Registration Act and the registration renewed each year until their final adoption and naturalization as US citizens. Doc read the letter with growing panic. Bill made it all sound so inexorable; if there was a problem with Mary he would have to act fast.

Sean Ross Abbey,
Roscrea,
County Tipp.

27th January 1956

Dear Mr and Mrs Hess,

I was surprised to get your letter with the account of Mary.

You will remember that it was you who brought Mary to the Doctor and you had her with you all day, so there was nothing hidden from you.

If we had noticed Mary defective in any way, we would have told you. We would not have let you have her alone with the Doctor if we wanted to hide anything.

If you do decide you do not want to keep Mary, we will have no trouble with the placement of the children. There are thousands who would take Mary if we ask them. But don't make arrangements for any transportation until you have informed us, as it could cause you and us greater worry.

I am sorry this has happened. We know of nothing like this in Mary's family.

Until I hear from you again, God bless and keep you.

Sr M. Hildegarde.

PS If you decide to take another child, Doctor Hess had better come over and examine the child. I would not like myself to take responsibility. S.M.H.

Sister Hildegarde's somewhat terse reply to Doc's letter arrived in the Hess mailbox the same day the *St Louis Post-Dispatch* published its article. Marge had almost forgotten speaking to the reporter who had called weeks earlier and asked her to express her excitement on acquiring her new family. Now it was all written up in banner headlines, ST LOUIS DOCTOR AND WIFE ADOPT IRISH CHILDREN, followed by some lame prose: 'Bundles of joy from Ireland: St Louis Irish eyes were smiling as two Irish youngsters, Mary, two, and Michael, three, were getting better acquainted with their new family this month . . .' And printed beside the piece was the photograph Marge had loaned the fellow, the shot Doc had taken at the airport with young Mike clinging to his toy plane from Roscrea.

The coincidence of the two events, the letter and the article, sent Doc into a fury. He approached Marge, newspaper in hand, as she washed dishes at the kitchen sink.

'Look here, Marge, this is damned inconvenient,' he said, slapping the newspaper down on the counter beside her and folding his arms across his chest. Marge looked at him, then down at the paper.

'Oh Doc,' she said, 'it's not—'

'Marge, listen. You know how I feel about these kids, the girl in particular. She's not normal, and we've taken on a great deal of trouble with her. I've been thinking very seriously about having her sent back to that convent – don't try to argue with me, Marge – but this damned story . . . Why'd you have to go and do a thing like that? Damn it, Marge, we can't send her back now – not with *this*.' He stabbed his finger at the paper and tossed the letter down beside it. Marge dried her hands calmly and picked up the letter.

'We can't send them back anyway, Doc. Not after what they've been through.'

'Well, hell! It's too bad. We should never have— We should have thought harder about this whole thing before taking on such a burden. I'm too old for this.'

Marge was stung. She had secretly, guiltily, been thinking the same thing herself. She laid a hand on Doc's crossed arms.

'Don't worry, Doc. I know it seems bad now, but things will get better. I'll give Loras a call and see if he can get someone to come take a look at Mary.'

'Well, go ahead and call your brother,' Doc said. 'But one thing's for sure – we have to get this whole thing fixed before the custody hearing.'

*

The next morning Marge was standing at the kitchen sink, watching Mike and Mary through the window. The ground was still covered in snow, and as soon as Doc left for work Mike had bundled his sister up in her winter coat and tugged her outside. The sun was shining and it made the red of Mary's hair glow like burning embers against the snowy garden; her cheeks were rosy and her eyes gleamed with energy. Watching as she chased Mike round the yard, sending clouds of snow puffing up around them, Marge could hardly believe her new daughter was a defective, whatever Doc said; she seemed so healthy and so lovely and full of potential.

What worried Marge was Mary's continuing refusal to speak to them. She opened the window quietly and listened in puzzlement to the incomprehensible words Mary was gabbling, wondering as she had so often how Mike seemed to understand it. Marge was sick of talking to her daughter through Mike: he had become a kind of interpreter, speaking to Mary in nonsense, then translating into English for the Hesses. Doc said it was unacceptable in a civilized house.

After Marge's phone call, Loras had rung Father Bob Slattery of St Louis Catholic Charities. Slattery was an Irishman himself, and when he showed up one morning in early March Marge took to him at once. She introduced him to the young ones, but Mary was her usual taciturn self and Michael too seemed strangely suspicious of the priest in his black robes.

'You see what I mean, Father? I'm at my wits' end and Doc's started saying Mary has something wrong with her.'

Father Slattery looked thoughtfully at the children.

'OK, Mrs Hess,' he said. 'Can you leave me alone with them? There's something I'd like to try.'

Marge went out to the store, and when she returned a half-hour later Father Slattery was beaming.

That evening when Doc arrived home from work, his wife was in better spirits than he'd seen in a long time.

'I have something to tell you, Doc Hess,' Marge beamed. 'It's real important for all of us and we have Father Slattery to thank for it. While I was out at the store, he spoke to Mike and Mary in Gaelic and they answered him back right away! That gibberish they've been speaking to each other is Gaelic, Doc. They're fluent in it! Bob says they must have picked it up from the staff in the nurseries at the convent. Isn't that marvellous news?'

Doc thought for a moment but didn't return Marge's smile.

'Well, I guess so. But what I want to know is how come they've been so damn tricksy and always speaking it over here? Didn't they know it was going to get us all spoiling mad?'

Marge tried to explain that for two scared children thrust into a world they feared and mistrusted, the secrecy of a language known only to themselves provided a refuge and a form of self-protection, but Doc wasn't interested in explanations.

'So tell me, what does Father Slattery say we should do to get the girl speaking English?'

Marge laughed.

'Well, Bob says she's pretty sure to understand English and probably just needs prompting to start speaking it. He says we should let her know very gently that we're not going to use Michael as an interpreter any more and she needs to start asking for things herself.'

Doc harrumphed. 'Well, darn it, woman, isn't that what I said all along! If the girl wants a cup of milk and she sees she ain't gonna get it till she asks properly, my guess is she'll start speaking English pretty damn quick!'

It was good advice. Within a couple of weeks Mary was beginning to speak, hesitantly at first but then with growing confidence. By the time Doc and Marge's twentieth wedding anniversary came round on 25 March, the family had regained some of its lost composure. In the evening Marge cooked Doc's favourite T-bone steaks and he raised a toast, 'To twenty years!'

Afterwards, they got through two bottles of champagne, and before going up to bed Doc whispered in her ear, 'Well, Marge, I guess we better keep them.'

FOUR

1956

In his first months in America Mike was an enigma – one moment loving and affectionate, the next withdrawn and rebarbative, shunning the company of those around him, retreating into silence. His innate trust of the world, his innocence and openness, had taken a knock after his expulsion from the serenity of Roscrea. The jolting transition to a new life in an unfamiliar country, the loss of all that had gone before – people, objects, faces, places, sounds, smells, clothes – had left him less sure of the world's goodness, less convinced he could rely on life to be dependable and benign. He had not forgotten the world he had been torn from; he saw it in his dreams, he spoke of it to Mary, and at times he yearned for it terribly.

It took a long period of ups and downs, of unpredictable sullenness and parental doubts, before Mike began to settle, but it eventually appeared to all who knew him in that year of 1956 that his sweet nature had finally resurfaced. His good behaviour and his earnest desire to please were noticed and admired. Marge's mother Josephine – Grams to her grandchildren – was especially fond of him and even Doc recognized his obliging disposition, though his praise for Mike was oftentimes implicit with criticism of Mary.

But there was an undercurrent in Mike's character that Marge found hard to figure. He didn't argue with his parents; he gave way promptly and meekly in clashes with the boys; he was constantly striving to please to the extent that Marge felt at times he was almost too good. She wondered just why he was so compliant: was it from some kind of fear? She couldn't say of what exactly, but it was somehow as if he were terrified of losing the good opinion of those around him, of those he depended on. Marge wondered what had caused such deep-seated anxieties.

By early summer Mike had made a handful of friends and the Hesses invited them over for his fourth birthday.

On the whole, the party had been a success. Marge had watched Mike closely and was relieved to see him enjoying the games, discovering a knack for hide-and-seek and giggling uncontrollably at the random collisions and unexpected bodily contacts of blind man's buff. He had loved pass the parcel, meekly handing over the mysterious bundle each time the music restarted and smiling when candy fell from the paper into the laps of the other children.

The only difficult moment had come near the end, when Mike was opening his presents. The biggest of them, and most alluring to four-year-old eyes, was a toy drum wrapped in silver-specked birthday paper that Mike had torn off in a frenzy of excitement, yelping with pleasure as the drum itself slid out. Ronald Casabue from over the way in Risdon Drive had made the mistake of trying to grab it from him and Mike had responded with the protective belligerence he'd learned in the Roscrea dinner lines, tussling and yelling, 'No, no, no, that's mine,' and – in his deepest Irish accent – 'Do you wanna fight, boy? Put your dooks up!'

James and Thomas, the older Hess boys, had laughed out loud at the incongruity of Mike's display of Irish defiance. For years afterwards they would taunt him – mostly good-naturedly – whenever his brow seemed to darken with anger or annoyance by shouting, 'Mike's got his "Do you wanna fight" look on! Put yer dooks up! Put yer dooks up!' Young Stevie, less understanding of his new brother's quirks, had taken to referring to him as 'that creep'.

*

At the end of the summer Marge brought peaches home from the store and offered one to Mike. He had never seen a peach before, and sitting at the sunny kitchen table he turned it over, cupped it in his hands and slid his fingers over the strange furry skin. Marge was charmed by his unselfconscious wonderment at things which to her seemed so everyday. He sniffed its sweet heavy perfume, like nothing he had ever encountered, pressed its warm yielding flesh, licked it and drew back his tongue in puzzlement at its forbidding texture, then jumped off his chair, ran with it into the sunshine of the backyard and plunged his teeth into its welcoming softness.

Marge laughed, finished her cup of tea and went upstairs to make the children's beds. The moment she was gone, Mike, overcome by temptation, sneaked back in and devoured the other eleven peaches Marge had bought. For the rest of his life he would love peaches – he loved them most when their yellow ripeness would melt under his thumb, when after the first delicate bite the flesh would fall away from the stone of its own accord, no need for teeth to pierce it, a gentle suck enough to entice it into his mouth. He loved the sweet, sticky juice that scented his lips and left its warm stain on his fingers. He was a sensual person, and when his senses took over he could not stop himself. Later in life, he would gulp down mugs of coffee to feel the surge of adrenalin, devour chocolate bars to give himself the sugar rush they brought and surrender to other, more complex delights.

He was slumped at the table licking his fingers when Marge came back in and let out a gasp.

'Why, Mike, what on earth have you been doing in here?'

The table was tacky with juice and littered with peach stones sucked clean. Mike's face and hands were flecked with little chunks of fruit. Thinking of the peach pie she'd been planning for dessert, Marge grasped him by the shoulders and lifted him from his chair with more force than she'd intended.

'Those peaches weren't just for you, Mike; they were for everyone. You did a bad thing just now . . . and you've probably made yourself sick too. Go upstairs and clean yourself up while I deal with this mess.'

The tone of Marge's voice made Mike panic. He grabbed the dishcloth and wiped the table frantically, but Marge took it from him.

'No, Mike – go upstairs. Just go upstairs and wash. And don't ever do it again.'

Annoyed more by her own reaction than by Mike's gluttony, Marge couldn't bring herself to look at him and set about cleaning up. Mike, close to tears, racked his brains for something to say that would make her love him again, but her back stayed resolutely turned.

That evening as they lay in their beds, Mike turned to face Mary.

'Are you awake?' he whispered in Gaelic. Mary rolled over quickly, her mouth open with surprise. Mike hadn't spoken to her in Gaelic for weeks, under instructions from Doc, and hearing it again made her feel cosy and secret.

'Yes,' she replied. 'What is it?'

'Shh! Or they'll hear us.'

The room was lit by a tiny nightlight in the shape of a red mushroom, and in its dim glow Mary saw Mike's eyes fixed on her.

'What is it?' she repeated more quietly. Mike was silent for a moment.

'Do you remember your real mammy?' he asked at last. 'Mom isn't her.'

Mary said nothing, but put her thumb in her mouth and looked at her brother with wide eyes.

'Our real mammies didn't want us because we were bad,' Mike whispered, then paused to reflect on what he had said. 'They hated us. So they sent us away. I did something bad today, and Mom got mad at me.'

He raised himself up on his elbow and leaned across the gap between their beds for emphasis.

'So we must remember always to be good. If Mom knows how bad we are, she'll hate us too. And maybe she'll send us away.'

He lay back down and looked at the ceiling.

'So we must always be good,' he repeated softly.

FIVE

1956–7

In September 1956 Mary McDonald and Anthony Lee legally became Mary and Michael Hess. Marge had been thrilled, showing the papers first to Doc, then to Michael and Mary, then to the older boys with exhortations that they must 'all be one happy family now'. Doc had patted his wife on the arm and gone to fetch the camera for a family photo. James and Thomas had humoured their mother with nods and smiles, but Stevie's response was less gracious. Posing for the camera outside in the driveway, he had placed a large, gloved hand on Mike's neck, given it a warning squeeze and whispered, 'Watch your back, *bro*,' through clenched teeth.

Watching Doc arrange the kids for the photograph, Marge had felt old doubts. He'd spent several minutes preening Stevie, getting his bow tie right, adjusting his collar and ruffling his hair, but he'd barely glanced at the two older boys. Doc had always blundered his way through parenting: he said what he thought even if it was tactless and offensive. Marge had known from early on that Stevie was Doc's favourite – he made little effort to conceal it – and she spent more and more time these days worrying about the effect this was having on James and Thomas.

To add to Marge's concerns, as Mike was growing steadily into the role of model child, Mary seemed to be heading in the opposite direction. Now she had found her tongue in English, she was not afraid to use it: she was becoming argumentative and difficult. Growing up with four brothers, she was changing from a self-effacing, almost catatonic child into a noisy, assertive tomboy. Marge dressed her in pretty dresses, but she abandoned her dolls for Mike's toy trucks, learned to run and shout, climbed trees and played rough. Doc still thought she was a problem child – no longer a defective mute, but now too rowdy and quarrelsome. Yet for all her force and energy, Mary would unaccountably burst into tears at times so prolonged and so violent that her whole body would shake and only Mike was able to calm her down.

Fall came and the acorns fell from the trees. Separated from Ireland by a fourth of their lives, the children's memories of life there – the half-formed products of developing brains – were growing dim. But for Mary acorns brought back memories of the fairies. Early one morning Mike found himself being shaken awake by strong little hands.

'What's wrong, Mary?' he asked in a sleep-muffled voice. 'What time is it?'

'After five – they're all asleep,' she whispered. 'We must go down to the garden before they wake up!'

Mary, impatient and excited, pulled the blankets off him and ran to get his clothes from the closet.

'Mary, stop that! Why d'you want to go outside this time of the morning?'

Mary rolled her eyes impatiently.

'*Because*,' she announced with a teacher's authority, 'we gotta find an acorn cup. An acorn cup filled with dew – that's where the fairies wash their faces. Then the fairies'll grant us a wish – and we can go home!'

The fairies did not send them back to Roscrea. They were, though, fated to leave St Louis within a year.

On 27 June 1956 Raymond Peter Hillinger had resigned on health grounds as fourth bishop of Rockford, Illinois and Monsignor Donald Carroll had been nominated as his successor. But Carroll himself had fallen sick within a month of his nomination and by the end of the year the Church had decided Rockford could no longer wait for its new bishop.

The nomination of Loras Lane as sixth bishop of Rockford shook up the Hess household. Loras was about to become the youngest full bishop in the United States. He was regarded as a future star of the Church, destined for great things. He was also beginning to earn a reputation among his clerical contemporaries for being hugely ambitious and more than a little cocky.

On 20 November 1956 Marge and Doc took the kids to Loras's consecration.

It was a six-hour drive from St Louis to Rockford, but for Doc and Marge it was like going home. They had both been born and raised in towns just over the Iowa border – Marge in Cascade and Doc in Worthington – and when they got to Rockford they looked at each other and wondered why ever they had left.

Mike was fascinated by Loras's consecration ceremony. The smell of the incense worked on him like a hypnotic drug; the murmured rhythms of the Latin ritual, the incantations and chants, the slow processing up and down the aisles captivated his imagination. He loved the colour, the glamour of the vestments: Uncle Loras's tall stiff mitre, his pale blue chasuble and the flowing robes with their yellow trim; Archbishop Binz's great gold crozier and long white pallium, his ruby ring and his pectoral cross; the dark cassocks and pink birettas of the attendants; the white surplices of the altar boys; the mystery of the '*Munire me digneris*' and the hint of a world beyond . . . The men gathered in solemn, hushed communion round the dimly lit altar seemed to the four-year-old Mike the most elegant, mysterious and romantic beings he had ever seen.

The bishop's residence on North Court Street was easily big enough to accommodate the Hess clan and Loras insisted they all stay on for Thanksgiving, which fell two days after the inauguration. It was a busy time for the new bishop and he was grateful to have his sister there to help. Doc took his boys bowling while Marge stayed home with the little ones, helping Mrs Brannigan the housekeeper assemble the ingredients for the Thanksgiving dinner.

When Loras came in from his day's work, he looked happier than Marge had seen him for a long time, full of enthusiasm for his new post and relishing the task that lay ahead. In an access of high spirits he picked Mike up under one arm and Mary under the other and twirled them round until they shrieked with excitement. When he came to an exhausted stop, both were shouting, 'More, more, more!' and Loras obliged with a final twirl before slumping in his armchair, where they immediately threw themselves on his knee.

Marge smiled to see how fond the kids were becoming of her brother. She was a perceptive woman – she knew Mike and Mary were troubled little things – and she was delighted to see a smile on their faces. Loras was tickling them and making them cry with laughter. It was, Marge thought, the first time she had seen them completely and unreservedly happy.

'Can you remember your mammy, Mary?'

Mike returned to the question for the hundredth time. He was whispering – even though they were huddled under the bedclothes they could hear the adults talking downstairs over the remnants of the Thanksgiving meal.

Mary shook her head. 'Can you remember yours, Mikey?'

Mike frowned as if concentrating on some elusive inner vision.

'No,' he said, 'I don't think so.'

When he thought of the old world now it came to him as a faded image of high windows, whispered talk and femininity; the old days, once sharp and individually delineated, were merging into a single generic memory.

'But *why* did our mammies give us away, Mikey? Did they never ever love us at all?'

Mike pondered the vital, half-remembered riddle.

'No, Mary, I think they never loved us. For if they did, they would not have given us away. I think they just had us and gave us to the sisters.'

Mary's eyes filled with tears.

'But Mikey, *why* did our mammies never love us? Did we do something very bad?'

'Well, Mary, I would say we did not do anything bad before they gave us away. We were only babbies when they gave us away, so we hadn't done nothing at all, even though we surely have been very bad since . . .'

Mary cast her eyes down guiltily as Mike continued.

'So what I think is this: they gave us away because they saw we were very bad inside, and that's why they never loved us. And now no one ever can love us because of what we are.'

Mary nodded and bit her lip. After a moment she said, 'But Mikey, sure Mommy loves us. I mean this mommy. So why did she take us if we are so bad?'

It was something Mike had thought about and found the explanation for.

'She took us because she didn't know what we are like – because we managed to disguise our badness. So that's why we must never argue or misbehave now. We must always do what they say – what Pop says and what the boys say – because if we don't, they will send us away again, just like our own mammies did . . .'

In the darkness Mike sensed that Mary was crying. The thought of being sent away terrified her and she hated when Mike spoke about it. How could they ever cope if their new mother gave them up like the old ones did?

'Mikey, don't say that!' she pleaded. 'You know I can't always be good like you. When I'm a bad girl, when I argue and cry, does that mean they will send us away? I can't bear it if they do, Mikey!'

Mary was working herself into a state and Mike knew it was time to drop the subject. He put his arm round his sister's shoulder and pulled her close to him.

'It's all right, Mary. I'll be here for you. I'll always look after you. I won't let them send us away.'

Mary sniffed and snuggled up to her brother.

'You love me, Mikey; you love me, don't you?'

Mike nodded and squeezed his sister's hand.

SIX

1957–60

The trip the Hess family had taken for Loras's consecration had set the wheels of Doc's mind in motion, but they needed plenty of oiling and Marge, having dreamt for years of living closer to her brother, worked on him tirelessly. She remarked more than once on the glaring absence of any professional urologist in the Rockford area . . . and suddenly one morning Doc made a triumphant, authoritative announcement: the Hesses would be moving to Rockford!

Loras was delighted and quickly found a suitable house for rent on North Church Street, just two blocks from his own residence. They moved in at the end of June 1957 but Doc Hess resented wasting money on rent, and almost as soon as they arrived began the search for a place to buy. He picked a plot in a new subdivision that was being carved out near the Rock River and engaged a construction company to build a large tri-level house at the head of a small cul-de-sac named Maplewood Drive.

Moving to a new city and a new home was good for Mike and Mary, and living so close to Uncle Loras allowed them to form close ties with an adult man for the first time in their lives, ties they never formed with the demanding and distant Doc. When the school year began, Loras took Mike and Mary to the kindergarten and introduced them to the teachers, setting up a vexed dynamic that followed them through their Rockford years: being niece and nephew of the bishop brought both respect and envy, both affection and resentment. Suddenly being special was a confusing, unfamiliar experience.

The final years of the 1950s blessed the American Midwest with a series of long, hot summers. Crop yields hit record highs and President Eisenhower was able to back up his doctrine of support for countries resisting communism with exports of tons of surplus grain.

On 9 October 1958 Pope Pius XII died and three months later his reforming successor John XXIII announced he was planning a great Vatican council, the first of its kind since 1871, which would modernize and liberalize the Catholic Church.

'I want to throw open the windows of the Church,' he told his advisers, 'so that we can see out and the people can see in.'

As a liberal himself, Loras Lane was encouraged by the Pope's promise and excited by the prospect of an impending trip to Rome.

The Hesses eventually moved into the new house on Maplewood Drive, and this meant a new school for Mike and Mary. Mike was seven now and growing tall and slim. His hair was gleaming black, his skin smooth and his blue eyes glowed with a limpid serenity. Doc insisted on Mike having a military-style buzz cut (he had tried and failed with Jim and Tom, who were now in their late teens and confirmed devotees of the Elvis quiff), and in spite of Mary's protestations – she said that with his high forehead it made his face look too long – Mike had, as ever, been happy to do what Doc wanted. Oftentimes Doc would make him wear bright, patterned bow ties that gave him the comical look of a preening cockatoo (Doc and Stevie wore them the whole time), but Mike never argued and had even learned how to tie them the way Doc liked best.

At school his eager compliance and sharp intelligence proved a winning combination. He loved reading; his appetite for learning was insatiable; the teachers adored him and he got the highest grades. He was sensitive to his sister's needs and helped her with homework, but for a long time she felt very much in his shadow: he was such a hard act to follow that after a while Mary gave up trying.

Mike loved to please and hated the thought of letting people down. He quickly sensed he was not meeting Doc's expectations and the thought tormented him. Doc boasted that he had turned his own boys into real men. Jim, Tom and Stevie played masculine sports – football, track, baseball – and Doc expected Mike to do the same. Mike was not cut out for sport but he forced himself to do what Doc wanted. He ran cross-country and went on treks that left his feet blistered and his legs bruised; but he forced himself to keep going because he did not want to disappoint his father. In bed afterwards he would lie awake with his feet throbbing and his body aching, berating himself for his weakness. *I gotta do better*, he said to himself as he drifted into uneasy sleep. *I gotta do better*.

Mary and Mike were constantly in church: Marge took them to parishes where Loras was celebrating Mass and they attended Church functions with their parents. The trappings of Catholicism were a part of their life and they accepted the Church's teachings because they never knew anything different. They believed in heaven and hell, in the devil and eternal damnation, and they looked up to the priests and nuns who ran their school on weekdays and their church on Sundays.

When Mike made his First Communion in summer 1961 it was taken for granted that he would become a server at St James' Pro Cathedral. He adored being an altar boy, and unlike some took his responsibilities seriously. When the others poked fun at the priest or sabotaged the serving of Communion, he kept out of it. He was the first to volunteer for early Mass, stayed on in the evening to tidy up the church and was never late for duty. His sweet singing voice made him a favourite of the priests and a star of the St James' choir.

Mike loved the theatricality of the Mass, the vestments and the incense, the incantations and prayers, the feeling that he was assisting in a rite that opened the doors to another reality. The ceremonies conjured up another world beyond the dull facade of material life, a world he hoped might transcend the injustices and anxieties of his own existence. The more Mike served, the more he fell under the spell of the ritual. Numbers, repetition, formulae became the bulwarks of his faith; following the liturgical forms, murmuring the responses and penances. If he could just do everything with no mistakes, if he never deviated, never stumbled over the words, he might perhaps stave off the malevolent forces he felt buffeting his path through life.

Confession was an important part of the bargain, but he found the build-up to the mysterious encounter in the confessional fraught with dread. How to confess? How to quantify his sins? He knew he was bad – that he had done, spoken, thought bad things – and the obsessive compulsion within him demanded he formulate his badness in the proper way, the *only* way that would work the miracle of absolution. So where other children sought out young Father O'Leary, the gentle pastor who would reply mildly and reassuringly, merely enjoining the sinner to 'go away and be kind', Mike chose Father Sullivan. Stepping into the musty half-light of the confessional, his eyes fixed on the latticed window beyond which his hopes of redemption lay, he felt his anxiety increase.

'In the name of the Father and of the Son and of the Holy Ghost. Amen.'

Mike knelt.

'Bless me, Father, for I have sinned. It has been a week since my last confession.'

There was a grunt from beyond the window as Mike began listing his shames, one by one in a stuttering rush. Father Sullivan was rigorous, stern and reproachful, demanding to know how many times the sin had been repeated, how many times the sinner had disobeyed his parents, how many times he had thought wicked thoughts. But without the severity Mike felt the ritual was inadequate, the magic not properly performed: the harsher the judgement and the bigger the penance, the greater were the chances of his salvation.

As always, the end of the confession brought sudden panic.

Have I missed something out? he thought desperately as Father Sullivan's throaty mumble blessed and forgave him, gnarled hands silhouetted against the grille, making the familiar sign of the cross. *Did I forget something? Did I withhold it on purpose?* As he scrambled to his feet, helplessly stammering the Latin, Mike felt the magic of the confessional slip tormentingly beyond his grasp. He was seized with the thought that he had not earned forgiveness, that some tiny imperfection in his confession – he had forgotten something; he *must* have forgotten something – had rendered the absolution worthless. As he knelt down at a pew to commence his Hail Marys a void opened beneath him, sucking him down to the emptiness below.

SEVEN

1961–3

School was a torment for Mary. Full of youthful energy, she found the discipline hard to take, and her grades were average at best. She could not settle with a book and longed to be out climbing trees or playing in the fields around Maplewood Drive.

Exasperated by her behaviour, Mrs Hummers asked Doc and Marge to come in for a parent–teacher conference. She explained that Mary needed to learn respect and obedience; she needed to calm down and sit quietly at her table, listen to the teacher and concentrate on the lesson instead of fidgeting and looking out the window.

'I can hardly believe she is young Michael's sister,' Mrs Hummers said. 'He's such a sweet, quiet young man, always diligent at his work and never any trouble. But she is more rambunctious than any boy!'

'Those darn kids,' Doc had growled in the car on the way home. 'They're the wrong way round.' Marge had looked at him in puzzlement. 'She should have turned out better behaved, like the boy,' he'd continued, eyes glaring fixedly on the road, 'and he should have turned out more like her. He's too damn girly by half!'

Mike hadn't made many friends among the altar boys – they regarded him as stand-offish because he refused to take part in their pranks and they worried he would snitch on them to his uncle the bishop – but he had become close to one of them. Jake Horvath was the same age as Mike and shared some of his earnest thoughtfulness. Jake's uncle was a monsignor in the Rockford diocese, and every morning as they wriggled into their white cassocks and lacy surplices they would exchange gossip they'd picked up from their priestly relatives. Mike loved these whispered, secret moments and, maybe even more than that, he loved the ritual of the dressing-up, the transformation they were going through – 'just like Clark Kent' – from ordinary Joe to purveyors of transcendent truth. For him, the swish of the soft white robes conjured fleeting images, never quite defined but redolent of the long-ago world he had once inhabited and lost. The ritual and the vestments gave him the chance to be *someone else*, to stop being the person he was, the rejected orphan he hated.

Loras Lane had been due to fly to Rome for the opening of the Vatican council in October 1962. He had renewed his passport, booked his plane ticket and made arrangements for diocesan affairs in his absence, but a week before he was due to depart he had collapsed in the parlour of his residence. Dr West, who had rushed out to examine him, concluded that all he needed was bed rest and a protein diet, but sent him for blood tests at Rockford Memorial Hospital all the same.

When the results came back, Dr West was less reassuring. 'Your Excellency,' he said dubiously, 'have you suffered any serious disease or sickness in your life that I am not aware of?'

Loras thought for a moment and mentioned the mysterious two months of pain he had been through as a teenager. It had kept him away from school, he had shed pounds in weight and his urine had been tinged with blood.

Dr West frowned. 'And did the medics never make a specific diagnosis? Because to me that sounds like a classic case of nephritis.'

Father Hiller was director of vocations for the Rockford diocese and had seen countless boys who thought they had a priestly calling. He could usually distinguish the serious candidates from the dreamers, but Michael Hess was an enigma. He said all the right things – and he was the nephew of the bishop – but there was something odd about his reasons for wanting to join the priesthood. Mike himself was unclear about his motivation: it was something to do with his compulsive obsession with the power of ritual, but he could put none of this into words. Hiller recommended Mike take part in a two-week retreat the diocese was organizing.

The vocation camp was at a diocesan centre south-west of Rockford in the woods by the Rock River. There were bonfires and singalongs, barbecues and prayers. Young priests came to share their experiences and answer questions from the boys about the demands of celibacy and the Church's view of homosexuality, the communist threat and the real presence in the Eucharist – is the Communion bread really transformed into Christ's flesh before we eat it? Some of the boys saw it as little more than a summer camp – there was horseplay and smuggled liquor – but Mike took it seriously. He respected the rules of silence and the periods of contemplation, ignoring the whispers, winks and grimaces that disrupted the retreat's solemnity. Mike prayed constantly and fretted about the authenticity of his vocation. He prayed for a sign and maybe he got it.

At the end of the two weeks the boys were told to spend the afternoon in private meditation before the bus took them home. Mike found a secluded corner by the stream and knelt to pray.

O Lord, teach me what You want me to be; give me Your sign and I will follow; give me a vocation and I will see it through; make me good, O Lord. Please Lord, make me good . . .

When he lifted his head the sun was gone and clouds were gathering. Looking at his watch, he was horrified to see two hours had passed. He returned to the retreat centre at a run, his heart heavy with foreboding, and was seized with panic when he found it deserted.

They've left you behind, a voice whispered, and all the old insecurities, the fears of abandonment and rejection swept over him. He ran through the empty rooms, hoping it was all a mistake, that they would be huddled together in deep discussion or hiding from him as a cruel joke – anything but the terrible reality: that they had forgotten him; that he was not worth remembering; that they had left him all alone.

When Father Hiller came back for him two hours later, mortified at the mistake, he found Mike slumped on the black and white tiles of the bathroom, tear-stained and staring through the window.

They travelled back together in silence, and although Mike continued his duties as an altar boy he would no longer discuss or even acknowledge the priestly vocation that had been his obsession.

EIGHT

1963–6

The doctors had diagnosed Bishop Lane's sickness as a recurrence of acute nephritis and its effects were becoming increasingly serious. By the spring of 1963 he was suffering from blinding headaches, vomiting, and pain in his stomach and joints; he was frequently short of breath and spent more and more time confined to his bed. The doctors concluded the virulent attack he experienced in childhood had damaged his kidneys and he had been living with the consequences ever since. They told him the disease was likely to prove fatal, although with treatment and rest its advance might possibly be slowed. In the short term, there could be no question of him travelling to Rome – his visit to the Vatican would have to wait.

Overcome with foreboding, Marge had set up a camp bed in the bishop's residence so she could help nurse him, but in spite of Loras's unwavering optimism his condition continued to decline. The Hess household had been disrupted and unsettled and Mike had fallen sick himself, his anxieties incarnated in a racing heart and violent nausea. But after eighteen months of treatment and bed rest Loras had rallied sufficiently to resume his diocesan duties, and at the end of 1965 he had finally boarded the plane for Rome. He sent Marge a cheery postcard: 'Arrived safe and sound after a good trip. Am feeling fine, although I still must take it easy. Went to the Council yesterday, for the first time. Only 14 speeches!'

The next September Michael Hess was in the 1966 intake at Rockford's Boylan High School; Mary would follow him a year later. Their Uncle Loras had laid the school's foundation stone and worked hard to make it a success; he regarded it as one of his greatest achievements. Since returning from Rome he had been a sick man, already concerned by thoughts of his legacy. Mike was horrified by the pale, emaciated figure his uncle had become; the old gap-toothed smile in the plump round face had been extinguished by kidney failure and the whisper of death.

Fears for his uncle darkened Mike's first days at high school, and when Marge too fell sick a few weeks later he felt the old panic rising in him. She was going to be operated on for chronic pain in her spine and all her cheery reassurances that it was nothing to worry about failed to calm his fears. The night Marge went into surgery, Mike and Mary sat out on the porch in Maplewood Drive and huddled together against the October chill. Mary rasped a match against a Red Cloud matchbook and lit one of Doc's Chesterfields – for all Mike's objections, she had dabbled with cigarettes since her thirteenth birthday.

'You know, Mike, if Mom dies, we will have no one,' she said quietly.

Mike's objection was half-hearted. 'We'll still have Uncle Loras.'

Mary looked at him with raised eyebrows and he shifted uncomfortably.

'Well, it might *seem* like we'd be on our own. It'll be OK, though,' he said with a smile. 'I'll always be here for you; you can count on me. And I was thinking something else too. You know how sometimes . . . we talk about our mothers in Ireland?'

Mary nodded, looking at him with interest.

'Well, I was thinking . . . Maybe it would be good if we could go find them. If we could find them and ask them about us. Then we'd know the truth. About . . . how we came to be here and who we really are.'

'But how will that help, Mike?' Mary looked dubious. 'We can't change things. We can't go back to what we were.'

Mike fell silent. He wished so much he could explain to her that he *wanted* to go back to the world before; wanted to rewind the clock and undo the terrible rupture that blighted his life. But he couldn't say it.

'I know,' he said at last. 'But don't you want to find out why you were given away? If we could just do that, maybe we could start to put things right.'

Mary smoked her cigarette in silence and Mike stared into the night sky. The orphan's sense of a life incomplete was strong in him, the feeling that he was robbed of his identity and must rediscover who he was and why he was rejected. In his heart he felt his true self lay elsewhere, tied up in the place they both came from, in that half-remembered feminine world of warmth and whiteness from which they had been expelled.

A week later, after Marge had been discharged from Rockford Memorial, Mike went to see his uncle. He had left his mom complaining she wouldn't be able to play golf any more but otherwise in high spirits: the pain in her spine and hips had been greatly reduced by the operation and she was about to start physiotherapy. His uncle, though, was dying. Mike had never witnessed the terminal decline of another human being before, and he found it sad and disturbing.

Loras had always treated Mike as a grown-up, an equal, and their conversations were serious and honest. Mike had asked him many times about his illness and Loras had always replied that he was fighting it but could not be sure of the outcome. They frequently discussed the Church, and today they were discussing politics. Rockford was blue-collar Republican – Doc and Marge were lifelong supporters of the Grand Old Party – and looming Senate elections were mobilizing the party's forces. Loras had explained the current political situation and the Church's involvement in it, telling Mike about Illinois's senior senator, Everett Dirksen, the long-standing Republican leader in the Senate and a staunch ally of Joe McCarthy through his rise and fall in the 1950s. The state's other seat was occupied by a Democrat, the now elderly Paul Douglas, but LBJ's pursuit of the conflict in Vietnam

had made the Democrats vulnerable and the Republicans had identified Douglas as a key target.

'Just take a look at these,' Loras said, thrusting a bundle of sermons
and diocesan letters in Mike's direction. 'I've been given these by my
bosses in Chicago. They're so hell-bent on getting Douglas out of
the picture they want *me* to spread the word with this kind of nonsense.
They send me stuff like this practically every week – they aren't taking
any prisoners.'

As Mike flicked through the draft sermons unsettling phrases
leapt out at him – warnings that the Democrats 'would place us
squarely on the road to suicide as a people'; references to the 'sacraments of their secular culture, namely abortion, sodomy, contracep-
tion and divorce . . . which are the seeds of the destruction of our
nation'. 'It is the duty of every Catholic,' one sermon concluded, 'to
work for the extirpation from our society of all those who would in
any way foster or promote these things.'

'Jeez,' breathed Mike, 'that's terrible!'

Seeing the horror on his face, Loras patted his arm.

'Don't worry, son.' He smiled. 'I won't be using any of that. The
bosses can say what they like, but I have only one authority to answer
to now . . .'

NINE

Apollo 1 burned up on 27 January 1967. As America mourned the astronauts who had lost their lives on the launch pad at Cape Kennedy, Boylan High observed a minute's silence and the students wrote letters of condolence to the Grissom, White and Chaffee families. In physics Mr Strom abandoned his lesson plan and instead reviewed the scanty information that had emerged about the fire. The principle of Brownian motion had been on the curriculum for next fall, but he had decided to bring it forward – this, he said, was as good a moment as any to examine the way gases interact.

No one yet knew of the arbitrary, minor events that had caused the tragedy, the chance electrical spark from the friction of an astronaut's nylon spacesuit which had ignited the blaze, but Mr Strom explained how the oxygen-rich mixture of gases in the pressurized cabin would fan a tiny flame to the point where an aluminium stanchion would burn like a piece of wood. The students watched as he introduced a phial of bromine gas into a diffusion tube. He told them to observe how its brown-coloured particles moved chaotically as invisible speeding molecules in surrounding gases smashed into them. He asked them to imagine how the tangled zigzag movements of a bromine particle were actually the result of hundreds of tiny random impacts nudging it from its intended trajectory – great brains including Einstein had attempted to describe it in mathematical models.

But Mike's thoughts were wandering a path of their own. The swirling gases had crystallized a notion – it had long been on his mind – that powerful invisible forces were shaping his own existence: that chance collisions and impacts over which he had no control were deflecting his own trajectory, and that their effect was to a large extent a negative one.

He thought of Mrs de Boer's geography class the previous week when she had told them there were 3.5 billion people in the world; now, watching the random, frenzied collisions inside the diffusion tube, he was haunted by the notion that he could have ended up in the hands of any one of them. It was not, he said to himself, that he resented Marge and Doc. What upset him was the lack of any reason why he should be there: nothing made it more natural for him and Mary to be in Rockford, Illinois than to be in Peking, China. He looked at his classmates, who had real mothers and fathers, and envied them because they were where they should be, anchored in the place life had reserved for them. He could never be in that place unless and until he found his mother. The image of his life as a particle in some cosmic Brownian motion preoccupied him now; the sense of his existence rootless and spinning out of control was always with him.

'I will arise and go now, and go to Innisfree,
And a small cabin build there, of clay and wattles made;
Nine bean rows will I have there, a hive for the honey bee,
And live alone in the bee-loud glade.
And I shall have some peace there, for peace comes dropping
    slow,
Dropping from the veils of the morning . . .'

Sister Brophy's cracked, gentle intonation roused Mike from his sombre thoughts. He raised his head, suddenly alert. The English teacher sighed with pleasure.

'That's one of my favourite poems by Yeats. Beautiful,' she mused. 'William Butler Yeats was an Irish poet and his Irish heritage features strongly in his poetry.'

Mike was dumbfounded. He had recognized something of himself in the poem Sister Brophy had read out: a smallness, a humility, a desire to escape from the life that was his prison and find the peace of elsewhere.

The bell sounded and the classroom emptied – except for Mike. Sister Brophy sat at her desk, rereading the poem with a smile on her face.

'Yes, Mike? Did you want something?'

Mike smiled eagerly.

'Do you have any other poems by . . . Yeats?' he ventured, slowly putting his books into his bag. Sister Brophy looked delighted.

'Why, Mike! I might have known you'd be interested . . .'

Mike had studied a little poetry before, but nothing like this. He spent the weekend lying on his bed, reading and rereading the *Collected Poems* Sister Brophy had given him. His brothers sneered and Doc shook his head disapprovingly – he disliked and distrusted poetry – but Mary and Marge were enthralled by his dramatic recitations of the haunting, beautiful verse.

In the weeks that followed Sister Brophy introduced him to John Donne, Robert Frost, Baudelaire and countless others until his mind swam with gold-tinted images and his heart floated on a sea of words.

Loras Lane reached his fifty-seventh birthday in October 1967 and felt well enough to enjoy a quiet celebration with his family at the bishop's residence. The following day he sent word that he would like to speak to Michael, who arrived to find his uncle propped up on pillows in bed and looking exhausted. For a moment Loras struggled to speak. When he did, his voice was hoarse and came from somewhere deep inside him.

'Thank you for coming, Michael. I asked you because I shall not much longer be in this world.'

Mike made as if to object; Loras silenced him with a smile.

'Don't trouble yourself, my son. You're a good, kind boy; you always have been. But there are matters I wish to resolve before . . .' Loras hesitated. 'Before it is too late. You and I have always spoken frankly with each other and I know you have followed my advice in many things. What I wish to understand, Michael, is why I sense such unhappiness in your life.'

Mike looked hard at his uncle and nodded. The question did not surprise him and this was not a time for denial or flippancy. In as measured a tone as he could manage, Mike told the dying bishop about the fears which underlay his life, about the helplessness he felt in the face of a world that buffeted him one way and another, and about the sense of rejection that stemmed from his secret certainty of his own worthlessness. He spoke about the fleeting hope he had found in the idea of entering the priesthood and the comfort he still took in the rites of the Church, the talismanic rituals and magic formulae that, repeated hard enough and often enough, might ward off life's cruelty. It was a strange kind of religion and he knew Uncle Loras could not approve of it, but it was one that a frightened boy could cling to.

When he finished, Loras squeezed his hand. In a voice charged with emotion, he whispered, 'Thank you, my son. Thank you for coming into my life. I would like so much to tell you that God will provide the answers you seek, that He will clasp us back to the sanctuary of His paradise, but now – as I prepare to meet Him – I cannot be certain what to think. If I could know the truth of the world beyond, I would reach out and tell you of it; but all I can say is, seek for answers, seek to know who you are, and do not forget the love that is within us. When I am gone, please be kind to my sister, Mike, be kind to your own sister . . . and be kind to yourself.'

Within a month, Loras was dead.

Marge, desperate with grief herself, suggested Mike take time off school to cope with his uncle's death, but he insisted on going. He walked through the corridors in a daze, barely comprehending anything that went on in class, but welcoming the distraction school offered: home felt like a tomb. The second day after Loras died, Mike sat in English class and felt his cheeks flush with emotion as Sister Brophy read out a poem which seemed to him to sum up his life in two stanzas.

'It's a translation of a work by the Russian poet Michael Lermontov,' she said by way of introduction. 'Humanity's sin made God expel us from Eden, and our fate is to suffer the memory of Paradise in the torment of exile . . .

'An angel was flying though the midnight sky, and softly did
    he sing;
And the moon and the stars and the clouds hearkened to that
    holy song.
He sang of the bliss of the innocent souls in the gardens of
    paradise;
He sang of the great God, and his praise was sincere.

In his arms he carried a young soul, destined for the world of
sorrow and tears;
    And the sound of that song stayed, wordless but alive, in
the young soul's mind.
    And for a long time the soul languished in the world,
filled with a wonderful longing,
    And earth's tedious songs could not replace for it those
heavenly sounds.'

TEN

1968

Mike's sixteenth birthday came in the summer of revolutions. The
events of May '68 in France had roused the campuses of the US. In
August the National Guard in Chicago beat and gassed the foot
soldiers of the revolution, spawning legions more. Robert Kennedy
and Martin Luther King were shot dead.

By September the mood at Boylan High was febrile. The world
was rising in protest and Mike was tormented by thoughts of revolt
and escape. Erik Erikson's theories were circulating on the pages of
psychology journals, and students were recognizing themselves in the
bastardized word-of-mouth versions that reached places like Boylan.
Mike's classmates saw themselves through the mirror of Erikson's teenage
identity crisis, but Mike knew that orphans alone were truly without
an identity.

The new music that blew in with the spirit of revolt made Mrs
Finucane, Boylan's music teacher, feel she was fighting a losing battle.
She was teaching Mozart and Beethoven, but John Lennon and Jimi
Hendrix filled the students' hearts. She announced auditions for the
school's annual musical, *Mame*, without great hopes, but was surprised
by the turnout.

When Mike saw the flyer, his head had filled with thoughts of
music and dressing-up, of poetry and greasepaint. He pictured Doc
and Marge applauding. To be admired was to be accepted, and he

didn't hesitate: he was first to arrive at the audition, and when Mrs Finucane asked him to sing his favourite song, his performance of 'Danny Boy' brought a tear to her eye. With two other hopefuls, he was given sheet music to practise at home before returning to try out for the male lead, Patrick.

When he got in from school, Mike took advantage of Marge's daily half-hour among the backyard petunias to tell her about it. She smiled and gave him a kiss on the cheek.

'Oh Mike, how wonderful! You'll be a shoo-in with your lovely voice – and it's so nice to see you taking an interest in good music. All this rock and roll going on the whole time is so annoying, don't you find? You must tell Doc the moment he gets home. Are there any nice girls in the show?'

Mike blushed and seemed embarrassed. Marge understood – her son was discovering the attractions of the opposite sex. Everything was as it should be. Doc *would* be pleased.

Mrs Finucane had no hesitation in picking Mike for the role of Patrick. His voice was good – there was no doubt about it – but his brooding good looks were his trump card. 'Film-star looks,' she told the head of English in the staffroom after the audition. 'All the girls will swoon to see him up on stage. If I were twenty years younger myself . . .'

Picking a female lead had been harder – there had been many more girls at the audition than boys – but there was one whose beauty and charm had brought her enormous popularity at Boylan High, and she didn't have a bad voice either. Her name was Charlotte Inhelder.

As usual when big things were in the air, Mary was Mike's first confidante. She was fifteen and full of enthusiasm for her brother's exploits.

'So I guess you'll be wearing lots of fancy costumes?' she whispered excitedly. The rest of the house had gone to bed and they were sitting in Mary's room, dimly lit by a little table lamp. 'That's real neat, Mikey. Do you get to wear glitzy make-up and all that stuff?'

'I guess so.' He shrugged, trying to play it cool. 'My character, the hero' – he stopped to give Mary a saucy wink – 'is a young guy called Patrick from Des Moines, and I go on this big adventure to New York, where I get to stay with my Auntie Mame, who's rich and moves in high society. Then I fall in love with two girls and stuff, so I'm sure to get some cool costumes to wear and make-up and all.'

Mary looked at him.

'So who plays the two girls, Mikey?'

He laughed.

'Aw, just a couple of girls from eleventh grade. The real big role is my Auntie Mame, and she's gonna be played by Charlotte Inhelder.'

Mary gave a little gasp. 'Oh, Mikey! Charlotte Inhelder's soooo beautiful!' Her eyes grew misty. 'I wish I looked like her. She's so popular – and you're gonna get to know her!'

Suddenly Mary felt oddly frightened.

'I bet you'll fall right in love with her.' She laughed, but her eyes were serious. 'And then . . . you'll run away together and forget about your stupid sister.'

She gave a strange little giggle, which sounded more like a sob.

Mike put his arm around her gently.

'Oh Sis, don't be so silly. You know it's me and you forever. I'd never dream of leaving you – and definitely not for Charlotte Inhelder! You and me, we're two peas in one pod, and that's how it's going to stay.'

Rehearsals took place after school each evening for an hour or more in the Bishop Boylan auditorium. Mrs Finucane marvelled at Mike's enthusiasm and application: he didn't just learn his own part, he knew everyone else's too and could sing all the big numbers in the show with a startling, flamboyant theatricality. His love duet with the beautiful ingénue, Pegeen, was charmingly sweet and moving, but the musical's central relationship was between Patrick and his Aunt Mame.

Charlotte Inhelder had blonde hair that reached to her shoulders, pale blue eyes and the lithe figure of a gymnast. For all her intimidating beauty, she spoke in the hushed, respectful tones her

Bavarian parents had taught her were proper. But when she burst into song, she was transfigured, absolutely believable as the booming, iconoclastic heroine bent on shaking up the dull proprieties of hidebound America. Mike was excited when Charlotte sang with him. He was intrigued by the boldness of her gaze and the message she seemed to be sending him. He liked the brash, noisy, vulgar music and he liked the theatrical dame Charlotte turned into when she entered her role.

Mrs Finucane said she wanted the show's main relationship to have chemistry and vitality, and she asked Mike and Charlotte to come for one-on-one rehearsals.

'The first thing to bear in mind,' she told them, 'is that Mame is older and more worldly-wise than Patrick, but there's definitely a spark of sexual attraction between them.'

Charlotte stifled a giggle and Mike felt his cheeks burn at the mention of the S-word. Mrs Finucane pretended not to notice.

'Mame is a great beauty and a very sexual being; Patrick's just an innocent young country boy in short pants, and when they first meet Mame's way of speaking to him is actually pretty risqué. Over the course of the play, though, Patrick becomes a man, with his own . . . manly desires.'

Mrs Finucane paused for a pensive moment and Charlotte's eyes met Mike's with a twinkle of amusement. At the end of the rehearsal, she took his hand.

'Old Finucane's a saucy one, isn't she just?' Charlotte laughed. 'Bishop Boylan must be turning in his grave to hear all that in his school!'

Mike blushed, but he didn't pull his hand away.

'I've fallen in love with Michael A. Hess,' Charlotte declared. Lucy, her best friend, gaped at her from across the table where they were sharing a soda in Don's Café.

'Lucy, he's the most beautiful, sensitive boy in the world,' she said, staring rapturously at the tablecloth. 'He's perfect – tall, dark and handsome! And he's German too, thank the Lord, so my parents are bound to like him. I'm going to take him to the prom this year, just you see if I don't.'

Lucy sighed enviously.

'Those Hess boys are all pretty cute,' she said, dreamily, 'but Mike's definitely the nicest. And he's so mysterious – no one knows what he's really like.'

'Well, guess what,' added Charlotte, glowing with pride and excitement, 'Tomorrow night I get to put my arm round him and hold his hand. And . . . *he's going to be wearing short pants*!'

When he told Mary about the rehearsal, Mike was agitated and he didn't know why. He paced the room as he spoke of Charlotte's beauty and the friendly way she had treated him. Mary sat watching him.

'Mikey . . .' she said after a while. 'Could I maybe come see you rehearsing with Charlotte sometime?'

Mike was delighted.

'Sure, you can come tomorrow night. We're rehearsing the start of Act One and we're trying out our costumes for the first time. It's gonna be so cool, and the music is so lovely you'll just die!'

The following evening Mary sat at the back of the Boylan Auditorium. Mike appeared onstage wearing an old suit jacket that was too small for him and grey pants that didn't reach to his knees. He was carrying a suitcase and looking bewildered. A woman in a ragged linen skirt and faded blue blouse was holding his hand and leading him through the streets of New York. She was evidently Patrick's nanny and it seemed they'd got lost looking for his Auntie Mame's mansion on Beekman Place. To keep their spirits up in the cruel new world they'd tumbled into, Nanny Gooch addressed a trembling musical prayer to the litany of Catholic saints: 'Saint Bridget, deliver us to Beekman Place, / Away from the wicked and depraved; / [. . .] Mame's dear arms reach out for his embrace.'

Watching from the semi-darkness, Mary felt herself shiver: she hadn't realized her brother was playing an orphan and was surprised he hadn't told her. His arrival in the fake New York of the painted stage set seemed a mocking mimicry of the real trauma they had lived through, and, worst of all, Mikey was about to find salvation in the arms of a beautiful woman.

What if Mike falls in love with Charlotte Inhelder? What if he leaves me all alone? she thought as she watched them meet on stage. *He can't keep his eyes off her* . . . She screwed up her eyes and huddled deep down into her seat. She wanted to crawl into the darkness and never come out.

ELEVEN

1968

In the midst of the upheavals, in the sixth year of the US war in Vietnam, with tens of thousands on the streets of American cities and black power challenging the established order, Michael and Mary Hess became US citizens. Twelve and a half years of alien status, during which their Irish passports had to be renewed and registered annually with the Immigration Service, came to an end on 3 October 1968.

Doc Hess arranged for their naturalization to be held in the Rockford courthouse under the auspices of US Circuit Judge Albert O'Sullivan. Judge Bert was a regular at Doc's urology practice, and both men belonged to Rockford's great and good, so O'Sullivan had agreed to bend the rules and give Mike and Mary a private ceremony while thirty-five other applicants were lumped together for a communal oath-taking afterwards. Mike and Mary were singled out for coverage in the following day's *Rockford Register* under the headline IRISH HESSES BECOME AMERICAN CITIZENS:

Michael and Mary Hess, Boylan students, became American citizens at a ceremony at the courthouse on October 3. Michael, who was born in Tipperary, Ireland, came to America at the age of three and a half. He remembers little of his native land and lost his brogue soon after arriving. Mary Hess was born in Dublin and came here at the age of two. Chief Circuit Judge Albert S. O'Sullivan presided over the ceremonies. Mary Hess said, 'It was a beautiful and moving ceremony, one that I will never forget.' Michael remarked, 'I've felt American ever since coming here twelve years ago, now I have a right to claim it.' Thirty Italians, two Englishmen, two Swiss, and four-year-old Rickey McDowell of Castlepollard, County Westmeath, Ireland, were naturalized later.

Reading the newspaper the next morning, Mike and Mary were outraged.

'"It was a beautiful and moving ceremony"? Yuck! Who *says* that kind of sentimental stuff?' yelled Mary. 'How can they put stuff in that we didn't say? He didn't even talk to me!'

'And who says I can't remember my own country?' asked Mike as the article was read out at the breakfast table. 'Who says it? That's a lie!'

He brought a clenched fist down on the table that made the coffee cups rattle, and his brothers chorused in amused delight, 'Put yer dooks up! Put yer dooks up! Do ya wanna fight, boy? Put yer dooks up!'

Doc smiled, ignoring the ruckus. 'This is the way of the press,' he said wryly. 'You must never trust what you read in the newspapers.'

But Marge was delighted by the article and particularly pleased with the photo that accompanied it. It featured Mike standing in front of an American flag in his new tweed jacket and dark brown tie, his thick hair glossily combed in a neat side parting and his wide smile and gleaming white teeth making him look for all the world like one of the Kennedy boys, while at his side Mary was standing with a ribbon in her hair and a Bible in her hand looking up with admiring eyes at her brother. The caption underneath read, 'Mary and Mike Hess, who came to America from Ireland at the ages of 2 and 3, are glad to be American citizens now.'

Another photo, taken by Marge after the ceremony, showed Mike shaking hands with a stern-looking Judge O'Sullivan in his long black robes and Mary in profile looking on with a half-smile on her lips. It was this photo that Mary studied with rapt attention for many days afterwards, for she noticed something that others did not. She had never previously realized it so clearly, but here was incontrovertible photographic evidence that her nose was big, long and crooked. With a teenager's uncompromising self-criticism, she decided then and there that something must be done about it – something to improve herself, she told Marge.

'Oh honey, you don't need your nose fixed. Lots of young girls feel that way.'

Marge knew all about teenage insecurity. 'I remember being a teenager and hating every part of myself! You'll grow out of it. You have a lovely nose. The most important thing is to go out and have fun. If you love yourself, others will love you too!'

But Mary was furious. Was nobody listening? Her problem was that she *couldn't* love herself – she *hated* herself. Eventually, unnerved by the ferocity of her daughter's apparent self-loathing, Marge told her to go ask Doc about it.

Mary was stumped. She knew that, of all the people in the world, Doc was the least likely to sympathize with her feelings, but she also knew that nothing could take place in the Hess household without his approval. She approached him when he was at his most malleable – as he smoked a cigar in the den, following *The Liberace Show*. She told him her nose embarrassed her and made her feel bad; she could never be happy until it was fixed. She told him he was a doctor and he ought to find her someone who could straighten it out. But Doc laughed his annoying laugh.

'Doctors are for curing people who are sick, young lady. And having a crooked nose don't make you sick. Many folks have much worse things to deal with, so don't you go making a fuss about your nose, OK?'

Mary stamped her foot and stormed out, feeling more alone than ever.

*

When Mike and Mary became US citizens, they had been amused by the arcane paperwork, the fingerprinting and the exaggerated solemnity of the ponderous ceremony. They had smiled complacently as they swore to 'support and defend . . . the United States of America against all enemies . . . and bear arms on behalf of the United States when required by the law'. It had all seemed academic – Mike was a juvenile and Vietnam was a long way away – but no sooner had they become Americans than the draft became the defining issue of Americanness. Suddenly it was the touchstone people were measured against: you were for it or against it and all the rest followed on behind.

The undertaking Mike had sworn before Judge O'Sullivan seemed distinctly less academic when Congressman Alexander Pirnie drew 30 April out of the lottery pot and James Hess, the eldest of Doc's three boys, found himself drafted on the random chance of his birth date into the US Army. Mike's cohort, those born in 1952, was scheduled to enter the draft lottery in three years' time.

As the election campaign unfolded and Nixon harried LBJ over Vietnam and the draft, *Mame*'s American razzle-dazzle filled the rehearsal room with energy and noise. The show was a glitzy re-creation of an earlier age when the gulf between America's haves and have-nots could be bridged by a champagne party and a brassy song from a camp musical dame. On stage Charlotte was loud and brash; the costume and the make-up turned her into a splendid forty-year-old – her teenage sexuality was attenuated, her maternal qualities enhanced – and Mike found it reassuring and attractive. The hours they spent studying each other's expressions taught them to read the meanings that flickered hesitantly in each other's faces; if one of them stumbled over their lines, the other would be there with a timely prompt.

After rehearsals, they took to drinking sodas together in the parlour of Don's Café. Marge and Doc were thrilled. They shrugged their shoulders knowingly and mouthed, 'Teenagers!' to each other. But Mary, who was used to sharing her evenings with her brother, brooded and fretted in her room.

Mike felt an ambiguity about what was happening to him: he loved the big show tunes, the make-up and the glamour of becoming someone else in the blaze of the footlights. Onstage he felt safe – he loved his role and he knew it would carry him smoothly forward on a sea of music to a preordained happy ending that no one could take away from him. On top of all this, maybe – maybe – he was in love with Charlotte Inhelder. Charlotte had already starred in Boylan's previous musical, *The Pirates of Penzance*. She guided Mike and fussed over him, and he was flattered by her attention. Charlotte didn't hide the fact that she liked him and he felt a sort of obligation to return her devotion. It worked that way onstage, and Mike vaguely sensed that was how it should work in life; by the eve of their opening night, they had already exchanged kisses in the leafy privacy of Oaks Park, over the road from the school on North Main Street. But Mike was finding that he loved her more when she was in character than when she was in the tricky unpredictable seas of real life. Mike had fallen in love with Charlotte as Mame; he didn't know if he loved her as Charlotte.

TWELVE

1968

Mike paced and fretted backstage, but Charlotte squeezed his hand and told him he would be great. In an auditorium packed with parents, teachers and students, Mary closed her eyes as the curtain went up. She knew what was coming and she was worried what Marge and Doc would think about Mikey playing his orphan role for the whole world to see. But as Nanny Gooch warbled on about 'dear St Bridget', she sneaked a glance at her parents and saw they were entranced. Mike was the focus of attention and they were revelling in his performance. By the time orphan Patrick sang his first big number, Mary was excited and thrilled by the smiling faces and ripples of applause. She basked in her brother's success.

In the second half of the show Mike grew into a dazzling society beau, his short pants swapped for an elegant, tight-fitting tuxedo, his glossy black hair gelled into place with one cute curl strategically placed on his whitened forehead. Rouge on his cheeks and a slash of red across his lips gave him the surreal, impossibly perfect air of a 1930s movie idol. When he sang, his voice welled from deep within him and filled the auditorium with lilting harmony. Mary and 300 others fell under the spell of this magnificent creature they knew to be but refused to believe was Michael Anthony Hess.

The reception in the school hall after the show brought Mike his first taste of adulation. The boys pumped his hand, the girls sought to catch his eye. In the back of Doc's Cadillac on the way home, Mary welled over with love and pride.

'It was just *so* neat, Mikey! You were just *so* fantastic! How does it feel to have all those people clapping like crazy every time you open your mouth?'

Mike ruffled her hair.

'Well . . . it's a buzz. When all the lights go up it's pretty scary, but when the music starts it's like you know exactly what to do and how to behave. You don't feel like some insignificant little nobody any more; you feel like some big time hero or something, and you know everything's going to work out in your life.'

Mary nodded, transfixed by the thought.

'And when you kiss Charlotte and tell her you love her, are you acting it, like you do onstage? Or are you being yourself?'

Mike looked at his sister in the shadows of the back seat and didn't know how to answer.

When the pictures of Mike and Mary's naturalization ceremony had arrived, Marge had got one framed and hung it on the wall by the front door. Arriving home now, exhilarated by Mike's success, Mary felt her spirits fall the minute she saw it. She couldn't see anything else in the picture but her nose, and long after everyone else had taken off their coats and retired to the den to chat excitedly about their glamorous young star-in-the-making, Mary remained standing in front of the picture, weighing it up and thinking tormented thoughts.

James had been watching the calendar. His call-up date was drawing closer and Marge, frantic at the thought of him leaving, had pleaded with Doc to do something. The morning after the show the mail brought the first sign that Doc's efforts might be paying off. A letter from the Department of Defense indicated that James M. Hess was to report for a six-month intensive training programme at the US Army's Officer Candidate School. Doc's contacts had reassured him that if his son completed the training, he would graduate with the rank of lieutenant in a unit scheduled to serve in Panama. It would be hot, but it wasn't Vietnam. Marge took the letter to her bedroom and read it over and over again. She kissed it and held it to her heart. She said a silent prayer of thanksgiving to Our Lady. Her eyes filled with grateful tears.

In the evening the phone rang and Marge picked up the call. Charlotte wanted to speak to Michael, but she didn't object when Mrs Hess engaged her in conversation. Charlotte laughed when Marge said what a lovely couple she and Mike had made on stage and how much Mike had been talking about her and what a pleasure it would be to have Charlotte and her family over for lemonade on Sunday. And when Marge told her the good news that James would not be going to Vietnam after all, Charlotte was genuinely pleased for her. Her own brother's birth date would be in next year's lottery and she knew her parents were going through agonies. When, eventually, Marge said, 'I'm sure you've heard enough of me. I guess I'd better get Mikey for you,' Charlotte laughed again and thanked her. She was calling to say she and her brother had got a loan of their father's Buick for the evening.

A half-hour later Marius and Charlotte Inhelder pulled up outside the Hess house in Maplewood Drive and Mike jumped in back. The car was pulsing with excitement: endless vistas of possibility stretched ahead and Mike felt grown-up and powerful. Charlotte introduced him to her brother, who responded with a conspiratorial wink. Marius had the same Saxon beauty as his sister – the same blond hair, the same lithe elegance. Sitting behind him, Mike gazed at the slim curve of his neck above the whiteness of his T-shirt, delicate shoulder blades rising and falling as he manipulated the heavy steering wheel, and he was shocked by the intensity of his admiration. An overwhelming longing came over him to reach out and touch the gleaming skin that glowed only feet away from his own face.

In the front passenger seat Charlotte bounced around with feverish excitement, eschewing her seat belt with a teenager's faith in her own immortality. She chattered excitedly, on a high, swivelling her gymnast's body this way and that, turning to Mike in the back and then to her brother beside her. They were going to Marius's favourite bar, Mr

Entrance to the dormitory for unmarried mothers, Sean Ross Abbey.

Ruins of the medieval monastery and the old graveyard.

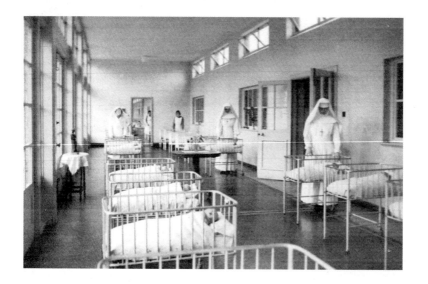

Above The new
newborn babies'
nursery in the 1950s.

Right The babies
on the terrace.

Below
The children's
dining room.

Above Philomena as
a young girl.

Left Philomena after
leaving Roscrea.

Left Sister Annunciata in the Abbey grounds.

Below Sister Annunciata with Anthony.

Right Anthony on the slide.

Below right Anthony in the convent parlour.

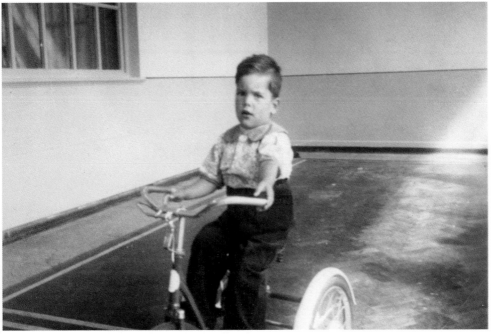

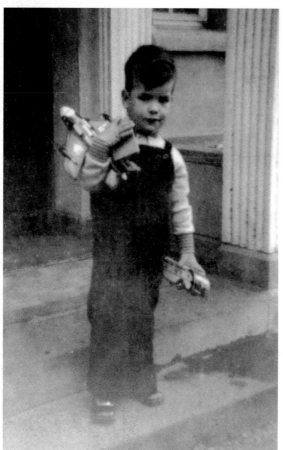

Above Anthony and Mary outside the children's nursery.

Below Anthony ready to leave for America, December 1955.

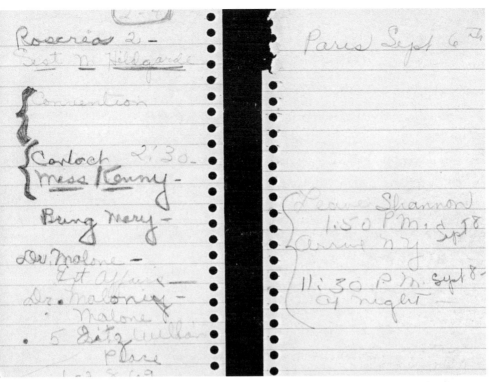

Marge's Irish notebook, summer 1955.

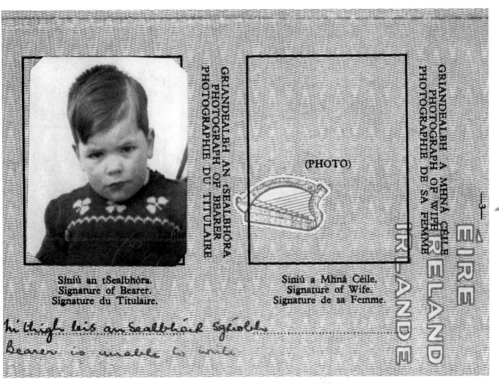

Anthony's passport, December 1955.

I, Philomena Lee of Limerick, Ireland, aged 22 years make oath and say:-

That I am the Mother of Anthony Lee who was born to me out of wedlock at Sean Ross Abbey, Roscrea, Co. Tipperary, Ireland, on 5th July 1952.

That I hereby relinquish full claim forever to my said child Anthony Lee and surrender the said child to Sister Barbara, Superioress of Sean Ross Abbey, Roscrea, Co. Tipperary, Ireland. The purpose of this relinquishment is to enable Sister Barbara to make my child available for adoption to any person she considers fit and proper, inside or outside the State.

That I further undertake never to attempt to see, interfere with or make any claim to the said child at any future time.

Philomena Lee

Subscribed and sworn to by the said Philomena Lee as her free act and deed this 27th day of June 1955.

Desmond A. Houlla

Notary Public,
Birr,
Co.Offaly,
Ireland.

Notary Public during the pleasure of The Chief Justice for Ireland.

Philomena's renunciation oath, giving up her son.

PART TWO

Henry's on State Street, she said, where his friends were dying to meet
Mike and see the boy who had captured his little sister's heart. Marius's
eyes met Mike's in the rear-view mirror and he gave him a little smile,
man to man, amused by his sister's enthusiasm.

Mike had never been to Mr Henry's. He liked it at once. It was
dark-panelled, pub-like and crowded, the tables pushed close together
and covered in plastic checked tablecloths. An old upright piano sat
on a dais at the end of the room and one wall was covered in the
kind of nude paintings that might have been risqué once, before
the seen-it-all nonchalance of the 1960s. Marius was the only one
old enough to drink legally, so they sat at a shadowy corner table
and ordered a pitcher of beer.

Mike was enthralled by the noise, the dim, sexy lighting and the
sweet, grimy smells of spilled beer and cheap perfume. He watched
excitedly as men in biker jackets and women with close-cropped hair-
cuts gathered in little knots at a bar that stretched the length of the
room and waiters with brightly dyed hair sailed through the throng
like ballet dancers.

Mike, Charlotte and Marius, young, fresh-faced and beautiful,
were themselves the object of admiring glances from those around
them. Marius's friends were only slightly older than Mike and Charlotte,
but they could have come from a different planet. Their bright T-shirts
and jewellery, long hair and earrings made Mike feel staid and dull.
They babbled breathlessly about art, music, poetry and a festival they
were all going to in upstate New York. A young man in a black shirt
and yellow pants recited a strange poem by some guy named Leonard
Cohen and a lazy-eyed girl announced she had slept with Andy Warhol,
a claim that was greeted with jocular scepticism.

Marius had told his friends about Mike and Charlotte's 'fabulous' performance in the school musical and someone suggested they
should get up and sing. The piano had been in desultory use during
the evening, but no one had succeeded in stopping the chatter and
commanding the room's attention. After five or six rounds of beer,
Marius's friend Joey, a tall, willowy boy with long hair and a sly
smile, took Mike and Charlotte by the hand and led them to the dais.

To their intense embarrassment, he raised his hand and called for silence.

'Ladies and gentlemen,' he announced, 'pray quiet, for it is that time of the night when we welcome our star turn. Mr Michael Hess and Miss Charlotte Inhelder will – for your exclusive benefit – reprise their award-winning performance of Mr Jerry Herman's most beautiful, fabulous runaway Broadway success, erm . . . Help me, Michael, what was it called?'

The room tittered and Mike blushed, but Charlotte was made of feistier stuff and hit the opening chord on the piano. Mike took his cue and added his voice to hers. For all their hip sophistication, the crowd in the bar loved the glamour of musicals, and by the first chorus those who knew the words were joining in. The number got a round of applause and an older man with an earring asked if they knew any Judy Garland numbers.

'Sure.' Charlotte shrugged and smiled. 'But you'll have to play the piano part.'

Without a word, the guy jumped up onstage and the three of them let rip with a string of songs that drew wild applause. Free drinks were forced on them, and by the time they responded to the audience's demands for *The Wizard of Oz*, their inhibitions were a thing of the past. Mike slipped effortlessly into the role of Dorothy (it was one of Marge's favourite movies so he had seen it a hundred times) and he put his heart into 'Somewhere Over the Rainbow' because he so wanted to *be* the bird that flies away – 'why oh *why* can't I?' When they left the stage, they were offered drinks by half the bar and it took Marius's good sense and fear of paternal retribution to drag them out and bundle them into the back seat of the Buick.

THIRTEEN

1968

Mike and Charlotte were the talk of Boylan High, and Mike's male classmates were quick to tease him, hinting at their envy of his good fortune in bawdy comments he tried to ignore. Unsure if he was being mocked or admired, Mike responded with a sheepish smile that only confirmed his peers' suspicions of his sexual prowess. Jake Horvath alone spoke seriously to him. He wanted to know if he really loved Charlotte and what it was like to be in love. Mike sensed the earnestness of Jake's questions, but had no answers. 'I don't know,' he said. 'I don't know what I feel.'

Charlotte's girlfriends made a show of congratulating her, then whispered to each other about the 'plastered on' make-up that made her look 'such a hussy no wonder the boy couldn't resist'.

On the Sunday the Inhelders were due to call, Doc and Marge scurried around tidying the house. The Inhelders had a reputation in Rockford – they were regarded as an 'arty' family. Everyone knew Charlotte's mom played Brahms and Mendelssohn on the baby grand her forebears had brought with them from Germany; her brothers painted the scenery and served as stage hands for Boylan High's annual plays; and her dad Otto, well, he collected cigar wrappers.

The afternoon turned out to be one of those embarrassing occasions when everyone knows something is hanging in the air, but no one broaches the subject. Otto did his best.

'*Bravo, junger Mann,*' he barked at Mike with an encouraging pump of the hand. '*Sie haben ja eine schoene Stimme!*'

Mike smiled awkwardly, but Mary burst into laughter.

'Ain't no use talking German to Mikey, Mr Inhelder: he's all Irish through and through!'

Otto turned to Doc with a confused frown. 'But Mr Hess, I was thinking your family are all German through and through. Is this not so?'

Doc shrugged. 'They're adopted, him and Mary. Adopted from Ireland. That's the way it is.'

Otto looked across to Charlotte and saw his daughter was as surprised as he was, but before he could say anything his wife nudged him and he coughed stiffly.

'So,' he said to Mike, 'as I was saying, young man, you have the lovely singing voice.'

Mike smiled again and thanked him, but he was watching Charlotte from the corner of his eye.

On Monday in school Charlotte was distant and Mike asked her to let him explain things – the need to apologize hovered over him his whole life like an ever-present albatross – but Charlotte was hurt and didn't want to know.

'Look, Mike,' she sniffed. 'I just don't understand you. I thought we were being honest with each other. I thought we were telling each other everything. So how d'you think it made me feel yesterday when I found out pretty much the most important thing about you in front of everyone?'

Mike tried to object, but Charlotte was in full flow.

'You know your problem, Michael Hess? You never let anyone get close to you. You're like a closed book and you don't want anyone to see inside – not even me. Why don't you want people to know you? Why don't you want people to love you?'

Mike was about to say this was nonsense, but something was telling him maybe she was right. Before he could grasp the thought, Charlotte had jumped in with another reproach, this one clearly intended to give him a way out.

'I suppose you're going to say being Irish doesn't mean much to you,' she said. 'Is that what you're going to tell me?'

Mike looked down. 'No,' he said quietly. 'It does mean a lot to me. It means an awful lot.'

Charlotte's eyes flashed with bitter triumph.

'Well, that's just as I thought, then. The most important thing in your life and you don't bother to tell me about it! You know what that means, Michael? It means you don't love me.'

Mike shifted on his feet and lifted his gaze. Charlotte's eyes were glistening and he felt a sudden surge of sympathy for her pain at being rejected.

'Don't say it means that, Charlotte. I don't know why I never told you about Ireland, about being adopted. Maybe I thought it would put you off me.'

Charlotte looked thoughtfully at him.

'Well, I gotta tell you, Mike, my dad doesn't like the idea of me seeing someone who pretends to be German but is nothing of the sort.'

'I never pretended to be German,' Mike replied indignantly. 'I never *wanted* to be German! I wanted to be what I'm *meant* to be. It's not my fault where I ended up. Sometimes I feel . . . like I was never meant to be here. Anyway, I don't like talking about it. That's why I never told you. I hate talking about it.'

Charlotte looked doubtful. 'You're missing your real mom, is that it?'

'I don't know. Sometimes I think I don't remember anything about her and other times it's like . . . I can remember the *feel* of her.'

He struggled to put his thoughts into words.

'You know, it's like . . . you've heard a song and really loved it, and can't get it out of your head, but then it fades and you can still recall the feeling of it but it won't come back to you. That's how it feels.'

Charlotte put her hand on Mike's arm, thinking how different he was from other boys. All her old feelings for him came back in a rush. He was so sensitive and vulnerable. All the tension she felt with other boys – the suspicion they were always looking down her brassiere, always thinking of putting their hands on her – Mike made her forget all that; he made her feel at ease, and she loved him for it.

'Oh Mikey,' she soothed. 'I understand. We all get sad and lonely. We all need someone who cares about us and thinks about our feelings instead of just what *they* want. That's how I feel about you and I think – I *hope* – that's how you feel about me . . . Isn't it?'

Mike thought for a moment and decided that it probably *was* how he felt about Charlotte. What he wanted from her was not the kisses and the embarrassed fondling in the woods in Oak Park; he wanted the sympathy and concern and – yes, maybe – the love she was offering him.

He put his hand on hers.

'Yes, it is,' he said softly. 'I'm sorry about . . . Sometimes I get pretty down. I can't figure it at all, because I got a good life here and my mom and dad look out for me and stuff. But it still feels like there's always something missing—'

'Well *I* can be that something for you, Mikey. I can be there for you . . .'

Charlotte had interrupted him and he had lost his train of ideas; he wasn't completely sure that was where his thoughts had been taking him, but Charlotte's certainty made him forget what else it could have been.

'Yeah, you can,' he replied a little uncertainly.

Mike told Jake Horvath about Charlotte and about the doubts he couldn't shake off.

'You know, Jake, she says I never open up to her and I guess it's true. It's like there's something inside telling me not to get too close to people in case they let me down . . . like I know I'm going to get rejected so there's no point even trying. Do you know what I mean?'

Jake nodded. He was kind of shy himself.

'I see what you mean, Mike. But you'll never find out how things might end up if you don't take a gamble on it. I'd say you've got to let your defences down sometimes.'

When Mike told Mary about it, she understood at once. Every orphan has been rejected, and not just by anyone – their rejection has come from the most important person in the world.

Mike and Charlotte saw less of each other in the weeks that followed. Charlotte told her friends and maybe told herself that it was because her dad had forbidden their love – they were studying *Romeo and Juliet* in English and Charlotte was thrilled by the tragedy and romance of it all – but she knew Otto's complaints were more show than substance. The real reason they were drifting apart was because their relationship had trespassed on areas where Mike was far from comfortable. He had opened his heart to Charlotte and he was regretting it. The more he found excuses for not seeing her, the more Charlotte was mystified and offended.

That's just like him, she thought. *You get close to him and straight away he draws back . . .*

Mike began spending more and more time with Jake Horvath. When he invited him over to Maplewood Drive, Jake said how much he adored Marge for her selfless devotion to her husband and her children, but when he heard Doc cursing the government, calling LBJ an ass and a schmuck and demanding 'someone put a bomb under those goddam Democrats before they destroy the whole country', Jake looked at Mike and grimaced. The two boys were spending most evenings at each other's houses now, and although they hadn't officially broken up, Mike avoided Charlotte's eye as they passed each other in the school corridors.

The phone call changed everything. It came while Doc was at work and the kids at school. Marge was watering plants in the backyard and stripped off her gardening gloves as she raced into the house to catch it. The voice at the other end was raspy and broken – it was no longer the voice of Otto the phlegmatic burgher; it was some poor, broken man dialling every number in his address book, hoping that by sharing his sudden, terrible burden he might somehow lessen its unbearable weight.

'Marge? Marge? That you? It's Otto.'

Marge sensed his urgency. 'Yes, Otto, it's me. What's wrong?'

The line seemed dead for a second, then thrashed wrenchingly into life.

'Charlotte . . . It's Charlotte. Last night . . . She was going to the drugstore. That's what's most . . . That's what I can't understand. Can you, Marge? Can you understand it?'

Marge swallowed and hesitated.

'Otto, you're going to have to tell me what's happened. Tell me slowly. I'm listening. Just tell me what's happened.'

The line heaved with Otto's grief.

'My girl, Marge. It's my girl. They killed her . . .'

Marge listened to twenty minutes of pain and sorrow.

Charlotte and her brother had taken the Inhelders' Buick for an evening drive into Rockford. They'd planned to meet some friends and stop for a couple of Coca-Colas at the drugstore on State Street, but they never got there. On North Second Street a drunk in a blue pickup had crossed the centre median, veered through the left-hand lane and ploughed head-on into them. Charlotte, who never wore a seat belt, was thrown clean through the windshield and hit a truck. Her brother was saved because the steering wheel caught him in the chest and pinned him to the seat. He was in hospital, Otto said; the doctors had promised he would be OK.

'But Marge' – his voice was hoarse and faint, as if grief had tugged him away to some distant, untrodden land, stretching and beating to airy lightness the copper line between them – 'I had to . . . identify her body . . . at the morgue . . . Oh God, Marge, she was so beautiful . . . No father should have to do that, should he? No man should have to do that . . .'

Rumours of the Inhelders' tragedy circulated in Boylan High for much of the morning. After lunch the principal called the school together to announce that one of their most promising and most gifted students had been called to the bosom of the Lord.

Mike listened in silence, picked up his bag and walked home to Maplewood Drive. Marge met him at the door and he crumpled in her arms. For a quarter-hour they stood together, hugging each other and sobbing.

Death changes things. It changes how we think about people; it changes the living and it changes the dead. That evening as Mike lay on his bed staring at the ceiling, he felt he was finally beginning to understand the relationship that had existed between him and Charlotte. The way Mike saw it now, he had never had *any* doubts about committing himself, about putting himself at her mercy; he had never hesitated at all. They were lovers and would have been lovers for life. He had placed his fate in her hands and she had accepted his love forever.

In this new version of events there could be no regrets about how he had behaved. In Mike's mind now he and Charlotte had been practically engaged. It was a comforting thought, a relationship that could be viewed in complete serenity – he would never have to fear the rejection of a dead sweetheart, and the aspic-fixed emotions of the past were far safer territory than the anxieties of the present. But when the school held a remembrance ceremony for Charlotte a week later, Mike was shocked to hear that Greg Tucker would be singing a lament in her memory. He knew Charlotte had once been sweet on Greg, but he had always believed their relationship was over when he first met her at Mrs Finucane's auditions. Now he realized with a jolt that it was Greg, not he, who was being enthroned as Charlotte's boyfriend.

FOURTEEN

1968–9

'Don't you tell me what to do . . . and *don't* tell me how to feel!'

Marge looked on as the flaming row between Mike and Doc approached its final, fiery stages. It was the latest in a series of furious arguments Mike had provoked in the weeks since Charlotte died, and Marge could see by the bafflement and fury in Doc's face that he was thinking the same thing she was. *Whatever happened to our perfect boy? Who is this moody, quarrelsome stranger?*

Marge couldn't even remember how this fight had started. Mike seemed to be living on an emotional knife-edge, and could lash out at the slightest thing. Mary had gone to hide in her room – even she had felt Mike's anger in recent days, and as soon as he showed signs of flaring up she would slip away, bewildered and hurt, keen to be out of his range. The deaths of Loras and Charlotte had taken their toll on Mike: he felt abandoned, responsible, and picked fights to deflect the pain. Years of stifled resentment and frustration, all the years of striving constantly to be 'good', were being released in concentrated, furious bursts.

'Go to your room, young man!' roared Doc, hurling open the door and pointing up the stairs.

'That's right – get rid of the problem. Send the little Irish boy out of sight so you don't have to look at him! I've had *enough* of living by your rules and regulations. Go to *hell*!' Mike screamed. He swept out of the room and slammed the door. Marge and Doc looked at each other, exhausted.

'Oh Doc,' Marge whispered. 'Where did we go wrong?'

'That boy,' Doc sniffed, still reeling with anger and indignation, 'that boy needs discipline, Marge. *Discipline*. He will not act like that in *my house*!'

The older children kept out of it. James, whose relationship with Doc had always been difficult, tried to offer Mike support, but he and Thomas were no longer living at home and didn't see the full extent of it. Stevie, who saw everything, seemed unmoved.

Mary was saddened by her brother's pain and unsettled by his fury, but when she tried to talk to him he waved her away. His behaviour was so aberrant, so out of character, that Mary too was thrown off balance. Her quarrelsome demeanour, the shows of defiance, the troublemaker's temper that had characterized her previous conduct disappeared overnight. Suddenly she was quiet, docile, obedient, as if she were withdrawing before Mike's crisis, giving him room to articulate the emotions he had long repressed. Marge found Mary's behaviour almost as disconcerting as Michael's.

The stand-off continued through the winter. Marge fretted, Doc fumed and Mary watched anxiously as Mike dragged himself wearily to school. Stevie got lucky in the lottery and avoided the draft; Thomas, who was also spared, began studying to be a dentist; James, newly commissioned as a lieutenant in the US Army and now stationed in Panama, wrote home announcing his intention to marry Shirley, his old girlfriend from Rockford. Doc read the letter with trembling hands and furious disapproval. It was never clear what he didn't like about Shirley, but he was unshakeably categorical: Shirley was not a suitable wife for his son. His reply to James was terse: he did not approve, refused to consent to any such match and had no intention of offering the least financial support should Jim pursue the idea. He hoped he had made himself clear.

When Jim wrote back immediately, declaring that he would marry her anyway and didn't care what *anybody* thought, Doc hit the roof.

'Goddam that boy!' he declared, screwing up James's letter and throwing it in the trash. 'Can't he *ever* do what his father tells him!'

Marge remembered the way her own parents had tried to stop her marrying Doc – how they'd had to elope, and the bad blood the affair had caused for so many years afterwards. She thought how short Doc's memory must be.

'Oh Doc, come on. It isn't so bad,' she soothed. 'If he really loves her—'

'Marge, all the things we've done for that boy over the years – the *money* we spent on him, the presents, the holidays, the treats – the letter I wrote to the Department of Defense! And now he . . . he *shames* me – shames the whole family by going against my will . . . Well, I won't hear of it, Marge! I *will not hear of it!*'

Doc strode the room, incoherent with rage that *yet another* son, his *eldest* son, would dare challenge his authority.

'But Doc,' pleaded Marge, 'he's a grown man now and if he wants to—'

'Grown man?' He turned on her. '*Grown man?* Is he still my son, Marge? Did I not raise him? Do I not have a right, as his father, to—'

Mike, who had been glowering in the corner, suddenly stood up.

'*Stop* shouting at her and leave Jimmy *alone!*' he yelled, hating the self-righteous obstinate tyrant who stood before him more than he ever had before.

'How *dare* you raise your voice at me!' countered Doc, and before he could stop himself he had raised his right hand and slapped him.

Marge gasped – '*Doc!*' – and Mary, who was trembling on the sofa, burst into tears. Mike was still for a moment, then, to the astonishment of everyone in the room, he pounced. The blow caught Doc on the temple, and he reeled against the open door, banging it into the wall with a resounding crack. Marge let out a scream and Mary leapt up like a frightened cat, darting past Doc, who was clutching his head, and through the doorway into the hall. As she hurled the front door open, the hated photograph caught on her sleeve and she shrieked with frustration and despair, dashing it to the ground, where it smashed to pieces. An hour later she returned with her face covered in blood and her nose broken in three places.

The shock of Mary's injuries brought a temporary truce. Marge carried her through to the family room, laid her on the sofa and Mike swabbed her face with damp cloths until the bleeding stopped.

'Jesus, Mary,' he whispered, 'what have you done?'

Doc knelt on the floor and examined her nose.

'Can you breathe OK?' he asked, his face pale with concern.

'Not through my nose,' came the muffled reply, 'but I can through my mouth.'

Doc poked a little at where a large blue swelling was beginning to rise – he was concerned about the possibility of a septal haematoma – but eventually concluded the damage was confined to the bone, which was badly smashed.

'And just how did this happen?' he demanded, once he was certain it was nothing more serious than it appeared.

'I went out to play basketball,' Mary sniffed, 'and some kids were playing rough . . . My nose got smashed by the ball.'

Doc grunted; Mary avoided his eye.

'That doesn't *look* like a basketball injury to me,' he said, leaning in close and raising his eyebrows.

'I said my nose got smashed by the *ball*!' she shouted, bursting into fresh tears so violent that her nose began bleeding again.

Doc's resolve faltered. 'Well,' he said, getting to his feet, 'it's broken, there's no denying it. And it doesn't look too good. So I guess we better get it fixed.'

That night in bed her nose hurt and her head pounded, but Mary managed a little smile – the drama and the pain had been intense and it had taken some courage on her part, but she had made it work and got what she wanted. In the morning Dr Habbakuk carried out a closed reduction of the nasal fracture followed by a rather neat septorhinoplasty that would leave the patient with a short, straight nose ending in an attractive rounded tip.

The days that followed brought an interlude of peace. As Mary convalesced from the surgery, Mike seemed to regain some of his composure. He fussed over his sister, brought her soft drinks and snacks and recommended books for her to read while she waited for the swelling to go down. The arguments with Doc became less frequent and Mike seemed to be returning to something like his former self.

But Marge's anxiety would not go away. She was worried about Michael – she sensed his unhappiness had been suppressed, not vanquished; that it could resurface at any time – and she told Doc that Mike needed help just as much as Mary did. Couldn't Doc, with all his expertise and countless contacts who no doubt had the utmost respect for him, recommend someone to whom Mike would be able to open his heart?

FIFTEEN

My fellow Americans. We have found ourselves rich in goods, but ragged in spirit; reaching with magnificent precision for the moon, but falling into raucous discord on earth. We are caught in war, wanting peace. We are torn by division, wanting unity. We see around us empty lives, wanting fulfilment . . . To a crisis of the spirit, we need an answer of the spirit. To find that answer, we must look within ourselves. When we listen to 'the better angels of our nature', we find that they celebrate the simple things, the basic things – such as goodness, decency, love, kindness.

First Inaugural Address of Richard Milhous Nixon,
20 January 1969

New Year 1969 had brought blizzards to the Midwest and a new man to the White House. Doc had gathered the family round the TV set to watch Richard Nixon's inaugural and accompanied the broadcast with his own commentary. He applauded as Justice Warren administered the oath of office and yelled, 'You can say that again!' when Nixon spoke of the spiritual crisis America was living through.

'Thank God those goddam Democrats are finally out on their asses and we've got a real man running the country! You know, boy'

– he turned to Mike with a serious expression – 'you should pay attention to what this fellow says. This man knows what America's about all right. Yep, he sure does.'

Doc leaned back in his chair with a smile of satisfaction and Mike nodded dubiously. He had a tough time agreeing with Doc's political views – if pressed he would classify himself as a liberal on most issues – but he liked the message of tolerance and inclusion Nixon seemed to be offering: 'We cannot learn from one another until we stop shouting at one another, until we speak quietly enough that our words can be heard as well as our voices. We will strive to listen in new ways – to the voices of quiet anguish, the voices that speak without words, the voices of the heart – to the injured voices, the anxious voices, the voices that have despaired of being heard . . .'

'Politics is a real important thing to learn about, son,' Doc said, leaning forward in his chair again and looking Mike in the eye with a serious, interested expression.

'Sure, Pop, I know that.' Mike felt the familiar yearning to create a rapport with his father. 'I've followed the election and I don't agree with everything Nixon says, but I think he has . . . some good views on equality.' He hesitated before playing an inspired ace. 'Anyway,' he shrugged significantly, 'I've been thinking about studying politics and government at college.'

The following day Doc approached Mike with what he saw as a more than generous proposal. He had set the wheels in motion to arrange an internship for him with Everett Dirksen, who had been Illinois' senior senator in Washington for nigh on twenty years. Dirksen was a former patient of his and Doc was sure he could make it happen. Mike, though, was unsure about the whole thing – Dirksen was a Republican and he didn't like the man's conservative views. He didn't like Doc running his life either, and he told himself he should really stand up for what *he* wanted. But Doc was enthusing about the idea, saying what an unbeatable introduction it would be to the world of big politics and talking like it was a done deal. Mike thought for a moment, decided if he was going to object and was surprised to hear himself say, 'Thanks, Doc. That would be great . . .'

His Washington trip was scheduled for the summer of that year.

Gustav Heinlein was a busy man, but he was prepared to squeeze a colleague's son into his schedule. Mike had been deeply unconvinced about the idea of seeing a shrink – *Do they think I'm actually crazy?* he'd wondered, half amused, half uneasy – and he had gone to the first session reluctantly. It had, inevitably, turned out to be awkward – Mike was diffident at the best of times and he didn't like the fact that Heinlein was a friend of his father – but little by little he had opened up to the solemn-faced doctor in the grey suit.

In the first month they had discussed his reaction to the deaths of Loras and Charlotte and his strained relationship with his father, and then – at Heinlein's cautious suggestion – they moved on to a new topic. 'Now Mike, I'd like you to tell me how it makes you feel when you think about your real mother, the mother who gave birth to you.'

Mike stared at his feet, crossed neatly at the end of the couch, and closed his eyes.

'Oh, sometimes I miss her . . . and sometimes I hate her,' he heard himself say. 'But I know – that is, I *feel* – that she can't have been a bad person. Sometimes I think I remember her . . . and I remember her being good. But that means . . .' He trailed off, frowning.

'What do you think that means, Mike?'

'Well, I think it means . . . *I* must be bad. She must have hated me for something . . . something I did or . . . the person I was. Otherwise, why did she give me away?'

Two tears made their way slowly down Mike's face.

'OK,' said Heinlein softly. 'Let's think about this. You say your mother hated you, but I wonder why you think that. There's no way you can know the reasons for what your mother did, now is there? So what are you basing these fears on, Mike? Did someone say something to you?'

'My mom – I mean, Marge – she told my brother Stevie how it

all happened, and he told me. How my real mother hated me and didn't want to look after me.' He began to sob. 'It hurts, Dr Heinlein; it hurts to know you're no good . . .'

Heinlein shook his head sadly.

'So you believed what your brother Stevie told you?' he asked, his voice so gentle it was almost a whisper. 'Did you never consider the possibility he was lying to hurt you?'

Mike thought for a moment.

'Yeah, sure I did. Maybe I even knew he was lying. Maybe I know everything's much more complicated. But the thing is, I can't stop hating myself. My mother abandoned me and never tried to find me. If *she* didn't love me, it means no one can, and I certainly can't love myself.'

'But Mike,' Heinlein said, 'have you never thought that maybe your mother left you with the nuns because she was just a girl herself, that she couldn't give you the care you needed even though she loved you as much as any mother loves her child?'

Mike frowned and thought for a moment.

'If I had a child,' he concluded, choosing his words with great deliberation, 'I would love that child more than anything. Even if I had no money and no home and no clothes, nothing would come between us. Mom – Marge – once told me there was nothing she wouldn't do to make me happy. So I can't believe my real mother would have given me up forever without a second thought just because she was too young, or too poor, to bring me up right. She should have known I'd have been just as happy with nothing, so long as I had *her*.'

It was a perfect warm early-spring evening and Doc was sitting opposite Gus Heinlein in a coffee shop around the corner from Heinlein's office.

'Now Gus,' he began, getting down to business immediately, 'I know all about this doctor–patient confidentiality business – I'm a doctor myself, for God's sake – but this is my son we're talking about, and whatever's going on in that head of his, I need to know about it because it affects all of us living under one roof.'

Gus nodded. 'Sure. I understand that, Doc. But I gotta say, whatever it is you're hoping to hear from me, it isn't all good news. You maybe don't realize that orphans make up just 2 to 3 per cent of the general population – but they make up 30 to 40 per cent of the inmates at residential treatment centres, juvenile detention facilities and special schools . . .'

Doc grunted and sipped his coffee, feeling – not for the first time – that those children of Marge's were more trouble than they were worth.

'. . . and they also present a high incidence of delinquency, sexual promiscuity and alcohol abuse. Now, I'm not saying your boy is going to be in any or all of those categories,' Heinlein went on, 'but you should know the facts. These people are addictive personalities. They're always trying to make up for something that's missing in their life or for something they think they've done wrong.'

Gus paused and munched on a cookie, studying Doc's reaction.

'Mike's a smart boy,' Doc said after a moment. 'He gets real good grades and he thinks a lot, maybe too much. The strange thing is, when we first got them it was the girl who gave us all the problems. Mike was quiet, did what he was told and never kicked up a fuss. It's only recent that he's become such a crazy schmuck, always arguing and fighting and punching people . . .'

'That's classic,' Heinlein said. 'The orphan is always looking for acceptance but always expecting rejection. It's like they feel they're never wanted and can never fit in. Their birth mother rejected them so they think there's something wrong with them: they expect everyone else to reject them too. So you get the orphan who spends his whole time being obliging and docile in the hope his new parents won't send him away. Then you get the other type who's always causing trouble, like he's saying, "I know you're gonna reject me, so screw you – I'm gonna reject you first!" That behaviour's called testing-out and it can get pretty extreme. Now to me it sounds like your boy's got a bit of both in him. And I'm sorry to say it, but that sort always end up pretty screwed up: they have problems with trust and intimacy, with sex and relationships. Half the time they're fretting about conforming and living blameless conventional lives, and the other half they're giving in to crazy impulses and addictions and taking risks that end up killing them.'

Doc sighed into his mug.

'Yeah, well, I guess I read something similar to that. So what's to be done about it?'

'Not much, I'm afraid,' Heinlein mused. 'It all goes back to our earliest experiences and the way they shape the rest of our lives. Did you know babies can pick out their mother's face minutes after they're born? Forty weeks in utero means they're already pretty bonded, so being abandoned is a big thing. Even though your kids were given away the minute they were born, they're still going to remember it at some level, and it's still going to be devastating for them.'

Doc chewed this over.

'Actually, it's worse than that, Gus. They were with their moms for three whole years,' he said finally. 'And when they left, it was against their mothers' wishes. We've never told them about that.'

Gus stared in amazement at his colleague's disregard for his children and, with a supreme effort to retain his professional detachment, forced himself to nod sympathetically.

At the next therapy session Dr Heinlein tried hard not to look guilty. He was fond of Mike and felt bad about speaking to Doc behind his back. He was keen to make it up to the boy with a really probing, cleansing session, so he started with a really tough question.

'Would you say, Mike, that you find it impossible to allow people to get close to you?'

Mike was momentarily thrown.

'Gee, Dr Heinlein. Nice to see you too,' he joked. But Heinlein's face was serious.

'Many orphans feel that way, Michael, and you've mentioned before that you found your relationship with Miss Inhelder very difficult.'

Mike shifted to make himself comfortable.

'I wish I'd never been in that show,' he said. 'I wish I'd never gotten close to her.' He paused. 'Uncle Loras too.'

Heinlein looked up.

'You regret the close relationship you had with your uncle?'

'Whenever I get close to people, they always disappear.'

Heinlein made a note on his notepad.

'Death is a natural thing, Mike – a terrible, tragic thing, but a natural thing. We all fear it, we all experience it. It's OK to mourn, but blaming yourself will get you nowhere.'

Heinlein decided he needed to lighten the mood – he hadn't intended the subject of death to crop up so early in their relationship.

'Anyway, I'm sure you don't really regret taking part in the show – you've told me before that it was one of the highlights of your life!'

Mike gave a little shrug.

'Yeah. It was.'

'So why do you think you enjoyed it so much, Mike?'

Mike thought for a moment.

'It was . . . an amazing feeling, being up onstage with everyone watching me . . . loving me.' He blushed, conscious that he sounded arrogant. 'And . . . I loved dressing up. I loved playing Patrick. It seemed . . . so simple to be up onstage, saying lines I'd already learned, going through motions I'd already rehearsed – knowing where I was heading and how things would end.'

'You loved the pretence, is that it? You loved the mask? Getting to be somebody else – having everybody watch you without really *seeing* you?'

Mike looked sharply at the doctor. That was exactly how it had felt.

'So you like to disguise parts of yourself,' Heinlein probed, 'behind performance, behind charity work, behind conformity and obedience . . . because you're frightened of letting people see and maybe judge the real you?'

'It's hard to relax when you're worried about that stuff,' Mike assented.

'But *why* are you trying to hide, Mike?'

There was a long pause before Mike said, in a tiny voice, 'I don't know.'

'What would happen if you stopped pretending and let the world see the real you? I think they might find you quite wonderful.'

Mike looked at Doctor Heinlein with gleaming eyes. 'They wouldn't . . . believe me, Dr Heinlein – they wouldn't. I'm . . . not like other people. I'm . . . different, like someone deformed.'

'Slightly *un*formed maybe – but not *de*formed, Mike. If you told me the innermost part of yourself, the part you're more afraid than anything of other people seeing, I guarantee it would be nothing that I hadn't heard before. What are you most ashamed of, Mike? There's nothing you can say that would repulse me or shock me. You are safe from judgement here.'

Mike began to cry. He wanted so much to tell kind Dr Heinlein the truth, and before he knew it he was telling him all about Marius Inhelder of all people: how beautiful he had seemed in the car that night they drove to Mr Henry's; how like Charlotte but so much more powerful . . . In rushed, hitching breaths he described the attraction, the complicity he had felt watching Marius laugh and chat with his friends, the way his neck had glowed in the moonlight as he'd driven them home, how he had wanted to reach out and touch it.

'I felt like there was something wrong with me . . . something wrong inside,' Mike explained, desperately looking to the doctor for help, explanation, reassurance.

Dr Heinlein, leaning forward in his chair with rapt attention, suddenly looked at the clock. 'Time's up, Mike,' he said softly. 'This has been a very good session and we can continue where we left off next week.'

When Mike left, Doctor Heinlein reluctantly called Doc Hess.

'Doc,' he began determinedly, 'I need to ask you something. Have you ever thought there is a chance your son might be – excuse me for asking this – a homosexual?'

For a brief moment there was silence on the line and then Doc burst out laughing.

'You know what, Gus? Spare me the Freud. Mike may be a lot of things, but if there's one thing he most certainly is not, it's a goddam faggot!'

Shortly afterwards Doc announced that the counselling sessions with Dr Heinlein were over.

SIXTEEN

1969

Arriving in Washington DC that summer was like taking a crash course on street politics. President Nixon's promises to wind down US involvement in Vietnam had not been matched by deeds, and public opinion was turning as American GIs continued to come home in body bags. Descending from the Greyhound at the back of Union Station, Mike found the streets leading to the Capitol filled with crowds wearing black armbands and carrying anti-war banners. He heard them chanting, 'Hell no, we won't go!' and, 'I don't give a damn for Uncle Sam, I ain't going to Vietnam!' There was an atmosphere of solidarity and purpose among the demonstrators that drew him in; most were young and serious-looking, fired by an intensity of feeling that Mike found exhilarating. He let himself be carried along, inhaling the sense of history and the sweet odour of pot. He felt he was at the centre of important events – his years in Rockford and the concerns of his youth seemed suddenly trivial. He needed to be *here*, where he could make a difference on the big things, like the shame of Vietnam and the injustice of poverty and discrimination.

He stayed with the demonstration for an hour, but he was carrying his backpack and starting to get hungry. As darkness fell, he went looking for Webster Hall, the congressional dorm where he would be boarding for his four weeks in Washington. He had the address and knew it was close to the Supreme Court Building, but the DC system of geographical quadrants – NE, NW, SE and SW – confused him and he found himself wandering through a series of neighbourhoods north of the Capitol where burnt-out houses lined the streets and shopfronts were boarded up with painted signs warning against looting. The race riots following the death of Martin Luther King had left an enduring scar on the face of the nation's capital, a reminder of the tensions that ran beneath the affluent society Mike was used to, where such things were glimpsed on the TV news if at all.

By the time he reached Webster Hall Mike was feeling agitated and disoriented but strangely excited. He was in the heart of the nation's capital, and this was where he could change things for the better.

Michael's official title was Page to the Senator. He had been told broadly what his duties were: delivering documents and mail within the congressional complex, taking messages for Senator Dirksen, calling him when he was needed on the phone and carrying papers to his desk in the Senate. He was looking forward to meeting Dirksen and telling him exactly what he thought about the key issues facing the nation and about the older man's lamentable record on them. Dirksen was a fiscal conservative, a protectionist and one of Congress's leading hawks on the Vietnam war; Mike was going to tell him he was wrong on all counts.

In his seventies now, big-handed, big-boned, white-haired and jowly, Dirksen had the air of a man supremely at ease with life, comfortable with his role, unhurried and friendly. His welcome to Mike seemed genuine.

'Well, well, a young Hess,' he boomed, striding across the room. 'Come here and shake my hand, young man. You are indeed welcome and not just because your dad was the one who spotted my prostate back in the day and maybe – I say maybe – saved my worthless old life.'

Dirksen saw the look of surprise on Mike's face and smiled.

'Oh, don't pay no heed to me, son. I'm just a farm boy from

Illinois and I say what comes into my head. Dirksen, Hess – we're all Deutschers, you know. Anyway, what do you make of the place?'

Mike looked around him at the plush carpets and wood-panelled walls. The place looked fusty, self-absorbed, apprehensively protected against the real world.

'Well, it's pretty impressive, Senator. But I think—'

'You think it all looks fuddy-duddy and out of touch – that what you think? Well, I can't blame you. Think the place needs shaking up, huh?'

Mike was clearly not the first Young Turk Everett Dirksen had come across. His remarks were made with amused bonhomie and Mike's inherited reflexes made him smile back. He didn't mean to, but somehow he couldn't help it.

'Well, Senator, I don't say that, but—'

'But we could do with some new thinking, could we? "Senator, Congressman, please heed the call . . . The times they are a-changing"?'

It was said without malice and with such self-mockery that Mike couldn't avoid liking the man.

'No, that's not what I mean to say. But I do think the country needs to do something about the war and how to use our resources to help the poor and the underprivileged.'

Dirksen's face grew serious.

'Well said, son,' he shot back. 'Your opinions are honourable and I for one share them. It's a sad fact that politics doesn't always allow you to do the right thing; sometimes you just gotta choose the least bad one. But you can rely on this: everything I do is with the interests of this great country at heart, and I would be honoured if you would give me your support, as a member of our young generation, in the efforts we're making to ensure this country's future. What do you say, young man? We'd sure like to have you with us.'

Mike looked at him and knew it was a speech he had given a thousand times – he could see why he was known as Oily Ev, the Wizard of Ooze – but something about the appeal and the way it addressed him, Michael Hess, as an individual, a person worth

courting, got to him. Despite his best resolutions, he shook the proffered hand. The senator was opening the door to a world people
respected, solid, enduring and reliable. Mike desperately wanted to
belong, and he wanted to be wanted.

Dirksen gave him a grin.

'Good to have you on board, Michael Hess. Good to have you,
son. Now I gotta go vote, but we're having a cocktail this evening –
very informal and very exclusive – so I want you to be sure and ask
Miss Gregson in my office for all the details. I'm counting on seeing
you there.'

When Dirksen was gone, Mike mulled over the conversation. It
felt like he'd been taken by a clever con man, but it also felt good to
be part of his stable, reassuring world with its unquestioned rules
you could live your life and judge yourself by.

The month in Washington went by in a buzz of working days and
partying nights. Dirksen worked his staff hard but rarely failed to
make them feel loved and wanted. And that was the drug that kept
Mike hooked, the reward that made him forget his scruples. The price
of belonging was a minimal one – commit yourself to the party and
the party will give you the acceptance you crave.

When he returned to Rockford, he said little about his experiences and replied cursorily to Doc's questions about the senator. But
he told Mary his stint in Washington had opened his eyes to a different
world and a different way of thinking about himself. He felt he was
on the threshold of doing something worthwhile at last.

'You feel like you're part of the new generation,' he told his sister
the night he got back. 'It's like you're knocking on the door of the
establishment and – amazingly – they're opening the door and letting
you in.'

'Wow.' Mary grinned. 'That sounds so cool, Mike. I'm . . . kinda
surprised by the Republican thing though. I thought you hated them.
Every time Doc says what a great party the Republicans are, you
always pull a face.'

Mike looked a little embarrassed and said quickly, 'Yeah, well, the key thing is to be accepted, Mary. To be a member of the big boys' club. Then I can think what to do next.'

Mary frowned. 'I guess,' she said uncertainly.

Mike's optimism was clouded by two events that followed soon after.

In late August James wrote to say his wedding would take place in the fall. After he finished with the army he and Shirley were fixing to settle in Iowa City, where he planned to resume his law studies and train as an attorney. The letter gave the time and place of the ceremony and James said he really hoped Doc and Marge and all the family would come. In a last attempt at reconciliation with his father, he said he was sorry if he had offended anyone and it had never been his intention to do so; he had always tried to be a good son and he was sad if other people didn't see it that way.

At breakfast on the day the letter arrived, Doc read the three handwritten pages in silence before announcing that no one would be going to any wedding. He destroyed James's note and wrote a reply that he didn't show to Marge. When she asked what he had written, he said it would be a long time before they spoke to James again. He didn't say he was disinheriting his son, but he told his other children they were no longer to contact him in any way. Mike said nothing, but he recalled his Uncle Loras's dying injunction and resolved he would follow the dictates of his conscience before those of his father.

Then in September, just weeks after Mike had returned from his internship in Washington, he picked up the *Chicago Tribune* and read the front-page report: 'Everett Dirksen, dead at 73. Sen. Everett McKinley Dirksen was eulogized today as a Senate man and a leader whose unique style is the stuff of legends. The Senate met for 12 minutes and adjourned in tribute . . . President Nixon called him an individualist of the first rank, who belonged to all of us because he always put his Nation before himself . . .'

Dirksen had died in Washington DC after unsuccessful surgery on a rapidly metastasizing prostate cancer that had spread to his lungs.

SEVENTEEN

1970

Mike graduated from Boylan in June 1970 with the best grades of any male student. He and Joy Heskey, the top female student, were honoured at a ceremony in the school auditorium by Bishop Art O'Neill, who had filled the post after Loras Lane's death. Marge and Doc loved the pomp and prestige, the speeches and the congratulations. They were delighted with Mike's performance and they told him so. His grades guaranteed his acceptance by the University of Notre Dame, which both he and Doc had been hoping for. Mike had thought of studying theology – Notre Dame's Catholic heritage and Irish connections made it seem the logical thing – but after his time in Washington, and with Doc's encouragement, he had elected to take a BA in government.

Back home after the graduation ceremony, they sat around the table and drank champagne. They toasted Mike and Doc said he hoped they would be celebrating again next year when Mary graduated, but she pulled a face and said, 'Don't hold your breath, guys.'

For Marge the occasion was a sort of vindication. As she watched Mike and Mary fooling around, taking turns to wear Mike's mortar board, she thought back to the day they had arrived from the airport. It seemed a long time ago now; there had been tough times, plenty of them, Marge reflected, but moments like this made it seem worthwhile.

At around eleven Doc stood up and said, 'Ah well, there is work to be done in the morning', which was usually the signal for everyone to go to bed. But when the others went upstairs, Mike stayed in the kitchen and took a beer from the refrigerator. The eulogies at the graduation had left him with a sense of elation that wouldn't let him sleep.

A little later, when Marge came down in her robe to get herself some water, Mike surprised her with a long, heartfelt hug.

'I love you, Mom,' he said, slurring his words a little. 'I wanna thank you . . . for everything. All the things you've done for me and Mary over the years. You're a wonderful mom and we're lucky to have you.'

Marge was touched.

'Oh Mikey,' she sniffed, 'you know how much we love you guys. You needed someone to look after you all those years ago and we were just happy to be there for you. You've always been such a good boy – right from when you came here – and you've repaid our love many times over.'

Mike took her hand, suddenly feeling very sober.

'Mom, there's something I've been meaning to ask you.'

'Sure, Mike,' Marge replied. 'What is it?'

He hesitated for a moment – the subject was not an easy one for him, or for Marge, and he didn't want to hurt her. He dropped his gaze momentarily, then met her eyes.

'It's about Ireland, Mom. I mean, about me and Ireland. You know how you've always told us you got us from the orphanage and how you took me because I was Mary's best friend and held her hand and stuff? Well, I was just wondering what you knew about us *before* that all happened. Did you, like, know where we came from or who we were?'

Marge looked at him. He had asked her similar questions in the past and she was aware her answers had left him disappointed. She began to repeat the usual story, the family legend of How the Kids Were Adopted, but Mike interrupted.

'The thing is, Mom – and it's nothing to do with you – that is, you've been the best mom I could have had, and all – but I want to know about my other mom, the one who gave birth to me and gave me to the nuns.'

'Well, I don't know how much I can help you on that, Mikey,' Marge stammered, but Mike persevered.

'Because there's something that has always bothered me: it's a long time ago and I'm not sure if I'm imagining things, but sometimes it seems I can remember my Irish mom, like she was right there and I can picture her face and hear her voice.'

Marge shook her head gently.

'No, honey. I'm sorry but I don't think that can be right. So far as we ever knew, your mom gave you to the nuns right after you were born. She left you in the convent and went to get on with her life. We simply have no idea who she was or what made her give you up or where she went afterwards. But I'm sure she wasn't there with you in the orphanage.'

Mike sighed, his hopes fading.

'OK, Mom. I guess you're right. It's only vague memories, you know, like everything is kinda fuzzy and unclear.'

Marge squeezed his hand. She felt for her son but it wasn't as if he was ever going to go back to Ireland, and it was surely best for him to forget the past and focus on his future.

'Well, that's OK,' she said. 'Just don't torment yourself over all those things. You're Mike Hess now, the all-American boy' – she laughed – 'and you're doing real well for yourself. We're proud of you, son.'

Mike kissed her goodnight and finished his beer a little dejectedly at the kitchen table.

As Marge got into bed she whispered to Doc that Michael had been asking about his Irish mom.

'Well,' Doc asked groggily, 'what'd you say?'

'I kept to our agreement. I told him what you said I should.'

Doc grunted.

'It's for the best, Marge. There's no point telling them about all that stuff with their moms; it'd just make things harder for everyone.'

*

When Mike's formal acceptance at Notre Dame came through, Mary said she would miss him: Jim, Tom and Stevie had already left home, and now, she said, Doc was talking about selling up and retiring to Florida. Mike found all this unsettling. He was moving away to college while the others were scattering to distant places. And he was worried about Marge, who had seemed a little fragile in recent times. She'd fretted and lost weight since Loras's death, which had hit her badly, and she oftentimes seemed overwrought and unhappy.

Uncertainty about the future reinforced Mike's need for certainty about the past. With his imminent release from the bonds of his adoptive family the quest to discover his real identity seemed more urgent than ever, and he found a way to take it forward.

The Notre Dame Admissions Office had written asking Mike for his birth certificate, social security number and naturalization papers. When Doc put the papers in an envelope to mail to the university, Mike offered to take the letter to the post office, where, with glances to left and right, he carefully opened it and noted down the details: 'Anthony Lee, a male child having been born on the 5th day of July 1952 at Sean Ross Abbey, Roscrea, Ireland; and Philomena Lee, mother of the said child, having relinquished full claim forever . . .'

Anthony Lee, son of Philomena Lee. Mike stared at the piece of paper for a long time. That night he wrote a letter, the first step on a journey he hoped would lead him to his mother, and to himself. He addressed it to the Mother Superior, Sean Ross Abbey, Roscrea.

EIGHTEEN

1970

Mike loved Notre Dame from the moment he arrived. It was such a heady, unlikely mixture of smells and bells, Catholicism and stage Irishness that he almost suspected the place was a private joke deliberately aimed at him. The twin presiding spirits of the campus were the gilded statue of the Blessed Virgin looking down from the dome of the Sacred Heart Basilica and the gigantic Christ with outstretched, celebrating arms that the jocks nicknamed Touchdown Jesus. Priests with Irish names presided over morning Mass; the Fighting Irish battled most weekends in a stadium where 60,000 raucous spectators, many with green-painted faces, led by cheerleaders in leprechaun outfits, sang thunderous renditions of the 'Notre Dame Victory March' ('Rally sons of Notre Dame, / Sing her glory, sound her fame / . . . Rah, rah, rah for Notre Dame, / Wake the echoes with her name'); and Irish pipe bands marched through the leafy quadrangles and across the rolling lawns to the twin lakes of St Mary and St Joseph, where long rows of black crosses marked the graves of generations of teacher brothers called to their heavenly reward.

Mike was assigned to Fisher Hall, where he had a bedroom to himself and shared a bathroom down the corridor with a half-dozen other freshmen. He covered the walls with Santana and Led Zeppelin posters and settled down to read the texts for his US constitution module between duties as a eucharist assistant serving Communion in the basilica and stints as the dorm DJ hosting noisy parties late into the night. His love of music got him singing in the chapel choir, playing piano for Aloha celebrations and jamming in the campus nightclub. He was beginning to acquire the encyclopedic knowledge of rock and pop music that would stay with him and grow throughout his life. Word spread through the university about his talents as a DJ and his services were increasingly in demand, but he did not lose sight of prayer and contemplation. Time spent at the Grotto of Our Lady of Lourdes alternated with volunteer work at Riverside Hospital and mentoring at South Bend's Juvenile Justice Facility.

In 1970 Notre Dame was still a male-only institution, with a testosterone-charged reputation fuelled by exploits on the sports field and a deliberately fostered image of aggressive masculinity. But Mike did not play football and did not thrill to the exploits of the jocks. The coterie he moved in was cerebral and sensitive: his friends were intellectuals and aesthetes interested in poetry and the arts; where the jocks wore tracksuits and baseball caps, they revelled in their flared trousers, flowered shirts and long hair. Tall and naturally slim, Mike made a fine clothes horse: he attracted a following among the girls of the adjacent St Mary's College and from certain of the boys in Fisher Hall. It was a period of exploration and self-discovery; he felt liberated after the constraints of family life, uncovering new things about himself, readjusting his projections of the future. His studies were going well; his grades were good; he felt more at ease with himself than he had done for many years.

Kurt Rockley, a sophomore English major and budding poet with a shock of blond hair that flopped over his pale forehead, took a particular interest in Mike. They would sit together for hours in the Memorial Library or the social lounge of Fisher Hall discussing the beat poets, Andy Warhol, Miles Davis and Stanley Kubrick. Mike found Kurt's attention flattering and his conversation inspiring. He felt relaxed in his presence; they understood each other and were able to discuss important things. When they spoke about their plans and ambitions, their hopes for the future and regrets about the past, Mike confided in him about his adoptive family and his Irish roots. He told him of the quest he had embarked on, the search for the mother who abandoned him and whom he was now trying to contact. But, he said, there had been no answer from Sean Ross Abbey and the passing weeks were fanning his ever-smouldering sense of foreboding.

'How romantic!' Kurt exclaimed when Mike reached the end of his story. '*Die Frau Ohne Schatten* produced a Boy Without a Shadow . . .'

Mike gave a helpless smile, but Kurt was a Californian and convinced that every problem must have a practical solution.

'So, listen! If the nuns won't write you, then you better just pick up that telephone and call them,' he said, as if the answers to the riddle of life, fate and identity were simply a phone call away. Mike laughed.

'So how do you suggest we get the phone number, Einstein? Look in the South Bend directory?'

But Kurt was enjoying the challenge of the quest and the prospect of intimacy with Michael it conferred on him. Two days later he appeared at Mike's door brandishing a scribbled note from Father Benjamin in the Notre Dame Secretariat. 'Roscrea 220!' he announced triumphantly and handed over the paper.

'How on earth did you get that?' Mike asked, grinning, but Kurt shook his head teasingly.

'Well? What are you waiting for?' he said. 'Go dial the number!'

Next morning, standing in the international phone booth at the South Bend post office with the scrap of paper in his hand, Mike stared at the phone and told himself to pick up the receiver. He stood for a quarter-hour and felt the sweat break out on his palms, but when the clerk came and asked him if he intended to make a call, he shook his head and walked out onto the windy street.

NINETEEN

1971

Mike spent the summer at Notre Dame, working as an administrator for the university's summer extension programme. The campus filled up with earnest adults attending courses on life sciences, writing for the stage and screen, and biblical exegesis. Most students who stayed on to provide support services were guys like Mike – without a home they wanted to go to, or too poor to take a vacation. When Mike asked Kurt Rockley why he had remained instead of flying back to his parents in San Francisco Kurt raised an eyebrow and said archly, 'Well, I'm surprised you need to ask. I stayed here to be with you, of *course*.'

Doc had found a house in St Petersburg Beach on the Gulf Coast of Florida and they had moved as soon as Mary graduated from Boylan High in June. In August Mike phoned to say he wanted to come down for a week to see them and, if it was OK, he'd like to bring a friend. Marge was delighted and said she was sure Doc wouldn't mind, so eight days later the two of them descended the steps of the Eastern Airlines 727 at the newly opened Tampa International Airport and jumped a Greyhound to St Petersburg Beach.

Mike lay on the poolside, listening to the hypnotic beat of his own heart and the lapping of the water. Tiny beads of sweat trickled over

his closed eyelids. The universe was sailing away into airy nothingness and a half-remembered tune from some place in his past was
hovering on the fringes of his mind. He didn't hear Kurt slip out of
the water and glide over the hot path; didn't see the trail of moist
Rorschach blots that marked his passage; felt nothing until the boy's
lips were on his own and warm droplets were falling from Kurt's hair
onto his cheeks and neck.

That evening at dinner Doc asked Kurt how he had gotten to
know Michael, and Mike replied quickly that they played football
together for Fisher Hall.

At the end of the week, the night before the boys were due to fly
back north, Mary asked Mike if she could speak with him alone.
They sat in the dark by the pool and talked about how different it
was here from the cold nights when they sat on the porch in Maplewood
Drive. Kurt was inside, playing cards with Marge while Doc watched
TV, and Mary put her hand on Mike's arm.

'That friend of yours sure is nice, Mikey. Cute too.'

'Yeah,' Mike agreed, 'he's a good man.'

They spoke about Marge, and Mike said he was worried about
her – how frail she seemed and how unhappy. Mary said it was hard
starting over in a new place, and there were tensions in the family.
Then she fell silent. Mike asked her if she was OK.

Mary hesitated and whispered, 'Mikey, I've been seeing this guy
and . . . I think I'm pregnant.'

Mike was quiet on the plane up to Chicago. He was quiet on the
Greyhound from Chicago to South Bend.

At first Kurt respected Mike's obvious desire not to talk, but his
irritation finally got the better of him. 'Hey,' he hissed, jostling Mike
with his elbow. 'What's with the Greta Garbo act? What's with the
big sulk? Did I say something? Did I do something?'

Mike apologized and said it was nothing Kurt had done. But when
they got back to Notre Dame he said maybe it would be better if
they didn't see each other for a while.

TWENTY

Father Adrian knew the students who came regularly to confession. In theory the screen and dim light of the confessional were guarantees of anonymity, but the reality was you got to recognize their voices – and often their sins. Tonight, he could tell that Mike was agitated and struggling to find the right words. Father Adrian tried to guide him but the conversation was awkward, like they were avoiding something, and they both left the booth feeling things that needed saying had gone unsaid.

He wasn't surprised to find Mike waiting outside the basilica. When he asked him if he could help, Mike replied, 'I don't know.'

Adrian smiled. 'Let me try then.'

Over coffee in the priests' residence, they chatted about academic life, books, music and movies. Adrian did not push Mike to talk about the things he had on his mind, and it was Mike who brought the subject up.

'Father, I'm feeling guilty . . . .'

Father Adrian asked if he could be more specific and Mike said, 'Well, for one thing, my brother James has been kicked out of the family and I haven't done anything to try and contact him or tell him how bad I feel for him.'

The priest nodded. 'It is always sad when families quarrel. But from what you tell me, it hardly seems your fault that your brother has been sent away. And anyhow you can remedy your sin of omission by contacting him and expressing your love for him, can you not?'

'I guess you're right, Father. I should just write him and Shirley, I know I should. I'll do it tomorrow.' He paused. 'But there are other things too . . .'

And suddenly he was telling Father Adrian how worried he was about Marge; how guilty he felt for not taking care of her after all she had done for him; about Mary's pregnancy and how he wished he could be there to support her as he always had been.

Father Adrian listened with sympathy in his eyes.

'Well, sure, Mike,' he said when Mike had finished. 'We all could do more to help others. But you are beating yourself up too much. Really. You can't go through life blaming yourself for everything that happens to people you love, feeling responsible for every bad thing in the world. I can tell you are a loving son and brother, so why do you feel so bad about yourself? What makes you think you're always to blame?'

Mike took a breath. He hadn't planned on saying anything more, but Father Adrian seemed such an understanding guy that maybe he would understand this.

'I feel bad about myself because I *am* bad, Father. Everyone who gets close to me sees it and runs a mile. And I don't blame them. I look inside myself and I see things that scare me.'

Father Adrian leaned over and put a hand on Mike's knee.

'Oh come now, my son. What sort of things can there be? You're a mere innocent at your age. You confess your sins, but in reality your sins are nothing at all.'

The priest smiled encouragingly but Mike was growing agitated and shook his head.

'You're wrong, Father. I'm not innocent . . . My sin is that I love men.'

LONDON

Present Day

The photo on my desk now is of a young man in a bright short-sleeved shirt and sunglasses in the Florida sunshine. He is sitting by the side of a swimming pool and the ocean is glinting through the trees behind him. Beside the picture a slightly older copy of the *Rockford Register*, from summer 1970, carries the headline TODAY'S GOOD NEWS: PUPILS ARE HEROES AT HOME FOR AGED.

> Shopping with your mother can be a drag, but when you help an elderly woman go to the grocery store – and she's not even your mother – you're somewhat of a hero. That's what the boys of Boylan High School's Key Club do each Wednesday afternoon for the women at North Main Manor Home, 505 N Main St. 'We're a service organization,' explained Michael Hess, club president, 'and we got the idea of helping these women.' Two or three of the boys come each Wednesday to the retirement home and take the ladies 'wherever they want to go, but usually it's grocery shopping', Hess explained.

The photograph with the article is of a serious-looking teenager in a shirt and tie, his black hair flopping over a clean-cut attractive face in half-profile, ushering a frail-looking lady in a headscarf into the passenger seat of a parked car.

Going back further, the footsteps of the distant life I have been following resound faintly in the cavernous archives of the Catholic Church. A photograph of Bishop Art O'Neill shows him presenting graduation prizes at Rockford's Boylan High School to a female student in white robe and cap, and a smiling young man wearing a purple and black gown with the tassel of his mortar board hanging casually over the side of his face. A splendid 1965 print from the annals of the Vatican captures Pope Paul VI preening for the camera in the Vatican Library, flanked by a beaming Bishop Loras Lane in Rome for the closing sessions of the Vatican council and an old lady in widow's black, hair carefully curled under a lace mantilla with black purse and white gloves, standing unsteadily on painfully swollen ankles. Worried by her son's health, Josephine Lane in her late eighties appears to have made a final journey across the Atlantic to be with him, and this is the last picture of her. While the two men smile at the camera, she is staring into the distance beyond.

Sporadic traces and disparate evidence – newspaper extracts, photographs, state and Church documents, and a distinctive toy plane – had taken me from Anthony Lee to Michael A. Hess, from Ireland to America, but now the trail was growing cold. Apart from confirming his dates and academic record, Notre Dame would not respond to my enquiries about Michael, citing federal privacy laws. The US Senate had a list of interns and pages for every year since the Second World War, but no details beyond their names and home towns. I did, though, have two reels of Standard-8 home movies dating from the 1950s that had come into my possession by a circuitous and somewhat mysterious route. It was these old films, together with newspaper cuttings of a Washington scandal and a series of chance events, that would bring me into contact with the key figures in Michael's adult life.

PART THREE

ONE

Mike agonized about the confession he had made to Father Adrian. Sometimes he regretted opening his soul to the scrutiny of another human being; at others he felt liberated by what he had done. Back at Notre Dame he threw himself into his studies. He opted for courses about the political machinery the country depended on. He loved the complexities of the American electoral system and was fascinated by the case law on gerrymandering, the art of redrawing electoral boundaries for partisan purposes that dated back to the eighteenth century. He filled his social life with hectic activity, accepting DJ engagements, volunteering for hours of religious duties and charity work, acting and singing in university drama productions and concerts. He knew – but did not want to admit – that he was stuffing his existence with noise and commotion to block out the troubling thoughts he was striving to forget.

Mike had taken at least part of Father Adrian's advice. He had composed a conciliatory and sympathetic letter to his brother James, offering congratulations on his marriage and saying how sorry he was about the split in the family. He said he would be happy to help if ever James and Shirley wanted to try and patch things up with Doc. Then, spurred on by the adrenalin rush of *doing something,* he had phoned Marge in St Pete to apologize for not visiting more often and promised to put things right in the future. Her response had been so touchingly grateful that Mike had promised to come down to see them that weekend, and on Friday morning he skipped class and flew home.

On Saturday afternoon Mike was sitting opposite his sister in one of the booths of the Paradise Café in St Petersburg Beach. Beside Mary was the soon-to-be father of her child, Craig. Mike eyed him over his milkshake and was pleased to see that his hair and clothes were neat and there was a seriousness in his eyes that spoke of responsibility and decency. Mary herself had undergone a subtle change: the old 'I want' frown line between her eyebrows had smoothed, and her smile was relaxed and easy. When she spoke to Craig, Mike saw the intimate, knowing looks that passed between them – a comfortable familiarity and understanding so achingly absent from Mike's own life. A pang of unexpected envy peppered the happiness he felt at his sister's apparent good fortune.

While Mary was in the ladies' room, Craig leaned forward and looked at Mike intently.

'Hey, Mike, you know I'm going to . . . You know I'll take good care of her, right?'

Mike almost laughed at the earnestness of his gaze – it was a look he himself was used to using.

'Oh man, I know that. Come on, Craig, you don't have to—'

'No, I want to,' Craig said. 'You know, she talks about you all the time. She thinks the world of you and I know she misses you a whole lot. So it's important that I tell you – that I'm going to do the right thing by her. I've already spoken about it to your dad' – Mike frowned at the mention of Doc but said nothing – 'and he was . . . He seems OK about it all now. I know it wasn't planned, but, jeez, I don't know. I mean, I love her.'

He paused and looked at his hands. Mike was won over.

'That's great, Craig. Listen, I'm really happy for both of you. I'm sure you'll be wonderful parents and I couldn't leave Mary in better hands. I can't believe I'm going to be an uncle!'

'Well, you better believe it!' Mary laughed, easing herself back onto the bench and elbowing Mike in the ribs.

'OK,' Craig said, still blushing. 'I gotta go – I got soccer practice in a half-hour and I need to pick up my stuff.'

He kissed Mary on the lips and nodded to Mike, beaming a little sheepishly. When he had left, Mike turned to Mary.

'Well, he's a great guy! I like him a lot.'

Mary smiled proudly as she watched Craig through the window bounding to his car.

'Me too. Me *too*!'

'Hey, Sis . . .' Mike said, stirring the dregs of his milkshake with his straw.

'Hmm?'

'I want you to know I'm . . . Well, I'm sorry I've been such a bad brother lately. I know I should've called you more often and given you more support; I should've—'

'Hey,' Mary whispered, clutching at Mike's hands. 'God, Mike, don't beat yourself up. I know how busy you must be . . .'

'It's no excuse,' Mike insisted. 'I promised you I'd always be there for you. I *want* to be there for you.'

'You will be, I know you will,' Mary said with a squeeze of the hand. 'You're my big brother – I know I can always count on you.'

Mike went to see Father Adrian. He had avoided him since their discussion in the summer, going to confession elsewhere and keeping out of his way on campus. He had been putting off a resumption of their discussion, but the thought was tormenting him and on the Tuesday after he arrived back from Florida he knocked on the door of the priests' residence.

Father Adrian greeted him with a disappointed 'Ah.' They sat facing each other, each waiting for the other to begin. The atmosphere in the dimly lit cell, comforting and conspiratorial when Mike last came here, was combative. Mike could hardly meet Father Adrian's eye.

'So,' said the priest at last, 'have you had further sinful desires of the kind you told me about when we met?'

Mike was taken aback. Where was the laid-back confidant he had known before?

'I . . . I . . .' he stammered, struggling to express the complexities of human desire in the clumsy words that language attaches to it. 'I . . . haven't—'

'Perhaps this will be easier for you to answer: have you *acted* on your sinful desires?'

Now Mike could answer honestly. He met the priest's cold gaze. 'No, Father. I know that would be wrong.'

Father Adrian grunted a reluctant approval. Mike took it as the cue to talk. He spoke truthfully, tentatively, studying his counsellor for a reaction that was deliberately withheld.

'I know that I am subject to . . . lustful thoughts of an . . . immoral nature. But I have always resisted them except for—' He gasped at the memory of Kurt's stolen kiss; the sinfulness of it had faded with time, but now it came back to him in all its disgusting depravity.

He shuddered, and Father Adrian declared triumphantly, 'Ah! I see. Then tell me about it. Tell me what happened.'

'There was one . . . moment of . . . There was a kiss,' Mike acknowledged, his voice very quiet, praying that he wouldn't start to cry. 'But it wasn't my choice. It was . . . completely uninvited, completely unexpected.'

He gave Father Adrian an imploring look, trying to quell his own doubts about the sincerity of the explanation.

'Sin must be resisted,' the priest announced. 'Homosexuality is a sin, whatever form it takes. If you submitted to the sinful urges of another, the wickedness of that sin is transferred to you. Homosexuality' – he spat the word out – 'is a *disease*, a *sickness*. It is unnatural and *evil*. There is no place for homosexuality in the Catholic community. You must purge yourself of it if you wish to belong, if you wish to be accepted as part of the community.'

Mike thought back to the innocent pleasure of his stolen kiss with Kurt – the tenderness, the feeling of *rightness*, of things fitting in a way they never had before. He scrutinized the scene for the evil Father Adrian was talking about, and found none.

'But Father,' he protested, 'if God created all of us . . . if He

created *me*, why did He create me the way I am – if He disapproves
of it? If it's evil?'

Father Adrian sighed.

'*He* did not create you as a homosexual, Michael. In God's order
every creature is created heterosexual; the inclination to homosexuality is an *objective disorder*. Natural law, the Church and psychol-
ogists all agree: God does not create disorder, does not create disease.
It is a product of original sin, of the fall of man.'

He clasped his hands together in his lap and smiled with bitter
satisfaction.

'Well then . . . I mean . . . why are only some men . . . homosexual,
and others not? Is it, does it stem from their own . . . individual sinfulness?'

Father Adrian pondered this.

'Yes,' he mused. 'In many cases that is the objective reason. In
other cases it can be . . . more complex.'

Mike sat forward in his chair, his eyes lit with an earnest hope.

'Father, what does God want us to *do*? What can *I* do to . . . to
save myself?'

Father Adrian had a ready answer.

'People with this . . . this *disorder* must be called to chastity. They
must abstain from sexual relations for the love of God and the peace
of their own conscience. And when I say "chastity" I mean *no sex* –
no pornography, no . . . self-cultivation, no fantasizing.'

Mike blushed; it felt as if Father Adrian were looking right into
his thoughts.

'It may not guarantee salvation,' the priest was saying, 'but by
the grace of God they can, after prolonged effort, experience detachment from homosexuality as their core identity and attain the will
to live as the new creation the Blood of Christ won for them.'

He looked hard at the young man before him, and his face softened.

'I know people who have done this, Mike,' he said more gently.
'I know it can be done – through prayer, the sacraments, a life of
service and charity, and through living in obedience to the teachings

of the Catholic Church. In all things, holiness is the opposite of homosexuality.'

His words were meant to be reassuring, but Mike left Father
Adrian weighed down by visions of the long gloomy days of struggle
and denial that lay ahead.

In the weeks that followed, he sought refuge in ritual. He researched
the indulgences, those mystical rites that might lessen the punishment of his sin, and found that every religious practice, from reciting
the rosary to pious invocation ('Holy Mary, pray for us!') reduced
the time his soul must spend in purgatory: blessing yourself with holy
water brought a hundred days' remission; blessing yourself without
holy water brought fifty. He could not hope for a plenary indulgence,
a complete remission of his sins, because his offending thoughts were
still within him, but he strove as best he could to minimize the retribution he would suffer for them.

TWO

The times were confusing and certainties hard to come by. Richard Nixon went to China and stepped up the bombing of North Vietnam; George Wallace was shot in Maryland; the Church prayed for the defeat of communism, for peace in the world and for reconciliation at home. Mike tried to stay calm, worked hard at his studies and did his best to ignore the torment he felt inside.

In the summer of 1972 Mary had married Craig and had her baby, a boy with rosy cheeks and soft eyes who was christened Nathan. Mike went to Florida for the ceremony and was enchanted by him: he told his sister he had never seen a more beautiful child. Mary seemed more content than she had ever been and Mike envied her the fulfilment of parenthood. He loved children and somewhere among his other demons lurked the dreadful thought that he faced a future without them.

At Notre Dame his sessions with Father Adrian continued in the same tense vein: reprimands, promises and tangled explanations succeeded each other in a dreary carousel of recrimination and un-spoken resentment. It felt as if the conversation was turning endlessly round the same topics, the same irresolvable sticking points, and leading nowhere. Mike left the meetings with the impression that Father Adrian was playing a stalling game – as if he were keeping Mike talking to stop him acting.

He had, though, kept to his resolution not to see Kurt and had avoided situations where he would be tempted to give in to his desires. He rebuffed any chance advances that came his way, including one from a good-looking but shifty priest who had asked him, with a knowing expression, to accompany him to a Johnny Mathis concert in Chicago.

His resolve held for six months. Then, in the spring of 1973, he took the Greyhound into Chicago and headed for Rush Street.

He'd been here in daytime – it was where free speech was celebrated by quirky orators on soapboxes – but now it was night and the landscape seemed transformed. The neon lights shone, the shopfronts were bright and the music spilling out of the bars seemed to speak directly to him. He let himself merge into the throngs of men on the sidewalks around Bughouse Square. Like a novice in a gloomy cathedral, he followed the path through the darkness of the square gardens, glancing into the shadowy side chapels under arching trees, catching sight of the mysteries within. Groups of men leaning against the gnarled trunks threw him a glance, smiled or winked. But he averted his eyes, intrigued, excited, timid. He did not delude himself about his reasons for being here. *I could do this*, he thought hungrily. He coveted the muscled forearms and strong hands, bulging chests under white T-shirts, narrow hips in tight jeans. *But what if someone recognizes me? What if I meet someone?* To give in to his desires would be something that could never be undone.

Shoving his trembling hands into his pockets, he emerged on the other side of the square. Now the lights stung his eyes. On Rush Street he tried to look inconspicuous. He glanced at the signs on the shopfronts. A shabby open door was labelled MOVIES 4 MEN. He rummaged in his pocket for the three dollars and ducked through the curtain into a small theatre.

On the screen two youths locked in an embrace were unzipping each other's pants. He felt a rush of excitement followed by a powerful surge of guilt. The scenes he had been imagining in his dreams – and hating himself for imagining – were being played out here in a public place and no one seemed discomfited by them. The sensation was puzzling, anticlimactic almost, as if the pleasure were incomplete without its usual side dish of shame and self-loathing. He watched as the figures on screen enacted the fantasies he had regarded as his alone. The warmth and darkness of the movie theatre were comforting; he was beginning to unwind some of the wrenching terror that had screwed his stomach into tightly wrung sinews. But when he felt the hand of the guy next to him on his knee, he stood up and rushed out into the street. It was nearly midnight and he was torn between regret at ever having come here and fear of leaving without completing the task he had set himself.

Across the street was the Normandy Bar. Mike wandered inside in search of a drink. A large room with a long bar reminded him of the place Marius and Charlotte had taken him, back in Rockford. He was rocked by nostalgia for the days when his sexuality was just an unrecognized ache.

'Beer, please,' he muttered to the bartender, glancing at the other guys standing at the bar. He wondered which of them might be *hustlers* – he'd heard the term from the Notre Dame coterie who knew about these things.

An older, greasy-haired man with a thin moustache introduced himself as Ruggiero.

'Pleased to meet you,' Mike said with a guarded smile. 'I'm Dave.'

'So, you a student, Dave? Where you come from?'

'Actually . . . I'm a salesman,' said Mike. 'I . . . come from Detroit.'

'Ah, OK! So you got a bit of money, then? What you looking for tonight?'

Mike faltered, realizing his mistake. 'Well, I mean . . . business is pretty bad right now – it's not like I'm loaded.'

'OK, OK,' Ruggiero hushed him. 'So maybe you just got fifty, sixty dollars? What type of guy you looking for?'

Mike was relieved the man was not a hustler himself – he found his manner subtly threatening – but was surprised by the notion that he might have a 'type'. What *was* he looking for? Someone who would worship him, excite him, fulfil him, spend the rest of his life loving and understanding him? *But that's probably a little out of Ruggiero's league*, he thought with a small smile.

'Well?' the guy demanded.

How did transactions like this take place? What was the right thing to say?

'Uh . . . look, I've only got forty dollars,' Mike heard himself say, 'and I need some for the bus home.' He realized that he was actually haggling.

Ruggiero was contemplating his words with a businessman's concentration.

'OK,' he said at last, 'we can do a deal.'

He took Mike's money and beckoned him into the back bar. A tall blond guy in his thirties was lounging by the door in a flower-patterned shirt. Mike reeled. *Oh God, am I really doing this?*

'Howdy, stranger,' flower-shirt said to Ruggiero. 'And who's this beautiful little chickadee you're bringing me tonight?'

He looked Mike up and down with a predatory approval.

'Is she going to be a bad, bad girl, do we think?'

Mike was appalled – it was so different from what he had imagined, from the way he wanted things to be.

'Look,' he said nervously, 'I'm not sure this is—'

'Kid, kid, no worries. This guy knows what he's doing, trust me.' Ruggiero was taking Mike's arm, shepherding him through another doorway beside the smaller bar, into a dingy corridor.

This isn't right, a voice was saying in Mike's brain. *This isn't how it's meant to be.*

But Ruggiero and the hustler were leading him on and now he was alone with the blond in a cramped, dimly lit room with tattered blinds and an old stained couch in one corner. The blond had grasped him tightly from behind and was licking his neck. Then suddenly they were on the couch and the blond's tongue was in his mouth and Mike felt his inhibitions, his guilt, his shame drift away through the shredded blinds into the darkness outside.

*

He missed his pre-law seminar with a headache that just wouldn't let up. He had come home from Chicago in the early hours and gone straight to bed, where he lay sleepless and racked by drink-dulled memories. The camp affectations of the hustler, the offhand mocking treatment of their transaction, the sleazy pimp, the sordid setting of his first sexual encounter had left him shivering with revulsion and self-disgust.

He lay in his room with the blinds pulled, his head pounding in the darkness. But as his shaken emotions settled, something unexpected took hold of him, something he tried at first to ignore but that nagged at him: the more he thought about the encounter in the bar, and the more he dwelled on the shame and humiliation, the more he felt himself aroused by it.

Alone in bed he relived the excitement of the contact, the touch of the man's body, and each memory afforded him mounting gratification. The experience was far from the beauty and spiritual love he had dreamt of, but he felt its attraction with a power that frightened him. He had tasted the addictive charm of casual, irresponsible sensuality.

THREE

1973

Mike knew he should confess to Father Adrian, but he didn't. In the weeks that followed he returned to Rush Street as often as his time and funds would allow. He got to know the safe bars and learned how to avoid the confidence tricksters and clip joints. After a while he was able to distinguish between the different hustlers and pick 'his type', as he laughingly called them. He shunned the drag artists and effeminate queens who lisped and referred to each other as 'she', and sought out the smart preppy types who looked and dressed so straight they could be taken for happily married heteros. The more he experienced the exhilaration of the illicit transactions, the more he craved and needed them. He thought about them in class, fantasized about them as he listened to the priest in Sunday Mass and watched the hands of the clock in anticipation of the evening trip into town. After years of self-denial, the thrill of anonymous sex took a powerful hold on him.

Over the course of the semester he realized that the restraints on his behaviour were no longer ethical, but practical. He gradually stopped agonizing about what he was doing and no longer went to confession, but the ride into Chicago took almost two hours and the cost of his evening trips was draining his bank account. There were gay bars closer to home in South Bend – one on South Main Street and another on Lincoln Way – but the fear of exposure was high and

Mike hadn't the courage to visit them. Once or twice he had hung around the toilets at the train station on Washington Avenue and picked up some tough-looking guys who'd made him do things he hadn't enjoyed but felt too scared to refuse. He'd found the experiences terrifying while they lasted and immensely exciting in retrospect.

The sudden outpouring of Mike's sexuality, so long repressed and now so intense, brought him new knowledge not only of himself but increasingly of others. Now he could spot the signs in other men, the signals of another gay guy who wanted to be recognized and the mannerisms of those who did not. He was certain, for instance, that Father Adrian was himself gay and that his moral outrage masked his own desires. When their paths crossed on the Notre Dame lawns, they avoided each other's gaze.

Mike had come to a kind of private concordat between himself and the Church – he had carried on going to Mass and Communion, but told the monsignor he would have to stop serving as a eucharist assistant, saying his final examinations were approaching and he wanted to ensure he got the grades he needed for law school. He also had noticed, with vague concern, that he was drinking more frequently and in greater quantities. He had always enjoyed a drink, but some nights when he was DJ'ing on campus or in town he would down so many bottles he could hardly get back to Fisher Hall. He had a strong constitution and rarely suffered the morning after, but the drinking was becoming a habit and he suspected grimly that it was getting the better of him. By the end of the school year he was drinking beer with whisky chasers every single night and when he worked as a DJ – or when he stayed up late revising for class – he took the readily available amphetamine pills that were many students' essential accessory.

Alcohol gave him courage and the uppers gave him energy. At the end of May, when he had finished the bulk of his examinations, he got drunk in a downtown bar and fell into conversation with a group of men who invited him back for more drinks at their place. Outside the bar they beat him up, took his wallet and wristwatch and left him lying on the sidewalk with a broken finger and blood streaming from his nose.

In spite of the commotion in his life, Mike's grades had remained outstanding – so good that he was way ahead of his course and his supervisor recommended he be allowed to graduate ahead of schedule in December.

In the summer vacation of 1973 Mike flew to Florida to stay with Doc and Marge at the house in St Petersburg Beach. They were delighted by his academic success and the first weeks of the summer were among the happiest they had spent together. Marge seemed to have rallied: she had gained some weight back and the southern sunshine had revived her spirits. The house itself was delightful, set on the ocean front with a swimming pool and diving board in the backyard. Doc and Marge had a couple of schnauzers – good German hounds, Doc said – and Mike spent the sun-filled days walking them on the beach or swimming in the pool.

One day while Doc and Marge were out visiting (long afternoons and evenings playing canasta with other retirees) Mike pulled out a box of family movies that been in storage since the move from Rockford and threaded them into the Eumig Super-8 projector he'd found on the shelf in the garage. In the darkened family room he watched ghostly images of a young Doc and a tall, elegant Marge race across the walls, lips silently moving, waving to the camera, picking up the three boys and making them wave too. A series of 4th of July parades from someplace in Iowa gave way to scenes of holidays in Mexico and Cuba, with US flags and incongruous American tourists in downtown Havana, and then recurring annual footage from the summer cottage in Minnesota, where Doc and the boys swam in the same lake and fished the same walleyes from the same jetty, growing a year older every time one spool replaced another.

Mike watched the images for an hour or more and thought how strange that the colours of twenty years ago should come down so well preserved, so sharp and bright. He was packing up to go walk the dogs when he spotted a couple of reels in the very bottom of the box. The sun outside was still hot and the spools were unlabelled and intriguing, so he threaded one of them onto the projector. Heat-melted celluloid sent bubbles up and down the wall and then settled into jumpy images of rolling fields and a grey donkey cart winding down a dusty country lane. The remains of an old stone chapel appeared, just three ruined walls covered in ivy with an oak tree growing within them. Then Uncle Loras came into shot, wearing his cassock and a white straw panama that made him look like Alec Guinness as the vicar in *Kind Hearts and Coronets*. He was walking through a small graveyard containing a handful of black-painted crosses, then past a dark building, all squares and rectangles in plain grey concrete. It looked like a hot day wherever it was, and Loras was the only moving figure in a deserted landscape. A white maypole on a patch of bright green grass in front of a tall alabaster angel had long white ribbons trailing from it, awaiting dancing children who had vanished from the earth.

With the sudden shock that old movies produce, the frame jumped and a little girl appeared on the wall.

She looked about two and was wearing a woollen overcoat with a pink beret and little white socks inside red patent shoes. The back-ground was dark – Mike could make out little except vague, grainy shapes – but the girl herself was in bright sunlight and her auburn hair shone brilliantly. Her head was turned away, but an unheard voice called her to look at the camera, and as she swivelled towards him Mike felt his breath catch in his throat: staring from the long shadows of departed time was the sad, lost face of the girl who was now his sister, fixed forever with her lips turned down in an anxious pucker that spoke of impending tears.

Roscrea, thought Mike with a sudden surge of emotion. *The day they came to choose us.*

The scene on the wall shifted to a patch of dappled grass where the August sunshine of 1955 was filtering through a glade of trees and tiny figures trotted slowly into the frame. Little Mary was there again, but this time without the overcoat, in a pink and white cotton dress with a checked bow in her hair and a yellow fluffy toy snuggled to her face. Now she was holding someone's hand and the two of them were advancing towards the camera. She was clinging to the hand of a little boy, his face obscured by the camera strap that had fallen over the lens but wearing grey pants and a blue knitted jumper with white shamrocks. He was holding his other hand uncertainly to his chin, and when the obstruction on the lens fell away Mike came face to face with the boy he knew and didn't know, in a place he knew and didn't know and had wanted *so much* and for *so long* to rediscover.

FOUR

1973

Mike stayed in Florida for his twenty-first birthday and Doc and Marge invited a few neighbours over for drinks around the pool. As the sunshine and tequila relaxed the guests and loosened tongues, Mike played with his baby nephew. He tickled the little fellow and laughed as Nathan wriggled and chortled in his arms. He imagined the love a parent must feel for his child.

As the sun set, Doc rapped a knife on the side of his glass and called for silence. Mike and Mary looked at each other. For years they had bitten their lips when Doc insisted on entertaining dinner parties with his jokes – his gags were racist, misogynist and homophobic, but that was the tenor of the times and they had shrugged and let it go.

'Well, now, everybody,' Doc was saying, tapping his glass a couple more times. 'We're here today for one reason and one reason only – to toast the success of my fourth son Mike, the only son we got imported.'

His audience rippled uneasily as Doc told the story of Mike's Irish origins then launched into an anecdote about Irish drinking habits and stage-Irish simpletons before leading inexorably on to his repertoire of contemptuous, patronizing negro stories.

Sitting in the corner of the poolside patio, Mike was seething and embarrassed. If it wasn't his own birthday, it might have been different, but he felt Doc's speech reflected on him, and he could see from other people's expressions that he wasn't the only one finding the anecdotes discomfiting.

'Uh, Doc?' he called, in as polite a voice as he could muster. 'I'm sorry, I just . . . don't think this is the time for that kind of thing.'

There was silence. Mary held her breath and Marge peered anxiously at Doc. But Doc just smiled a little coldly and raised his glass.

'Well, as I said, we're here to toast my *son*, Mike. So here's to you, Mike.'

Everyone raised their glasses and Mike smiled, but as the party was wrapping up and people were saying their goodbyes, Doc sidled up to him and leaned in so his lips were almost touching Mike's ear.

'Now I'm only going to say this once, so listen good: this is my house and those people are my guests. So when I want to make a speech, I'll make a speech, and when I want to tell some jokes, I'll tell some goddam jokes.'

Alert to the hardness in Doc's voice, Mike turned and walked away. His heart was hammering with stifled rage.

The following day he stayed in his room feeling raw and irritable. It seemed like he had spent his whole life making allowances for Doc, letting him get away with his offensive remarks and authoritarian views, and now he felt like a coward for doing so.

But there was something more. This was the first time he had been with his family since he had given in to the demands of his sexuality and he had the uncanny feeling that he was made of glass. Images of the dark things he had done and the dark places he had been burned constant and vivid in his mind, so vivid that he felt the others must read them in his face. In the staid, domestic setting of his parents' house the memories of his sexual encounters took on a debauched quality which unsettled him.

Mike was sullen at dinner. He tried to be gracious and helpful towards Marge but the argument with Doc still hung in the air. Both of them had things they still wanted to say; each felt the other had gotten away with something. Doc was reading out loud from the *Miami Herald*, holding forth about the price of gasoline and 'goddam Ay-rabs' and how Nixon should 'go teach them a lesson'. Mike had always resented Doc's right-wing Republican views and now he was feeling vulnerable and combative, convinced everything was aimed at him, seeing hidden reproaches in everything that was said. *He's doing this on purpose – he's taunting me*, Mike fumed, but he kept his mouth shut and stared at his dinner in silence.

'Oh, Doc, I wanted to ask you: could you give Mary and me a ride to the baby clinic in the morning?' Marge asked, helping Doc to seconds. 'It'll be some time around ten I should think – I'm going to call her after dinner and make sure.'

'Oh, that darn girl and her baby – you're always fussing around her,' Doc grumbled, and was surprised to see Mike jump up and thump the table.

'*You're* the baby, Doc! Christ, look at you. You get fussed over more than anyone and you're a grown man! So don't call my sister "that darn girl" and *don't* bitch at Mom just for loving her and wanting to take care of her! You need to start treating people with more respect!'

Doc looked stunned – he had not intended to offend anyone; it was just his way of talking – but he too had resentments he wanted to put on the table.

'Well, I'm not sure you're qualified to teach me lessons, young man. I don't see you volunteering to help out your family. In fact, we never see you nowadays. You just go your own way and think about yourself, and now you're at college you think you're too good for us, is that it?'

'Hah!' Mike retorted. 'It's you who never thinks about other people! You're so caught up in your little universe of prostate conditions and bigotry and crooked presidents, you never stop to think how the rest of us are feeling. You treat Mom like a slave; you order everyone around; you behave like some Nazi dictator; and – and the saddest thing is, you've made it quite clear you never wanted me and Mary in the first place.'

Marge let out a sob and Mike immediately regretted his outburst. Even as he spoke, he realized he was saying things that could not be unsaid. Doc was yelling now, something about ungrateful children and a lack of respect, but Mike had already plunged into a much deeper panic, frantically trying to assess the damage he had done and terrifyingly aware of the convoluted impulses that had pushed him into it. Marge was blowing her nose, her body trembling, and Mike hated himself for the trouble he had caused.

'Wait, Doc.' Mike placed a hand on Doc's arm. 'I'm sorry. I was in the wrong. I'm really sorry. It's all my fault.' And he ran out of the house.

In the cab down to the Don Cesar he reflected on the events that had led to the fight. He sensed his row with Doc had something to do with attack as the best form of defence – the feeling that he was in the wrong had made him lash out. But how exactly was he in the wrong?

The houses on Gulf Boulevard were flashing by, lighted windows and cosy front rooms proclaiming happy families from which he, Michael Hess, would be forever excluded. He was adrift, struggling to fit his new, sexual self into this old, inhibited world. His secret life disadvantaged him here, made him feel at fault, like the child whose greatest fear was disappointing his parents. He felt guilty before Doc and he hated himself for feeling guilty.

The cab arrived at the Pink Palace and Mike got out, unsure why he had come here except that it was an escape from the tensions of the house. The Don was the oldest hotel in St Pete and its pink walls exuded stability and reassurance – everything Mike craved. Belonging was important, he thought as he trod the marble floors of the lobby, belonging to something established and solid. The orphan's sense of exclusion was redoubled in the gay man and Mike was only just coming to terms with it. Maybe that was why he resented Doc with his Republican views, his petty, bourgeois certainties, his effortless, self-satisfied masculinity – poor, bigoted, ignorant Doc, who stood for everything that Mike was not.

The self-loathing was all too familiar, and suddenly seemed trivial and irritating. He made his way to the bar and ordered a whisky. The room was practically empty, but it opened onto a pool area which was enclosed and dimly lit. Mike took a deep breath in the evening air. *I'm OK*, he told himself.

There were a few guys hanging around on the poolside loungers dressed in shorts and polo shirts, and Mike, adept at reading the signs, smiled at one of them and asked if he could sit down.

'Sure can,' the man answered, grinning. They chatted for a few minutes and Mike let his eyes wander up and down the guy's body. He was tanned and slightly balding, with chest hair that spilled over the collar of his shirt; his torso was not muscular, but neither was it flabby, and his hands looked well groomed.

'So . . . do you have any plans for the evening?' Mike asked.

The man cocked his head.

'Sure. I know a little motel over the bridge in Gulfport if you're interested . . .'

They smiled at each other in mute understanding and stood up in unison. Mike reached out a hand with an unembarrassed smile.

'I'm Mike, by the way,' he said, and the man laughed.

'I'm Paul. Glad to meet you.'

Mike left while the guy was still asleep. He felt groggy and unsteady – they'd shared a bottle of Jack Daniel's – and he'd suddenly thought he must get home before his parents woke. But as the taxi drew up at a quarter before six, Doc was already prowling the terrace sucking on a cigar.

'And what hour do you call this, young man?' he demanded as Mike lurched up the drive. 'Where have you been all this time?'

Mike forced himself to meet his father's gaze and prayed that the reek of the cigar would disguise the booze on his breath.

'I met up with a few guys to watch the ball game. You know how it is.'

But Doc was unconvinced. He smelt the whisky on Mike's breath and saw the flush in his cheeks. His questions were insistent, stiffened by the threat of retribution if Mike didn't tell the truth.

'So tell me: what guys are these that you know down here, Mike? Where is it that you spent the whole night out? What have you been doing?'

Mike's instinctual deference, his innate fear of alienating people, spurred him to politeness, but he was certainly not going to confess the truth.

'Look, I'm really sorry for getting home so late. I knew you and Mom would be worried, so I tried to get back before you woke up, that's all. I'm sorry. I just want to take a shower and go back to bed for a couple hours, OK?'

He pulled the blinds in his room and lay in the darkness, gripped by the inescapable fear that Doc knew exactly where he had been and exactly what he had been doing.

Things calmed down towards the end of the vacation. Marge played the peacemaker, as usual, and it was she who broached the subject of Mike's future: if he was going to graduate early, he needed to decide what to do next. Mike said he wanted to study law – he'd been taking pre-law courses at Notre Dame – but the question of which school he would go to still had to be resolved. Doc was categorical.

'To study law you must go to the University of Iowa,' he declared, as if announcing a universally acknowledged truth. 'Many Hess luminaries have been through their law school and with the Hess name you will be well received by the top men in the faculty, which is a big factor in getting the sort of degree you're gonna need in that business.'

Mike bristled. Doc was always telling him what he should do, trying to run his life for him.

'I don't want to go back to the Midwest,' he said in as calm a tone as he could manage. 'I want to go to one of the big schools out East – I've already been in touch with a few of them.'

'*What?*' Doc boomed.

Marge cut in with a pleading smile: 'Come on, you guys – time out, time out. I'll put on some coffee. We can all cool down and discuss this like—'

'You've already gotten in *touch* with them? Without telling us? Without asking our permission?' Doc was up and pacing the room. 'It'd be *crazy* to go all that way out East, where no one knows you and no one cares about you! And all you'll do is end up with a worse education than you'd have gotten in Iowa!'

The two men stared at each other. Both were simmering with resentment from their earlier skirmishes, and a conversation that might otherwise have ended with a sensible compromise degenerated into ferocious argument.

'I want to go out East,' Mike repeated, and Doc snapped.

'Dammit, boy!' he yelled, sweeping the pewter ashtray off the table with a swipe of his arm. 'You listen to me, and you listen good. When I say you go to Iowa, you go to Iowa. You go where I say or you don't go anywhere!'

Mike was shocked, but the momentum of the quarrel was sweeping him onwards and he could no longer put the brakes on.

'What do you mean, Doc? You mean you won't finance me to go anywhere except your precious Iowa?' Mike stood up and scowled. 'Well, fine! If that's the case, screw you! I'll do it myself!'

FIVE

1973

Back at Notre Dame for his final semester, Mike was beginning to regret his bravado. He had been shocked by the tuition costs at the East Coast law schools and had begun to despair of getting to one without help from his family. But part of him revelled in the challenge: if Doc thought he was so hopeless he could never pay his own way through law school, he would show him he was wrong; and, come what may, he would now be entering a new era of independence that would liberate him from the old debilitating reliance on his parents' goodwill.

For the next three months Mike worked hard and excelled in his studies. He no longer tormented himself over his night-time adventures in Chicago and South Bend and rarely paid for sex any more; on several occasions had even accepted money from men who approached him thinking that he was hustling. His confidence in his own powers of attraction had grown: he'd noticed that men looked enviously at his body; he had started taking extra care with his hair and skin; and his face was slender with a wide mouth that curled easily into a dazzling smile.

There was no question of 'coming out', of course – it was 1973, the tough-guy environment of Notre Dame made it virtually impossible to be openly gay, and anyway he did not want to be seen as some effeminate queen. He had abandoned the flares and flowers of his freshman year and dressed conservatively now, favouring the preppy Brooks Brothers look with casual jackets, buttoned Oxford collars, cable-knit sweaters, chinos and loafers, and he spoke in a deep mellifluous voice that announced him as a serious, thoughtful guy – not a jock, but not overtly queer either. *I may be gay*, he told himself, *but there's a lot more to me than that.*

The casual sex excited him, but he had emotional needs too, and in the course of that final winter in South Bend he began to feel increasingly they were not being met. When he asked himself what was missing, it dawned on him that, in spite of the countless men who came and went in his life, he was lonely.

Kurt Rockley couldn't have been more surprised when he opened his door to see Mike standing there with a bunch of flowers. He looked so taken aback that Mike laughed out loud.

'Sorry,' he said, getting control of himself. 'This isn't how I wanted to start.'

Kurt raised an eyebrow with the ghost of a smile.

'And how *did* you want to start?'

'I wanted to . . . apologize for the way I've treated you. I didn't mean to block you out. I've had a lot going on.' He tapped his forehead and shrugged. 'I guess I had to come to terms with . . . who I am.'

Kurt stood aside.

'Well, you better come in – or are you so comfortable with who you are that you want to talk about it here in the corridor?'

Over a pot of coffee they went over everything that had happened to them since their stolen kiss in Florida. Mike admitted to the countless hours he'd spent replaying the moment in his mind, to the guilt Father Adrian had made him feel about it, and to his more recent exploits on Rush Street.

'*You?*' Kurt laughed. '*You*, on *Rush Street?*'

Mike laughed too.

'Yeah, I know. But really it's been good for me. I understand things now: I know I'm not the only gay man in the world.'

Kurt cocked his head to one side. 'You're not the only gay man in the *room*, honey.' And they both cracked up again.

'Really though, I'm sorry for how I acted,' said Mike, putting a tentative hand on Kurt's knee.

Kurt looked at him, serious now. 'Mike, I can't do this if it's going to be like before. You know how I feel about you, but . . . those few months weren't easy for me.'

'The thing is,' Mike said after a moment, 'I still don't know if I can *do* relationships. And you and I . . . we could never just be lovers.'

He paused, realizing he was putting things badly, wishing he'd clarified things in his own mind. The idea of a relationship scared him. He pictured the commitment, the demands, the emotional ties and the ever-present threat of rejection, and then he thought of the hustlers and casual Johns he was used to. *They may despise you, but they can't hurt you.*

He took Kurt's face between his hands and brushed the blond hair out of his boyish eyes. 'You're pretty hard to resist,' he said softly, 'but it's got to be only this once, OK? When we leave this room, we leave *us* behind . . .'

Kurt smiled a little sadly and shrugged. 'I guess I don't have a choice.' And his lips met Mike's.

The pre-law tutor had told Mike that George Washington University was his best bet. It wasn't one of the top ten law schools but it was well regarded and the fees were not the highest. Its location, just a few blocks from the White House and virtually next to the State Department, meant you couldn't get much closer to the heart of power, and for Mike that was a powerful incentive.

At his interview he'd found the place buzzy and attractive and the faculty welcoming. GWU got over twenty applicants for every place, but they had been impressed by his grades from Notre Dame – he was about to graduate magna cum laude six months ahead of schedule – and were prepared to accept him for a doctor of law degree beginning September 1974. When Mike told them he'd be financing his studies himself, they had been dubious: tuition was over $4,000 and with living costs on top of that, he would have to work hard to pay his way. Mike had already planned to find a job between January and September, and the admissions office suggested that, once at GWU, he become a resident assistant in one of the undergraduate dorms. This would provide him with free accommodation and part of his tuition would be paid. Mike said the idea of looking after a couple of hundred undergraduates filled him with terror, but he was in no position to refuse and he signed the RA application along with his enrolment papers.

At Christmas Mike told Doc and Marge they wouldn't be seeing him for a while. He had landed a job as a salesman for Procter and Gamble based out of Atlanta, and he would be travelling the southern states selling cleaning products to hotels and restaurants. Marge looked sad that Mike would be away for so long, but Doc just turned his back and left the room. Later, he tried talking to Mike about politics, the oil crisis and baseball and the slump the White Sox were in. Mike sensed he was feeling bad about refusing to fund him through law school, but Doc said nothing that could be taken as an apology or an attempt to bridge the gap between them, and Mike felt no inclination to take the first step. He was sorry Marge had to suffer, but he wasn't unhappy with how things stood: from now on he would feel no obligation towards his adoptive father, and if their relationship was cold and distant he had no desire to warm it up. The years had stored up such complex emotions between him and Doc that it was a relief not to have to deal with him any more.

Mike spent a lot of time with his sister over Christmas; he saw Nathan's delight as he tore the wrapping paper from his presents and congratulated Mary on her beautiful son. Thoughts of his own childhood were in his mind.

'You know, Mary, I've been thinking,' he said as they watched Nathan play.

Mary laughed. 'Oh? That makes a change.'

But Mike was serious. 'I've been thinking about trying to go back to Ireland sometime, to see where we grew up . . . You ever think about that?'

Mary looked at him frankly. 'Not really, Mike. I've got my hands full with Nathan. And anyway, you couldn't go until after GWU – how would you afford it?'

Mike frowned. 'That's true. It's just . . . it's been on my mind. But you're right, it can wait. I guess my first priority is to get through the next eight months selling soap powder.'

'Yeah, and you know what they say about travelling salesmen – lots of bored housewives!' Mary said with a smile.

Neither Mike nor Mary knew it, but on the other side of the Atlantic Archbishop John Charles McQuaid, the man whose insistence on controlling the fate of Ireland's orphans had changed the course of their lives, was on his deathbed. According to witnesses, the prelate became agitated as death approached, saying he was frightened of dying and feared the judgement that awaited him.

SIX

1974–5

When Mike arrived in Washington DC in September 1974 he had money in his bank account and a spring in his step. He had not been in the capital since his internship with Senator Dirksen and he remembered the place with a surge of excitement and renewed anticipation. His BA in government had given him a taste for politics and he was becoming more and more convinced a political career was where his future lay. He knew homophobia – particularly within the Republican Party – might make things hard for him, but he put that out of his mind. For the moment his goal was a good law degree that would open doors for him to the political establishment.

His first impressions of Thurston Hall were not good. The 1930s red-brick on the corner of 19th and F towered above the sidewalk like a fortress. It had been an apartment block before George Washington University took it over, and its nine storeys housed a thousand or more undergraduates. Mike had been assigned residential assistant on the top floor, and as he stepped out of the elevator the noise that greeted him was overwhelming. The students lived in double rooms along a central corridor; stereos were blasting out rock music and voices seemed to be yelling from all of them at once. Mike had his own apartment with a kitchen and bathroom, and he dragged his suitcases along the corridor until he found it.

Inside, he locked the door and slumped onto the battered sofa wondering how he was going to survive a year, or two, or three, of this pandemonium. He pulled out his RA contract and read the list of duties: 'Providing supervision, behaviour modification and mentoring; ensuring students wake on time for class; ensuring students are dressed appropriately; monitoring personal hygiene and room/chore assignments; providing informal counselling related to stress management and personal problems; serving as a channel between students and staff . . .' The list went on and on.

Mike decided he needed a beer. He attached the name badge he had been given to the lapel of his jacket and ventured to the elevator. He was accosted en route by a group of freshmen demanding to know how come the refrigerator wasn't working and how come they pay their rent and don't get no proper service here . . . Mike looked at them, pondered briefly and told them to put it all in triplicate and send it to the dean.

In the weeks that followed he heard plenty of horror stories about Thurston – about the sit-ins and love-ins, the protests and riots, the all-night parties and the vomit constantly on the staircases, and about its reputation as the most sexually active dorm in the university if not the whole country. In practice, things weren't so bad: he got used to the noise and chaos, and after a couple of months no longer noticed it. The students he had care of were all freshmen, aged seventeen or eighteen, and most were well behaved. He found he didn't have to worry about most of the duties in his contract and struck up a good rapport with a dozen students who acted as his eyes and ears on the floor. The few troublemakers he couldn't get through to just carried on doing their thing. Mike figured it wasn't worth trying any 'behaviour modification' so he let them get on with it.

At the same time he was finding his feet in law school. After the relaxed atmosphere of Notre Dame, GW's students seemed driven and serious. Mike had learned the basics of the legal system in his pre-law classes and now opted to major in constitutional law. He was fascinated by the way legal issues influenced the country's political life and he decided to write his thesis about electoral redistricting – gerrymandering. The topic had been a hot one since the 1970 census had resulted in changes to the number of representatives each state sent to Congress. States whose populations had risen were apportioned more seats in Washington and those where voting numbers had declined were given fewer. Controversy had arisen over the way some states had redrawn their electoral districts to reflect their revised numbers of seats. In several cases there had been allegations that the party controlling the state legislature had fixed the new boundaries to group voters in the way most likely to get its own candidates elected. Some ludicrously shaped districts had been created and the most blatant cases of gerrymandering were being challenged in the courts.

While Mike admired the others in his class, he didn't warm to them as friends. He wanted a life outside the lecture hall and his talents as a DJ opened doors for him. In the middle of his first year at GW he landed a job at the university radio station WRGW filling in for one of the regular presenters who was off sick. He played a mix of music that spanned current chart hits from Bowie, Lou Reed and the Stones to 1960s Motown classics, Bob Dylan and sentimental ballads by Barbra Streisand and Dolly Parton. The management liked his eclectic tastes and his rich, moody voice. After his first show he got enough good feedback from listeners to be offered more work, and by the end of his first year at GW he was pretty much established as the station's number-one late-night DJ. In his second year he got his own show, *Mike at Nite*, which ran from 10 p.m. to midnight and was the station's most popular slot.

Afterwards, he would plunge into the gay clubs and cruise bars. Many were located in the worst parts of Washington, in the rough streets of South-East DC between South Capitol Street and the freeway, but Mike didn't mind; he liked the fact that it put some distance between his diurnal existence in the cosseted prosperity of comfortable NW and his other, nocturnal life. He was adept at compartmentalizing his world, and it was a kind of insurance policy to have the compartments far removed.

Most times he preferred understated bars where the clientele submerged their daytime identities in a uniform dress code that made a company president indistinguishable from a penniless hustler, a painter in oils from a house painter, a published author from a trash collector. All forsook their Armani suits, dungarees and military fatigues to don the gay uniform of tight T-shirt and jeans. They forgot their constraints in a warmth and solidarity that led to remarkable trust. Mike met guys who worked for senators and congressmen, for public figures and big law firms, and even a CIA operative who revealed his profession despite the security risk.

In the Lost & Found on L Street SE, Mike learned to dance the Hustle on a vast dance floor with light shows and a rain curtain; he got to know the cute DJ Jon Carter Davis, and laughed at the excesses of the flamboyant dressers and drag queens. The Appaloosa band played live for discos and for afternoon tea dances, and the Lost & Found lovelies, Roxanne and Rose, Dixie and Mame, dished out awards for style (best drag, best lookalike, most spectacular), for acting, for talent and for personality. The L&F's brand of twinkie disco bar amused Mike: it drew large numbers of effeminate white men to a tough, largely black neighbourhood and provoked outrage when it tried to bar African-Americans. But it continued to thrive and opened its own cabaret theatre, the Waay Off Broadway, where Wayland Flowers and gay boy bands alternated with female impersonators and fan dancers.

By the end of his first year in DC, Mike had done the rounds of the Plus One, Bachelor's Mill, Remington's, the Brass Rail and the original Mr Henry's, where Roberta Flack performed her 'Ballad of the Sad Young Men'. The biggest of the clubs and Mike's favourite was the Pier Nine, where tables were equipped with telephones to call other diners just like in the musical *Cabaret*. Few ever used them, but the idea – and the club as a whole – was considered a riot.

The health warnings that appeared on walls and flyers seem in retrospect charmingly naive. 'VD and thee', they headlined. 'Heard the joke about this guy who gets VD? If you haven't, it's because VD is no joke. Last year more than 13,000 guys got treated for VD in DC; a whole lot more never got treated and are still spreading it. Do your man a favour – get a blood test!'

The District's first gay bathhouse had opened on L street NW, an area that became home to gay bookshops and community centres in the blocks around Dupont Circle. Mike found the Regency Baths intimidating, with its brick-warehouse chic and steamy cubicles offering privacy for the fleeting, impersonal sexual encounters its patrons repeatedly and tirelessly sought. He got a thrill from visiting the baths but the place had the reputation of being raided by the police and it made him nervous. Most of all, he was intrigued by the leather thongs and harnesses, the bridles and rubber fetish wear on sale in the Leather Rack on Connecticut Avenue, with all their sadomasochistic promise, but he couldn't pluck up the courage to go inside, and he read the small ads in the *Gay Blade* with secret longing.

In his most reckless moments, usually when he had drunk a lot and feared nothing in the world, he rode the Blue Line from Foggy Bottom to Arlington Cemetery and walked the shadows around the Iwo Jima Memorial. It catered to his sense of the wild side, but it was lonely and dangerous: recent reports in the *Post* had coined the phrase 'queer-bashing' to describe the activities of gangs of homophobes who roamed the alleyways round the memorial beating up gay men.

The part of Mike's RA duties that he took most seriously was the requirement to provide informal counselling to students. Surprisingly few came to see to him, and those who did were usually worried about academic troubles, clashes with some prof or worries about a girlfriend who might or might not be pregnant. But at the end of the spring semester, just as GWU was about to pack up and go home for the summer, a young freshman appeared at Mike's door and asked if he could talk with him.

'Uh, listen, I'm sorry to bother you,' he said, obviously nervous and unsure how to begin. 'It's just, I don't have too many people I can talk to . . .' His hands were clasped, fingers twisting, and his eyes were darting about the room.

Mike put a comforting arm on the boy's shoulder and led him to the couch.

'OK,' he said, offering a handshake. 'First off, I'm Mike.'

The boy grasped his hand.

'David Carlin. I'm a freshman – English and drama.'

'Good to meet you, David. Want some coffee?'

David nodded and Mike went to the kitchen. He had noticed David before, had passed him in the corridor a few times and been struck by his brooding good looks and slender hips. There was something troubled and intense about the guy that made him alarmingly desirable.

When Mike came through with the coffee, David was opening a pack of cigarettes.

'Do you mind?' he asked, putting a cigarette in his mouth.

'Go ahead,' said Mike. He watched David strike the match a couple of times and fumble as it failed to ignite; he felt like reaching out and steadying his hand, but he held back. 'Want me to—' he began, just as David managed it. They looked at each other and laughed.

'So where are you from?' asked Mike. He was sitting at an angle to the couch and the boy appeared to him in an elegant half-profile.

'Pennsylvania,' David replied. 'My dad had this big auto business that he sold a coupla years back, so we're pretty well off, I guess. Oh God. I don't know why I just told you that.'

He looked uncomfortable and self-conscious.

'So anyway, my father wanted me to come here to GW, you know, and I just said OK. Sometimes I regret it – being so accommodating. Maybe I should have done what *I* wanted instead of what my old man told me.'

'It's OK, David,' Mike said. 'Don't think you're the only one who has problems with his parents – it's been going on since Adam and Eve.'

It was a thin joke but both of them laughed.

'The thing is,' David went on, 'I think maybe I'm on the wrong course, or even at the wrong university.'

Without knowing why, Mike felt disappointed; it seemed such a humdrum thing to be worried about. But what was it that had made him expect something more, he wondered. Sure, the guy seemed over-wrought, but then lots of eighteen-year-olds are that way.

Mike said, 'I guess you should talk to your course tutors and see if you can't get a transfer,' and was surprised how pleased he felt when the guy continued to look agitated. It was as if part of him were hoping the boy had a real problem, a proper problem, something he could help him with. He came to sit on the sofa.

'Are you OK, David?'

He saw the little shake of the head and then the sobs began.

'You know what? I guess I'm not OK, actually. I guess I'm pretty screwed up.'

Mike moved closer and took David's hand. 'It's all right,' he said. 'You can tell me. That's what I'm here for. And whatever it is, it won't go further than this room.'

He was struck by how like a priest he sounded, by the way his own years of Confession had imbued him with the solemnity and the magic formulae of the ritual. But now he also felt the prurient interest he suspected priests must enjoy as they probe the innermost secrets of a sinner's heart.

David looked up and blew his nose.

'Sorry, man,' he said with a thin smile. 'Have you ever been to see a shrink? If you have, you'll know what this is all about.'

Mike thought back to his sessions with Doctor Heinlein and hesitated before shaking his head.

'No, I haven't,' he said – his denial was something to do with power and self-protection, he thought vaguely; the guy was needy and vulnerable and Mike was finding him strangely, deliciously attractive – 'but don't worry, I understand lots of things . . .'

David looked at him and took the cue. The words came tumbling out. It was his father who had insisted on the psychiatrist, and that was OK, he said. He didn't mind that; he understood what his old man must have been thinking. That was the kind of family he came from: they didn't know anything different from what they were used to in their little world. His father was probably doing what he thought was best. 'But' – David hesitated – 'but *how* could he have sent me

231

for that goddam therapy? How could he do that to his own son? How could he, man?'

Mike squeezed his hand and told him to slow down. 'It's OK, David. Just tell me what it is that's making you so sad and we'll work it out. We'll talk about it and work it out . . .'

David pulled himself together. He told him about the aversion therapy: how they'd tried to cure his sinful desires by strapping electrodes to his genitals, by giving him apomorphine to make him vomit at the sight of pictures of naked men; how he was locked in a windowless room in a psychiatric ward; how it went on and on and on . . .

'It was terrible, man. And all the time I was in there I was thinking of my father and how he was the one who made me do it. And I don't know how I stayed sane or how I went back to that house and carried on living there after what they did to me.'

Mike had his arm round David's shoulder now. His thoughts were churning. He felt for the guy, but his sympathy was mingled with memories of his own father and how he had always suspected Doc knew about his sexuality and how he feared the retribution that might be visited on him. He was drawn to David and the guy's vulnerability increased the attraction – physical proximity and the hothouse atmosphere of shared emotions were stirring Mike's body into a state of desire. But he held back. He didn't know why. Thoughts of the responsibility of his position seemed neither here nor there; taking advantage of a vulnerable adolescent seemed not wrong but, on the contrary, natural and desirable. And it wasn't out of respect for the boy's pain; the sense that he was damaged goods served to strengthen the desire he aroused. So what was it?

Mike squeezed the boy's shoulder and stood up.

'Hey, David,' he said. 'That's some tough story. Let me go fix another coffee and then we'll take stock.'

But David was already on his feet, looking disappointed and puzzled. There was anger in his voice. 'Hey, man. I thought you understood. I thought you said we were going to work this out. What's with the coldness all of a sudden?'

'I'm not being cold,' Mike muttered. 'I'm . . . There are a lot of . . . issues to deal with here and I'm not sure I'm—'

'You wanted to kiss me, didn't you? Is that it? Don't deny you wanted to.'

'Whoa,' said Mike, backing away. 'Let's not—'

'No, it's OK, it's OK,' David insisted, walking towards him. 'Don't you see? Isn't it obvious? I came because I love you. I saw you the first day I came here and I've thought of you every minute since. I listen to you on WRGW the whole time. Your voice is never out of my head; I follow you in the halls; I dream of you when I'm in bed. And don't say you don't love me, Mike, because I know you do. I sensed it when we were sitting there and I sense it right now.'

Mike looked at him pensively. *The guy must be crazy* – he kept repeating the thought to himself, trying to convince himself to walk away. But he couldn't dampen the physical desire or the strange attraction that drew him to this soulful, tortured, beautiful man. After an eternity he cleared his throat.

'Look, David. I don't know what I feel, and that's the truth. It's getting late. And tomorrow you guys all go off for the vacation. I don't want to spoil things between us, OK? So go home to Pennsylvania and look after yourself. Don't get too down, think good things and come back next September. Then we'll see if we still feel the same way.'

David had been listening with gloom on his face but at Mike's last remark he seemed to light up with hope.

'See if *we* feel the same way? Hey, man, that's the coolest— If *we* feel the same . . .'

Before Mike knew what was happening David had given him an excited kiss on the lips and bounded out the door shouting, 'See you next semester, then! And thanks for the coffee!'

God, thought Mike, sitting down in a daze, *he's an emotional rollercoaster. What the hell have I let myself in for?*

SEVEN

1975

Mike spent the summer of 1975 appearing at the Kennedy Center for the Performing Arts in downtown Washington DC. He said it that way because it sounded impressive, but then he would laugh and add, 'Yeah, I appear nightly . . . in the south foyer during the intermission. I do a nice line in marshmallows, jellybeans and candy bars!'

The candy concession at the Kennedy Center had been run since the place opened in 1971 by an old couple who recruited vacation cover from students at the neighbouring GW University by offering a modest salary and the considerable attraction of free admission to performances in the concert hall and opera house. By the end of the summer Mike had seen Pearl Bailey sing live, the Berlin Philharmonic under Karajan, the Bolshoi Ballet dancing *Spartacus*, performances of *Cat on a Hot Tin Roof* and a dramatization of Steinbeck's *Of Mice and Men.*

Then there was the scope the job offered for meeting interesting strangers. Significant glances were exchanged over the Hershey Bars and Twizzlers with young men from out of town looking for a little contact and comfort in an unfamiliar city. He took them back to his rooms in Thurston Hall, where he offered them hospitality and tender care, but throughout the distractions of the summer thoughts of sad, crazy David Carlin stayed in his mind. He thought of him back home in Pennsylvania with the family that seemed to hate the very essence of his identity and had tortured him to change it.

When school resumed in September, the excitement he felt at the prospect of seeing David took him by surprise. He looked in the GW register and saw the university had listed David's address for the new school year as 2025 I Street NW. In the evening he pulled on his jacket and walked north from Thurston up 20th till he reached the triangular patch of greenery known as Monroe Park, where the hobos drank whisky and sprawled on the shabby wooden benches. Over the street he picked out the tall red-brick and saw a bunch of students with their moms and dads unloading suitcases and oversized radio-cassette players from cars with out-of-town plates. He sat down on a bench and he was still there when David emerged from the lobby with a cigarette in his fingers, exhaling smoke from rounded lips and watching it drift up into the neon-lit evening. Under the green canopy of the awning he cut a dark figure with the frowning brows and preoccupied air Mike found so enthralling. He was wearing a tweed jacket and brown cord pants and holding himself, Mike thought, very erect. For all the world he looked straight as a die, an eligible bachelor with long years of married life ahead of him. As he turned the image over in his mind, Mike found himself warming to it. If he had a type it was guys who dressed the same way he did – understated, low-key clothes, a little preppy maybe, with none of the excesses and fey mannerisms of overt gayness. His fantasy when he trawled the cruise bars was that he would pick up a straight, married man and open his eyes to the love he secretly desired but would never know until he met Mike. His thoughts were languorously slotting David Carlin into the role of his married conquest when a tall blonde girl with long stockinged legs and a short skirt came running from the building and threw her arms round David in a lingering, unmistakably amorous embrace. For Mike, not yet emerged from his fantasy world, it somehow fitted perfectly, the natural adjunct of the exhilarating narrative he was creating in his head. Then it hit him the girl was no fantasy and David was returning her kisses. For a moment he watched, taken aback, then rose stiffly from the park bench and disappeared into the shadows of Pennsylvania Avenue.

The evening shift at WRGW were starting to panic. It was after 9.45 and *Mike at Nite* was on air in less than a quarter-hour. The producer, Rick Moock, had tried calling Thurston, but the janitor said he hadn't seen Mike Hess since before dinner. Rick was discussing with the studio manager whether to run a tape of an old show or whether he himself should step into the breach when Mike walked into the production suite and flung his jacket over the chair.

'OK, guys,' he said. 'I know I'm late. Don't bug me. Just give me the first three plays and I'll pick it up from there, all right? Give me the new Art Garfunkel, will you?'

But Rick was pissed at Mike and wanted him to know it.

'No way, Mike. That's so unprofessional, coming in here with the show almost on air and thinking you can improv your way out of it. While you were out doing whatever you were doing Paul and I decided the playlist, and we're opening with Bowie, then Janis Ian and Glen Campbell – it's number one in case you didn't notice . . .'

Mike was in a state and didn't want to argue, but his rapidly churning mind had thrown up a plan.

'I know, guys. Look, I'm sorry, OK? We'll do the Bowie and all the others, but just let me open with Garfunkel, will you? It's no big deal.'

Rick glanced at the clock and saw there was no time to bitch. He handed Mike the record.

'OK, Mike. You win. But just as soon as we get the show done, you owe me an explanation.'

Mike smiled gratefully, took the disc and walked upstairs to deck five, where the DJ booth was waiting and the feed of the NBC newscast was just wrapping up.

'And a very good evening to you from Mike, Mike at Nite, that is.'

As the turntable whirred and Art Garfunkel crooned his resurrected love ballad, Rick Moock wondered at Mike's ability to jump from stressed-out life to the on-air epitome of calm.

'And that was Art Garfunkel, boys and girls,' his rich voice intoned as the track finished. '"I Only Have Eyes for You". Number eighteen on the *Billboard* Hot One Hundred, and tonight it goes out to a very special guy with a message from his old RA . . .'

Rick gestured through the studio glass and turned up his palms to ask what he thought he was doing, but Mike was already reading out the song lyrics with such intensity and feeling that the most hackneyed of them seemed suddenly vibrant with meaning.

'"My love must be a kind of blind love,"' he murmured, his voice soft and low . . .

'I can't see anyone but you.
Are the stars out tonight?
I don't know if it's cloudy or bright,
Because I only have eyes for you.
You are here; so am I.
Maybe millions of people go by.
But they all disappear from view,
And I only have eyes for you . . .'

After the show Mike didn't hang around. He ran back to his room in Thurston Hall and threw himself, exhausted, on the battered sofa. It was 2 a.m. when he looked at the fluorescent green digits of his radio alarm and realized the woodpecker that had been bugging him in his dream was someone tapping at the door. When he opened it, still half asleep, he saw David and clasped him in his arms.

That first night was the most wonderful Mike had ever known. Minutes of frenzied lovemaking, hypnotic in their rhythmic intensity, alternated with the deepest, most perfect tranquillity as they lay on the narrow bed by the window staring in rapt amazement at the Washington night. Before dawn Mike pointed out the glimmering constellations with exotic names that a now-dead bishop had once described to him, and in the morning they went to eat blueberries in the window of the Port of Piraeus on 21st and M, hardly talking then both suddenly speaking at once and laughing at their own clumsiness. They refilled their coffee mugs over and over till an unspoken signal passed between them and they rose as one to stroll back with arms linked to Thurston and the bed of their love.

The day went by and night came; then another day and another night, and still they clung to each other. They ordered in food from the Kozy Korner up near Dupont and shut out the world. The blinds were down, the phone unplugged; they lived in a realm where time and life hung suspended in honour of a greater, stronger force. Now, David said, he understood how Kathleen Ferrier could sing so beautifully about being dead to the world's tumult and living only in her wonderful heaven of beauty and love. Mike nodded and made a mental note to listen to Kathleen Ferrier's album in the WRGW archives.

It took Mike's RA duties to prise them apart. When the janitor knocked on his door to remind him about the hall's freshmen welcome party, Mike shook himself as if the hoi polloi had stormed the temple.

David laughed. 'OK, sweetheart, don't worry about it. You look after your little boys and girls. I need to go visit my apartment and maybe even do some work, you know . . .'

He sounded so serene Mike could not believe this was the same guy who three months earlier had burst into his life in such nervous turmoil. But when he thought about it, it struck him that he too felt so much calmer now, more at peace than he had been for months. It was as if he and David had been filled with dangerous, sparking electrical energy that their coming together had somehow discharged and neutralized.

EIGHT

1976

The last months of 1975 and the first half of 1976 were a happy time for Mike. He was doing well in his law studies and gaining a reputation as an authority on the arcane subject of political redistricting. His radio career was taking off – he had had interest from a couple of DC stations that were possibly going to offer him a guest slot in their late-night schedules – and he was DJ'ing regularly at dorm bashes and discos in the university and for private parties in Maryland and Virginia. He was also finding more and more to admire in his new lover: David was smart and cultured, sparky and artistic; he loved all sorts of music – not just Mahler, which had become a private joke between them – and he helped Mike enthusiastically with suggestions for his playlists; the profs in his English class had marked him out as an elegant and original writer; he was reviewing theatre and cinema regularly for the GW *Hatchet*.

The relationship with Mike seemed to have steadied David's nerves, and he stayed on an even keel for long periods. He smoked almost constantly, though – too much, Mike told him – and he was given to bouts of his old depression when small things went wrong. He saw the absurdity of letting insignificant events upset him – he'd read Aaron Beck's new book on something called cognitive therapy – and he would berate himself with caustic outbursts of 'Catastrophize! Personalize!' which he sang to the tune of Donovan's 'Jennifer Juniper'.

One thing he never mentioned, and Mike never enquired about, was the woman he had kissed on the sidewalk that evening back in September. Mike was with him so constantly now that he figured she must have dropped out of his life or, if she hadn't, was taking very much second place to himself. Sometimes, in moments when he felt particularly close to David, Mike was on the point of asking him about his *femme mystérieuse*, but he always held back. It was as if he were enjoying the idea that his partner had a wife somewhere. There was no jealousy on Mike's part and it made their lovemaking even more piquant.

They slept most of the time in Thurston Hall and ate out at least once a week. But David was not much of a social animal, and when Mike had late-night DJ engagements he would go back to his apartment on I Street. The building had a good number of GW students in it, mostly seniors and sophomores like David himself, and he got to know a few of them over the course of the year. When they asked why he was hardly ever at home and where he spent his time, he would wave his hand and answer with a vague, 'Oh, here and there. You know . . .'

David met Mark O'Connor in the lobby of the building on an evening when Mike was running a disco for a twenty-first-birthday party. They discovered their rooms were on the same corridor and David invited him in for coffee.

Mark was eighteen, a psychology major from Boston and happy to make new friends. He was struck by the gloom of David's room, by the books that lined the walls and the scholarly journals and sheets of scribbled-on writing paper that covered the carpet. Unemptied ashtrays sat on the table and smoke from hours of chain-smoked Marlboros gave the room a stale, hazy patina that Mark found tremendously sophisticated. After a minute's small talk, he was surprised to hear David say, 'So, I guess you're Irish, then?'

Mark laughed and said, 'Is it that obvious?'

He was of Irish descent, of course, fairer-complexioned and slighter of build than Mike, but with a very Celtic look about him. His father had traced the family back to County Fermanagh in the nineteenth century, and Mark was pretty comfortable about his heritage and his place in the world.

'Only, I have an Irish guy I'm pretty fond of,' David was saying. 'I don't tell too many folk about him because . . . because, well . . .' David thought through his reasons for not telling people about Mike and concluded, 'Well, because I just don't. But you seem like, you know . . .' He had guessed Mark was gay and liked his sensitive, sympathetic air but didn't want to just jump in.

'Anyway,' he said. 'Maybe you've seen him. He's an RA down in Thurston; his name's Mike Hess.'

Mark said he had noticed the guy but had no idea he was gay. David smiled and lit another cigarette.

'You know what? I think he doesn't want to advertise it. I think maybe he's planning to go into politics, and being gay's a bit of a downer in that line of business.'

Mark wondered why he was being told all this – possibly simply because of his own Irishness – but he was beginning to suspect David was looking for some kind of affirmation from him.

'Well, that's true for sure,' Mark said with a smile. 'I'm always amazed that Kinsey calculates one in ten of us are gay, yet the guys who run our politics are 100-per-cent red-blooded heteros without a single exception. Am I alone in thinking there's something dubious going on there?'

David laughed and said he'd pass the message on to Mike when he saw him next. Mark thanked him for the coffee and said he better get back to work, but as he was leaving he pointed to the piles of papers on the floor.

'You take care with those cigarettes now; you don't want to set the whole place on fire, do you?'

David kept up contact with Mark O'Connor for the rest of the school year and spoke fairly openly about his affair with Mike Hess. He told him how much he loved the guy and how much he'd come to depend on him in the months they had been together. Mark himself had had a few fleeting sexual experiences, but he was a young eighteen and the notion of a real romance filled him with excitement. He was aware David occasionally received visits from a girl with blonde hair, but she was never mentioned in their conversations. Latterly, Mark had sensed David was setting greater and greater store by his relationship with Mike: at times he was coming home looking jumpy, upset and more than usually gloomy. Mark wondered if he wasn't setting himself up for a fall.

As the spring semester wore on, Mike began casting around for a summer vacation job. Being a candy man at the Kennedy Center was his fallback, but he was almost a qualified lawyer now and he was hoping he could find something more suitable and better paid. A few of his fellow students had been taken on by law firms for the summer, but the places he applied to all seemed to have filled their vacancies and he was getting a little desperate.

Towards the end of March he and David booked a table at a new restaurant on M Street in Georgetown. The Bistro Français was run by a chef from the south of France and had gotten good opening reviews: a few of their friends had eaten there and said the eggs Benedict were heavenly.

The cherry blossom hung on the trees as they strolled up Pennsylvania Avenue. Mike was feeling irritable and worried about summer. He could see David had a spring in his step and, in the insidious way of these things, he sensed his partner's upbeat mood compounding his own irritability. David was chatting away about music and the weather, about poetry and Shakespeare, a production of *Hamlet* he had seen at Ford's Theater and a review he was writing that he wanted to 'make into a sort of thesis on the nature of parricide'.

'So I'm going to call it "Hamlet and us". What do you think? It'll explain why Hamlet is so tormented, why he thinks the times are out of joint. It's because he's been born at the wrong time in the wrong place and naturally he blames his father and his mother. The big theme in *Hamlet* is that he hasn't found the place in the world where he belongs, so all the other places including Elsinore are just arbitrary and meaningless. No wonder he says Denmark's a prison.'

They were on the bridge over the Parkway now and Mike sensed David was in one of his manic moments when boundless energy flowed through his synapses and he couldn't stop himself bubbling about everything that came into his head. But such moments were followed by deflation and despair, and Mike's heart sank at the prospect of the depression to come. David was stopping at all the art and antique shops along M Street, exclaiming at the beauty of the objets in the windows and how they really should buy this figurine or that decanter. They were nearly at the restaurant when Mike realized he was being asked a question.

'I *knew* you weren't listening, Mike. I was saying that *I* used to be Hamlet, but then I found you. And now everything feels so right, like there's one place on earth where fate intended me to be, and now I'm in it! Do you know what I mean? It's like this is where I should be and anywhere else would be wrong and just random. There would be no reason for me to be there . . . but now I'm in the place life has always reserved for me.'

Mike listened with a slow fascination. David's encomium sounded so exactly like his own long-held view of life's randomness that he wondered if maybe he had spoken about it in a drunken moment or in his sleep and David had somehow imbibed it and was regurgitating it to him in a grotesque parody. But David wasn't joking; he so palpably believed what he was saying that Mike began to reflect on it himself. It was clear he had become very attached to Mike, and Mike – if he were honest – had probably felt better in the past six months with David than he had in his whole life.

Mike was quiet during the meal – David was doing enough talking for both of them – and he was increasingly aware of a vague, nagging feeling that something was going wrong. He felt he really ought to be in a good mood. David was right, after all: their relationship *had* brought them stability and a sense of belonging where before they both had been tormented and adrift. But a bitter little worm was burrowing through Mike's thoughts and he was becoming more and more disturbed by it. If his time with David had brought him happiness, the worm was telling him he didn't deserve to be happy – he shouldn't be happy, he didn't want the happiness he had found.

Mike was used to responding to David's chatter with a tolerant smile, but this time the smile would not come. As they strolled back to Thurston together Mike was deaf to David's conversation; all he could hear was the worm telling him over and over, *You don't deserve it. You can't be happy because you don't deserve it* . . .

NINE

1976

In the weeks that followed Mike began to make excuses for not seeing his lover – he would discover he had a disco to go to or a friend he had to visit and would make it clear that David wouldn't enjoy it. At first David took it well – he was still on his manic high and nothing could touch him when he was feeling that way – but the more his mood began to deflate, the more hurt and rejected he felt. In early May, in the middle of his end-of-year exams, David demanded they sit down and talk. Mike could see he was sliding to the bottom of his manic slope, plunging helplessly into the depths of depression, and he felt scared by the force of what he saw unfolding. He knew he should comfort the guy, but something was holding him back. The fact that David was combative and accusatory made it easier for him to stay cold and noncommittal.

'You know what your problem is?' David began over dinner. 'Your problem is that you don't know *how* to love someone. You know that loving me is going to make me happy and it's going to make you happy, but you can't cope with that, can you? You can't bear to let yourself go, to give yourself up to someone . . .'

He stared at Mike. Mike mumbled a few placatory remarks, but David was not listening.

'It's been the same since we met. That first day, all those months ago, you led me on and then you drew back. And then I thought we'd sorted things out, but now I see you were never going to commit yourself. Come on, Mike. You're not being honest with me, are you? Have you found someone else? Is that why you keep turning me away?'

'*No*,' Mike said, rolling his eyes. 'I just need more space, that's all. There's no one else.'

But the idea had lodged in David's head and he wasn't going to let it go.

'OK, so prove it to me,' he implored, grasping Mike's hand over the table. 'Take me with you tonight. And don't say you've got something you can't take me to.'

'Sure.' Mike shrugged. 'You know where I'm going anyway – it's the drag award thing at the Lost & Found and I'm doing the music, remember?' He removed his hand from David's grasp. 'I don't think it'll be your scene, but you're welcome to come.'

They parted frostily. Mike couldn't give David a ride to the L&F because he needed to go with the truck transporting the sound gear, but David said he'd make his own way there.

When David arrived, around nine, the place was in full swing. In a cavernous space carved from an old warehouse and decorated with mirrors, black lights and rubber plants the bar was thronged, the pool table was busy and the main floor area was occupied by tables set for dinner. A spotlit stage was decked with flowers and a glittering silver banner proclaimed THE FOURTH UNIFIED ANNUAL ACADEMY AWARDS OF WASHINGTON. A svelte female impersonator in a backless ball gown and tiara was addressing the sea of tables, most of which were occupied by similarly dressed men of varying ages and sizes.

'OK, girls, settle down. I know you're excited, but I need to let you know that our panel of judges this evening will be made up of the fabulous Miss Fanny Brice, the heavenly Miss Mae Bush, the *real* Miss Liz Taylor and your president, the one and only, the *incomparable* Miss Mame Dennis!'

A ripple of applause went round the room as a large drag queen with an outrageous beehive and wearing a low-cut, sequinned blue dress tottered on very high heels onto the stage. Mame Dennis, alias

Carl Rizzie, blew into the microphone and, satisfied she could be heard, began announcing the plethora of awards that would be judged over the course of the evening. Her voice was nasal and affected and she twirled a long cigarette holder as she spoke. Most of her witty, scathing remarks were met with whistles and catcalls from the audience.

David grimaced. He found the place distasteful, but as long as Mike was there he was determined to stay. Mike was seated at a sound and light desk, pressing buttons and sliding faders, and made no effort to welcome David.

'I'll be tied up for a couple of hours,' he said without looking up. 'Why don't you go get a drink.'

David shrugged and made his way to the bar. Mike watched him go with a frown.

Two hours and six whiskies later David returned to find Mike sitting on a pink banquette chatting with the slim drag queen in the ball gown who had introduced Mame Dennis. When Mike didn't get up, David felt the alcohol kindling his anger and resentment.

'Whaddya think you're doing?' he slurred, louder than he'd intended.

His discomfort provoked a hoot of laughter from the drag queen. 'What does he think he's doing? Well, honey, that's no way to speak to a gentleman. He is squiring a young lady who demands his closest care and attention, and if you want my opinion, *you* would do well to take a cab and go home to wherever it is you come from!'

Mike looked at the floor and said nothing.

'Why are you doing this, Mike?' David asked, angry and humiliated. 'You know she's wrong for you: you hate queens. Why are you doing this to the person who really loves you?'

The drag queen gasped in mock outrage and wagged a stern finger.

'Honey, I'm telling you: you best be gone before the fur starts flying and someone enters you for the Most Boring Married Man award! This ain't a place for bitching and making trouble, you understand me?'

David looked to Mike for support, but he didn't respond. David hesitated for a moment then seemed to make up his mind. Turning on his heel, he walked unsteadily out of the club.

Mike got back to Thurston after two in the morning and was woken three hours later by the telephone. The hoarse, panicked voice on the line introduced itself as Mark O'Connor, checked that this *was* Michael Hess and said, 'You need to come quick. David Carlin's in the ER and I'm not sure he's going to make it.'

The emergency room of the George Washington Hospital was busy. Mike, still half asleep, walked in from the gloom of a deserted 23rd Street to the garishly lit foyer as if in a dream. It was 4 May and the radio on the nurses' desk was relaying the latest projections in the DC Democratic primary. Jimmy Carter seemed to be shading it from Morris Udall, Mike registered subliminally (he had a mild preference for Carter) as a hand tapped him on the shoulder.

'Mike Hess?'

'That's my name. Don't wear it out.'

'Mark O'Connor,' the man said shakily. Mike thought he looked more of a boy than a man. 'We spoke.'

'Yeah. I know who you are. David told me about you. What happened?'

'I don't know if you . . . got everything I said on the phone. There was a fire.'

'And how . . .' Mike rubbed his eyes and coughed harshly. 'How is he?'

'Well, they're saying close to 80-per-cent burns. But I saw him just yesterday and he seemed so . . .'

Suddenly, unexpectedly, Mark broke into desperate, hitching sobs.

'I just . . . I just . . . I think he's not going to make it. I *know* he's not − 80-per-cent burns − 80-per-*cent*—'

He collapsed into Mike's arms, gasping for breath. Mike squinted at him and saw he was in shock. He himself was feeling little or nothing at all – if anything terribly calm. He was taking things in yet at the same time was outside everything, in a private world where grief had no foothold.

'OK, Mark, take it easy. I think you need to sit down and drink a coffee. Wait here; I'll get you one.'

He walked over to the nurses' station.

'David Carlin?' he asked the tired-looking nurse. 'Burns. Came in this morning. I'm family.'

She was a middle-aged black woman who looked like she'd seen it all, but the mention of David's name made her start.

'Yes, sir. Mr Carlin is in surgery right now. We're – we're doing what we can for him. We have the best surgeons in the District . . .'

Her voice trailed off and her eyes dropped to the desk in front of her.

Mike nodded. 'Thanks. Mind if I get some coffee from your pot back there?'

He gestured to the coffee pot on the hot plate behind her and she got up to fetch it.

By the time Mike sat down next to Mark, he had collected his thoughts.

'OK, Mark. Here you go. Drink this. And then run me through what happened, will you? Take it nice and slow; start at the beginning.'

Mark took a sip of the coffee.

'Actually, I don't know what happened,' he said weakly. 'I was asleep and the fire bell starts going. We all thought it's most likely the usual false alarm, but there was smoke . . . I live down the corridor from David – I could see it was coming from his room. But the . . . the door was locked and the handle was real hot, way too hot to touch.' He shuddered and screwed up his eyes. 'The fire department was there in ten minutes and they told us to go wait on the sidewalk. They . . . they came down with a gurney. I couldn't see his face, but I knew it was David.'

Mike and Mark sat in the waiting room as day broke. Patients were being walked or wheeled through the swing doors to the rooms beyond, but no one came to tell them about David. They went to fetch muffins from the McDonald's at 19th and M. They sat and waited. When they enquired, they were told Mr Carlin was still in surgery. They smiled nervously at each other and said nothing. Mark felt terrible – he hadn't slept and the horror of what had happened kept sweeping over him – but the guy beside him was acting so calm, so confident, so together; it was hard to believe it was his lover who was hovering between life and death. He didn't admit it, but Mark was a little in awe – Mike was five years older than he was, a law student and an RA. He was dreamy too, with his dark eyes and thick black hair.

Late in the morning a doctor came to say David was out of surgery. Things had gone as well as could be expected and he was being moved to intensive care. Mike asked if he was conscious and the doctor said he had been, but now he was heavily sedated. Mike asked if he was going to make it, and the doctor said if they were believers, they should pray.

Outside on Washington Circle they were surprised to see life had continued in their absence. The sun was warming the sidewalks and office workers were appearing with sandwiches and bottles of Coke. The cherry blossom was gone, but the grass was scattered with tulips and George Washington on bronze horseback was offering shade to students in shirtsleeves who sat and lit cigarettes.

Mark looked at his watch. 'I missed my class. It was Jung and the meaning of dreams.'

Mike murmured something inaudible.

'I've got nowhere to go, you know. They said we can't go back in the building till the fire department has it all checked out.'

Mike nodded as if he had been expecting this. 'I guess you better come home with me then.' And they strolled in silence through the University Yard to Thurston. In Mike's room Mark asked, 'Do you smoke?' and Mike said he didn't. Neither of them went to class that day. In the evening they went back to the hospital and were told no one could see David. An old couple was sitting in the waiting room:

he was thin and bald; she had grey hair and her hands were shaking as she tried to unwrap a packet of Oreos.

Mike guessed immediately they were David's parents.

The cookies fell on the floor and he hastened to pick them up for her. She looked up at him as he handed her the broken pieces. There was so much gratitude in her eyes that he winced.

'Mrs Carlin? Mr Carlin? I'm Michael Hess. I was David's resident assistant and I came to see how he's doing.'

The woman took his hand in hers and squeezed it with the desperation of a mother's grief. The man coughed and said, 'Pleased to meet you, sir. They told us he's sleeping now. I think that might be a good sign.' He hesitated, wiped the back of his hand across his eyes and added quietly, 'We love him so much, you know. So much . . .'

David lived for another five days.

Mark had stayed on at Thurston. He could see that for Mike life was suspended; it was as if he were holding his breath. When the nurse told them the news of David's death, Mike had seemed relieved at first and then went quiet. In the evening he stood up and put on his jacket.

'I think I need to go for a walk,' he said, almost to himself. 'On my own.'

Mark nodded then, impulsively, gave him a hug.

It was forty-eight hours later when Mike reappeared, and Mark was almost hysterical. Mike had no idea where he'd been, and all he wanted was sleep.

'But Mike, where *were* you? I wanted to call the police but I . . . I didn't know if you . . . I've been so worried about you, Mike.'

But Mike's mind was a blank, and before Mark could say any more he collapsed on the floor.

'Jesus,' Mark muttered, smelling the alcohol and vomit on Mike's clothes. He tried to lift him into bed, but he was deadweight. He undressed him and washed him as best he could, then rolled him onto a blanket and covered him with a quilt. He sat with him for the day and a half that he slept and fed him pieces of cornbread in boiled milk when he woke. Mike's face and body were white; he shivered constantly; his limbs were stiff and his legs were convulsed by spasms. Little by little Mark nursed him back to life, brought him food from the Georgetown market, fielded calls from the university administration, intercepted students coming to wish him a good vacation. But Mike was oppressed by nightmares and slept badly; Mark struggled to boost his spirits.

After a week, Mike asked him, 'What the hell is wrong with me? You're the psychologist; can't you tell me?'

Mark laughed and said his undergraduate major hardly qualified him to psychoanalyse anyone. But Mike was serious.

'It's my fault,' he said. 'You know that, don't you? He did it because I treated him bad. And the terrible thing is I knew what I was doing. I loved him – he was my happiness, but I destroyed it. Why would I do that, Mark? Why would anyone do that?'

Mark shrugged his shoulders and looked away. David had told him about Mike's self-destructive impulses, his love of excess, and he had read about the orphan's internalized dread of rejection, the consequent difficulty with relationships and the urge to *provoke* the rejection he feels is inevitable.

Mike lay back and closed his eyes; Mark could almost feel him concentrating. When he began to talk, he told Mark everything: about the losses he had suffered in the past and how he blamed himself for all of them; about Charlotte, Loras and the mother who abandoned him; about how he had spent his own life rejecting and failing the people he loved; and about the tremendous guilt he felt. The only way out, he thought, might be to go back to where it all began: to find his birth mother, understand what happened all those years ago. Maybe that way he could halt the cycle of pain.

'Because until I do that, it just seems this thing . . . this tragedy . . . will happen over and over and over . . .'

Mark hesitated, then took Mike in his arms and rocked him back and forth like a baby.

TEN

1976

In the middle of May a letter arrived offering Mike a vacation job. It was from the National Institute of Municipal Law Officers on Connecticut Avenue. Mike barely remembered writing them and had only the sketchiest idea what they did, but Mark was enthusiastic – he wanted Mike to accept right away, fearing a summer with nothing to fill his time would leave him prey to destructive thoughts.

Before he left for Boston and summer with his family, Mark made Mike promise he would at least go see the NIMLO people and asked him where he would be living next year. Mike said he hadn't thought about it: his RA post at Thurston was for two years only, so he would have to find somewhere else. Mark said he had rooms lined up in a house on E Street down in South-East DC just below Capitol Hill, and Mike was welcome to come live with him. When Mike said, 'Sure; that sounds good' Mark was ecstatic.

Left behind in DC, Mike took Mark's advice. He accepted the NIMLO job and began work at the start of June. The organization's headquarters were in a tall brown 1960s building at the corner of Connecticut and K, and Mike turned up on his first day still unsure what he would be doing there. In a large open-plan office men in shirtsleeves were labouring over desks weighed down with files and legal tomes, tapping at typewriters, shuffling piles of papers and communicating in undertones. It was a Dickensian scene and Mike's heart sank. At either end of the big office were identical glass cubicles with nameplates on the doors. One of them eventually opened to disgorge a smartly dressed lawyer who introduced himself as Bill and apologized that the president could not be here in person.

Mike laughed. 'Well, I guess Gerry Ford's just too busy preparing for the election right now.'

But the lawyer did not smile.

'I meant *our* president, Mr Hess. You have no doubt heard of Charles S. Crane . . .'

Mike was about to say he hadn't, but was not given the chance.

'Mr Crane has been president of NIMLO since he founded the organization forty years ago. He led the US Bar Association for many years; he served as Richard Nixon's special ambassador to the UNHCR and he acted for the White House in the Watergate hearings. The two of them are personal friends, you know, ever since they were at Duke Law School.'

Mike adopted an expression that he hoped would suggest he was impressed, but he was thinking what a dreary Republican cabal the whole thing sounded, and he was amazed anyone should still think it a good idea to boast of connections with disgraced old Tricky Dicky.

'I see,' he said. 'And what sort of work does NIMLO do, exactly?'

The lawyer opened a file and passed him a small booklet. Mike glanced at an airbrushed photo of a distinguished-looking Charles Septimus Crane; the text proclaimed that NIMLO was 'a non-profit, professional organization that has been an advocate and legal resource for local government attorneys since 1935, providing its members with information about, and solutions to, the profusion of legal issues facing local governments today'.

Mike looked up.

'So you give litigation advice to city and state governments. Can you tell me why Mr Crane picked me to come work here?'

The lawyer smiled.

'Oh, a number of reasons, I should think. He's a GW graduate himself, an admirer of the Catholic Church, of course. He's been looking at your record and he liked what he saw. Your specialization in redistricting, for example . . .'

Mike thought it sounded like something out of *Great Expectations* with Mr Crane as some mysterious long-lost benefactor, but Bill was droning on.

'You no doubt know that Mr Crane fought the landmark Baker versus Carr case that made Tennessee redraw its electoral boundaries back in '62. That's what produced the Supreme Court ruling on one man, one vote that's allowed the current challenges to states gerry-mandering . . .'

Mike said he had, of course, heard of Baker versus Carr and that he would very much look forward to meeting Mr Crane.

'In the meantime,' Bill was saying, 'I will leave you in the hands of our capable legal secretary, Ms Kavanagh. If you need anything else, I will be in my office.' And with that he scurried back into his cubicle.

Susan Kavanagh shook Mike's hand warmly.

'I see you've met Bill Crane – Bill the boss's son,' she said with a broad smile. 'I wouldn't let him worry you – it's his pa who calls the shots round here.'

Mike worked hard at NIMLO and the summer seemed to fly by. He worked on the smallest of small cases – little towns in the Midwest wanting legal advice on planning disputes, wanting to know if they could plant a tree in a public square or build on the site of a former cemetery – but he liked the feeling of doing some real legal work at last, and he liked Susan Kavanagh.

Susan was from New York, fourth-generation Irish Catholic and just a couple of years older than Mike, but she had already been married and separated and had a young daughter to look after. Smart, witty and good fun, she was exactly what he needed that summer. However much he was feeling sorry for himself, he could not help smiling when she was around; when she sensed he was lapsing into his sullen, gloomy mode she would cheer him up with a joke or a droll observation about one of their work colleagues. She had studied

English at university but retrained as a lawyer's assistant after her husband left her, and saw the legal world with a sardonic, outsider's eye.

Bill Crane was the target of many of their shared jokes. Smug and self-regarding, he was heavily built and walked like a football player. According to office gossip, he had no friends. Susan produced a piece of paper he had dropped on the floor with a handwritten list of words he had evidently been trying to teach himself like *catalyst*, *symbiosis*, *prurient* and *disingenuous*. Bill was in his late twenties and had himself graduated from GW Law School just three years earlier.

'You better watch out,' Susan warned Mike with a smile. 'You're a GW lawyer yourself, younger than him, brighter than him and *much better-looking*. I think he's a bit jealous of you.'

Mike laughed and took an exaggerated bow. 'Then I shall have to challenge him to a duel,' he said, wielding an imaginary rapier in the air just as Bill emerged from his glass cubicle to enquire what was going on.

Over drinks in the Old Ebbitt Grill that evening, Susan and Mike guffawed at the look of incomprehension on Bill's face when Mike had told him he was practising for his fencing class. 'Honestly, Susan, that guy makes me feel like a naughty schoolboy. I don't know how you stay sane in that place. There's was no way I'm coming to work full time for a bunch of old fogeys like NIMLO – they'd drive me nuts!'

That summer saw the culmination of an unusually hard-fought season of presidential primaries. The incumbent president Gerald Ford snatched the Republican nomination after a lengthy battle with the conservative Ronald Reagan, but the Democratic race was wide open. Jimmy Carter was the front runner, hotly pursued by Governor Jerry Brown of California, the wheelchair-bound maverick George Wallace and the liberal Morris Udall of Arizona. As the only avowed Democrats in the NIMLO office, Mike and Susan had been following the contest with growing excitement, attracting mockery from fellow workers who laughed at their naivety and denounced them as dangerous commies.

Towards the end of Mike's period at NIMLO a senior member of Morris Udall's campaign team was murdered in Washington. Ron Pettine was a thirty-year-old practising Catholic who had no criminal connections. First reports hinted at a political motive – ever since Watergate, Americans were ready to believe that politics was rife with crime and conspiracies – but it emerged that Pettine had been found naked and battered to death by the Iwo Jima Memorial at the entrance to Arlington National Cemetery. His face was unrecognizable and he had been identified only by his ring. Shortly afterwards three young men were arrested who confessed they had 'gone looking for a faggot' to beat up and had found Pettine soliciting for gay sex. Horrified, Mike thought back to the times he himself had walked the lonely paths around the memorial. Reading the media accounts of the murder left him disturbed and depressed, and he began increasingly to rethink his own plans for a career in politics.

On the day he left NIMLO to return to student life, Mike bought flowers from the florist in Foggy Bottom and gave them to Susan Kavanagh with a sweetly worded note thanking her for helping him through a difficult time in his life. She was unsure if that was the only meaning the flowers conveyed and she hoped they might mean more, but there was something unfathomable about Mike Hess and she didn't want to risk offending him by being too upfront about her feelings for him.

'You will promise to keep in touch, won't you?' she said, but quickly added, 'You should keep your options open: you'll be qualified in eight months and you never know when you might need a job.'

ELEVEN

1976

As soon as Mark O'Connor returned from his summer in Boston, Mike moved in with him. Mark had found a large apartment in a neighbourhood the rental agent described somewhat hopefully as 'transitional'. It stood between the Capitol and the Marine Corps Barracks, and it was the area's reputation as a little less than salubrious which allowed a couple of students to afford the amount of space they now occupied. The sprawling apartment occupied the entire floor above a store; it had high ceilings, very little furniture, and was perfect for parties.

After the drama of his relationship with David Carlin, Mike had settled gratefully into his new life with Mark. It wasn't that Mark was boring – he certainly wasn't – but he had a grounded sense of serenity about him. He was intelligent and at ease with himself: being gay was not a source of torment, but a source of joy. And he was very, very beautiful.

When Jimmy Carter won the Democratic nomination, Mike rejoiced: he admired Carter and told Mark it was high time to kick out the Republicans and erase the last traces of Nixonian corruption. He also hoped a Democrat in the White House might temper Washington's innate homophobia. That said, he continued to keep his sexuality if not a secret, then at least something he did not advertise outside his own immediate circle.

At Christmas 1976 Mike and Mark gave a spectacular party in their apartment. It was not exclusively gay – straight friends, men and women, students from the law school and from Mark's undergraduate class were invited and came in large numbers. Some of them knew about Mike and Mark, while others took at face value the formula that they were just buddies sharing an apartment. At the start of the evening they toasted Jimmy Carter's election as president the previous month and drank to 1977 – America's bicentennial – being a better year.

Susan Kavanagh came along with her friend Karen, a bubbly brunette who worked as a paralegal for a DC law firm. When Karen caught sight of Mike, she grabbed Susan's arm.

'*That's* Mike? Oh sweet Lord, he should be in the movies! How come you didn't tell me what a dreamboat he is? There's something wrong with you, Susan Kavanagh – I'm *genuinely* worried!'

Mike was amused and flattered by Karen's interest in him. She spent the evening darting to and fro between his improvised DJ booth and the drinks table, much to Susan's embarrassment, and Mark watched from a corner with a wry smile. Around midnight Mike stopped the turntables, loaded a cartridge into the eight-track and came to join the party. Karen, who had been enjoying the champagne, pounced on him and dragged him onto the dance floor.

'Your friend's crazy!' Mike hissed into Susan's ear. 'But I like her style.'

By three in the morning the last guests were trickling out and Susan was helping Mike clear away some of the glasses that littered the room. 'I'm going to have a little trouble getting Karen to leave,' she warned him, nodding at her friend, who was sprawled seductively on the couch. 'She thinks she's going to get lucky tonight.'

Mike smiled, wondering if Susan had guessed the truth about him. He had been waiting for the right time to slip it into the conversation, but she got there before him.

'You know, sweetheart,' she said, stroking his hair, 'you sure do have a lot of Broadway posters on your walls . . . and the decor in here is *suspiciously* tasteful. Now I don't want to leap to conclusions but' – she looked round at Mark, who was chatting to a group of people by the door – 'I do think you two make a lovely couple.'

Mike looked at her, feeling happy and sad at the same time.

'Thank you,' he replied softly.

An hour later Karen was fast asleep on the sofa and Susan was drinking coffee with Mike and Mark, who were sitting on cushions with their arms around each other.

'She's dreaming about you, Mike . . .' Susan pointed at Karen's peaceful face. 'I think she's in love!'

'You know what? He has that effect on women.' Mark laughed. 'I don't know whether to be jealous or flattered!'

Susan sighed theatrically. 'Actually, Karen's not the only one. Ever since I first met him, he's been sweetening my dreams too. You're a lucky man, Mark O'Connor.'

Christmas '76 was the first of many gatherings at the apartment on Capitol Hill. Mike loved entertaining and there were frequent dinners and parties, with endless trains of people arriving for the evening and often staying for days. He was a good cook, and the pair of them gained a reputation as accomplished chefs whose dinners were not to be missed. It was a happy time in their relationship – they were not just lovers, they were also friends. Mark introduced his sister Ellen, who had recently married and lived in Washington, and she and Mike became close. They would go out together to the zoo up in Woodley Park, shop at Woodies and Lord & Taylor in Chevy Chase and meet up for lunch at the restaurants in Bethesda. When Ellen's marriage fell apart, it was Mike she turned to for support and understanding.

But Mark noticed that Mike had problems dealing with his own family. He talked frequently and adoringly about his sister Mary and her lovely young son; now and again he spoke fondly of Marge, but he was scathing about his adoptive father and the years he had spent trying to live up to his expectations. He was bitter about Doc's refusal to help with his law school tuition and he resented the homophobia his father did little to disguise. Listening to Mike's calls home, Mark could tell the relationship was a difficult one – they didn't argue and yell on the phone, but the conversation was strained and combative. As if to compensate, Mike spoke a lot about his origins in Ireland and about the birth mother he was determined to find. He was keen for people to know he was adopted – partly, Mark suspected, to distance himself from Doc.

Mark's own grandparents had come from Ireland to work as servants in the upmarket Beacon Hill district of Boston, but Mark considered himself American and had little interest in tracing his ancestry. For him, Mike's obsession with Ireland, his determination to find out the full story of his background, was charming and a little odd. But he saw how much it meant to Mike and encouraged him.

'Well, why *don't* you go back there?' he asked. 'What's stopping you?'

'Oh,' Mike said vaguely, 'there's a whole lot of stuff. It would cost a lot, for one thing, and I don't want to risk upsetting Marge.'

Mark frowned. 'So what . . . You're going to live your life complaining the whole time about how you can't go to Ireland and how it's breaking your heart? You keep saying that going back there would answer your questions about yourself, so why not? Marge will understand; she sounds like a sympathetic woman.'

The following night Mike returned from his show at WRGW brandishing a record he had been sent to play on air.

'Mark, Mark!' he shouted. 'This is the weirdest thing. And after that conversation we just had . . . It's so amazing!' He put the record on the stereo. 'Listen to this – they're an Irish band. An *Irish* band.'

Mark listened as a haunting female voice intoned a lilting melody.

> *Do you love an apple, do you love a pear?*
> *Do you love a laddie with curly brown hair?*
>
> *He stood at the corner, a fag in his mouth,*
> *Two hands in his pockets, he whistled me out.*
> *He works at the pier, for nine bob a week,*
> *Come Saturday night he comes rolling home drunk.*

And still, I love him, I can't deny him,
I'll be with him wherever he goes.

'Well?' cried Mike. 'What do you think?'

'It's beautiful,' Mark said. 'But I still don't get it – what's the amazing coincidence?' Mike sat beside him, flushed with excitement.

'Well, we were talking about me going back to Roscrea, right? How it would – what did you say? – "make me complete". And all day I've been trying to remember things about that place – the place I grew up in. Then I get to WRGW and this album by a group called the Bothy Band – who I'd never heard of – is lying on my desk. But as soon as I played it I thought *I've heard this song before.* But that seemed so crazy, because the album only just came out. So I asked Rick Moock about it, and he says it's an old Irish song they revived from somewhere.' He paused. 'You know what, Mark? I think I must have heard it over there when I was a baby. I think they must have sung it to me, and it got stuck in my brain. Now it's like . . . like a message coming to me from that other world I came from.' He smiled at Mark, his eyes glistening. 'And you know the strangest thing? There are moments when I can almost picture the woman who sang it to me . . . I can almost see her face.'

Mark took his hand. Mike's eyes had filled with tears and he suddenly looked uncertain, as if he wanted to tell Mark something but was afraid he'd get laughed at.

'It's OK, Mike,' he whispered. 'What is it?'

'Maybe you'll say I'm being stupid, but it feels like my mother is . . . sending me a message; like she's trying to contact me, as if she can tell what I'm thinking all the way over here and I can tell what she's thinking even though we're parted by all those years and all these miles . . .' He hesitated for a moment, then came out with it. 'What I think is that my mother is looking for me, Mark. I think she's searching for me right now. And I think she's sending a message for me to do the same. Do you think that's crazy? Do you think those sorts of things can ever happen?'

Mark smiled, but it wasn't a mocking smile.

'Sure I do, Mike. I think if you love someone long enough and hard enough you can always get through to them. And there's nothing stronger than a mother's love. You hear so many stories of mothers and children communicating – mothers who can hear their children cry even when they're miles apart. I'd say you've got to go over there and find out if she *is* looking for you. Think how desperate she must be.'

Mike breathed a sigh of relief and happiness.

'What else is there to say? Off I go to Ireland!' He wiped his tears and hugged Mark. 'Thank you, sweetheart. You're so good to me.'

TWELVE

As well as his legal work Mike continued to do shifts at the Kennedy Center, and Mark got a job there too, working evenings in the cloakroom. Between them they got to see all the new theatre productions, including the big event of the 1976/7 season, the musical *Annie*. The first time they saw it they loved it so much that they went back, and Mike ended up seeing it six times. Mark figured the story was something Mike was never going to resist: eleven-year-old redheaded little Annie, growing up in an orphanage where she is bullied and threatened but never gives up her dream of finding her parents and eventually discovers happiness through the intervention of President and Mrs Roosevelt. Mike bought the show's full-size publicity poster and hung it in the kitchen of their apartment.

From his two jobs Mike had amassed enough savings for the summer trip to Ireland and Mark could see he was excited and anxious. Towards the end of the school year, Mike announced that he had been offered a full-time post at the National Institute of Municipal Law Officers to begin in September and was thinking of accepting.

Mark was surprised. 'I thought you hated the place, Mike. You're always saying how boring and petty it is.'

Mike bristled. 'The point is they came and asked me. They want me and I think that's important, even if you don't.'

Mark shrank at the vehemence in Mike's voice and made a mental note not to underestimate his need for external validation. For the next few days Mike was gloomy and quiet. On Friday afternoon he packed an overnight bag and left a note for Mark saying he was going away for the weekend, but he didn't say where.

At the end of the school year Mike picked up his Juris Doctor law degree. There was no magna cum laude this time: he knew he hadn't put his soul into the work and was just thankful he had done enough to qualify. Doc and Marge flew up from Florida to attend his graduation at the end of May and afterwards they joined the crowd of smiling parents in the shade of the plane trees on University Yard. It was a hot day. Mike was wearing his heavy academic gown and they were all hungry, so they rushed through the obligatory photo session. Mike held up his degree certificate for the camera and smiled while Mark snapped him with his parents. The photos showed that Mike had put on quite a bit of weight, but Doc was looking older and thinner, and slightly bent where before he had been straight and erect. Marge had a fixed smile on her face, clung tight to Mike's arm and hid herself behind him a little as the photos were taken. Almost as an afterthought, Doc offered to take one of Michael Jnr with his 'buddy and roommate', who stood a respectable distance from his lover and smiled sheepishly.

In the evening they went out for a celebratory meal at the Bistro Français in Georgetown. Doc and Mike split the check between them.

Mary had not been able to come to Washington for Mike's graduation and he missed her. The day after, as soon as Doc and Marge had left, he picked up the phone and called her in Florida. She thought he sounded excited and soon discovered why.

'Is that you, Sis?' he shouted into the phone. 'It's me. Listen. I've had an amazing idea. I'm going to go to Ireland in August and I would really like for you to come with me. You don't have to worry about paying for plane tickets or anything, because I'm going to get them, and I have to get a hire car and a hotel room anyway, so that will be the same whether you're there or not . . . Say you'll come,

Sis, won't you? It'll be so fantastic to go back, don't you think?'

Mary said she would have to think about it. She would need to make arrangements for little Nathan, who was coming up to five now, and she'd need to fix some leave from her own job, but Mike was insistent and Mary didn't take too much persuading. She called him back the following day in a panic to say she didn't have a passport, but Mike reassured her that applications were processed within eight weeks and she would get it in plenty of time.

In early August they met up at Kennedy Airport in New York. On board the Pan Am 747 Mike asked his sister if she could remember anything about the last time they had flown across the Atlantic and she shrugged. 'Not a thing. How strange is that?'

'Not that strange, I guess, if you haven't been trying,' Mike said. 'I've been thinking about it a lot just recently. I think there was a nice man who looked after us for part of it. I remember being absolutely terrified when we took off and landed, and I felt sick as a dog the whole time.'

'Well, that's great.' Mary laughed. 'You've really made me feel good about flying now. But you know, one thing I do remember – and it's maybe only from looking at the photos – you had some toy airplane thing that you carried all the way from Ireland right to Chicago. Do you remember that?'

'Yeah, of course,' said Mike. 'I think Stevie trashed it in one of his fits of brotherly love.'

Mary laughed, but Mike seemed pensive.

'I've always wondered where that plane came from – who bought it for me, I mean. Do you think maybe it was my mother when she heard we were going on an airplane to America?'

'I dunno, Mikey,' Mary said dubiously. 'How could she have bought it for you if she gave you up at birth?'

'Yeah. I guess,' Mike replied. 'I just thought maybe she enquired about me and found out I was going to America . . .'

His voice trailed off and they sat awhile in silence.

'Do you ever wonder what we would have been if we'd stayed in

Ireland instead of coming to the US?' Mike asked finally, and Mary nodded.

'Yeah, sure I do. I would have ended up panhandling on the streets of Dublin, I guess, and you'd probably be in the IRA!'

They both laughed.

'It's true, though, isn't it, Sis?' Mike persisted. 'You've got to say Ireland is our home. It's where we come from, and even though we're US citizens and everything, when people ask "Where were you born?" that's really where your home is.'

Mary said she felt the same way.

'If you're adopted and you know you're from a special place and there's probably other people related to you, you kind of want to say, "OK, I'm a part of this place first and this is where I belong." But you know another thing I've been wondering, Mikey? How come Marge and Doc ever went to Ireland to adopt in the first place?'

Mike shrugged. 'I guess they couldn't do it in America. They had three healthy sons so they would be at the back of the line for adopting in the US.'

'And what are we hoping to find out now, Mikey? It's not like we're going to run into our moms just like that, just on the street one day. And it doesn't look like the nuns want to help us – they never answered your letters, did they?'

'Well,' said Mike, 'it's like they say: if you never try, then you'll never find out. And what if our moms are looking for us too? That would make them easier to find, right?'

'But Mikey, even if they were, I'm not sure how they'd ever find us – we're both Hesses now, and you don't even have your same first name any more.'

Mike frowned. 'I guess the only way would be if the nuns kept records of who they sent where and who got new names. And then it would need the nuns to give all that information to our moms. Or maybe they'll give *us* the information so we can go find them.'

They had decided to spend a couple of days in Dublin before heading for Roscrea. They wandered through the city, drank pints of Guinness in quiet pubs and chatted to the locals, who were friendly and interested in their Irish heritage. But they were impatient to get to Sean Ross Abbey. On their third morning in Ireland they collected the rental car, got lost in the Dublin traffic and took nearly three hours to complete the seventy-mile journey. It was lunchtime by the time they reached Roscrea and pulled up outside Grants Hotel on Castle Street. It was an eighteenth-century coaching inn and the door from the street led straight into a low, gloomy room with worn leather sofas, an open fireplace and an unstaffed long wooden counter. From an adjoining room they could hear the rumble of a television set broadcasting some kind of sporting event, so Mike left Mary with the bags and went to investigate. In the saloon bar a trio of middle-aged men were staring intently at a black and white TV showing burly fellows with long sticks running up and down, periodically launching a kind of puck in apparently random trajectories. Mike coughed, and one of the men stood up reluctantly to introduce himself as the owner.

'I suppose you'll be wanting something to eat?' he muttered as he showed them into a small twin room.

Over a lunch of beef and boiled potatoes, Mike asked the fellow where they would find Sean Ross Abbey.

'Ah, the abbey,' he growled. 'That's only a couple of miles up the road – past the petrol station, over the roundabout and then you'll see a sign on a gatepost. But it's no use going today. It's a high holy day and the nuns'll be busy with all the prayers and the spastics.'

'What do you mean, the spastics?' Mike asked.

'Well, the disabled lot,' the man said, scratching a stubbly chin. 'The people the nuns look after.'

'So it's a home for disabled people, is it?' Mike asked. 'Don't they have children there any more?'

'Haven't had them since 1970,' the fellow said. 'These last years it's all been folk in wheelchairs and shaking from the palsy. But they keep themselves to themselves, the nuns do. You'll not see them in town at all and they get all their provisions sent up to them. You wouldn't know they were there if you didn't know they were there.'

THIRTEEN

1977

They found the place easily enough – a wooden sign in vaguely Celtic lettering confirmed this was indeed Sean Ross Abbey. In the fields around the gatehouse new low-rise institutional housing had sprung up with signposts pointing to Marian House, Lourdes House, Dara House, Edel House. A half-mile up the undulating drive they could see the convent at the top of the hill. The ruins of the ancient monastery rose against the skyline; the windows of the Georgian mansion glinted in the August sun, and to its right a line of square grey concrete buildings with small windows set high in their walls closed off the side of the front courtyard.

Mike looked at Mary. 'What do you think? Should we go knock?'

Mary shook her head. 'No, Mikey, you heard what the man said: I don't think we should disturb them when they're busy. Let's come back tomorrow.'

Mike did not argue. Like his sister, he was apprehensive at the thought of revisiting the place. He turned the car around and drove back into Roscrea, where they spent the afternoon visiting the remains of the town's castle and the evening drinking Guinness in the bar of Grants Hotel.

Next morning they woke early. When they arrived at the abbey the mist was still hanging over the fields and the place seemed deserted. They saw no one on the drive from the gatehouse up to the convent and when they rang and knocked at the door of the old house nothing stirred. The windows on either side were heavily curtained and too high to look into. Mary tugged at Mike's sleeve.

'Let's go, Mikey,' she whispered. 'Let's go, shall we? I don't like this place. Shall we just go back to the hotel?'

Mike was nervous too, but he had come and was determined to see it through. He had important questions to ask and this was the only place they would ever be answered.

'Come on, let's go round back.'

Their footsteps rang on the cobbles of the courtyard, echoing from the walls and sending Mary glancing nervously for signs of life. Like trespassers in a forbidden garden, they walked the length of the building and found a path that led behind it.

'Do you really think we should, Mikey?' Mary asked breathlessly. 'Don't you think someone might see us?'

Mike tightened his grip on her arm.

'What are they going to do? Shoot us or something?'

They reached the rear of the building and were standing on what had once been a lawn but was overgrown now with tangled weeds. In front of them was a single-storey structure whose French windows opened onto the concrete flags of what to Mike seemed a dimly familiar terrace. Mary hung back but Mike took her hand, led her up to the windows and looked inside. The long narrow nursery was derelict – a couple of broken cots lay by one of the doors, and the windows still bore the strips of adhesive tape that had sealed them shut in winter – but in Mike's memory the place had sprung into radiant life: in a sudden rush of emotion he felt again the sunshine that had lit his first days on earth, saw again the long high ceilings and polished wooden floors that had been the boundaries of his childhood universe; he saw the two rows of cribs – tall and narrow, then wide and low – and the nuns in white habits who had walked among them, brushing the side of his cot with a soft rustle of cloth; he smelt the lilac floor polish, the long-boiled vegetables and the lingering perfume of incense. In his memory the place was bustling with people, as if the hundreds of babies now scattered to the corners of the earth had been sucked back to where they all began, as if the hundreds of mothers who had suffered and grieved here, the hundreds of nuns who had prayed and died and were buried in the churchyard, as if all the shades of the past had returned from their wanderings and gathered once again in the rooms they once inhabited. He saw them peering through the windows, drinking in the sunlight, a hundred pale faces at the windows, quizzical, lost, staring out at him, looking for answers. And somewhere in the background, in the darkened part of the nursery behind the hosts who jostled at the window, a young woman with jet-black hair and blue eyes, short and slight, little more than a girl, was walking slowly out of sight.

'May I ask what you are looking for?'

The woman's voice startled them, shrill in the quiet of the garden. A nun in a black habit and old-fashioned wimple was staring at them with her hands clasped before her. Mary gave a shriek; Mike shook himself.

'Good afternoon, Sister. We knocked at the door but no one answered. I hope we haven't disturbed you.'

The nun smiled coldly. She was young but her face was hard.

'You have not. Do you have business at the abbey?'

Mike hesitated. 'Yes. Well, yes. We have something we want to ask you . . .'

The sister smiled her opaque smile.

'Then you had better follow me.'

Back they went to the big house, up the steps to the front door, into the entrance hall, where the grand staircase was hung with old-fashioned prints of the Virgin displaying her bleeding heart at the pain of losing her son. Two elderly nuns were chatting in a corner.

The young nun called out to them, 'Sister Bridget, Sister Rosamond, be off now!' She ushered Mike and Mary into the high-ceilinged Georgian parlour, bowed slightly and asked them to be seated. 'I think we had all better introduce ourselves. I am Sister Catherine. And you are . . . ?'

'My name is Michael Hess, and this is my sister Mary. We were both born here, or at least I was born here and Mary was born in

Dublin, but her mom came here with her when she was very little and then—'

Mike realized he was speaking way too fast and needed to slow down. He took a couple of breaths.

'So the purpose of our visit is actually to ask, to ask if you will help us with something – if you will help us find our mothers. Is that possible? Can you give us any help . . . any information?'

Disconcertingly the nun made no reply but sat and looked at them in silence as Mike stammered on. When he came to a halt, she rose to her feet.

'I shall need to fetch Mother Barbara. Would you be kind enough to wait here a moment?'

When they were alone, Mike grabbed his sister's hand.

'I've been in this room, Mary. I know I have. I was here with two men and a woman, and the woman was not a nun. I was very little, but I'm sure – I'm sure the woman was my mother!'

Mary frowned.

'I don't like this place, Mike. And I don't like that sister – she gives me the creeps. Did you see the way she ordered those two old nuns to clear off? I think she wanted to keep us away from them.'

'Yeah, that's what I thought,' Mike whispered. 'I wonder why they don't want the old nuns speaking to us? Maybe they remember things about us . . .'

Sister Catherine swept back in, accompanied by another nun who introduced herself as the abbey's mother superior.

'Welcome to Sean Ross Abbey,' Mother Barbara said in a tone that suggested she had been dragged away from more important business. 'I understand you were born here, and it is of course natural that you wish to see the place. You are welcome to look around the grounds, but I must ask that you do not disturb the tranquillity of our sisters by asking questions. I am at your service for any information you require.'

Mike thanked her. 'That is very kind, but actually . . . it's a little more than just seeing the place, Reverend Mother. We would like your help, if possible, in finding out something about our mothers, in finding out – in fact – what has happened to them and where they are now.'

Mother Barbara turned her head slightly and looked at him from the corner of her eye.

'Well, that, I'm afraid, is the one thing we cannot help you with.' Her voice was categorical. 'We are not at liberty to divulge details about our girls: it simply would not be fair to violate their privacy. The rules are particularly strict.'

Mike didn't know what he'd been expecting, but the peremptory tone of Mother Barbara's rebuff shook him. He heard himself stammering a pathetic protest: 'But – but – Reverend Mother, you are our only hope. We'll never find our mothers if you don't help us.'

A look of distaste came over Mother Barbara's face.

'I do not wish to be insensitive, but is it not the case that we *found* mothers and fathers for you many years ago? I assume from your accents that you were adopted in America, and I assume you have parents there, do you not? Is it not unfair to them to come here looking for someone who gave you up many years ago and whom you have not seen since?'

Mike and Mary looked at each other. They had discussed the issue of their adoptive parents at great length and they were indeed concerned that searching for their birth mothers might be hurtful to Marge.

Mike sensed Mary was on the point of letting the matter drop and cut in quickly: 'Yes, Reverend Mother. You did find us new parents and we are grateful to you. But I find it hard to believe we are barred from finding our birth mothers. I assume the convent has kept records of all the babies who passed through here and that they would include both our names at birth and the new names we were given by our adoptive parents. So why would you not agree, at the very least, to pass on a letter from a child to his mother? Her identity would be protected and her privacy would not be violated.'

Mike was beginning to sound like a lawyer and slightly regretted the tone he heard himself adopting. Mother Barbara did not like being lectured.

'I am afraid that is certainly not something we could do. Imagine the distress such a letter might cause, not to mention the scope for mistaken identities or even impostors. Without wishing to cast aspersions, how could I even be sure you are who you say you are? I believe you said your name was Michael Hess, but I have no recollection of any baby by that name.'

Mike felt the argument was slipping away from him. He decided to try another tack: 'We've always been told our mothers abandoned us at birth, but I have strong memories of my own mother being here with me at some stage. Could that be the case, Reverend Mother? Did she stay here and look after me?'

Mother Barbara was losing patience.

'It is possible some of them were here for a while,' she said sharply. 'I cannot be expected to remember every case that has been through our doors. We had hundreds of mothers and babies.'

Mike sensed the nuns were getting ready to bring the proceedings to a close: he would have to hurry to get his remaining questions in.

'Of course, Reverend Mother, I understand. But I do believe you were personally involved in arranging our adoptions; I think I've seen your signature on some of the documents. My sister's name at birth was Mary McDonald and mine was Anthony Lee. My mother's name was Philomena Lee.'

Mother Barbara seemed to start at the mention of Philomena's name. Mike noticed it and felt sure something had registered with her, so he was all the more surprised by her reply.

'No, Mr Hess, I am sorry to disappoint you, that name means nothing to me. I have no recollection of being involved with your case, or with that of your sister.'

But Mike was suspicious now, his intuition telling him to push the point.

'Because, Reverend Mother, I have reason to believe my birth mother has been looking for me and that she may have contacted you or even visited you here as part of her search.'

It was a lawyer's bluff and it did not work. Mother Barbara had regained her composure and simply rose to her feet as a signal that the interview was over.

As they turned and pulled away from the house, Mike pointed wordlessly to a white maypole standing on a patch of bright green grass in front of a tall alabaster statue of an angel.

FOURTEEN

1977

When he came back from Ireland, Mike was preoccupied and uncommunicative. When Mark asked him what he had found out, he just mumbled, 'Not much,' and lapsed into silence. After a week, he apologized for his sullenness.

'It's just so disappointing. I really thought we were going to get somewhere, but it was like a stone wall. I'm positive they're covering something up. But the bummer is I've been researching the legal position and under Irish law the nuns are correct: neither adopted children nor their birth mothers have any legal right to obtain information that might lead them to each other. It's so unfair, and I can't see any way around it.'

In the days that followed, Mark watched Mike's dejection turn, as it always did, to hopelessness and self-loathing. Now all the setbacks and rebuffs seemed to him the result of his own inadequacy: the orphan's rootless insecurity, his sense of not belonging, left him feeling adrift, helplessly tossed by life's tempests. These were the moments in which his desire to belong became paramount, when any chance to be part of the established order was sought like a refuge in a storm. NIMLO was part of the establishment – it offered the prospect of acceptance and security – and Mike signed the contract.

Susan Kavanagh was delighted. Now that Mike was a qualified

lawyer and full-time attorney for the firm, he got to pick an assistant to work with him. Naturally he picked Susan and they resumed their old partnership. The legendary Charles Crane, the old white shoe Washington lawyer who had founded NIMLO forty years earlier, had finally shown up again – and now that he was back he seemed to think his position as president gave him the right to commandeer paralegals to do his private research. Mike stood his ground and refused to let Susan be diverted from her proper work – Susan was grateful, but Mike sensed he was in the boss's bad books.

If Charles Crane was angry with Mike, it was nothing compared to the way he treated his own son Bill. From their glass cubicles at either end of the NIMLO office, the two of them seemed engaged in a constant war of attrition. Susan told Mike that Bill Crane was adopted and that Charles had always treated him atrociously. Bill was endlessly trying to live up to his father's unrealistic expectations.

'The problem with Bill Crane,' she said, 'is that he's a man of modest talents who can never be good enough for his father. Charles was one of Washington's top legal honchos and he obviously hoped Bill would be the same. I feel sorry for the guy, but the office is no place for family warfare.'

Mike took Susan for a drink after work. Sitting in the bar of the Four Seasons in Georgetown, he told her about his history of adoption and his own problems with his adoptive father. 'You know, if I'd known Bill was adopted I'd have understood his behaviour a whole lot better,' he said, nursing his drink. 'I know exactly what it's like to feel you're never going to be good enough. It's an unhealthy feeling – a terrible feeling.'

Over a series of cocktails, they talked about their common backgrounds and Irish Catholic inheritance in a conversation that began as intimate and searching but ended up very jovial. By the time they stood up to go home they were in high spirits, but at the cloakroom Susan became serious.

'Listen, Mike. I know we laugh about him, but I think you gotta watch your back with Bill Crane. He's not a bad guy – he's doing his best to cope with the job and with his father – but he gets jealous of the other attorneys. I've seen him really mad at guys he thinks are shining too bright or impressing old Charles too much. I'm not saying it's going to happen to you, but you need to know that Bill can be pretty ruthless in the way he treats people.'

Mike smiled.

'You know what? If he fired me, he'd probably be doing me a favour – I know for a fact I could earn a stack more working for a private law firm.'

Susan looked at him with exaggerated puppy-dog eyes.

'But you'd never dream of jumping ship and leaving me, right, Mikey?'

Mike put his arm around her shoulder as they emerged onto the M Street sidewalk.

'You know, Susan, sometimes I think you're the only thing that keeps me at that place. When I look back, the only reason I joined is because I was so depressed I was ready to grab anyone who would have me. It's amazing how willing I am to sell out my principles for the flattery of someone who says they want me!'

Susan laughed but she sensed it was not entirely a joke.

A week later, Charles Crane sent word that Mr Hess should attend him in his office. Mike was expecting a dressing-down but the old man's welcome was effusive.

'Mr Hess. Delighted to see you. Do have a cigar.' Mike smiled and shook his head, trying to repress a shudder at the memory of Doc's habit.

'No? You don't mind if I do? Sit down and I'll tell you what I have in mind.'

Crane had the easy air of an insider, a man whose life has been lived in the cosy corridors of the establishment. His feet on the desk, his pungent cigar, his elegant suit with its unbuttoned vest and gold watch chain exuded power and confidence.

'First, I want you to know I've had my eye on you; that I brought you into this organization for a purpose. We've reached a turning point in the political life of this country, Mr Hess. I'm not talking about Carter or Ford, but about the principles on which *all* power rests. Our future depends not on individuals but on how our electoral system functions – or can be made to function. And the man who knows how to pull those levers can be powerful indeed.'

He leaned back in his chair as if he had made his point. Mike wondered if he was supposed to chip in, but Crane was merely pausing for effect.

'What I want you to do is go look at the Iowa decision and see how we can use it. What has happened in Iowa opens the door for all sorts of litigation and we need to be on top of it to stay ahead of the game.'

Mike had read about the Iowa case, but since leaving law school he had not followed gerrymandering issues with as much attention as he perhaps should have.

'Of course I will, Charles,' he said, vaguely hoping they were on first-name terms. 'I'll read the papers and write a report for you.'

Crane nodded.

'I want to you understand the importance of this work. Redrawing electoral boundaries will be the hot button for politics in this country. If the party in power can force out opposition congressmen by cutting up their districts and putting them into seats they can't win, the face of American democracy will be changed forever.'

Mike remembered the idealism with which he had condemned the evils of gerrymandering in law school and decided to venture an opinion: 'It sure is, Charles. It's a scandal that a ruling party can draw these crazy new boundaries to shoo in its own candidates. We lawyers need to oppose such abuses.'

Charles Crane let out a guffaw. 'Mr Hess, you don't get it! We're not gamekeepers in this jungle! NIMLO's role is to tell our clients how to *exploit* the rules. Sure, we help Republicans and Democrats alike, but they take it and go do what they have to do, including gerrymandering – even,' he added with a wink that was intimate and derisive at the same time, 'if that offends your conscience.'

Mike made to object, but Crane waved a hand.

'You go make yourself an expert on redistricting law and you can be a powerful man: politicians will come running for your help. Gerrymandering is the future, Mr Hess!'

As Mike slipped out of the boss's cubicle he felt buoyed and confused, pleased at being picked for a big assignment but worried by the prospect of working in a field he found morally dubious. At the other end of the office, he could see Bill Crane gazing in his direction. He wasn't sure if he was imagining things because of his talk with Susan, but he got the distinct impression that Bill was looking jealous and a little threatening.

In the months that followed, Mike kept out of Bill's way and saw Charles Crane only rarely. He swallowed his scruples and threw himself into the research. He uncovered case law from across the nation, including examples of Republican states drawing electoral boundaries to prevent black voters electing Democratic congressmen; he saw districts so strangely shaped – long and meandering, sprawling and jagged – that they clearly violated the spirit of the law; and he saw Democratic legislatures splitting seats to maximize their own candidates while packing opposition voters into as few districts as possible.

Mike told Susan he was uncomfortable with the way the electoral process was being subverted. He calculated that the balance of power in the House of Representatives now depended on the results of gerrymandered seats, and the party better equipped to exploit the legal loopholes would soon be able to swing control of Congress in its favour. Both parties had recognized the crucial importance of legal advice, and with key decisions pending on the future of redistricting the whole political direction of the country could soon depend on smart young lawyers like Michael Hess. Susan listened to Mike's concerns and tried to reassure him.

'You're too good for this business, Mike. Really. It isn't an attorney's job to worry about right or wrong; it's his job to help his clients make the most of whatever the legislation allows.'

'I guess so,' Mike said. 'I love constitutional law – I love debating all those gerrymander schemes. You pit your wits and you take pride in building a case that'll stand up in court, then you get the adrenalin rush of winning for your client. But the problem is, you get so caught up in the game that you forget it has real consequences – like people getting disenfranchised, like parties winning power through litigation instead of policies. In the long run, we lawyers could make the difference between a Republican or a Democrat in the White House, and that's got to be wrong.'

FIFTEEN

1977–9

In the three years he was at NIMLO, Michael Hess built a reputation as one of Washington's leading experts on redistricting. The calls from state officials and party lawyers began as a trickle and swelled to a torrent: pretty soon the majority of phone enquiries coming in to the switchboard would open with the words, 'May I speak with Attorney Hess?' Bill Crane said nothing, but it was clear from his demeanour that he was jealous. Someone had succeeded in fulfilling old man Crane's expectations, where he, his son, had failed. Susan told Mike to watch out, but Mike just laughed.

'What are they going do to me? They'd be lost without the stuff I've got stashed up here.' He tapped his forehead. 'Redistricting is big potatoes: the politicians are fascinated by it and the lawyers are going to have a field day. So many cases are due in court these next few years that they'll need every attorney who's got even the remotest understanding of the issues.' He paused before producing his clinching argument. 'And the key thing is that what I'm working on right now could be gold dust, Susan. I'm getting close to constructing a Fourteenth Amendment defence that would get a whole stack of these gerrymanders struck down by the courts. It'll have to be argued, of course, but it could change the political landscape.'

Susan sighed. Mike was a good attorney, but he had made enemies and he needed to be on his guard.

*

With his star high, Mike had engineered a part-time job for Mark in the library of the law firm NIMLO shared premises with. Mark was in his final undergraduate year at GW and about to go to law school, so working evenings and weekends at Williams and Connolly was perfect for him.

The two of them were still living in the apartment in South-East DC, but things between them had been strained in recent months and Mike knew it was largely his fault. He had been unpredictable and moody, curt and offhand for no reason. He was worried about his NIMLO work, and always lurking the back of his mind was the memory of his failed expedition to Ireland, but he knew there was no excuse. Mark knew how to avoid stoking his anger, but after a while his very reasonableness had become annoying. Mike watched himself as if from a great height, slowly beginning to destroy the relationship that meant so much to him, just as he had done with David Carlin. More and more frequently, he found himself guiltily packing a weekend bag while Mark was out of the house and sneaking to the train station with sheepish, backward looks, not returning until Sunday afternoon, refusing to meet Mark's eye and hating him for not asking where he'd been.

One Monday late in October Mike and Mark were home eating dinner when three fire trucks raced past the junction at the corner of E Street.

'Wow. It's usually the cops who are in a hurry in this neighbourhood,' Mike joked, but Mark looked serious.

'They're heading down 7th Street, Mike. That's down to the Lost & Found. I hope nothing's happened, after all those crazy threats.'

A few crank letters had appeared recently in the local press threatening to firebomb a gay bar in DC. No one had given them much credence, but Mike said he would ring the L&F just to make sure. It took a while for the call to go through, and they were relieved when the barman answered that everything was OK.

A couple of hours later the doorbell sounded and an obviously shaken John Clarkson ran up the stairs.

'Thank God you're here,' he panted. 'I didn't know where else to go.'

John was a friend of theirs, a genial Texan who had come to Washington a decade earlier to study at GW Law School and stayed to work for a Democratic senator on Capitol Hill. He was a regular at the Lost & Found.

'Are you OK?' Mark asked. 'You look awful.'

John was an elegant man, usually perfectly groomed, but he was sweating, his hair awry and his face and hands stained with soot.

'Let me have some water, will you?' he gasped. 'It's terrible, absolutely terrible!'

Mike ran to fetch a glass as John sank onto the couch clutching his head.

'It's the Cinema Follies,' he said. 'Burned down. It's gone, guys. I was going to the L&F but I never got there. I was on L Street and I saw this smoke. I thought, God, where is that? And when I got close I saw it was the Follies on fire.'

John paused to gulp down the water.

'There was a pile of bodies. The firemen were dragging them out but they were dead, I'm sure of it. There were no windows in the place . . . No one could escape . . . They must have choked to death . . .'

Mike turned to Mark; his face was white.

'Go fetch some brandy, Mark. And three glasses.'

Mark nodded and hurried to the drinks cabinet. The three of them drank in silence. The Cinema Follies was a popular gay club that showed twenty-four-hour X-rated films for men. It had been premiering a new biker movie called *Harley's Angels* and the auditorium on the second floor had been crowded with guys from the leather crowd. Because the side rooms off the main theatre were reserved for private sexual encounters, the management had bricked up all the windows in the building, turning it into a fire trap.

Mike, Mark and John had all been in the Cinema Follies at one time or another and now they sat imagining the smoke, the screaming and panic in the dark crowded room. Mark broke the silence, turning to Mike with an accusing look.

'*You* wanted to go see that movie,' he mumbled. 'You *said* you wanted to see it. You nagged me about going! Don't you realize we could have been there? We could be dead! Why in God's name did you want to go see some leather flick, Mike? Why?'

Mark was shouting now. John Clarkson was taken aback by his sudden fury, but Mike knew the outburst stemmed from months of suspicion and resentment.

'What is it with you?' Mark was yelling. 'Where has all this fascination with bikers and fetishes and violence come from? What's so attractive about hog-tying people and whipping them and violating them? It's so *dirty*, Mike; it's so alien to us and our relationship, but suddenly you're fascinated by it all. God! I hope you're just talking about it, not *doing* it!'

Mike looked like he was going to say something, but then changed his mind, stood up and walked out the door.

The DC Fire Department determined that the fire at the Cinema Follies had been caused by a spark from a faulty rug-shampooing machine which ignited flammable cleaning fluid that had seeped into a carpet, setting alight drapes and wooden stairs. Smoke from the blaze had billowed up the narrow staircase into the movie theatre, sending the patrons running for an emergency exit that was locked from the outside. Nine people had died from smoke inhalation, their bodies found clustered round the padlocked door. Identifying the victims had been difficult because men visiting homosexual establishments usually didn't carry ID, but the DC authorities eventually revealed that many of the dead and injured were married with children and held a variety of professional jobs. One man who escaped with minor injuries was Jon Hinson, a senior aide to a conservative Republican congressman and campaigning himself for a seat in the House.

Because of his job at the law library, Mark began to see Susan Kavanagh frequently. He liked her and he knew she was a confidante of Mike's. He called her one afternoon when Mike was at a conference and asked if she would meet him after work for a drink.

It was the start of winter but temperatures had been holding up so they sat at one of the sidewalk tables at Rumors on M Street. They talked about the collapse of Jimmy Carter's presidency and the worrying rise of Ronald Reagan and the conservative right and how he was sure to be back in next year's presidentials, and then without warning Mark put his head in his hands and began to sob. He was so worried about Mike, he said, and about his mysterious absences, which were souring their relationship. Mike had begun to make a habit of the unexplained weekend trips and Mark found the secrecy surrounding them humiliating. When Mike came back from them he seemed so different that it frightened him.

'Do you know where he goes, Susan? He isn't going somewhere with you, is he? God, I wish he *was* going somewhere with you. I just have no idea what he's getting involved in. We always used to tell each other everything – we said we'd never have secrets and never cheat – but this thing's broken the trust between us.'

Susan said she would like to help, but Mike had said nothing to her. Mark put his hand on Susan's and said he was grateful to have her to talk to.

'It's like he and I don't speak any more. And I have to talk to someone, so it all gets dumped on you. I'm so sorry . . .' Mark gave a rueful laugh. 'But there's something else too. You know Mike's always been so preppy in the way he dresses and behaves – like a real college and law school kid, with all his great clothes, so clean cut and chic. That's how I've always known him and that's how I love him . . . But Susan, I think there's another side to Mike. He's started talking about leather and sadomasochism and stuff . . . and he's got this biker jacket I found in his closet . . . It's just not Mike . . . or it's not who I thought he was.'

Susan liked Mark a lot. She didn't want to see him hurt and didn't want to see Mike hurt either. For the next few weeks she looked for a suitable occasion to talk to him, but the office was busy and the chance didn't come.

*

In mid-December 1979 Washington's lawyers gathered for the Bar Association's Christmas party at the Hay Adams Hotel, and Mike and Susan went along as a couple. Mike kept his sexuality a secret in his professional life – prejudice and homophobia were less overt in the Carter years but there were still very few openly gay men in the legal or political communities. Mike had got into the habit of taking Susan to social functions where he might be recognized, and he chaperoned her to events she was invited to.

He enjoyed the feeling of being normal when he was with her, of not having to look over his shoulder every time he grasped her hand; he liked dancing with her and she enjoyed being with him – he had seen her flush with pleasure at another woman's envious glance. They both loved the Hay Adams – it had such style and old-world charm, with its Tudor-style wood panelling and Elizabethan ceilings and the White House just over the street. As they entered the lobby, they saw Charles Crane looking distinctly proprietorial, as befitted a grandee of the Washington scene.

'Welcome,' he cried, as if the Hay were his own townhouse. 'Welcome, my dears. How lovely you both look—' then he spotted John Dean, Richard Nixon's former counsel, and rushed off to glad-hand him instead.

When they were out of earshot, Mike leaned towards Susan with a suppressed grin. 'Well, how Victorian,' he whispered. 'Was that Mr Hay or was it Mr Adams, do you suppose?'

Susan laughed. 'What I want to know is: where is the noble scion?'

Mike made a show of looking around for Bill Crane and gave an exaggerated shrug.

'No idea. Skulking behind some column, I guess.'

The evening passed in a glitzy succession of vintage champagne and soft music. After dinner, Mike sat Susan down with a drink and headed for the men's room. The evening was going beautifully – what he felt like now was a dance. As he walked back towards Susan, he noticed a red-haired woman in a green dress had sat next to her and was chatting animatedly, gesturing and laughing in a manner which suggested she'd had too much to drink. As he approached, she caught sight of him and whispered something urgently to Susan before slinking off in the other direction.

'Well,' exclaimed Mike. 'What was all that about?' Susan looked uneasy.

'Just some nosy little bitch. She asked me if you were gay.' Mike's face fell. 'She said the girls in the office have been talking about it, and she had a bet going. She wanted me to confirm it.' Susan's eyes were dull with rage and Mike felt the sweat break out on the palms of his hands.

At around ten o'clock the MC tapped a glass and called for silence. The speeches were the usual mixture of pomposity and bad jokes and Mike noticed a few people looking at their watches long before the microphone was handed to Senator Hepton to make the closing remarks. A Republican from somewhere in the Midwest, Hepton was one of the right-wing conservatives who had been in the wilderness since the Democrats came to power but were becoming pretty chipper now that Carter was sliding towards record lows in the polls. Hepton made a few wisecracks about the Iran hostage crisis that had been battering the president for over a month, sang the praises of the revolution Margaret Thatcher was carrying out over in England and promised the same reinvigorating conservatism in the US if only the country would have the good sense to elect Ronald Reagan next year.

'And I'll tell you a couple of things about Ron,' he said. 'He won't let America be pushed around by mullahs and fanatics; he'll fix this economy of ours that keeps on breaking down; and he'll clear out the degenerates and perverts that've got their tentacles into the vital organs of our nation. You can rest assured that Ronald Reagan in the White House will heed the warnings of Christians like Reverend Falwell when he says the homosexuals are on the march in this country. We need to remember homosexuals do not reproduce, they recruit! And many of them are after my children and yours . . .'

Mike felt faint. He clenched his hands so tight that his finger-nails dug into his palms. He felt Susan take his arm and at the same time knew that someone was looking at him. Glancing to his left he saw Bill Crane smirking in his direction.

At the end of the evening, Mike drove Susan home. He pulled up in front of her apartment and was jumping out to open the car door for her, but she stopped him.

'Mike, can you just wait a moment? I need to say a couple of things.'

He nodded and turned off the motor.

'Well, first, I want to say that what that guy said tonight was terrible. It was stupid, insulting and wrong. But I'm worried, Mike. I think those people – Jerry Falwell, Pat Robertson, Anita Bryant, all the religious right – are going to be a lot more powerful if Reagan gets elected. I think the whole atmosphere could change. They've felt snubbed for years – even under Ford they were frozen out – and I think they're looking for payback. I heard some of the guys in the office talking at the water cooler and saying they're going to vote Reagan because . . . he'll crush the faggots, and other redneck crap. I know they're shooting their mouths off and maybe they don't even mean it, but I think the time's coming for a lot of people to keep their heads down.'

Mike nodded. He felt suddenly old and very tired.

'Do you think . . . anyone in our office knows about me?'

'No, I'd say most of them just think you're a handsome, single guy.' Susan hesitated. 'But there's a lot of homophobia about and I don't like this Reagan–Falwell thing. Once the guys at the top start using that sort of crazy language, how long before Joe Blue Collar gets to thinking it's OK to go beat up gays in the park? I'm just saying you need to be discreet, Mike. You're already in some people's bad books around the office, and they'll use anything they can against you.'

Mike sat for a moment, looking through the windscreen at the street ahead, suddenly picturing himself at the Iwo Jima Memorial late at night and a group of men with baseball bats.

'Thanks for caring about me, Susan. You're right – about discretion and everything . . .' He wanted to lighten the mood: they'd been so happy in the car on the way to the party. 'Of course, it'll mean lots more of these social outings for you,' he added, laughing. 'And lots more times that Mark gets left at home minding the cat.'

'Yeah,' said Susan, unsmiling. 'Actually, that was the other thing I wanted to ask about. How are things between you two?'

From her hesitant tone Mike sensed that she knew something. He thought for a moment and decided he was glad she knew, glad she was giving him the chance to talk.

'You know, Susie, I love Mark so much, but I think there must be something wrong with me because I seem to be doing my best to destroy us.'

Susan told him what Mark had said about the missing weekends and the leather fantasies, and Mike raised his eyebrows.

'Well, I guess you know all about it, then.' His cheeks reddened slightly. 'And there was me keeping it a secret because I didn't want to hurt him.'

'Keeping *what* a secret, Mike?' Susan asked imploringly. 'It's the secrecy that's doing the damage.'

Mike reached forward to the dashboard and turned on the heater. It was a chilly evening and the windows were fogging up with condensation.

'Keeping Harry a secret,' he said dully, without looking at her. 'Keeping the sex a secret. Keeping it all a secret.'

Susan took his hand. She had trespassed on territory she really had no right to venture into, but Mike wanted to tell her. He told her about Harry Chapman, the guy he had met at GW Law School, who had called him when he moved to New York City and invited him to come visit. Harry who had taken him to the sort of clubs Mike had always wanted to explore but never had the courage to enter; Harry who had introduced him to the exotic pleasures of bondage and sado-sex that excited him so much. And when he'd finished giving Susan the details he looked at her with puzzlement and shame on his face.

'But the crazy thing is, even while I'm doing all that stuff, even when I'm with Harry and we're in all those places, and even when it's so intense and so exhilarating . . . even then, I know *this is not where I want to be.*' He paused and corrected himself. 'That's to say, it *is* what I want and it's *not* what I want. I do it, but I don't know what *makes* me do it.'

Susan frowned, trying her best to understand.

'I guess . . . maybe . . . because it's so different from . . . from your other life—'

'It's because I find it addictive, Susan. That's what it is. It's because I can't help it.'

'So don't you love Mark any more? Is that what—'

'No, no. I do love him . . . I love him.'

'Then why are you so hell-bent on wrecking your own happiness? Can't you see Mark thinks the world of you? And you always seem so in love, like you were made for each other, and yet here you are throwing it all away.'

'I know, I know. It makes no sense. There's a side to me . . .' Mike thought for a moment. 'There's a side to me that I can't control. It's bad and wrong and it's self-destructive. I know it will spoil everything in my life, all the love and all the joy, but it's always there and it's always beckoning, always whispering, "You are unworthy of this happiness; therefore you must destroy it."'

SIXTEEN

1980

Mike and Mark spent a quiet Christmas and New Year together. Mike made no mention of his conversation with Susan, but he seemed chastened. When Mark asked if he was OK, Mike smiled and kissed him on the cheek. On Christmas Day they spoke of their shared years, from the tragedy that brought them together to the periods of domestic contentment, and their hopes for the future. But they did not broach the issue that had sown discord between them and neither really knew if they were putting it behind them or simply to one side.

January 1980 dawned with their relationship in limbo and America holding its collective breath: the economy was hurting, unemployment high and gasoline supplies running out. With the Iranian hostage crisis in its third month, the lines for gas last seen after the Arab–Israeli war of 1973 were back, and Jimmy Carter was taking the hit. For the Republicans, Ronald Reagan was mobilizing the right, and his only challenger – former CIA Director George Bush – was so bland and ineffectual that the nomination looked a shoo-in.

Mike volunteered to work for the Democrats and Jimmy Carter, went canvassing and helped with registering voters. At the end of February, after the Iowa and New Hampshire primaries, he raised a few eyebrows in the NIMLO office by turning up with a CARTER FOR PRESIDENT button on his lapel. Someone took exception and a message was relayed to him that Charles Crane wished to see him. This time there were no cigars and no avuncular charm.

'I won't hide the fact from you,' Crane began, 'that there has been dissatisfaction, Mr Hess. Partisan buttons can have no place in a non-partisan organization like ours. But this misjudgement on your part is not my only reason for wishing to speak with you.' Crane paused, preparing to utter something he obviously considered of great moment. 'No one here has any quarrel with your abilities; indeed, we can see you have a remarkable understanding of constitutional law. But there have been suggestions that you – how shall I put this? – are building your own private contacts in the world of politics and that you've been using the NIMLO name to help you do so.'

Mike looked shocked and made to interrupt, but Crane had not finished.

'Some of our attorneys feel you have established too much of an independent reputation with our clients – that clients are now calling you directly for advice instead of coming through the proper NIMLO channels, and that you may have ulterior motives for encouraging this to happen.'

Mike laughed. 'Whoa! You're accusing me of being too helpful to our clients? This is crazy, Charles. They come to me because I give them the advice they need. Like the Amendment Fourteen defence I've been working on for redistricting cases – I told you all about that, didn't I? That's something that'll help boost the NIMLO name: it'll make us indispensable to both political parties.'

Charles Crane grunted and raised his hand for him to stop, but Mike was angry.

'So who *is* it that's been snitching about me? Who says I'm not being a team player? Who says I'm acting too smart? It's Bill, isn't it? He's come running to Daddy, right?'

Mike thought Charles looked a little embarrassed – apologetic almost – but he was a man accustomed to winning arguments and he wasn't going to lose this one.

'Mr Hess, I wish you to take to heart what I have said to you today. From now on I wish you to make NIMLO your number-one priority – your *only* priority – and to forget about furthering your own ambitions by exploiting your position here. And one final thing . . .' Crane focused his eyes firmly on the desk in front of him. 'I want you to be very clear about this: we at NIMLO cannot, and will not, tolerate any . . . irregularities in the *personal lives* of our staff. I trust you understand what I am referring to?'

That evening, Mike sat in silence through dinner. He told Mark he was tired, but Mark knew him well enough to see there was something going on. Just before they went to bed, Mike said he had decided not to go to the fancy dress ball they had been invited to at the weekend.

'What?' exclaimed Mark. 'Why on earth not? We've been looking forward to it for weeks. Did something happen at work? What's up?'

Mike bit his tongue. He knew it was wrong, but he was mad at Mark for being surprised – though he had every right to be – was mad at him for not somehow magically understanding, was mad at him, Mike realized glumly, for simply being there.

'I've just changed my mind, that's all,' he said, not looking up.

Mark sensed there was more.

'Mike, if you're doing this to hurt me, then please don't. I'm getting weary of never knowing where we're up to nowadays. One minute you're loving and tender and the next you're as cold as—' He gestured to the snow swirling in the light of the street lamp outside the window. 'If you must know, I'm pretty pissed with the whole thing.'

He regretted the words as soon as they left his lips; he knew immediately he had given Mike the pretext he needed. Mike felt a surge of triumphant indignation – if his refusal to go to the party hadn't hurt Mark enough, he had another bullet ready loaded in the chamber: 'Well, if you *must* know,' he said with a frozen smile on cruel lips, 'the reason I'm not going to the party is because I'm going away for the weekend.'

The spring of 1980 came in and things went from bad to worse for Jimmy Carter. He severed diplomatic ties with Iran, and the Ayatollah taunted him by parading blindfolded American captives before the world's press; he announced a boycott of the Moscow Olympics, and footage of him collapsing while out jogging ran in all the news bulletins; he sent military helicopters to rescue the hostages and, inevitably, they crashed in the desert.

Mike's emotional state followed the plunge in the president's ratings. He told Susan Kavanagh that everything was going wrong in his life and the world was slowly closing in on him. He was still campaigning for Carter, but he told his fellow volunteer John Clarkson that the whole thing was a hopeless cause. John's Texan optimism would not allow him to throw in the towel, though, and he did his best to rally Mike's spirits. 'If we don't campaign for Carter,' he said, 'we'll get Reagan and the Christian right. Did you hear what Jerry Falwell's been saying about us? He told a rally, "Gay folks will just as soon kill you as look at you." So whaddya think about that, then?' He laughed. 'Do I look like a killer?'

The one thing that did not wane with Mike's plunging mood was his fascination with the law. However badly his life was going, its cut and thrust still excited him. He knew so much about redistricting now, and like a chess grandmaster he was building a line of attack that would provide powerful ammunition for politicians of either party to challenge their opponents' gerrymandering. The old arguments of racial discrimination had run through the courts with limited success, but Mike had scoured the 1965 Voting Rights Act and concluded that the fatal flaw in the practice of partisan gerrymandering was its inherent conflict with the provisions of the Fourteenth Amendment. If the constitution guaranteed that 'no state shall make or enforce any law which shall abridge the privileges or immunities of US citizens', he argued, then redistricting to disadvantage opposition voters would surely qualify as a curtailment of their rights. If a redistricting plan were to interfere with an opposition party's ability to participate in the electoral process, a violation of the Fourteenth Amendment must surely have occurred. And since the whole point of partisan gerrymandering was to do exactly that, Mike concluded the schemes should undoubtedly be struck down.

On the face of it, it was a dry, arcane formula, but a stack of redistricting cases were going through the courts and the legal profession was braced for many more that would surely result from the new round of reapportionment following the 1980 census. If a party could argue down its opponents' manoeuvres, it would gain a significant political advantage.

Susan Kavanagh put up with Mike's sullenness with good grace. She made allowances for him; he had shown her a great deal of kindness in the three years they had worked together and had brought a lot of fun into her life. So now when he got mad and yelled at her, she didn't answer back or hold it against him; and the following day he would invariably bring her flowers, ask her to excuse his behaviour and take her for a conciliatory drink after work.

She didn't ask him directly about his relationship with Mark, but she had a sense of how things were going. She was aware of the argument over the fancy dress party and knew it had left things tense between them, but as spring retreated before the dazzling Washington summer, she felt Mike was beginning to come out of the woods. His demeanour was brighter, the bags had gone from under his eyes and he was smiling again like the Mike she had known before. She had done much of the research that Mike was putting into his redistricting paper and shared some of his excitement about it. He still complained bitterly about the bungling and bad luck that were making a Democratic defeat in November look inevitable, but his comments about Reagan and the new conservatives were combative now, barbed and pugnacious where before they had been filled with terrible, haunted anxiety.

'Can you believe these guys?' he said one morning, brandishing a copy of the *Post*. 'Now they say if they're elected they'll repeal any anti-discrimination legislation that could be used to give guarantees to gay people, and they'll fight against the abolition of DC's anti-sodomy laws. What a bunch of antediluvian cretins! They're like puritan Rip Van Winkles waking up after 300 years and thinking America's still in the seventeenth century!'

When the phone rang that afternoon, Susan covered the mouthpiece

Above Arriving at
Chicago airport,
December 1955.

Left Michael
and Mary's first
Christmas in America.

Below Michael's
fourth birthday,
July 1956.

Doc Hess, Michael, Stevie, Thomas, Mary, James. September 1956.

Mary and Michael (front) in the garden in St Louis, with brother Stevie.

Above Michael aged five on vacation in Minnesota.

Right Michael aged seven.

Mary's first Communion.

Above Michael's
confirmation,
July 1961.

Left Loras Lane,
Pope Paul VI and
Josephine Lane
in the Vatican,
October 1965.

Below Michael and
Mary take the oath to
become US citizens,
3 October 1968.

Above Michael in Florida,
August 1971.

Right With Mark (left)
at Michael's law school
graduation, May 1977.

Below Michael with Susan
Kavanagh, Christmas 1979.

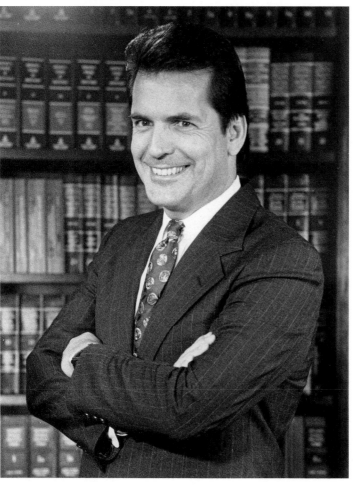

Left Pete Nilsson, Sally and
Michael at the cottage in
West Virginia.

Below left Official portrait of
the Republican Party's new
Chief Counsel, 1988.

Right Michael with Sister Hildegarde
at Sean Ross Abbey, August 1993.

Below right Mary and Michael,
sick with AIDS, in West Virginia,
Easter 1995.

Above Mary at Michael's grave, 1998.

Below Philomena's first visit after discovering her son's grave, summer 2004.

and called over to Mike, 'A Mr Van Winkle for you. Republican National Committee on line three – they say welcome to the seventeenth century!'

Mike picked up the phone and found it full of the thunderous nasal diphthongs and curtailed consonants of south Boston.

'Ron Kaufman here, Mr Hess. Tom Hofeller told me I could call you. Says you've got some crackerjack scheme on redistricting I need to know about. Can you do lunch this week?'

When Mike put down the phone he told Susan with a laugh that he would be out for lunch on Thursday.

'I'm supping with the devil now,' he said. 'Better get me the long spoon!'

June 1980 saw the beginning of the longest heat wave since US meteorological records began. Temperatures in Washington DC rarely fell below ninety degrees, the blacktop melted on the Beltway and over a thousand people died from heatstroke. A nationwide drought caused damage estimated at upwards of twenty billion dollars, and while Jimmy Carter was scaring voters by reintroducing the draft in response to the Soviet invasion of Afghanistan Ronald Reagan was triumphantly anointed as Republican candidate – and now odds-on favourite – for November's presidential election.

Mike had behaved himself at his lunch with the Republicans. Ron Kaufman was a sharp, witty operator in his mid-thirties who had been a senior field director for the Bush campaign but moved seamlessly into the Reagan camp after the nomination went his way. Mike had tackled him about the party's willingness to cosy up to the bigots of the religious right, but Kaufman had smiled and refused to rise to the bait. Then they had discussed Mike's ideas for the redistricting litigation and Kaufman had thanked him for his advice.

'Just don't go talking to the Democrats, OK?' he'd joked as they were leaving the restaurant.

Mike had heard nothing further and assumed the conversation would have no follow-up, but at the end of the month he was again summoned to see Charles Crane.

'Mr Hess, I'll get straight to the point,' Crane said, before Mike was even through the door of the office. 'We've had a phone call from the Republican National Committee. They were full of admiration for you and for your Amendment Fourteen strategy, which they're planning to use in some case or other.'

Mike heard the words of praise and wondered why he was not cheered by them. There was something in Crane's tone of voice which clashed with the content of what he was saying.

'Well, good. It's great to get an endorsement from the guys who run the political platform of one of our nicest parties. And it'll help NIMLO too. You were concerned about that, remember?'

Charles Crane looked at him with expressionless eyes.

'I think your tone is inappropriate, Mr Hess. And no, I do not think this will help NIMLO. I understand from some of our attorneys that your meeting with the Republican National Committee was intended to further your own interests, not ours.'

Mike blinked at the unfairness of the accusation and the suggestion that he was somehow courting the Republicans.

'Well, I don't know who's told you all this, Charles,' he said with a growing sense of unease, 'but I can tell you I was acting solely in NIMLO's best interests: I had no personal agenda whatsoever in speaking with Ron Kaufman.'

Charles Crane, though, had decided his line and he was sticking to it.

'I'm afraid that is not what I am hearing. What I hear is that you deliberately engineered that meeting to promote your own interests, to promote your own future with the RNC.'

Mike laughed: the idea was so crazy he couldn't stop himself.

'But I *hate* the fucking Republicans! How could I possibly go ass-licking guys I hold in the deepest contempt? The whole idea is ludicrous!'

At Mike's words, a look of triumph swept across his interrogator's face, as if Charles Crane had been waiting from the outset for a cue that could lend some legitimacy to what he had always planned to say.

'Mr Hess, your tone is offensive and your conduct unbecoming. I am afraid I have no option but to inform you that your contract at the National Institute of Municipal Law Officers is being terminated. I would be grateful if you would vacate your desk.'

Mike stumbled into the main office, called Susan over and slumped into his chair. 'Susan,' he said, 'I just got my pink slip. They fired me!'

SEVENTEEN

1980

Mike was in a foul mood and Mark could not rouse him from it. Losing his job in the depths of an economic downturn was a harsh blow, but Mark sensed there was something deeper. It was as if the NIMLO setback had tipped some sort of balance inside him, as if Mike were giving up on life as a whole: he stayed in bed with the blinds closed when Mark left to go to class and would be lying there still when Mark returned in the evening; he turned down invitations to go out and refused to pick up the phone; even Susan's messages went unanswered.

Mark was solicitous. He comforted Mike and fussed over him, put up with his curt, dismissive responses and kept a smile on his face despite the gloom Mike seemed determined to bring down on them. Mark was young and Mike was his first love – their relationship still seemed special to him, still worth fighting for. He reassured him endlessly, willing him not to despair.

'Don't worry, Mike. The main thing is we love each other. That's where your happiness lies, yours and mine. You can have happiness if you want it – you know that. It's here at your fingertips and nothing else matters.'

Mike knew he was right: he wanted the happiness and love as much as Mark did. But the more Mark was supportive and loving, the more Mike's anger grew. He didn't know why but sensed it was something to do with jealousy: he had convinced himself that he could never be happy and something inside him did not want anyone else to be happy. If his own happiness could only exist by Mark being happy, then he would sacrifice both.

Mark came home from class to find Mike up and dressed.

'Mike!' he exclaimed. 'God, it's great to see you back on your feet again. How are you feeling?' He made as if to hug him, but when he saw the look on his face took a step back. 'What's going on, Mike?'

'I'm dressed because I'm going away for the weekend.'

His voice was expressionless but his words were bullets.

Mark pleaded, asked him to stay, but Mike was unmovable. Mark glimpsed the gathering crisis and tried one last time to avert it.

'If you go, you'll ruin everything we've built together. I thought we were over these lost weekends, Mike. Please don't start it all again; it'll destroy everything.'

Mark held his breath, waiting for his lover's reply, and then heard the note of pleasure and triumph that betrayed how much Mike wanted to hurt him. 'I'm going, Mark. You can't stop me. That's what I want. That's where I want to be.'

'If you go,' Mark said, 'I won't be here when you get back. I'm serious . . .'

He saw Mike hesitate for a moment, saw the fleeting frown that darkened his face, then saw him pick up his bag and walk through the door.

Mike looked in the mirror and was startled to see himself there. The train was reaching top speed, bumping and swaying over the points. Tired and unsteady from the reckless abandon of the weekend, he could barely stand, but as he saw his reflection he paused for a moment, peering into the mirror for a closer look. How strange it was, this need to seek assurance of his own existence. He saw the eyes, the familiar nose and mouth, and told himself, *Look! There you are; you are there.*

The weekend in Manhattan – the weekend he had just spent with Harry – had ended a couple of hours ago but already it seemed like a black void. The drink, the pills, the sex – the memories existed somewhere in his brain, but distant now, veiled in the fog of forgetting. He peered again into the rattling, splash-stained mirror of the bathroom, but could not dispel the awful thought that Michael Hess did not exist. He laughed. How people dismiss you – 'He's a nobody!' – and now it was a reality.

In the lobby at the end of the carriage he stood by the door and pressed his face to the cold window. Outside the tracks were flashing past in the midnight darkness, clattering down below him, illuminated with rhythmic bursts of light in a Morse code he could not decipher. He examined the door handle – one of the old manual locks that could be flicked open with little effort. His hand was on it, beginning to lift, beginning to imagine the cold impact of the unforgiving steel. Then he heard a voice that seemed to echo in his mind – quick, stumbling phrases, a woman's voice: 'Don't let them put him in the ground . . . It's dark down there . . . It's cold down there.'

He gripped the hand on the door lever – his own hand, Mike Hess's hand. The flesh felt warm and alive.

'Don't let them bury him . . . They're burying him in the ground . . .'

He gave a short, muffled moan and sank to the floor.

When Mike got to the apartment on E Street, he found a note from Mark scribbled on a page torn from a yellow legal pad. 'I spoke to the landlord. You need to clear your stuff out by Friday. Leave the key with Spangler.'

When he looked in the bedroom, Mark's side of the closet was empty.

He phoned Susan Kavanagh and she drove over. She said she'd been alarmed when he didn't answer her phone calls. She had spoken with Mark and heard about them breaking up. A few of the guys at NIMLO had been trying to contact him to say how sorry they were to see him leave. Then she looked at him and sighed, 'Mike, you look awful. I think you better come stay with me until you get sorted out.

My daughter's at summer camp for another couple of weeks, and after that I think I can find you someplace to go.'

Susan nursed him and fed him. She cleared away the alcohol from the shelf in the kitchen and made sure he stayed home in the evenings. Mike seemed a little embarrassed – there was enough familiarity between the two of them that he could accept her kindness, but enough distance to keep him polite and grateful, to stop him sinking into the self-pitying depression he had used as a weapon against Mark.

At the beginning of September, a few days before her daughter was due back, Susan said she had spoken to a friend of hers who was willing to sublet the spare room of his apartment. The guy's name was Bob McMullen; he was the same age as Susan, a couple of years older than Mike, and he was gay. Susan invited him over to dinner and he explained that he and his partner had taken on the lease of a very grand apartment in the upmarket Wyoming Building on Columbia Road in Adams Morgan, a few blocks north from Dupont, but the two of them had recently split up so there was now a spare bedroom Mike might like to rent. The three of them agreed to meet at Bob's place the following day.

The Wyoming had been constructed around the turn of the twentieth century with high ceilings and marble and brass fittings, and its location could hardly have been better: after the rough streets of South-East DC, Mike found Adams Morgan very swanky, with its wide tree-lined avenues and funky restaurants. The apartment itself was spacious and comfortable: Bob had his own bedroom and private bathroom; Mike would have the same, and they would share a large lounge area and dining room. Mike did not warm to Bob McMullen, but the rent was reasonable, Susan knew the guy and Mike was in no position to go elsewhere. He signed a brief, informal document that would serve as a lease and the three of them walked round the corner for a celebratory beer in the Lemon Tree bar.

EIGHTEEN

1980–1

The heat wave of the summer had broken in late September and fall had come swift on its heels. Ronald Reagan had co-opted George Bush as his running mate and the Republican bandwagon was rolling towards inexorable victory in November. Mike had barely kept himself on an even keel, spending his days looking through the legal journals in search of a job but making no headway: every ad he responded to seemed to have been placed too late – he was sick of hearing the voice on the phone offering saccharin commiserations: 'We're *so* sorry, Mr Hess, but that position *has* now been filled . . .'

He was getting on OK with Bob McMullen but little more than that. Susan sensed the lack of warmth and told Mike she was worried she had put two of her friends in a situation that wasn't working out, but Mike said everything was fine – he had far bigger problems to worry about.

On 4 November Reagan won in a landslide, condemning Jimmy Carter to the worst defeat of an incumbent president since Herbert Hoover. Mike met up with John Clarkson and they drowned their sorrows in the Numbers Bar on the far side of Connecticut Avenue. John was a committed Democrat – he had worked for a Democratic senator and seemed to take the defeat as a personal rebuff – so Mike made it his business to cheer him up with a constant and copious supply of drink. When Susan arrived she said she'd been trying to call Mike all day and gotten no reply.

'I've been really wanting to find you, Mike. There's been a couple of calls for you from Ron Kaufman at the Republican National Committee, and they sound urgent. He says he told his boss about you after that meeting you had. They just discovered you were fired from NIMLO and, well, it sounds like they want to offer you a job.'

Mike said nothing but John spluttered through a mouthful of beer, 'What? Mike go work for the Republicans? You *cannot* be serious!'

Mike went to the meeting in a panic of indecision. He wanted a job – needed a job – but John Clarkson was right. On the Metro from Dupont to Capitol South he agonized and changed his mind a dozen times. The escalator carried him up from the subway into a wintry sun that wavered uncertainly above the Capitol. The row of low-built white-fronted offices across the street gleamed in the morning light, the headquarters of the Republican high command preening with the assurance of status and power. In the main lobby of 310 First Street Mike came face to face with a life-size image of Ronald and Nancy Reagan, waving and smiling with the Hollywood confidence that had charmed a nation. Mike shivered and asked the receptionist to let Mr Kaufman know he was here.

Kaufman came down himself, chatted in the elevator as if they were old buddies and led Mike through plush carpeted corridors where secretaries looked up from their keyboards to wave good morning and brass nameplates adorned oak doors. Mike thought how good it must be to have a brass nameplate . . .

'Welcome to mission control.' Kaufman laughed as he ushered Mike into a smallish office equipped with expensive-looking furniture and poured them both coffee. 'I take it you know what we do – coordination for the party across the nation, development and promotion of the party's political platform, fundraising, election strategy. High-powered and serious. But we also organize the convention every four years and now, praise be, the president's Inaugural – that's the fun stuff and that's what we'd like you to come and help out with. How does that sound?'

Mike blinked. Kaufman was a fast talker and he felt maybe he hadn't taken everything in.

'Tell me again – you want me to work on the Inaugural?' Mike wasn't sure what he'd been expecting, but this sounded like a job labelling envelopes for invitations to a presidential party.

'Sure. The Presidential Inaugural Committee's being constituted this week and it'll run for a couple of months – Reagan gets sworn in on January twentieth.'

Kaufman explained that the RNC needed volunteers to help with planning and staffing, arranging transport and staging the inaugural events like the parade and the ball, and marketing the official commemorative book and other souvenirs.

Mike gave a little laugh. 'So it's basically selling hot dogs. Is that what it is?'

Kaufman smiled.

'That's about the measure of it. But don't forget the golden rule of politics: if you want to get on, you need to be in the right place at the right time.'

Susan Kavanagh and John Clarkson snickered when Mike told them what he had been hired for, but he worked his time, labelled the envelopes and shuffled the papers. His most arduous task was to help draft hire contracts for the eight ballrooms in DC hotels and convention centres where 50,000 Republicans from the nation's four corners would gather to celebrate the inauguration of their man in the White House. On January twentieth his reward was a seat in the staff bleachers on the West Front of the Capitol. He was there at 11.30 a.m., as Reagan stepped up to be sworn in as fortieth president of the United States; and he was there at 11.35 a.m., the minute a UPI flash confirmed the hostages had taken off from Tehran after 444 days in captivity. Reagan's triumph was Carter's humiliation, and Mike felt both; his unease at the advent of the Republican right was attenuated by the exhilaration of the occasion and the sense that he was part of the machine which had put it in place.

In the evening he took Susan to the Inaugural staff ball at the Washington Sheraton. They floated through waltzes and jumped about to Kool and the Gang's 'Celebration', which had hit number one in the charts. 'There's a party going on right here, / a dedication to last throughout the year,' the young Republicans sang. 'We gonna have a good time tonight; / let's celebrate, it's all right . . .' Mike and Susan drank in the atmosphere and the free wine till their heads were light, their thoughts raced and their emotions were torn in a thousand directions. Mike smoked a joint in the men's room, its effect infinitely magnified by the knowledge that he was doing it in the heart of the Republican beast.

On the stroke of midnight an excited young guy with a West Coast accent got up on stage and asked for silence, the ballroom lights dimmed and suddenly they were there: Nancy, slender and shimmering in her ten-thousand-dollar gown, and the Gipper himself, impossibly tall and erect with his glossy hair swept into its perfect quiff and his perfect teeth smiling from his manly actor's face. Susan grabbed Mike's arm and joined in the collective scream of excitement; Mike felt his body quiver with the warm, tingling pleasure of nervy anticipation. As Frank Sinatra sang, the president did his 'Aw shucks' routine, thanked his staff and kissed his wife. Mike's head was spinning. The Reagans were among the crowds on the dance floor now, led this way and that by a beaming Ron Kaufman, who whispered the names of important staffers they needed to greet. Reagan's head towered above the throng and Mike pictured him as handsome cowboy, a muscular doomed athlete – as his own lover. Kaufman was whispering again and Reagan was right there beside him, taking his hand in his and delivering perfectly the line he had been told to say.

'Well, Mr Michael Hess, I presume. I've heard a lot about you and I would be honoured if you would give me your support, as a member of our young generation, in the efforts we're making to ensure this country's future. What do you say, young man? We'd sure like to have you with us.'

LONDON

Present Day

Constructing a portrait of an absent person is an exercise in extrapolation and verification. For all the research and detective work, there must be a black hole at the centre – where a man once stood and is no longer. His form can be surmised: the testimony of those who knew him offers a series of spotlights against which his silhouette emerges in dark, fleeting relief. Hundreds of people knew Michael Hess, or Anthony Lee, and I have spoken to dozens of them. But each spotlight focuses on a separate angle – at times, it seems, on an entirely different man – and where some remember a thing one way, others remember it otherwise. Some informants appear under their own names in the text of this book; others have asked to appear under a pseudonym or not to appear at all. Most have spoken with honesty and goodwill – the exceptions are those in public positions who have something to hide.

I will describe at the end of the story how we contacted the three or four people who played the most important roles in Michael's later years and how the arc of his life emerged from the accounts they gave. There are new photographs and documents on my desk now to guide me in the final stages of my search: a group of smiling young men at a West Virginia cottage; official White House portraits from the 1980s Republican heyday; a forty-year-old man in earnest conversation with a fragile elderly nun at the door of a country convent; a brother and sister, older again, sitting huddled on the wooden steps of a back porch in the country with sorrow written in their faces . . .

PART FOUR

ONE

1981

Michael Hess signed his contract of employment with the Republican National Committee on 27 March 1981. It was a Friday afternoon and the guys at the RNC said that if he didn't mind hanging around for an hour they would take him for a drink to celebrate. At 6.30 p.m. Ron Kaufman and Tom Hofeller collected him from the bare room with the single window and the thumb-tack-spotted walls that was destined to be his office and the three of them walked the eight blocks up to D Street. As they passed the Dirksen Senate Office Building (renamed for the late senator in 1972), Mike nodded to the nameplate and told his companions about the time he had been Ev Dirksen's page. Everyone laughed, and Mike was pleased that he had bolstered his threadbare Republican credentials. The Monocle was still pretty empty when they arrived and Nick, the Greek maître d', greeted Ron and Tom by name.

'Nick, I want you to meet Michael Hess,' Ron said. 'He's our newest recruit and he's Irish, so I guess you'll be seeing a lot of him in here.'

They all smiled, and Ron ordered a bottle of champagne. Mike liked him: he had a sharp brain and a sharp tongue and he was undoubtedly a coming man in Republican ranks. He was less than ten years older than Mike. His neat brown moustache, spectacles and tight waves of dark hair made him look like a cross between Groucho

Marx and Henry Kissinger, and his grumpy gravitas impressed senior senators and even the president himself. Kaufman took Mike by the arm and showed him the black and white photos on the walls of every Republican president and most of the party's leading senators from the thirty years the Monocle had been in existence. Tom Hofeller stayed at the table, flicking through briefing documents and news-paper cuttings. Mike found him hard to pin down. He appeared younger than Kaufman, with a full soft-looking face and hooded eyes that seemed gentle if you were on his side of the aisle or cruel if you were an opponent. He was one of those committed party operatives who eschewed small talk and seemed to spend every breath discussing party affairs. It was Tom who raised the business of the Indiana redis-tricting.

'OK, listen, guys. Mike needs to hit the ground running and the main thing on our plate right now is Indiana. Mike, I don't expect you to know about the case – in fact, I sure as hell hope you don't, because we've been trying to keep the thing quiet – but it could be big for us. The problem is our guys who control the state legislature have been a little too darn smart and it looks like they've got caught with their pecker in someone's pocket, as LBJ used to say.'

Mike smiled at the image.

'What's the case about?'

'Well, I know as much about redistricting as the next guy, but this one's a can of worms,' Tom said. 'When you come in Monday you need to hook up with our general counsel, Roger Allan Moore – he's our top legal guy. Reagan rates him and the VP thinks the sun shines out of him. Roger will fill you in, but we need to act pretty quick to stop this getting out of hand.'

Mike's first full day at the Republican National Committee was spent sorting out keys and passes and accreditation for the Senate and the White House. He was fingerprinted by the Secret Service and had his photo taken a dozen times. He left a message with Roger Allan Moore's secretary to fix an appointment, but no reply had come through by the time he left in the evening.

The following day had seemed to be going the same way. He'd spent the morning visiting with the Republican leaders in the Senate and the House when suddenly the office was thrown into turmoil. Reports on CNN, the newly opened television news channel, were talking about some disturbance outside the Hilton Hotel, where the president had been making a speech to the Construction Trades Council. By 2.30 p.m. it had become clear that CNN had been covering the president's speech and their cameras had filmed him leaving the building. The footage showed Reagan smiling and waving, then jerking forward with a grimace before policemen and Secret Service agents rushed up to grab him and bundle him into his limo. Every time the images were repeated, the hysteria in the office calmed momentarily as people turned to watch, shaking heads and wincing as Reagan fell.

For the rest of the afternoon business was suspended and Mike found himself at a loss. The news wires reported that the president had been wounded by a bullet from a would-be assassin and rushed to George Washington University Hospital; three other people in his entourage had also been hit. Dallas and JFK were in everyone's mind. Mike's thoughts sped back to the time he had spent in the ER room of GWH and he felt his stomach contract: the awful, protracted death of David Carlin and now the imminent danger to the president folded into a single, sickening nightmare. By mid-afternoon, Mike had heard that a policeman and a Secret Service agent had been wounded and that the White House press secretary James Brady was hovering between life and death with a bullet in his brain. Washington was in a state of febrile uncertainty.

Things began to settle down only when the networks carried news that the president was conscious and apparently in good spirits. NBC reported that his first words to a worried Nancy were, 'Honey, I forgot to duck,' and an ER nurse who asked him if he was OK said she heard him whisper, 'All in all, I'd rather be in Philadelphia.' The jokes were feeble, but they brought tears of relief to Mike's eyes. Sitting in his office, staring out at the dome of the Capitol, he was lost in thought, wondering how the fate of a man he had long despised should now affect him so deeply, when the door opened and a tall, elegant figure slipped in.

'Ahm, hello.' The voice was patrician, refined New England. 'Roger Allan Moore. So sorry about all of this.' He gestured vaguely to the television set in the corner. 'Not the best way to welcome you to the RNC, I suspect.'

Mike was taken aback. Amidst the panic, Moore exuded an unruffled serenity that was almost breathtaking.

'So, first things first,' he was saying. 'I've spoken with the surgeon and Ron's out of danger. The bullet was a ricochet – hit the limo, then caught him under the left arm. Didn't explode – thank the Lord – but made a mess of his left lung and stopped an inch from his heart.'

Mike listened in amazement to what he was hearing. Moore was pacing across the carpet, six foot four, gaunt and slim, with a craggy face and protruding ears under coiffured grey hair. He looked around fifty, the picture of an English gentleman in his tweed suit, size-fourteen Oxfords and woollen socks, with a briar pipe that never seemed to leave his hand.

'Yes. Thank God,' Mike offered. 'Thank God the president is safe. I'm Michael Hess, by the way.'

Roger Allan Moore stooped and shook the proffered hand.

'Yes, indeed you are. Welcome. I would have come earlier, but I was caught in the constitutional wrangle. I'm sure *you* know all there is to know about the presidential succession protocol – I just wish Al Haig did! I had to tell him that in fact he is *not* in charge despite what he's been saying all over the networks. The slight drawback is that it's a little uncertain who actually is.' He chuckled and looked skywards. 'Ah well, it'll be sorted out in an hour or so when Bush gets back from Andrews.'

For Mike, the sudden sense of being so close to the epicentre of events shaping the nation's future was exhilarating. Six months ago he had been a constitutional lawyer with no prospect of a particularly distinguished future, and now he was discussing the fate of presidents with people who had responsibilities for the constitution and the exercise of power.

'I know you must be busy, Roger,' Mike said deferentially. 'Why don't we put a date in the diary for when all this calms down?'

But Moore waved his hand.

'My dear fellow, there's no need to stand on ceremony. Do please pop into my office whenever you like. Mark Braden and I always have a couple of whiskies to help the day go down – or at least I do, and he sips something or other. Come and join us tomorrow, will you?'

The feeling of being accepted into a world he had thought was beyond his reach swept over Mike with a gratifying warmth.

He felt absurdly nervous as he walked down the corridor the following evening. Roger was finishing some paperwork when he walked in, but he motioned for Mike to help himself to a drink. A few minutes later Mark Braden appeared. The RNC's deputy chief counsel was younger than Moore, sharply dressed, with a broad, friendly face and neatly trimmed beard.

'So you're the third musketeer, are you?' he said. 'We've been awaiting your arrival. The party's been chasing us to get on top of this redistricting strategy – they think it could make or break the next elections – and we've been needing a extra pair of hands. Things'll go quiet for a while with all the fuss over the president, but it looks like he's on the mend. Shame about Jim Brady, though – permanent brain damage is what they're saying.'

Moore had finished off his pile of papers and joined them with a whisky glass in one hand and a lit pipe in the other.

'Ahm yes, gentlemen. No rest for the wicked as my old mother used to say. Now I want to fill Michael in on the Indiana debacle and also explain the revenge we're plotting over the California districting.'

Sitting in the comfortable surroundings of the general counsel's office, sipping his single malt whisky, Mike savoured the sensation of having arrived. He listened to the talk of constitutional law and gerrymandering, the looming political confrontations and the Republican Party's battle plan, and he felt himself aching to be a part of it. He was being drawn into the mindset of the place in the same way a new foot soldier submerges his identity in the needs of his regiment: he may disagree with the army's goals, but he devotes himself to attaining them. From his first days at the RNC, Mike was fascinated with the intellectual challenge of fighting its electoral battles and determined to do what he could to entrench the Republicans in power.

A couple of setbacks arising from an infection and a bout of fever meant Ronald Reagan did not return to the Oval Office until the end of April 1981. He was given a standing ovation by the White House staff and sent a message of thanks to the party's officials for the way they had coped during his absence. At their evening meeting Roger Allan Moore read out the president's letter.

'I am so proud of the way you carried on,' it read. 'I don't think this city has ever seen such a team. I want to thank all of you for all you've done and for all your good wishes. I don't have the words to express my pride in all of you.'

Mike felt a lump in his throat and a surge of affection for the men who were now his co-workers, potentially his future friends.

The RNC's spring ball followed a couple of weeks later, and the atmosphere was one of relieved celebration: the narrowly avoided tragedy had left the Republicans shaken but doubly determined to push ahead with the political changes they had promised as well as the new conservatism on social questions. Mike took Susan to the party and introduced her to his colleagues. As they glided together across the dance floor, she scrutinized his face with concern.

'This is all wonderful, Mike, and your colleagues seem like . . . nice people. But I'm still a little, you know, *uneasy* about you working here. Do you really feel like this is where you belong?'

Mike laughed and squeezed her waist.

'I know what you mean. These are lovely guys, but they're pillars of a community we don't belong to – Ivy League, married, kids, and most of them born to a life of ease. You know, Roger owns an apartment in DC, a farm in Charlestown and a house on Beacon Hill that has twelve fireplaces!'

Susan frowned. 'Well, that's fine and dandy – let them be rich, that's their concern – but what about the gay thing, Mike? There's no way you can be open about that.'

Mike made a little flapping motion with an exaggeratedly limp wrist.

'Darling, I've no *idea* what you mean.'

But Susan was serious. 'The media would go to town on you, Mike: TOP OFFICIAL IN HOMOPHOBIC PARTY IS GAY. You know what they'd make of it.'

Mike gripped her tight and executed a neat swirl.

'Well, that's what I depend on you for, now isn't it?'

Susan laughed and dropped the subject.

'On a pleasanter note – I hope – how's the love life?' she asked. 'Still seeing that male model, you lucky thing? Or did you cast him aside like all the others?'

'Oh, you know,' he said. 'I'm still looking for Mr Goodbar, but having a bit of fun in the meantime.'

Mike suddenly didn't feel like talking about his love life. When the band struck up a tango, he pulled himself up to his full height and struck a theatrical pose. 'Madam,' he growled, 'shall we?'

Two weeks after the RNC's collective sigh of relief for the return of the president, the US Centers for Disease Control issued a report on five gay men in Los Angeles who were suffering from a rare form of pneumonia. The strain seemed resistant to antibiotics and the men's condition was not responding to any treatment. On 4 June a summary of the report was included in the White House's daily briefing pack because the National Institutes of Health were worried the disease was infectious and they were unable to trace how it was being passed on. The item was listed so far down the president's agenda that the meeting finished before he got to it.

TWO

1981

Pete Nilsson had seen the guy on the Metro as he rode to work each morning. After a few days he had taken to waiting on the platform and letting trains go by until the striking dark-haired man showed up. They had been introduced at a reception on Capitol Hill and he was sure the guy recognized him, but he refused to return Pete's glances and Pete was beginning to lose hope.

Pete was twenty-eight, tall and blond from his Swedish ancestry. He had been in a relationship for the past five years, but it had broken up a few months ago and he was missing the comfort of a steady partner. He was a nester by nature, and all the freedom of being single, all the opportunities for brief exhilaration and casual sex, could not make up for going home to an empty house in the evenings. He had come close to speaking to the man on the train a few times – one morning he had appeared with a lump of shaving cream behind his ear and Pete had had to struggle not to scoop it up with his finger – but he was put off by the man's distant attitude and apparent lack of interest.

As Washington baked in the first hot days of summer Mike threw himself into his work and put his personal life on hold. He met people at parties, got chatting, sometimes swapped details, but no real friends were made: he may have been lonely, but he didn't have time to notice it. In one of the gay bars on a Monday night after work he'd struck up a conversation with a local couple who'd invited him to their house-warming party the following weekend. They'd given Mike their address and he'd stuffed it in his pocket.

The following Sunday he was going through his wardrobe when the scribbled note fell from a pair of jeans. It was a Georgetown address, very classy. *What the hell*, he thought. He spent a long time choosing his clothes – he was feeling nervous and excited about the party and nothing seemed quite right – so it was already half past midnight by the time he settled on an outfit.

The couple giving the party were old friends of Pete Nilsson, and as Mike was hurling shirts around his bedroom Pete was wrapping a house-warming gift he'd chosen that afternoon. A week earlier he had broken his ankle in a volleyball game and was hobbling with a cast on his leg, but he'd decided to go anyway and arrived at one in the morning to find the house overflowing with people, music and noise.

His hosts made a fuss of him and installed him with a drink on a sofa in the living room. He couldn't help wondering what the neighbours must be thinking of their new arrivals: half-naked men were coming and going from the bedrooms in a constant stream, and groups were shouting and yelling in the backyard. Pete was enjoying the party and the attention he was getting because of his leg, but his mood was deflated when he recognized his former long-term lover among the revellers.

Patrice was a Frenchman, a little older than Pete, and they had met in Aix-en-Provence when Pete was studying there after university. Patrice was from an aristocratic French family and his mannerisms and way of dressing were decidedly effeminate – looking at him now, Pete was amazed that he could ever have loved such an effete guy. But Patrice was edging his way through the room towards him and waving cheerily.

'Peter,' he called out, 'I want you to meet my fiancée!' With a flourish he introduced an attractive young American woman. Pete hardly knew what to say. Patrice was kissing her and she seemed happy, but Pete was taken aback. The guy already had a green card so it wasn't as if he needed to get married, and the thought of him in bed with a woman made Pete want to laugh out loud. He managed to congratulate the two of them and was about to say he needed to leave when the guy from the train walked in through the front door.

The following morning the Reagan White House got its first chance to tackle a problem that was destined to haunt it. The report from the Centers for Disease Control which the president had failed to read in the Oval Office had been passed instead to one of his domestic policy advisers. Gerry Hauer was a smart young law graduate from a tough area of Ohio. He had fought hard to get where he was and was keen to make an impression in the new administration, so he scanned the document in front of him to see if he could justify taking it back to the president. He made a disapproving face when he realized the new disease was largely confined to gay men – Hauer was about to be named chairman of the President's Working Group on the Family so he was on the lookout for material about degeneracy and perversion – but in the end he decided there was nothing to it and slid the report into his out tray.

Mike spent his morning at the office feeling strangely excited. He was meeting Pete Nilsson for dinner.

Mike had recognized Pete as soon as he'd walked into the party – handsome, svelte, muscular body. *It's that guy from the train who always looks at me.* The guy had beckoned to him. Mike had spotted the cast on his leg and the empty glass in his hand, and had fixed them both a drink. He'd held out a hand for the guy to shake, but to Mike's surprise and amusement Pete had raised an eyebrow and cocked his head to one side with a half-smile, ignoring the proffered handshake.

'You know, you're pretty rude. We were introduced at the reception on the Hill, but ever since then you've just looked straight through me.' To his own amazement, Mike had blushed. So *that* was where he'd recognized the guy from.

'Ah. You're the train guy.' He'd smiled.

'The train guy!' Pete had exclaimed with mock outrage. 'Is that all I am to you? The train guy . . .' He'd shaken his head in disbelief and knocked back some of his drink. Mike had studied his profile for a moment, then proffered something not far from an apology.

'I thought you were someone else. Someone who stole a boyfriend from me back in the day. But' – his voice had lowered – 'now I can see it wasn't you. I can see you are someone very different – someone very different indeed.'

Mike arrived at La Colline, a Republican haunt on Capitol Hill, five minutes early, but Pete was already sitting at the table, injured leg outstretched.

'Hi,' said Mike, smiling. Pete looked up at him and giggled.

'What's so funny?' asked Mike.

'Well, I decided not to wear loafers because I figured you'd be so smartly dressed I'd feel embarrassed about them – or about *it*.' He lifted the black leather shoe on his unbroken foot. Mike was dressed in a button-down shirt and penny loafers, and he looked down at himself with a deprecating grin.

'Well, I guess we're Lady and the Tramp, then.'

There was a sexual pull between them – they both felt it – but neither was sure what the other intended. For long sections of the meal the conversation could have been a business discussion between two straight acquaintances. Mike spoke about the work he was doing for the RNC and the redistricting cases they were trying to tie up before next year's mid-term elections; Pete talked about his job at the Food Marketing Institute – it paid well, he said, but he regarded it as a temporary stop on a journey to bigger things. Mike told him a little about his family background and his sister in Florida; Pete recounted his own peripatetic youth, dragged all over the world by a father with a successful military career that took him from Hawaii to Japan to Holland and finally to California. His father's family was Swedish, his mother was French, and he had come to DC to take a degree in international affairs and marketing at GWU. His sister also lived in the District and they were both keen swimmers and horse riders.

Mike and Pete discovered the coincidences – their close relationships with their sisters, their overlapping year at GWU, their birthdays four months apart (Pete was the younger). By the end of the meal they had drunk a couple of bottles of wine and their inhibitions were evaporating.

'I, uh . . . I only live ten minutes' walk from here,' Pete said.

Mike pointed at his broken foot. 'Ten minutes for me, maybe, but half an hour for you, Hopalong!'

They laughed. Mike flagged down a cab and they rode in comfortable silence. Outside a small townhouse ten blocks from the Capitol Pete said, 'I need to let you know – I share the place with a roommate, and he's a Democrat, press secretary for Senator Simon, actually, but he's gay himself and you don't need to worry about anything. He's a good guy.'

Mike squeezed Pete's hand and helped him up the steps, thinking how excited the guy looked, how different this all seemed from the quick trashy fade-to-lust of his usual dates.

Pete's housemate chatted for a couple of minutes before making a show of yawning and excusing himself to go to bed. Left alone, they embraced. Both were experienced lovers and each knew what they wanted from the other.

In the morning Pete toasted a couple of waffles and they drank coffee until it was time to go to work. Mike said he could walk to the RNC, just a couple of blocks away, but Pete had to take the Metro up to K Street so they parted at the door. As he was leaving, Mike turned to look back.

'Come to my place Saturday night and I'll cook for you. I live in the Wyoming up on Columbia Avenue. Can you find it?'

As he strolled to the RNC building, he felt like leaping in the air.

THREE

1981

Mike had become fond of Roger Allan Moore – the guy was one of life's great characters and brought a touch of intellectual elegance and humour to their work. His professorial manner concealed a warm heart and sharp wit, and staff at the RNC had collected some of his pithiest aphorisms in a pamphlet that circulated like samizdat among the Republican faithful ('The Conservative's motto: "Don't just do something – stand there!"' 'Really important people don't carry walkie-talkies'; 'Prefer rogues to fools: rogues sometimes take a rest.') Roger was lovely, but he played his cards close to his chest.

Mike was nodding off over the morning's briefing papers, reliving the pleasures of his night with Pete, when the door opened and Roger entered.

'Ahm, Michael,' he said, 'I may have mentioned this – then again I may not – but the president is expecting us at 11.30 to run him through what we're proposing on redistricting. It's important for him to understand the significance it has for the party, and it's important for us to get the funding we need to do it. Can you be sure and come along? The car will pick us up around eleven.'

The Oval Office was busy: White House staffers were milling around two beige sofas on the huge rug in the centre of the room, a uniformed maid was distributing tea and coffee, and a knot of officials were waiting with papers for the president to sign. Reagan himself was reclining in a dark leather captain's chair behind the massive presidential desk, looking a little drawn but smiling and joking with the doctor who was trying to take his blood pressure. Roger Allan Moore nodded to Mike and Mark Braden to take a seat, and they waited in silence until James Baker, the White House chief of staff, called the meeting to order.

'Mr President, the RNC are here in force to see you. Roger you know of course, and he has the deputy chief counsel Mark Braden with him and also Michael Hess, who is our redistricting attorney. Roger, the floor is yours. We have a quarter-hour and then we need to go see the Teamsters before lunch.'

Reagan pulled a face about the Teamsters meeting and nodded for Roger to begin.

'Mr President, I'll, ahm, get straight to the point. Redistricting in the United States never used to be much of a deal. Electoral boundaries rarely ever changed. Then in 1965 we had the one-person, one-vote revolution and by the end of the sixties every state had redrawn its districts. Sadly for us, '65 happened to be a high-water mark for the Democrats so they were able to draw lines that were substantially to their advantage. And that was pretty much the reason why they remained in total political power through the late sixties and seventies. What we are trying to do is redress that injustice by using the legal process to undo the Democrats' partisan gerrymandering.'

Moore stopped and checked the president was following him.

'So, Mr President, we are setting up a redistricting division for which Michael Hess here will act as counsel. I understand the funding is close to being agreed and we are grateful for that. Now I just want to let you know there may be a few . . . surprises in store. For instance, we are planning on supporting a judicial case *against* our own people in Indiana. Ahm, you may know that we briefly held the balance of power in the state legislature and some of our guys up there took advantage to do a little gerrymandering of their own. The Democrats were furious, of course, and they brought a suit to get our gerrymander overturned. Now we are planning to support the Democrats in this, and you may be puzzled why we're doing so. Well, the answer is that the suit – it's known as Davis v. Bandemer, by the way – will, if successful, establish the principle that the courts *do* have the right to overturn gerrymanders under the Equal Protection Amendment. And once we've got that principle established, we know we can use it across the whole of the Democrats' own gerrymanders in all the other states of the Union! In fact, they did us a favour when they took our guys to court because with both parties supporting the action, the courts are pretty likely to grant it!'

Moore looked up with a QED sort of smile on his face.

'Now I'm telling you all this, Mr President, because I suspect there'll be quite a few angry voices in the party when they hear we're supporting the Democrats and the National Association for the Advancement of Colored People, and, ahm, they may try to get you to stop us doing it. So I just wanted you to know that if we succeed – and Mr Hess is a most competent expert in this field – then we could change the whole face of politics in this country. We could undo the electoral bias that has favoured our opponents and kept us on the sidelines for decades. We haven't controlled the US Congress, the Senate and the House for so many years that everyone assumes it's an automatic Democrat privilege to be in charge. But if you give us the go-ahead, Mr President, I believe we can change all that and start a revolution they won't be able to stop!'

Moore had become unusually animated in the course of his speech, and after he finished he was gripped by a fit of coughing he seemed unable to control.

The president got up from his seat to pat Roger on the back and offer him a glass of water.

'Well done, Roger. You can be my 007 any day,' Reagan joked. 'And as far as the funding goes, by the way, you got it!'

In the car on the way back from the White House Moore continued to cough sporadically, and at one point Mike thought he saw flecks of blood spattering his linen handkerchief.

FOUR

1981

Pete Nilsson spent forty-eight hours wondering what to do about the cast on his leg and eventually decided to saw it off. It should have stayed on for two more weeks, but he was impatient to meet Michael on equal terms.

Mike was in the kitchen when Pete arrived. He kissed Pete, gave him a drink and sat him down with Bob McMullen while he finished cooking the John Dory and roast potatoes. Mike was wearing light-blue jeans, very tight with the cuffs rolled, and a bowling shirt; the combination, Pete thought, gave him a kind of 1950s James Dean look that he found very sexy. The meal was superb and Pete gushed with compliments. Bob laughed as Mike flushed with pleasure.

'You *do* realize that is the *only* thing he can cook, don't you? We can't go praising Mr Wonderful too much or he'll think we *all* have to fall down at his feet!'

Pete laughed, but he was so in awe of Michael that anything he did seemed just perfect. Mike looked across at Pete and smiled. *This could be it*, he thought suddenly. *I could be happy like this all the time.*

'Right,' announced Bob, rising from his seat, 'that was delicious, Mike. Thanks. Look, you know I'd stay and help clear and all that . . .' He walked out, slamming the door.

Mike eyed Pete. 'I made dessert, but—'

'It can wait, right?' Pete whispered. 'Why don't you show me the bedroom?'

They woke late on Sunday morning, and Pete suggested they go round to his friends in Georgetown for brunch. A crowd of guys were already there when they arrived and they walked in to a chorus of wolf whistles. Pete was delighted their partnership was already the talk of the group.

For Christmas and New Year they rented a cottage outside of Shepherdstown, West Virginia, with snow on the ground and a log fire in the living room. They tramped the hills in the dazzling winter sunshine and skated on the frozen Potomac. In the evenings Mike made mulled wine and chose the music to suit their mood, then they switched off the cassette player and lay in each other's arms drinking in the silence. On Christmas Eve they went carol singing to their neighbours in the farm up the road and were invited in. At midnight they said they must go, but the invitation to return the following day for Christmas dinner was irresistible.

Twelve people came to Christmas dinner, among them an elderly couple introduced as Mr and Mrs Shepherd. Henry Shepherd was ruddy-faced and jovial; his wife was a southern belle who had grown up raising orchids in Charleston; and their daughter Sally, who was in her early thirties, was beautiful.

After a few glasses of wine Mike was feeling festive. 'So, some coincidence, huh? You guys being Shepherds and this being Shepherdstown. Part of the reason you moved here?'

To his surprise, the whole table burst into laughter.

'Well, to tell you the truth,' Sally said with a shy smile, 'we were here before Shepherdstown was. We're the eleventh generation of Shepherds – it was my great-great-whatever who founded the place.'

'Yes, yes,' barked Henry Shepherd. 'Thomas Shepherd arrived here 1734. He built Bellevue, the house our family has lived in for two centuries.'

'It's a beautiful house,' Mrs Shepherd said softly, smiling at Mike and Pete. 'You must come see it sometime.'

'The Shepherds are the heart and soul of Shepherdstown society,' another neighbour said.

'Oh, come on, George, stop it,' Sally grinned.

'Quite true, quite true,' remarked Henry. 'And while the rest of the world is hell-bent on tearing itself apart, what we have in Shepherdstown is a real community. Neighbourliness,' he stressed, tapping his fork handle against the table. 'Loyalty. Courtesy.'

Pete raised his glass. 'To Shepherdstown and community spirit! I can't thank you enough for having us here.'

'Well, well,' Henry rumbled. 'Pleasure to have such fine boys in the neighbourhood – eh, Sally?' He turned to his daughter and gave her a nudge. Sally blushed.

Mrs Shepherd put a hand on her husband's arm.

'Now, Henry,' she murmured affectionately.

Mike locked eyes with Sally and both burst into giggles.

Gerry Hauer had spent his Christmas break with his family, but he was a man who took his work home with him. As soon as he returned to the White House he asked his secretary what she had done with the report from Los Angeles that had come in a while back about the mysterious pneumonia outbreak, but she said it must have been filed away somewhere and she couldn't find it.

Hauer shrugged and picked up the phone to his boss, William Bennett.

'Bill,' he said, 'have you seen the December issue of the *New England Journal of Medicine*? No? Well, I read it over Christmas. There's a study of this new homosexual disease they've been reporting in California and now in New York as well. Seems they've documented forty-one cases and eight of them have already died. Let's see . . .' He flicked through the pages. 'OK, here we are: "Twenty-six of the cases presented with Kaposi's sarcoma, an uncommonly reported malignancy in the United States . . . persistent diarrhoea, skin or mucous membrane lesions, often dark blue to violaceous plaques and nodules" – sorry about the yucky details – "necrotizing toxoplasmosis of the central nervous system, candidiasis, cryptococcal meningitis . . ."

Ah, yes, here's the bit: "The reason for the appearance of these unusual illnesses remains unclear. It is likely that sexually active, young homosexual men are frequently reinfected through exposure to semen and faeces of sexual partners. Such reinfection – before recovery from the cellular immune dysfunction induced by previous infection – could conceivably lead to the overwhelming immunodeficiency we are witnessing. All surviving patients have continued to have a severe wasting syndrome . . . " and blah, blah, blah. Can you imagine, Bill? It sounds like they're giving each other the plague by sticking their dongs up each other's you-know-whats . . .'

At the end of January Mike met up for lunch with Susan Kavanagh, bursting with stories about the two weeks he had spent living with Pete over Christmas. She smiled at the enthusiasm in his voice.

'Michael Hess! Correct me if I'm wrong, but I do believe you might be in love.'

Mike made a 'What, *me?*' kind of face and pulled out a photo of the two of them together.

'What do you think? He's cute, isn't he? Pretty sporty too – plays volleyball, goes swimming, loves horse riding – he's got a body to die for!'

Susan grinned and wiggled her eyebrows.

'He's *gorgeous*, Mike! But this is more than just a physical attraction, right?'

'Well, *he's* head over heels for sure!' He laughed at his own cockiness. 'And, you know, I'm feeling good about things too. Living with him out in West Virginia made me think maybe we could be together for the long term. I'm . . . I'm actually thinking of suggesting we move in together.'

'That's great, Mike. I think that's great. I guess you just need to be sure it doesn't get spoiled like it did with Mark. I still see him from time to time, you know.'

'Oh,' he said shortly. 'And how is he?'

'Well, he's about to graduate from law school – got a good job offer in Philadelphia.' Susan toyed with her food. 'I think he's over you now, Mike, but he was cut up at the time. He's got a new man in his life – Ben Kronfeld. Works for the government; he's very nice. But what I wanted to say . . . You're not still seeing that guy up in Manhattan, are you – the one who caused all the trouble?'

'Harry Chapman? I'm not seeing him, no. But I got a letter from him a couple of weeks back, and . . .' He hesitated. 'I think I maybe should write him. He says he's pretty sick with some crazy thing called Kaposi's sarcoma.'

FIVE

1982

The funding for the Republican Party's redistricting division had come through and Michael Hess was named to lead it. He had been working for the RNC for just a year and had risen so quickly he was already considered a veteran. Junior staff were now reporting to him and his opinion on issues of constitutional law was sought and quoted.

Mike, Roger Allan Moore and Mark Braden were regarded as the Republicans' swashbuckling musketeers, battling for the party's interests in courts around the country and constructing increasingly ingenious legal arguments to fight for its electoral rights. They met up each evening for drinks and vied like competitive teenagers, revelling in the intellectual challenge of finding answers to whatever their opponents might throw at them.

Mike still kept his sexuality a secret. Roger and Mark were family men, with photos of their kids on their desks, but they asked Mike no awkward questions and made no reference to his private life. All Mike's immediate colleagues were educated, civilized people with no personal sympathy for the homophobic paranoia the party was stirring up in the country at large. At this level in the leadership it was understood that the campaigns against abortion and equal rights for women and homosexuals were simply useful things to do – they kept the religious right happy and they appealed to the redneck bigots.

Mike saw the hypocrisy and told himself he understood it: the guys making the party platform had only one goal – to get Republicans elected wherever and whenever possible – and if a policy which victimized minority groups brought in majority votes, then it was going to be adopted. Apart from a small clique of extremist true believers and fanatics, the operatives who ran the Republican Party were largely pragmatists concerned with getting re-elected.

One morning in March Roger Allan Moore knocked on Mike's door and said he had had a message from Gerry Hauer.

'What he wants, it seems, is, ahm, a copy of the District's antisodomy legislation. I know you're busy with Davis v. Bandemer, of course, but I wondered if you wouldn't mind . . .'

Mike looked up at the tall figure prowling round his office and felt a surge of affection. Roger could have located the legislation himself, but this was his tactful way of alerting Mike that something was afoot that he should be aware of.

'Ahm, yes,' Roger continued. 'Seems the White House have been talking to Reverend Falwell and his, ahm, Moral Majority people about this and, you know—'

'I do, Roger. Thank you for giving me—'

'Yes, yes,' Roger cut in. There was evidently something he wanted to convey and he was having difficulty expressing it. 'It's to do with the repeal campaign, of course. The legislation's a nonsense – leftover from the puritans in the seventeenth century; been a godsend for blackmailers and the police wanting to coerce gay men for far too long; bosses using sodomy charges to fire people. Quite despicable. It darn well should be repealed, but I don't think it's going to be . . .'

Mike looked up at Roger and tried to read the meaning in his eyes.

'No. Ahm, unlikely to be repealed, because the Reverend has been agitating against it and it looks like the administration are going to go along with him.'

Mike nodded and this time Roger let him speak.

'Thank you, Roger. That's useful to know. I'll get the legislation out and send it to Mr Hauer.'

Roger was about to leave when a spasm of violent coughing gripped him. Mike rushed to help and saw blood in the corners of his mouth.

'My God, Roger, are you OK? What's wrong with you?'

'It's nothing. Nothing at all.' Roger stifled his coughing. 'But I just wonder, you know, are we all a little guilty – you and I included – of blindly devoting ourselves to keeping the party in power, and never pausing to think exactly *what* we're keeping in power? Remind me to talk to you about Chaim Rumkowski one day, will you.'

And with that he disappeared through the door.

In the summer of 1982 Pete Nilsson was offered a job in the marketing department of the National Restaurants Association. His contract with his former employers obliged him to take two months' time out before beginning his new position, and he decided to spend it with his family on the West Coast. It would be the longest period Pete and Mike had been apart for many months' and it came at a moment when they were both thinking seriously about their relationship. Just before Pete left, Mike asked if he would like to move in with him at the apartment in the Wyoming Building when he came back. Pete tried to contain his excitement.

'That's a possibility, Mike. Definitely a possibility. But, you know, I'd be kind of sad to give up my place on the Hill. You know what? We both loved Shepherdstown, didn't we? If you go find us a cottage out there in West Virginia, then how about I give up my place in DC and we split our lives between weekdays in your apartment and week-ends in the country?' The pretence at playing it cool had gone now. 'It would be so great, Mike. I could get some horses and we can have dogs . . . and think of all the parties we could have out there. We'd be like local squires inviting people to our country estate.'

Pete sounded so much like an excited little boy that Mike couldn't help laughing. He resolved to find the most beautiful cottage in West Virginia, with roses round the door.

While Pete was away Mike travelled out to Shepherdstown and met with Sally Shepherd. In the coffee shop on German Street he explained, cautiously, that he and Pete were a couple.

Sally laughed. 'Don't you think I know that? We're not all country bumpkins out here – or not all as naive as my dear old father, anyway.'

'Well, it's not something we really want to broadcast, you know.' Mike fell silent as the waitress appeared with a refill for their coffee. 'It can be difficult in the world I work in. But anyway, we really loved the time we spent here and we're thinking of looking for a little place to buy. I don't suppose you happen to—'

Sally didn't even let him finish his sentence. 'The perfect place! I know the perfect place for you. There's a cottage near the estate that's vacant and you can have it for a song – or half a song! How does that sound?'

'That . . . sounds . . . *marvellous.*'

Bellevue, the big house where Sally lived with her parents a mile out of town, was an old colonial-style mansion sitting atop an escarpment surrounded by tall trees, with a beautiful southern portico and wrought-iron balconies. The whole estate was thickly wooded and lay in a bend of the Potomac. The cottage was much more modest, but it had four rooms and breathtaking views down to the water. It was far enough away from Bellevue to be private, but close enough not to feel cut off.

Mike loved it at once and gave Sally a delighted hug.

'*Behave* yourself, Mr Hess!' she giggled, hugging him back. 'Or my father will be hiring the church and the hotel for the wedding reception before you can say, "I do."'

That evening they had supper with Sally's parents, who were enchanted by the idea of the boys moving into the cottage.

'Leave it to me,' declared Henry; 'I know everyone in Shepherdstown. I'll get you the best bargain you ever had in your life!'

A week later Mike flew out to California to spend a weekend with Pete and his sister Diane at the Nilsson family cabin in the mountains near Lake Tahoe. He brought photos of the Shepherdstown cottage, and the three of them spent the evening marvelling at the good fortune of finding such a wonderful place to live and at how fabulous life would be once Pete and Mike were settled there. The cottage came with a range of outbuildings – a hayloft and a silo and enough space to stable horses – and it was fifty minutes by train from DC to Harper's Ferry, followed by an easy twelve-mile drive.

'. . . so we can keep the old Fiat at the Harper's Ferry train station, go out to the cottage every Friday after work and get the early train back on Monday morning,' Mike announced.

They chatted for hours that night.

'So, Mr Michael Hess, tell us about this Irish ancestry you mentioned,' Diane said.

Mike stretched back on the sofa and put his hands behind his head. Pete poured them all some whisky and Mike told the tale of Marge and Doc, how they had wanted a little girl back in the 1950s and how Marge had come to Ireland for Mary.

'. . . but when Marge came to see her in the orphanage, Mary only talked to this little boy named Anthony. Whenever Mary was around, Anthony was around; if Anthony wasn't there, Mary would withdraw into herself. So Marge got to know Anthony as well, without ever really thinking about it. Then the night Marge was leaving she went into the nursery to say goodbye to Mary and Mary was sleeping, but little Anthony was standing in his crib and she said goodbye to him and started walking out. And he's saying to her the whole time, "Bye-bye. Bye-bye. Bye-bye." She turned around and looked at him waving in his crib and went right to the telephone in the convent and said, "Doc, can I bring back two of them?"'

Pete looked at his sister and saw she had tears in her eyes.

'Do you remember anything about the place?' she asked.

'Well, I once went back, actually, and there were places I definitely remembered. I remember the nursery; I remember this hall or that staircase . . . but nothing about my mother, and that's pretty tough.'

At the end of the evening, Pete asked his sister what she thought of Mike.

'He's lovely, Pete, and I like him a lot, but that's some sad story about Ireland, isn't it? He's . . . He seems like a pretty complicated guy.'

Pete nodded. 'Yeah, he's cut up about not being able to find his mother, so I think he pictures Ireland as some kind of lost paradise he's been expelled from. I think it torments him but it gives him his security too. He's never really felt like a Hess, so Ireland is this unattainable, wonderful thing out there that he can wrap around him like a warm blanket . . .'

Two days later, Mike and Pete agreed they would buy the cottage. It was an unspoken confirmation that now they were partners and committed for the long term. At the airport in San Francisco they hugged and kissed and cried.

'I love you, Mike,' Pete whispered. 'I don't think I ever said that to anyone before.'

'I love you, too, Pete. I want to be with you and live with you and grow old with you.'

In the airport terminal Mike bought a copy of the *Bay Area Reporter*, a San Francisco gay newspaper. He opened it on the plane but the man sitting next to him in the business suit that reeked of cigars kept looking over his shoulder, so he put it away until the guy fell asleep. The front page carried an article that Mike read from start to finish with a growing sense of alarm.

> A baffling and often deadly sickness is claiming hundreds of lives in the gay community. Young, otherwise healthy gay men are dying of diseases their immune systems would normally see off. But something is allowing these innocuous infections to overwhelm them.
>
> The new disease has a nightmarish quality – fungi grow round its victims' fingernails, once handsome faces sag with lesions – and it has no name: physicians in San Francisco sign death certificates with FUO (fever of unknown origin), but elsewhere they speak of KSOI (Kaposi's sarcoma and opportunistic infections) or GRID (gay related immune deficiency);

the latest issue of the *New York Magazine* has called it The Gay Plague.

As Larry Kramer says, those who have been stricken do not appear to have done anything that many gay men haven't done at one time or another. We're appalled this is happening to them and terrified it could happen to us.

It's easy to become frightened that one of the many things we've done or taken over the past years may be all it takes for a cancer to grow inside of us.

But this is our disease and we must take care of each other and ourselves.

Mike caught the Washington Flyer from Dulles Airport to downtown DC and the Metro up to Dupont. On the table in the living room Bob McMullen had left Mike's mail in a neat pile. Inside a large envelope with the logo of a New York law firm he found another envelope labelled in Harry Chapman's distinctive handwriting: '*To Michael Hess – to be mailed only after my death.*'

SIX

1982

The house-warming party Mike and Pete threw at the cottage made a stir in Washington's gay community. It was the end of August 1982 and the weather was welcoming – a stroke of good fortune for the 300 young men who arrived in Shepherdstown by car, bus, bike and cab because the hotels for miles around had been booked up weeks before and most of them would be sleeping in tents. The party started on a Friday night and lasted until Sunday. They hired a DJ from New York and set up two walls of speakers in a field, with hay bales marking out an impromptu dance floor that stayed floodlit throughout the night. Mike and Pete agreed to invite only gay buddies – the presence of work colleagues or straight friends would have been inhibiting – so the atmosphere was one of relaxed sexual indulgence. Those who had hotel rooms shuttled back and forth with various different partners, and those who did not would disappear into the surrounding woods or the tents which stood in the adjoining meadow.

An observer might have thought the legion of America's gilded youth had pitched its camp here, striking boys wandering in skimpy shorts and Speedos through the feather grass down to the water. On Sunday a dozen of them remained, lying on the hay bales in the warm evening air. As night came Mike sang 'Danny Boy', quietly at first, then letting his voice rise clear and loud into the darkness. Pete said the night made him think of Baudelaire's sensuous traveller embarking on his voyage to the realm of luxury and love: 'How sweet it is to live in the land of love, love until death, where the world falls asleep in a warm glow of light and ships sail the oceans to satisfy your slightest desires. *Là, tout n'est qu'ordre et beauté, / Luxe, calme et volupté.*'

Pete's French was good, but another voice rose from the shadows, a voice both familiar and unidentified.

'Baudelaire also wrote, "The island of Venus is no more,"' said the voice.

The sweet fair isle of secrets and flowers which filled our minds with love and languor is become a barren rock, where on a three-armed gibbet ferocious birds peck open the ripening corpse of a hangèd man whose heavy intestines fall down along his thighs and sharp beaks castrate him like razors. Ridiculous hanged man, your sufferings are mine! At the sight of your dangling limbs I feel the bitter river of my sorrows rise up like vomit to my teeth. O Lord, give me the courage to contemplate without disgust my lacerated body and poor infected soul!

A week later the nameless dread was given a name: a bulletin from the Centers for Disease Control in September 1982 contained the first reference to acquired immune deficiency syndrome (AIDS), and shortly afterwards the *Wall Street Journal* reported that non-homosexuals were also among the sick: NEW, OFTEN-FATAL ILLNESS IN HOMO-SEXUALS TURNS UP IN WOMEN, HETEROSEXUAL MALES.

The plague was no longer confined to a community the straight world could isolate and condemn, and gay men were blamed for endangering all of society with 'their' deadly disease. The stigma of AIDS opened the floodgates of poison: Patrick Buchanan of the Moral Majority said homosexuals had declared war on nature and nature was exacting awful retribution; Jerry Falwell said AIDS was God's judgement on a society that did not live by His rules.

In December 1982 the CDC reported that three heterosexual haemophiliacs had died from AIDS-related infections. They had had no homosexual contact but all had received Factor VIII concentrates, a transfusion product made by pooling blood from hundreds of donors. The realization that AIDS could be transmitted through the transfer of contaminated blood spread panic. Falwell seized on people's fears by telling a Moral Majority rally, 'gay men are going out of their way to donate blood three times as often as ordinary folks because they know they're going to die and they want to take as many people with them as they can'.

The White House remained silent, and its silence was taken as a go-ahead to the preachers of hate. In the anti-gay hysteria the campaign to repeal the DC sodomy laws fell at the first hurdle and Republican Party conventions in several states added another plank to their platforms – that homosexuals should be denied the social, political and economic rights guaranteed to others.

SEVEN

1983

On a Saturday afternoon in May 1983 Mike and Pete were in Shepherdstown when Mary called, sounding alarmed. Marge had been having back trouble on and off since her first operation in 1966 and the doctors had recommended she go in again to have some spurs of bone removed. It was a routine procedure and Doc had consulted his colleagues to see which hospital had the best record, eventually deciding on Mayo Clinic up in Rochester, Minnesota, not far from the Hesses' summer vacation cottage.

Marge had been admitted on Mother's Day, 8 May, but Mary was ringing to say there was some bad news: routine pre-operation tests had revealed a spot on her left lung that the doctors thought might be cancerous, and they had decided to operate on that instead of the bone spurs. Doc was in Minnesota on his own, and since it now looked like Marge's treatment would be more complicated and last longer than expected, he had asked if any of the children could go up and help him out. Mary wanted to go, but she was having trouble finding someone to look after Nathan.

'Don't worry,' Mike said at once. 'You stay where you are; I'll go on the next flight I can get onto. Do you know when they're planning to operate?'

'Well, tomorrow,' Mary replied glumly. 'And Mom'll probably be in for two weeks or more.'

*

At Mayo Clinic Mike found Doc in the waiting room smoking a cigar. He steeled himself.

'Hey, Pop.'

Doc shook his son's hand.

'Michael,' he grunted.

'How is she?' Mike asked.

'Well . . . the operation went OK, it seems. She's in bed now, resting. She seems pretty well, all things considered. You know your mother. She won't complain to nobody.'

They visited her that afternoon and found her in remarkably good spirits. The nurses said she was a model patient, calm and focused on making a full recovery. The X-rays showed the surgery had removed the tumour, so the goal of the coming weeks would be recuperation and physiotherapy to get her fit and mobile.

Relieved, Mike returned the same evening to sit with Marge as she drifted in and out of sedated sleep. Alone at her bedside in the quiet half-light, he gazed at the woman who had changed his life, reliving the events of the childhood she had given him. Without her he would never have known America, never have risen to the position he held at the heart of the world's most powerful nation; above all, he would never have met the man who had brought him happiness and with whom he planned to spend the rest of his days. He squeezed Marge's sleeping hand.

'Thank you, Mom,' he whispered. 'Thank you for everything.'

Pete was pleased to hear from Mike that Tom and Stevie Hess were on their way to relieve him at their mother's bedside. If all went well, Mike said, he could be back home in a few days.

'The main thing is it looks like she's going to be fine. But you know, Pete, it's amazing how it makes you think. I just sit there at her bedside and I remember everything. She's been a good mom to me and Mary, but' – he hesitated – 'there are so many things I need to ask her, you know? Just in case something happens to her.'

Four days went by and the doctors said Marge was making excellent progress. The nurses were getting her back on her feet, walking her slowly up and down the ward. Mike, Doc, Tom and Stevie felt confident enough to go out for lunch, but when they returned Marge's bed was empty and unmade, and when Doc asked at the nurses' station no one seemed to know where she was.

Mike looked around and saw the bathroom door was closed. He knocked softly.

'Mom?'

No answer.

'*Mom?*' The door was locked from the inside.

Mike ran to the desk and demanded a key.

'I'm coming in, Mom, OK?'

The door opened a crack, but something inside was blocking the way.

The door yielded slightly when he pushed but not enough to get through.

'*Mom?*' he called again.

She was wedged against the door, slumped on the floor.

He eased the door forward and felt something shift on the other side.

'Mom, can you hear me? Mom? Marge? I'm coming in for you. Everything's fine; you just fell. It's gonna be fine, Mom. OK, Mom?'

Mike groaned when he saw her: she was crumpled on the floor and a stream of blood trickled across the tiles. He picked her up in his arms and was amazed by how light she was. Staggering out of the bathroom into the ward, he slipped on the polished floor but managed to keep Marge aloft in his arms even as he jolted painfully to his knees. The nurses took Marge from him, bruised and barely breathing with a gash in the side of her head from her fall, and lifted her into bed.

When the doctor came from her bedside, his face was grim. 'It's bad news, I'm afraid. Her pulse is faint. For all intents and purposes she's in a coma. We'll have to carry out a scan, but I fear there may be brain damage.'

Doc clasped his palms to his face and sank into a chair. 'Marge, Marge, where are you?' he was sobbing. 'Don't leave me, Marge!'

Mike turned away.

Stevie tried to comfort Doc but he leapt up angrily to harangue the hospital staff. 'What in God's name were you thinking about?' he yelled. 'Why the hell did you let a fragile post-op patient go to the bathroom alone? And when she was in there, why the hell did no one come and get her out? I'm a doctor, you know. I'll sue this goddam clinic for every cent it has!'

Tom and Stevie took their father by the arm and led him away. For the next two days Marge hovered between life and death. Mary flew up at once, but Marge was comatose and did not respond to voices or the touch of hands. The results of the scan came back and the doctor said they indicated severe damage to the brain stem. He took Doc and the children to a consulting room and explained that Marge was being kept alive on a ventilator.

'I'm afraid the outlook is not good. Her injuries mean her chances of coming out of the coma are infinitesimal. She is unlikely to survive without the machine she is attached to, and if she stays on it she will likely be in what we call a persistent vegetative state, or PVS.' He paused and his voice grew very quiet. 'I am sorry to have to ask you this question, but you will need to decide whether or not you wish the ventilator to be switched off.'

Doc rose angrily to his feet, but the children calmed him down.

Mike turned to the doctor. 'Look, we're gonna need some time to talk about this.'

In the end they all agreed it would be cruel to keep Marge artificially alive, but Doc was adamant that if she had to die, she must first be taken 'back home' to Florida. When they explained this to the hospital administrator, they discovered that the clinic would not sign the papers for her to be released while she was still attached to the ventilator. Doc was furious.

'So that we can't sue you for negligent release if she dies?' he snarled. 'Well, let me tell you I already have so much I can throw at you that we're gonna sue your ass anyway. Your staff are to blame for what happened and there's no way you're gonna get away with it!'

The stand-off continued for three days. On the fourth day Doc hired a private jet with a nurse and doctor, arranging for it to be at Rochester Municipal Airport the following morning. But the hospital administrator continued to refuse to sign.

In the end it was Mary who settled it.

'You know what?' she said, her voice trembling. 'Tomorrow morning there's going to be an airplane at the airport and I want my mother put in an ambulance, and I want her taken to the airport with my father, and I want them to be able to fly out together tomorrow. Do you have any objections to that? Because if you do, I'm gonna have something to say about that right now.'

In the face of Mary's indignation and heartache, the administrator signed the release form. A week later in Florida the family unhooked Marge's ventilator. She died on 2 June.

Doc was angry and confused: the sudden loss of the wife on whom he had depended for all practical matters had left him wounded in the world.

Marge's death was traumatic for everyone, but the shared sorrow brought Mike and Mary together again. Sitting on the porch in the Florida sunshine waiting for the day of the funeral, they chatted about their lives.

'Nathan, well, he's just changed my life, Mikey. I know it sounds sappy, but I *live* for him. He's just . . . He's everything to me. I realize that even more now, with Mom gone.'

'Yeah? And still doing well in school?'

'He's the smartest eleven-year-old *I've* ever seen – since you, at least.' Mary laughed. 'And what about you? What's making your world go round? You seem different now – more settled . . . more *yourself*. I don't know. You seem happy.'

Mike looked at the ground and smiled, unsure of what to say. Mary shifted a little.

'Do you . . . do you mind if I ask you a question, Mikey?'

'Go ahead,' he said.

'Well, ever since you bought that place out in West Virginia, Doc's been asking me who exactly Pete is. He just says, "So who is this guy that Mike lives with?" and I don't really know what to tell him.'

She wished she'd said it better – something to make him want to confide in her – but Mike took her hand anyway.

'You know, I've been meaning to tell you, Mary – I should have told you a while ago – Pete and I are partners.'

Mary looked at him and blushed. 'You mean like sexual partners, Mikey? Lovers?'

'Hey, don't say it like that, Sis! It's not so bad, is it? That we love each other, I mean.'

'I'm not saying it's bad, Mike,' Mary said quickly. 'I'm really happy if you're happy, you know that. You're my brother and I love you whatever. I just – you know – all this in the papers about AIDS and stuff . . . It makes me worried for you.'

Mike nodded and looked serious.

'I know, Mary. It's a terrible thing and no one's doing anything about it except yell and curse at gay people and talk nonsense about the wrath of God. Society's pretty cockeyed when it comes to stuff like that. People listen to whoever shouts the loudest.'

Mary asked the question that Mike had been asking for months. 'But Mikey, how come the government isn't talking about it? You know, telling people what's causing all the sickness and telling them how to avoid it and stuff? Is there nothing you can do in your job to make them tackle it, Mike? *Someone* has to talk sense, don't they?'

Mike shifted and looked away. 'I think the problem is Reagan depends way too much on the Moral Majority or whatever stupid name they give themselves. He can't rock the boat, and he's got a bunch of conservatives around him, so even if he wanted to say something or do something, it gets blocked.'

But Mary was not going to let it drop. 'Sure, I mean, don't like go and encourage people to be gay or anything, but at least explain how to avoid catching it. That would help everyone, wouldn't it? Is there nothing you could do to get them to do that?'

Mike said nothing. The question simply had no answer.

'Anyway, Mikey,' Mary said, 'it's you I'm worried about. You don't know anyone who's got AIDS, do you?'

'No . . . No, I don't.'

'Well, that's the main thing. I guess you don't want Doc to know about any of this, do you?'

'God, no!' Mike exclaimed. 'I always thought one day I could tell Marge – I think she would have understood – but Doc's such a . . . such a . . . well . . . And the tragic thing is it's too late to tell Marge anything now.'

EIGHT

1983–4

Mike returned to Washington, still grieving, still angry. His mother's death seemed senselessly random in a world that turned on the whim of chance. He blamed the hospital and he blamed himself. When Pete tried to comfort him he snapped.

'Don't tell me it's not my fault! That's too damned easy. Everyone looks the other way; no one takes responsibility!' He paused, sensed the antagonism in his voice and apologized. 'Sorry, Pete, it's my guilty conscience speaking. Not for Marge, though God knows that's bad enough. It's all the stuff I see going on around me every day, you know, in the administration. I never do anything about anything and I guess everybody else just looks the other way too. I keep telling myself, if *I* don't stand up and do something, then who on earth will?'

Pete was surprised. 'What do you mean, Mike?'

'I mean if I keep on keeping quiet – pretending to be straight and ignoring what's going on – then I must be responsible for what's going on. I see all the briefings, you know. There are 4,000 AIDS cases now and over a thousand dead, but every time someone suggests spending money to deal with the thing, the zealots jump in and block it because it would "reward homosexuality" or some specious crap. It's like there's a holocaust beginning and no one will offer a helping hand. When the Health Department proposed direct-mailing a fact sheet about how it spreads and how to avoid catching it, Bill Bennett at Education opposed it, and this guy Gerry Hauer in the White House writes to say there's no need because "There isn't a breathing American who doesn't already know you get AIDS from sex. And if there is, he's probably not the kind of person who reads his mail anyway." Can you believe the complacency of it?'

Pete nodded. 'It's not just complacency, it's madness. What on earth does Reagan think he's doing?'

'He's an enigma, Pete. I don't know if he's scared of the born-again Christians or if he thinks this thing is like measles and it'll just go away.'

During the week Mike and Pete lived in the apartment in the Wyoming Building; on Fridays they fled to the country. In Washington Mike was forced to live a double lie: concealing his sexuality in his official life and dissembling about his work in his social life. Several gay friends who were aware of what he did had already dumped him and those he knew who were suffering from AIDS he could no longer look in the eye. Keeping his two worlds apart felt like wrestling with two sparking electrical cables that flailed uncontrollably in his hands – any connection could be fatal.

Weekends in Shepherdstown were an escape, breathing spaces when Mike and Pete could relax and enjoy their relationship. Knowing Sally Shepherd and her parents was an entrée to the community – they were invited to dinner parties and country fairs and people greeted them in the street like old friends. When the weather was good, they would spend weeknights there too, catching the early commuter train to DC in the morning. At the end of 1983 they bought two dogs to share the cottage with them. Mike christened them Finn McCool, for the legendary Irish giant, and Cashel, for the Tipperary town thirty miles from his birthplace. Walking them in the centre of Shepherdstown the following day, he was amazed at the number of people who knew about the dogs, even their names; when he asked how they had heard, the universal reply was, 'Oh, we know everything that goes on around here.'

Mike looked at Pete. 'My God, there are no secrets in this place! I wonder what else they know about us.'

In the spring of 1984 Pete bought a horse, which they stabled at the cottage and employed a local farmhand to feed while they were away. Mike used the modest inheritance Marge had left him to buy a new Harley Davidson FXST Softail with customized chrome frame and wheel arches. He got a leather biker jacket, pants and boots – although since they had been together Mike had resisted the lure of the leather cruise bars. For the first time he was finding life with a steady partner satisfaction enough. They were content with their own company out in the country and for the most part shunned the DC party scene. In Shepherdstown they cultivated their garden and Mike made preserves from the fruit they grew on their land; he baked bread and cooked while Pete rode out with Sally Shepherd. They invited friends over for tea and swapped recipes with the local ladies. Mike started canning his produce to enter in competitions at the county fair and won ribbon after ribbon. He printed his own labels and called his products the Almost Heaven range – he thought that was what he had found.

To those who knew him, Mike's life seemed to have reached a plateau of contentment. He had told no one about Harry Chapman or about the sad final missive he had received from him – *'Dear Mike, I'm writing to all my lovers because I fear there is something I need to tell you . . .'* – but the thought of it was always in the back of his mind. The image of Harry sitting down to write those letters as death approached in his loveless, empty apartment cast a shadow over Mike's happiness, and it gave added personal urgency to the stings of his conscience. The administration he worked for was dragging its feet in the battle against a disease that was cutting down thousands of young men and leaving millions feeling they were under the shadow of the gibbet, and he was doing nothing about it.

Roger Allan Moore had been away from the office for several weeks 'feeling a little under the weather'. His workload had been picked up by Mark Braden and by Mike, but without Roger the place seemed bereft. Davis v. Bandemer, the vital gerrymandering test case, was making its way towards the Supreme Court, and Braden and Mike missed Roger's reassuring evening drinks, where they had tested out each other's ideas and the arguments they planned to deploy in court.

Roger phoned from his country home in the middle of May to check how 'the boys' were getting along without him. He said he was feeling better and hoped to be back at work soon; he would certainly be coming to town for the White House reception at the end of the month.

'Ahm, in fact I've two tickets for the reception – there's a concert and a dinner – and since Mrs Moore can't come, I wondered if Michael would like to take her place? Ahm, the reason I say Michael rather than you, Mark, is that Ron and Nancy are hosting an Irish delegation that night before they go to Ireland to seek out – don't either of you laugh, please – Ron's Irish roots.'

Mark and Mike did both laugh. Reagan's ability to endear himself to vast swathes of the electorate was legendary, and the trip to Ireland was shamelessly aimed at securing the shamrock vote.

'Whoy, oi don't moind bein' patronized if it means oi get a ticket to yer ball, Mr Moore,' Mike replied. 'So sure and oi'd be deloited to come along widja.' And then, more seriously, 'I'm just happy you're feeling well enough to go, Roger. It'll be marvellous to see you again.'

On the day of the White House ball Mary called to say Doc was not doing too well. He had been pretty depressed in the twelve months since Marge died and seemed to have lost much of his old energy. He had hired lawyers to sue Mayo Clinic and they had subpoenaed the hospital's records, but having seen all the evidence they advised him there were insufficient grounds to bring a negligence suit. Doc had taken the news badly and was floundering.

'You know how Marge always used to say Doc could do nothing for himself?' Mary asked. 'Well, she was dead right. I've had the last year driving down every weekend to his house, doing his laundry, making meals and cleaning. He can barely make coffee. And I'm thinking in a couple of years, you know, it's possible he might be gone. So, anyway, I just wondered, do you want to come down and see him? Just in case – you know.'

'Look, I'm sorry, Sis,' Mike replied, 'but there's no way I want to see him. Maybe in a few years when things are way in the past, but right now I can't stop thinking of all the stuff he did to us as kids and the way he treated everyone, including Marge and James and all. Let me send you some money to help out with caring for him, but please don't ask me to forgive him. I'm sorry.'

NINE

1984

After the austerity of the Carter years, the White House under the Reagans was dazzlingly reborn as a social venue. Where Carter had ordered thermostats turned down and low-wattage light bulbs in all federal buildings, Reagan had switched the glitz back on. Mike had arranged to meet Roger Allan Moore in advance and they chatted as they stood in line with the other black-tie guests waiting to go through security.

'It feels good to be back in town after what has been . . . an uncomfortable few weeks,' Roger said, looking at the bustle around him.

'So . . . are you OK now?' Mike asked.

'Ahm, yes. Well, I stand with old Marcus Aurelius on that one. "Give thyself relief by doing every act of life as if it were the last," you know. Don't look so upset, my dear fellow! I am content with where I am. "When a thing tempts you to be bitter, say not 'this is a misfortune' but 'to bear this worthily is good fortune'." ' I am dying, Michael. That's the short of it; but for the rest I intend to find the happiness of life within me. I'm sorry to shock you.'

Mike felt an overwhelming desire to put his arm around the man and clasp him to himself, but some scruple – the proximity of the White House or the TV cameras? – held him back.

'Roger, that's terrible. What is it? What did the doctors say?'

'Oh, that it's the oesophagus and much too late now, you know.

Too much of this' – he tapped the lit pipe in his hand – 'too much, too much, too much.'

They entered the East Room to the sound of an Irish harp playing traditional melodies and found their place cards on the dining tables. They were not seated together and Mike toyed with the idea of moving the cards, but Roger shook his head.

'Enjoy yourself tonight,' he said quietly. 'As I shall be doing. And don't fret about things. I'll see you later.'

Mike's seat was at one of the lowlier tables, far from the podium and close to the service door. On his right a very old lady said she was representing the Hibernian Societies of America, but her deafness made conversation impossible; and the place on his left, labelled 'Robert Hampden', remained empty for an hour or so after the meal began. As the harpist played continuously, irritatingly, Mike felt his mood sliding from initial excitement to gloom. The gravity of Roger's news made the evening seem trite and empty.

Reagan was speaking now, welcoming his Irish guests and talking of his forthcoming trip to some village called Ballyporeen, which had clearly been picked at random as 'the ancestral home of the Reagans': 'President and Mrs Hillery, distinguished guests, and I want to add with the greatest of pleasure – I'll try – *A chairde Gaeil.*' There was laughter from part of the room. 'How did I do?' Applause. 'Welcome to the White House. Next week I shall stand on the ancient soil of my ancestors and I want you to know that for this great-grandson of Ireland, this is a moment of joy.' More applause. 'So much of what America means and stands for we owe to Ireland and to your indomitable spirit . . .'

Mike grimaced. At other times he might have enjoyed the ham Irishness, but now he found it grating.

'America has always been a haven of opportunity for those seeking a new life,' Reagan was saying, 'and Irish blood has enriched America. Your smiles, mirth and song lifted our spirits with laughter and music. And always you reminded us by your faith that wisdom and truth, love and beauty, grace and glory begin in Him – our Father, our Creator, our loving God.'

Mike cringed as Reagan launched into an Irish ditty.

'Ireland, O Ireland / Country of my father / Mother of my yearning / Love of all my longings / Home of my heart / God bless you.'

'My God, where did he get that from?' Mike said out loud, just
as the occupant of the seat on his left sat down with a laugh.

'My, my! Well, he got it from me. I tell you, it was either that or
"Mother Macree". Robert Hampden, by the way; very pleased to
meet you.'

Mike saw a slim, handsome young man in his late twenties, with
smartly slicked-down hair and a tuxedo that oozed style. Despite his
gloom Mike reciprocated the stranger's laugh and stretched out his
hand.

'Mike Hess, RNC. Pleased to meet you. I take it you're in White
House communications?'

'Surely, surely am! Work with Mike Deaver. We keep the president handsome, on message and well lit. It's responsible work!'

Mike laughed again – the fellow had a smooth southern charm
about him, and he was undeniably attractive. Reagan was onto serious
topics now, in the pulpit for the elections six months ahead that would
crown or break his presidency.

'When we Republicans took office we were determined to make
a new beginning, and our message as we approach this year's election
is simple: our country's best days are still to come. And with faith,
freedom and courage, there's no limit to what America can accom-
plish. If we do everything in our power to carry that message to the
voters on November sixth, they'll respond by keeping Republicans
where we belong: on the job, in the House, in the Senate, and in the
administration . . .'

Mike smiled at Robert Hampden.

'Did you write that bit too?'

Hampden shook his head.

'That's the big boys' stuff. I chose the flowers, though – real pretty,
don't you think?'

They fell silent as they sensed the president was wrapping up.

'Ladies and gentleman, the challenges to peace and freedom in
the world today are not easy. But face them we must. Edmund Burke's

warning of nearly two centuries ago still holds true: "The only thing necessary for the triumph of evil is for good men to do nothing." Thank you, and have a wonderful evening!'

As the applause rang round the room, Mike realized Robert Hampden was standing up and about to leave with the president. He grabbed his sleeve.

'How can I get in touch with you? Will you leave me your number?'

Robert took a Mont Blanc fountain pen from the breast pocket of his jacket, leaned down to scribble a phone number on the back of a menu card and walked quickly off.

Roger Allan Moore's driver picked them up from the North Portico. It was nearly eleven and the evening had left Mike feeling troubled. Roger seemed in a bubbly mood, though, chatting happily about the president's performance – 'He says he wants a majority in Congress, but he's not going to get it unless you and Mark Braden can bribe the Supreme Court to hurry Bandemer through in six months!' – the company – 'What a bunch of doughy old Republicans, don't you think? Thank goodness the Irish were there to brighten things up' – the food, the music and a dozen other things. The car was already approaching the intersection of Connecticut and Columbia when it dawned on Mike that Roger had been hogging the conversation to steer him away from more serious topics. Pulling up outside the Wyoming, Mike opened his mouth to broach the subject of Roger's sickness, but Roger lifted a finger to silence him.

'Goodnight, Michael. The estimable Ronald was far from Ciceronian tonight, I feel, but his closing lines from Edmund Burke may be something you could perhaps think about. I'll be in touch about the future and, ahm, other things. Delighted to have seen you, my dear fellow.'

Roger did not return to work. His retirement, on grounds of ill health, led to a reshuffle in the top legal posts, with Mark Braden becoming chief counsel and a competition opened to replace him as deputy chief. The Republican National Committee went through the motions of interviewing candidates, but Braden made it clear he wanted Mike to get the post and he did. At the age of thirty-two Michael Hess had risen from illegitimate birth in an obscure Irish convent via the lottery of adoption to a position of influence in the world's most powerful nation. At times a feeling of vertigo came over him. His appointment should have satisfied his striving to belong, confirmed his acceptance by the world, but the lurking sense of his own unworthiness did not leave him: *I don't deserve to be where I am; I am an impostor, just waiting for my secret to be exposed.* He was a gay man in a homophobic party, a rootless orphan in a world of rooted certainties.

When he called Mary to tell her about his promotion, she shrieked with delight. 'Mikey, that's amazing! To think one of us – well, it was always going to be you of course. To think: deputy chief counsel of the Republican National Committee! Wow!'

'Well, yes. I guess . . . It's sad Marge didn't live to see it, though – she would have been proud. And then, you know, I always wonder what my real mom would have thought about it all. I guess she's back there living in Ireland someplace and she's got no idea whatever happened to me. I just wish I could tell her, Mary.'

'Sure. I hear what you're saying, Mike. It makes everything seem kind of . . . incomplete, you know what I mean? To think my mom will never hear what we've become and what we've made of life . . . To think she'll never meet her grandson . . .'

'Yeah. Unless . . .' Mike hesitated. 'Unless I go back again and make those nuns tell us what they know. It's so frustrating knowing they've got the information, and I don't understand why they won't give it to us. Or maybe I do understand. Maybe they think they've got something to hide . . .'

'Yeah, I thought that too,' Mary said. 'But I wouldn't care, would you? Whatever we found out, whatever the big secret is, all we want is to find our moms . . .'

TEN

1984

Mike and Pete were invited to a house party the following weekend, and the hosts decided it would be fun to make it a celebration of Mike's new job. The place was a clapboard townhouse not far from Market Square in Old Town Alexandria. It had a little pool in the backyard and the July weather drew the forty or so guests out onto the terrace. Midway through the evening Mike saw Mark O'Connor walk in. It was the first time he had seen him since they split and he felt the blood rising to his cheeks.

'Oh, hi, Mark,' he mumbled, embarrassed. 'I want you to meet Pete Nilsson. We've been together for three years now. And Pete, er, this is Mark – I think I told you about him.'

Mike's worries were groundless: Mark did not bear a grudge. He had a promising law career and a new boyfriend he loved and trusted.

'I'd like you both to meet Ben Kronfeld. Ben works for the government.'

Kronfeld was a dark-haired man with a moustache and calm, serious eyes.

'Hello, Michael; I've heard a lot about you.'

'Right . . . So which part of the government do you work for, Ben?' Mike asked.

'I work at Interior – mainly labour policy and statistics. And I liked it until this administration came in. Then we got James Watt as interior secretary and everything went crazy.'

Mike sensed the antagonism in Ben's voice and wanted to walk away, but Pete was already asking, 'How do you mean "crazy"? What did he do?'

'Hey, don't get me started.' Ben grimaced. 'James Watt is the worst bigot you ever met. First day on the job, he called the policy staff together and he says, "Do you *all* work here?" In a couple of weeks he was handing out pink slips. And it wasn't like just reducing numbers, it was ideological. Everyone who didn't fit in, everyone identified with the Carter years, got fired. Then he moved onto minorities, including us right at the top of the list. Gay guys were the first to go, then all the others. He really did a number on the thing. And he even boasted about what he was doing. You remember that speech he made last year saying how he had "a black, a woman, two Jews and a cripple" on his staff? What a Republican hypocrite!'

Mike tugged Pete's arm. 'I think maybe we should go get a drink?'

'No, no, this is interesting.' Pete shook himself free. 'And I want to get to know Mark. Maybe you could fetch the drinks, Mike?'

By the time Mike got back he could hear the other three in heated conversation.

'What I can't understand,' Ben was saying in a voice tinged with exasperation, 'is why he agreed to go work for them in the first place. How can anyone work for a party that's got people like Pat Buchanan in it? How can you have one life where you're liberal and Democratic and open about being gay, and then have this secret, closeted life where your co-workers don't know you're gay and you're helping people do things that are not beneficial to the gay community? I can't understand how he can live with that.'

Mike coughed and handed over the drinks.

'Look, Ben, I heard what you're saying and I know it looks bad, OK? But don't be judgmental – we can all get on our high horse – and so far as I know you're working for the same government I work for, and you didn't get fired, did you?'

Ben Kronfeld was a reasonable man.

'OK, but let me say one thing: I survive in my job because I'm discreet about my private life, but that's not something any grown man should be forced to do. It's just bizarre to see men in their forties and fifties still hiding. I know in my chain of command right now there are at least two gay guys, both formerly married with children, and I know they're gay because they said so to one of my friends, but they both said, "Don't tell my boss because he doesn't know." And the other thing is I work for the government; I don't work for the Republicans. I don't work for the people who're doing those things . . .'

As Ben was speaking, the group was joined by a small, balding man with an overbite and a flamboyant dress sense who introduced himself as Rudy.

'Hey, this is no good time to be gay in America,' he said firmly. 'But it's suicide to hide away and pretend we're not there. Reagan doesn't care a nickel about us getting sick and dying. You remember Alvin Tranter, don't you? He died last month – pneumonia on his death certificate so as not to offend his parents, but it was AIDS. Hiding doesn't help. We need to start making ourselves visible and making things—'

He was interrupted by a spoon tapping on a glass and the announcement of a toast to congratulate Michael Hess on his new job. Mike responded with a brief expression of thanks, but the argument had left him feeling uncomfortable, as if he were somehow being held responsible for people getting sick and dying.

After midnight Mark managed to get him alone. 'Hey, Mike, are you avoiding me? I'm not going to attack you. I was hoping we could treat each other as grown-ups and be friends. You and Pete seem pretty happy and Ben and I are too.'

'Sure, Mark. No hard feelings. It's just that everyone seems to be on my case nowadays. It's like working for the RNC makes you some kind of pariah.'

Mark shrugged. 'Actually, I was going to ask you about that myself. It's a pretty strange choice, don't you think?'

'Hey, don't you start as well! I was looking for work. I needed a job, OK? I know a lot of people are pissed about it, but that's the way it is. We all have motives that move our lives and we don't always understand them. I thought your Ben was a little harsh, you know.'

'Ben's lovely, Mike. He likes you a lot, but I guess he's worried about you, and I am too. You know that Alvin Tranter guy Rudy mentioned? Ben knew him and he's been pretty cut up since he died. I think in some ways you remind him of Alvin. He was very beautiful and outgoing and sexually active. We met him at a party a couple of years back where the living room was covered in plastic and Alvin was doing everything – you know, I mean really everything – and he chided me and Ben for being so reserved. I can remember him saying, "Why should I be concerned about getting sick? Why go through life not having as much fun as I can?" And now he's dead. It's hard to understand that frame of mind, Mike. I hope you've been careful.'

By 2 a.m. a lot of alcohol had been consumed and a group was inside the house watching porn movies on the VCR. Some were making out, but the atmosphere was relaxed and sleepy. Mark and Ben had left, and Pete was outside on the terrace in quiet conversation with four or five other guys. Mike poured himself a whisky and sat by the pool. In the darkness he felt very alone.

ELEVEN

1984

Mike had left a couple of messages for Robert Hampden, but there had been no reply. One Tuesday in late July he returned from lunch to find a note from his secretary asking him to call 'Mr Horden at the White House'. Mike didn't recognize the name but checked the number and realized it was Robert.

'Mission Control, Hampden here.'

Mike chuckled. 'Michael Hess here, Robert. Is that how everyone answers the phone over there, or is it just you?'

'Oh, just me, of course. I'm glad you called. I have a walking assignment I'd like you to help out with. Are you free this Friday lunchtime by any chance – Chevy Chase Country Club, 12.30?'

'Well, sure. What kind of walking do you have in mind?'

'Oh, no actual walking,' Robert said. 'Just wear a smart suit with a silk handkerchief in your top pocket and look lovely. Can you manage that?'

Mike laughed. 'I'll try.'

Robert was waiting for him outside the sprawling half-timbered club-house.

'Michael, it's very good to see you. Now, Nancy has got Jerry Zipkin walking her – do you know Jerry? I'm squiring Jennie Edelman and you will take care of the delectable Laura Thurgood. The ladies don't arrive for another half-hour, so we've got time for a drink if you like? Let's go straight to the Gable Room and I'll order up some grog.'

In the slightly gloomy high-ceilinged room with its wood panelling and tables set for lunch the two men sat and drank Prosecco. Robert, in double-breasted grey herringbone with shiny black Oxfords on his feet, was clearly a regular: the waiting staff greeted him as 'Mr Hampden' and asked what the ladies would be wanting for lunch.

'Oh, something light. Mrs Edelman doesn't eat meat, as you know; the First Lady will have her usual two courses and Mrs Thurgood will be delighted to eat whatever Mrs Reagan has.'

Turning to Mike, Robert winked.

'As you may have deduced, our happy lot is to accompany the beautiful wives of powerful, busy men. When your husband is tied up in the White House or the Senate, the essential accessory for any woman is a charming walker who'll be your companion, not to mention your card partner and confidant.'

A week after the lunch in Chevy Chase Robert invited Mike over to the White House and the two men sat and drank coffee in the West Wing office of Robert's boss, Mike Deaver, who was out of town.

'I must congratulate you, Michael,' Robert said with a sly smile. 'Nancy told me she found you quite charming and if she weren't committed to the wonderful, marvellous Jerry she would love to have you walk her in the future. What do you think of that?'

Mike leaned back in his chair and laughed.

'What do I think? I think Mrs Reagan is very kind and I liked her a lot. But to be honest I don't see my future as a walker for other people's wives, however important they are. It's really not my style, you know.'

Robert pulled a little face.

'Oh, I see. You're the serious type with no time for frivolity, is that it? Always slaving away over your law books and worrying about the future of the party? More interested in gerrymandering than Jerry Zipkin?'

Robert slapped the desk and guffawed at the awfulness of his own joke. Mike rolled his eyes.

'Yep, that's the measure of it, I'm afraid. All work and not much play.'

Mike liked Robert's energy, wit and enthusiasm for life; he liked the way he made a joke of the most serious things, and he found him physically very attractive.

'But what's with Jerry Zipkin, anyway?' Mike asked. 'Where on earth did he spring from? And why does Nancy set so much store by him?'

Robert looked at Mike as if he were a hopeless case.

'Where have you been all your life, Michael? Jerry Zipkin is *the* original walker and most probably the third most powerful man in Washington – if you count Nancy as a man, that is. Get on the wrong side of Jerry at your absolute peril. His tongue's sharp as a razor and one word from him can ruin careers and reputations. But if Jerry likes you and you treat him right, he can be the most loyal and most useful friend you ever had.'

'Oh, come on.' Mike laughed. 'He's a raging queen!'

'My dear,' Robert said, 'he is indeed. And what's wrong with that, I might ask. You may have noticed that all three of us chaperones at the Country Club had at least one thing in common, did we not? Just think about it and you'll see it makes sense: if the sultan leaves someone in charge of his harem, he doesn't want anyone who'll be tempted to dip his hand in the honey pot, if you'll pardon my revoltingly mixed metaphor. In olden times the preference was for eunuchs but they come a little expensive nowadays, so we're the next best thing. *Voilà!*'

'And do you do much walking yourself?' Mike asked, fascinated by the thought of a hidden network of gay men escorting the wives of the rich and powerful through Washington society.

'Oh no, it's merely a sideline – I'm much too busy with Ron. And anyway, it's people like Jerry the ladies really want – much older and grander than we are, reeking of eau de cologne from red silk handkerchiefs and wearing perfect toupees on their perfectly bald old

heads, but willing to take them to fashion shows and society balls
and advise them on hair colour and make-up and shoes and hand-
bags and lingerie and the pros and cons of HRT. Jerry's squawky and
surly, a scold and a snob; he's waspish and persnickety and they all
love him and fear him. He's the closest they'll ever get Oscar Wilde
and they're wild about him. Get the picture?'

'Yeah, I do,' said Mike. 'But what I don't get is how guys like
that survive and prosper around the Reagans. I thought this was
the president who excoriates homosexuality and sends all gays to
hell.'

'Oh no, my dear fellow; I think you must have some other Ronald
Reagan in mind. *This* Ronald couldn't give a damn what people get
up to in the privacy of their bedrooms. He and Nancy cut their teeth
in Hollywood, don't forget, and all their actor friends are gay. Why,
some of them come and stay at the White House – it's Jerry Zipkin
who advises on the guest lists, you know. Just last year when they
had the place remodelled, they had their designer Ted Graber spend
the night there with his lover Archie Case – and a lovely couple they
were too. Ron's not a closet bigot, he's a closet tolerant.'

Robert's tone was bantering, but Mike didn't laugh.

'OK, so why does he kowtow to the bigots? Why does he let
Falwell and Robertson and Buchanan speak on behalf of the party?'

'Hey, I know what you're saying. But it's the old problem of politics and the Faustian bargains these guys have to make to get elected.
Sure, Ron talks the gay-bashing talk, but trust me: he doesn't walk
the walk.'

Robert was inviting him to drop the subject, but Mike didn't.

'Well, just answer me one thing, then: how come this administration has presided over the biggest threat to the lives of gay men
this country has ever known and not lifted a finger to do anything
about it? How come Reagan employs people like Gerry Hauer and
Bill Bennett to block funds for research and information campaigns?
If that's not walking the walk, then I don't know what is!'

Robert's face fell.

'I'm sorry, Robert,' Mike said. 'I know it's not your fault – it's not you I'm yelling at. It's just, this whole thing has got me scared. It's got me in a panic and I don't know what to do.'

'You and millions of us, Mike. All we can do is stay calm and be safe.'

Mike nodded. 'One other thing you and I can do is stay in touch and share what we hear,' he said, spotting an opening to keep in contact with Robert. 'You get information at your end and I get information at mine, so why don't we pool what we know?'

'Now that sounds like a fine idea,' Robert agreed, 'and an even better one if we do it over a good lunch or dinner, wouldn't you say? Are you going to Dallas for the convention next month?'

'Sure. The RNC runs the show, so I'll be there – the president's boring old legal adviser while you and Mike Deaver do the important things like arranging the flowers and keeping his nose powdered. Sounds like a winning combination, don't you think?'

Dallas was hot and sticky at the end of August, and the hundreds of officials who flew down to celebrate Ronald Reagan's nomination ran from air-conditioned cars to air-conditioned auditorium to air-conditioned hotel rooms. Mike had gone ahead with an advance party to oversee arrangements in the Reunion Arena, where the convention was being staged. By the time Reagan arrived on the morning of the 22nd proceedings had been under way for two days and Mike was feeling frazzled. With the rest of the Republican National Committee he was ferried downtown to Loew's Anatole Hotel to greet the presidential party and was mildly chagrined to see Robert behind Ron and Nancy looking his usual immaculate, unflustered self.

'Well, I'm pleased to see someone's had a relaxing day,' he whispered as Reagan made his arrival remarks to the staffers.

Robert smiled smugly. 'It was champagne and caviar all the way. Ron's in fine fettle and it's *so* nice to have him unchallenged for the nomination and a shoo-in for re-election, don't you think? I might even be free for dinner. The boss will be taking a nap and watching the speeches on TV, I suspect.'

Mike laughed dryly. 'It'd have to be a late dinner. I'm gonna be in the Arena until the last of the speeches and the roll-call of the states. It could be midnight before I'm done. Why don't we make it breakfast instead?'

But the next morning Robert was preoccupied with arrangements for the president's speech and media coverage and they had little time to chat. Reagan was in fine form in the evening, emerging on stage to roars from the hall and deafening chants of 'Four more years!' and 'Reagan, Reagan, U-S-A!'

His acceptance address lambasted the Democrats over their plans for the economy, foreign policy and family values. 'For us, words like faith and family are not slogans to be dragged out of the closet every four years,' he said in a choice of words that Mike noted with a grimace. 'They are values to respect and to live by every day. May God bless you, and may He continue to bless our beloved country.'

Ron and Nancy both came to the staff celebration afterwards, and the party went on long after the first couple retired to bed. Mike drank so much that in the early hours he walked straight into a glass door and was knocked out cold. Robert Hampden found him with his face covered in blood and took him to ER. He needed seven stitches in a head wound and flew back to Washington the next day feeling shaky and unsettled.

TWELVE

1984–5

Mike took little pleasure in the landslide that Reagan won in November or in the festivities of the January Inaugural. It was as if the incident in Dallas and the shedding of his blood had startled him into an agonized recognition of his own vulnerability. Pete felt the gloom but did not know the cause. His cautious enquiries were met with rebuffs. It seemed to Pete that Mike was feeling frightened and somehow guilty – at times he would glare at Pete with hostility in his face; at others his look would be full of concern and pity.

The gloom did not dissipate until the spring, when Mike came home from work one evening with a bottle of champagne and a bunch of blood-red peonies. Suddenly, unexpectedly he was back to his former self, full of energy and enthusiasm, planning for the future as if a great weight had been lifted from his shoulders.

'Listen,' he said. 'I've had *the best* idea. I think we should throw an Easter party at the Shepherdstown house. You know how we always talked about Easter vigils when we were little – church and prayers and serious stuff? Well, I think we should have an Easter vigil that's totally fun. We could get everyone over on the Saturday night and just party on through to the morning. Then we all go to Mass on Easter Sunday and chill for the rest of the weekend. How does that sound?'

All their old friends came: Mark O'Connor, Ben Kronfeld, John Clarkson, Susan Kavanagh; Robert Hampden brought his wealthy, older boyfriend, who was one of the capital's leading property developers; Sally Shepherd came, along with their other Shepherdstown acquaintances; and they even invited some of the West Virginia mudflowers, the name they gave to the local gay set – because if you cleaned them up, they might be kind of cute.

Dinner began at eleven in the evening and went on until two in the morning. Then the rugs were rolled back, the music cranked up and the dancing started. By the early hours half the guests were asleep in armchairs and the others were playing pool at the table in the back room. At nine o'clock Mike announced it was time to go to Easter Mass. There were objections from the Jews and Baptists, and a sudden crop of self-proclaimed atheists, but Mike insisted and the whole group trooped off to church. Afterwards, he and Pete went to Easter lunch at Sally's parents and came back in mid-afternoon to join the remaining guests before they left to go back to DC.

In the evening the two of them sat alone amid the chaos of the devastated house.

'You were magnificent, Mike,' Pete whispered. 'You cooked and DJ'd just like in the old days. You know, you've been so down recently that I thought I'd never see you happy again.'

Mike squeezed his arm.

'I know I haven't been . . . the easiest person to live with these past months. I'm really sorry for that. There was something I should have told you . . . Maybe I was too afraid to tell you. You remember Harry Chapman, the guy up in New York? Well, he died.'

Mike took a deep breath.

'Just before he went, he wrote me to say he had AIDS . . . and maybe I had it too.'

Pete said nothing.

'I know, I know. But let me finish. I couldn't get the thought out of my head. It just ate away at me that maybe I was going to lose you and the happiness we've found together . . . to lose everything. But last month they started these serum tests that let you find out if you're positive or negative, so I went for one . . . and they gave me the all-clear!'

Pete let out a gasp and Mike's eyes filled with tears.

'It's amazing how different everything suddenly looks, Pete. It's like I dodged the bullet and I've got a whole new life ahead of me. But the worry and the stress were so awful . . . I don't want ever to go through that again. I'm so sorry for . . . for what I've put you through.'

Pete shook his head. Mike had kept something secret that could have had dire consequences for him too, but he forced himself not to dwell on that. The future was what mattered now.

'I'm glad you told me, Mike. I was wondering what was going on with you, but I understand now. Thank God you're all right.' Pete got up to wipe his eyes. 'I'm so happy we got this out of the way,' he called through from the bathroom as he splashed cold water on his face. 'It's like we can start all over again – a clean slate.' He returned to the sofa. 'You do promise, though, don't you? The leather stud thing, the bondage boy stuff and the crazy sex . . . that's all in the past, right? The biker gear's just for your image. There'll be no more lost weekends and no more sex with strangers?'

Mike looked him in the eye and nodded.

'I promise, Pete. You're all I need now.'

THIRTEEN

1985–6

By 1985 Michael Hess was an established figure in the Republican Party. The Indiana gerrymandering suit, Davis v. Bandemer, was about to come before the Supreme Court and the RNC was relying on Mike's strategy to win the case. Pete was still working at the National Restaurants Association but was steadily building up his own marketing business. They began looking around for somewhere in DC to buy and found the perfect place.

The Methodist Building on Capitol Hill was a grand 1930s Renaissance-style block in white limestone that had long served as the Church's headquarters in the nation's capital. Alone among all the buildings on the Hill, it had a residential wing with fifty-five private apartments, many occupied by senators, representatives and Supreme Court judges. Al Gore Senior was the block's elder statesman and the place was the epitome of establishment Washington. When an apartment came on the market, Mike and Pete bought it and moved in at once. The apartment was not large, but they decorated it in style, with beige walls and dark grey carpet. They filled the rooms with antique cherrywood furniture and leather armchairs, a Chinese chest and African wooden sculptures. Side tables were arranged to show off little knick-knacks – alabaster eggs in a wicker basket, a golden pineapple, a sculpted-metal hand, antique pieces of ivory and whalebone. A beautiful washed-out golden screen stood in one corner of the main room and African spears in the other. On the walls they hung prints by Picasso and Matisse, and Robert Mapplethorpe's photographs of male nudes. From their window they could see the Capitol and the Supreme Court.

Like a lot of his friends, Mike was a big fan of Doris Day. He loved her musicals and the romantic comedies she had made with Rock Hudson. His favourite was *Pillow Talk*, particularly the scene where the manly Hudson pretends to be gay to trick the beautiful but coy Day into his arms.

'Oh, you know,' he tells her, 'there are some men who, well, you know, they're very devoted to their mothers – you know, the type that likes to collect cooking recipes or exchange bits of gossip . . .' It was a line that made Mike rock with laughter and he was delighted when the networks ran the movie as a prelude to Day's new TV series, in which Hudson was scheduled to appear as her first guest.

When *Doris Day's Best Friends* aired on 15 July Mike and the rest of the viewing public were shocked. Hudson was no longer a sleek, muscular hunk; his face was gaunt and ashen, his speech was slurred and he seemed painfully thin and frail. He was fifty-nine but looked seventy. Mike and Pete watched the news bulletins in the days that followed and wondered at the explanations that were advanced – liver cancer or severe influenza – until Hudson's spokesman put an end to the speculation by acknowledging that Rock was gay, that he was suffering from AIDS and had known about it for over a year.

Many Americans were appalled that the man they had admired for his masculinity had been faking all along. Ronald Reagan, who had been one of Hudson's closest colleagues, called him to express his personal sympathy but still said nothing and did nothing about the epidemic that was sweeping the country he led.

In the weeks before his death Hudson, along with hundreds of other American men, flew to Paris to be treated with the experimental antiretroviral drug HPA-23. The Americans were in Paris because their own country had no similar anti-AIDS programme and had not issued a licence for the French drug to be used in the US. Over 20,000 US citizens were diagnosed with AIDS in 1985, and for nearly every one of them the diagnosis was a death sentence. Rock Hudson included in his will a bequest of a quarter of a million dollars to set up the American Foundation for AIDS Research, to be chaired by his old friend Elizabeth Taylor. The unspoken message was that if the government wouldn't do it, then gay men would have to do it for themselves.

Ronald Reagan was in hospital the evening the Doris Day show aired, receiving treatment for intestinal polyps. For ten days he ran the country from his bed, with his newly appointed chief of staff, Don Regan, liaising between him and Vice President Bush.

The president had been back in the White House for little more than a month and still looked pale and drawn when Mark Braden and Mike were summoned to the Oval Office. Don Regan had clearly prepared him well because Reagan glanced at a briefing note and launched into an impassioned, seemingly impromptu speech in the style of Henry V at Agincourt.

'It's been thirty years since we Republicans controlled the House of Representatives,' he said, looking almost accusingly at his visitors from the RNC, 'and that's too long, guys. It makes life a misery for a Republican president and it stymies some of our best legislation. More than that, it's simply not fair. The Democrats have a stranglehold because the electoral rules are slanted in their favour. Now I know this Bandemer case won't solve things overnight – I know it's just a start – but we need to win it to give ourselves the precedent we can use to unravel the injustices in other states. As you can see, I'm just an old wreck sitting here on my butt right now, so I'm counting on you guys to go to the Supreme Court and win this thing for me. Will you do that, guys? Will you go win one for the Gipper?'

Reagan smiled without a hint of self-consciousness at his performance. Mike had been thinking he should use his audience with power to raise the scandal of the administration's inaction on AIDS, but his good intentions melted away as he shook the man's hand.

'We'll give it our best shot, Mr President, you can count on that.'

*

Rock Hudson died on 2 October 1985. Five days later Mike appeared before the Supreme Court of the United States to present the Republican Party's testimony in the gerrymandering test case of Davis v. Bandemer. In his pocket he had a message of good luck from the White House.

Having heard the arguments from attorneys on both sides of the dispute, Chief Justice Burger announced that he and his fellow justices would consider the issues involved and produce their ruling at the end of the court session, probably in June.

In the middle of June 1986 the Statue of Liberty in the Bay of New York was reopened after two years of extensive renovation. The monument was rededicated in a televised ceremony attended by dignitaries from the US and abroad. In the broadcast the Reagans could be seen in the audience, sitting next to President François Mitterand of France and his wife Danielle. Onstage, Bob Hope was entertaining the distinguished guests and cracking jokes about France, the US and their shared statue.

'I just heard that the Statue of Liberty has AIDS,' Hope was saying with a knowing smirk, 'but she doesn't know if she got it from the mouth of the Hudson or the Staten Island Fairy.'

As the camera panned to catch the audience reaction, the Mitterands could be seen looking horrified. The Reagans were laughing.

A week later the Supreme Court pronounced on Davis v. Bandemer and gave the Republican Party the ruling it had sought – that examples of partisan gerrymandering can be challenged through the courts. Mike, Mark Braden and their team celebrated the decision with champagne at RNC headquarters and Braden made a speech of congratulations.

'Tonight,' he said, 'we have won a case that has the potential to alter the political landscape of our country. It was no easy struggle and many elements within the Republican family disliked our tactics. But we stuck to our guns like a band of brothers fighting for a cause we believe in. We have won a battle, but we have not won the war. Now we need to take this victory forward to undo the Democrats' gerrymanders wherever we find them. The judicial process means the impact of our work will not be felt for another half-dozen years, but if we are successful, I do believe we could set ourselves a target of the 1994 mid-terms. So I give you a toast: to Republican control of the House in 1994 and for many years after!'

Mike raised his glass. Life was going well for him. The feeling of having been accepted into the most important establishment in America – the party that ran the country – was something he had yearned for. It was the palliative that could soothe his pain and silence the doubts that accompanied his existence, the insidious voices that whispered *You are no good* in the ear of the orphaned gay man. And having made it to the heart of the establishment, he was going to defend his position.

FOURTEEN

1986–9

It was a while since Mike had seen John Clarkson, his Texan friend from the Mark O'Connor days. John had been working for the Labor Union on civil liberties cases, but had moved out to California and had not been in DC for a year. Mike liked him and was pleased when he called at the end of October to say he was in town for a few days and would have time to meet for a drink.

They sat in the bar of the Hyatt Regency on New Jersey Avenue and ordered a pitcher of beer. John hadn't changed much – a little fuller round the waist, but still with the same outspoken directness.

'The West Coast is just way more friendly than here,' he said. 'More gay-friendly, anyway. But my God, there's an epidemic going on! I don't know whether it's worse there than it is here, or whether you Washingtonians just don't *talk* about AIDS, but back in San Francisco, man, I never saw anything like it.'

'Tell me about it,' Mike said. 'Dark days we're living in.'

John stabbed a finger down on a copy of the *Washington Post* that had been on their table when they arrived. 'Did you see this, though?' he said, pointing at a headline in the news section. 'It's taken the Reagan administration five years to publish its first report on the AIDS epidemic and now they're trying to backtrack on it. It says the surgeon general's report calling for AIDS education and the wide-spread use of condoms is being blocked by conservatives. Your guy,

Gerry Hauer, he's quoted as saying, "I don't see why a third grader needs to know anything about condoms and I'm not going to give the go-ahead to the local school to talk to my daughter about sodomy." What planet do these guys live on, Mike? Don't they realize there's a holocaust going on?'

Mike shifted on his seat

'Yeah, it's a tough call, John,' he muttered. 'They're all politicians, you know, and they have lots of things to take into account . . .'

John had raised the issue partly as a test for Mike, and he was failing it.

'Hey, you're not defending those bigots, are you? You know they want compulsory AIDS testing for all gays, don't you? And where's that going to lead us – forcible quarantine? Leper colonies? William F. Buckley says he wants all men with HIV to have it forcibly branded on their buttocks, like some Auschwitz tattoo! And he's one of Reagan's closest friends. So what's your president doing except sitting with the blinds down and hoping it'll all go away?'

Mike was not quite prepared to back down.

'You're wrong to blame Reagan,' he said. 'He and Nancy are very gay-friendly: they even had their interior designer and his partner stay at the White—'

'Oh, big deal!' John laughed contemptuously. 'So they have gay friends. And yet they let gay men die while their party blocks the funds for AIDS research. You know, I think that makes it even worse – worse than the cretinous rednecks who believe gays have horns and a tail because they've never met any and that's what their preacher tells them.'

Mike was about to protest, but John was in full flow.

'And what about the Republicans supporting the Georgia sodomy decision? Bowers v. Hardwick, right? These are two guys who just wanted to have sex in the privacy of their own bedroom – consenting adults, OK, just like you and me – and yet your party, *your party*, wants to make it a criminal act!'

'Yeah, well, get real, John.' Mike knew he was on shaky ground but made a lawyer's fist of it. 'You know these statutes have been on the books for centuries and they're very rarely enforced. So what if some southern state wants to keep the Bible-thumpers happy with a show of puritanism – it doesn't hurt anyone, does it? And you know I don't think a lot of gay men do themselves any favours, especially out west in your neck of the woods – all those demonstrations and the Act Up crowd. Don't you think they do more than anything to alienate politicians and the public? All this talk of outing people and shaming them in front of their friends and families and work colleagues . . .'

'God, Mike! I hope you don't believe all that,' John said. 'I hope you're only saying it because you're a Republican and you have to say it – because you're just obeying orders.'

At the beginning of March 1987 Robert Hampden called and asked Mike to meet him in the Irish Times bar on Capitol Hill. Robert was still the same witty gadfly, mocking the job with wry detachment even as he did it, but he had noticed a transformation in Mike: from the hesitant, self-effacing young official he had first met at the White House, he had grown into a committed and zealous Republican. It was as if the victories Mike had won for the party had bound him to it; as if he now shared the responsibility for making the party what it was and felt compelled to justify and defend it because it was too late to go back. Robert had laughed at Mike's proselytizing zeal and called him a 'soldier', loyal and unshakeable. Today, though, it was Robert who sounded serious.

'Hey, good to see you, Mike. I don't know if you've heard but it looks like Deaver's going down.'

Mike shook his head. He knew the guy had been under investigation, but no one had mentioned prison.

'Yeah, and it could be bad. Looks like he could cop five to ten for perjury and corruption.'

Mike Deaver had stepped down as White House deputy chief of staff a year previously to set up his own lobbying firm, but it was no secret that he maintained close links with the president. Now he was accused of exploiting them for monetary gain. The Democrat-controlled Congress had run an investigation into how Deaver had won contracts for his clients to build America's new B-1 bomber, and he had allegedly perjured himself during testimony to a federal grand jury.

'I can tell you, there's panic in high places,' Robert said. 'If Deaver goes to jail and this Iran–Contra contretemps gets out of hand, Ron's going to be tarred with the same brush that did for Nixon. The irony is that the guy who spent years protecting Reagan's image is now the Democrats' best hope for tarnishing it.'

'Jeez, Robert, that's terrible,' Mike said. 'Does Deaver have a defence? And is Bush mixed up in it? It'd be a disaster for the party if he can't run next year.'

Robert smiled at Mike's earnestness.

'Well, I'm pleased to see the pragmatist in you, Mike. No worries about morals and ethics or anything – a perfect Republican. Actually, Deaver's defence – and it's pretty slim – is that he was a victim of alcoholism, and that's what made him perjure himself. Cynical, but it may work. And Bush is in the clear, you'll be pleased to hear. I think he's already plotting his campaign for the presidency.'

Mike's final encounter with Roger Allan Moore came in the fall of 1988 as America was gearing up for the first round of campaign debates between George Bush and Michael Dukakis. Roger had called him a couple of weeks earlier and asked if he would travel up to see him at his house in Boston. He didn't say why, but Mike sensed urgency in his voice.

It was a sad meeting. In the vast old house on Beacon Hill, the house famed for its history and twelve fireplaces, Roger sat frail and white in the drawing room. He was wrapped in a tartan rug and despite the warmth of the late-September day a fire was blazing in the hearth.

'My dear fellow, I'm, ahm, touched that you have come to see me.' Roger's voice had lost its resonant baritone and he spoke now with a painful rasp. He struggled for breath.

'I promised I would be in touch to talk about the future, Michael, and for me that future is now. You will not see me again. No, the future I want to speak about is yours. I have followed your career since I departed and have been delighted to see the success you've achieved. In fact, I believe your star may be about to rise even higher.' Roger managed a fleeting smile. 'I have spoken to Mark Braden and I understand he will not be remaining at the RNC after these elections, so the post of chief counsel . . . But let's not get ahead of ourselves. What I wanted to say is that the world of power is an alluring one, very easy to fall in love with, and it can confer a certain feeling of invincibility . . . Do you understand what I am saying?'

Mike nodded, but Roger looked dubious.

'I think I mentioned the name of Chaim Rumkowski . . .'

Roger's eyes fluttered and closed briefly, but he made an effort to stay awake.

'It's the morphine; I'm sorry. They give it to me with an hypodermic syringe . . . and it dulls the mind. But, ahm, power, Michael – a fickle mistress – and the lawyer's defence of blindly serving the law is a thin one. If we lose sight of our actions as having a meaning in themselves, if we think only of winning, rather than the purpose of what we are doing, we can easily lose our way . . .'

Mike was beginning to feel Roger was accusing him of something.

'But *you* always did your best to win, didn't you, Roger? I mean, when you were a lawyer?'

Roger tugged the rug a little tighter round his shoulders.

'Let me tell you about a movie, Mike – I doubt you've ever seen it or ever will do; it's more my generation's kind of thing – called *Bridge on the River Kwai*. Alec Guinness is a British colonel captured by the Japanese during the war. The Japs want their prisoners to build a bridge for them, and Guinness is the senior officer . . . His conscience tells him not to help the Japanese, but he gets so caught up in the act of building and the satisfaction of overcoming the problems he faces and the *beauty* of the thing he's creating that he loses sight of the purpose it's intended for and the consequences it will have.'

The speech had cost Roger an effort that seemed to leave him exhausted. He waved his hand and sank back into the armchair, where his eyelids drooped into sleep. Mike sat with him for a half-hour waiting to see if he would stir and, when he did not, let himself quietly out of the house to fly back to DC.

Roger was right. Mark Braden resigned from the Republican National Committee after George Bush's election victory in November 1988 to set up his own law firm, and the post of chief counsel fell vacant. The new president knew the party's legal staff from his time as VP and let it be known that he wanted Michael Hess to get the job. Mike inherited the large corner room with windows in two walls and a brass nameplate on its solid oak door. Now it was he who would lead the delegations that reported in the Oval Office; it was he who would control the party's strategy to dismantle the Democrats' electoral stranglehold; it was he who would represent the Republican case before the Supreme Court and the committees of Congress; and it was his name that would appear on the record of the party's court battles across the nation.

Mike found George Bush a patrician Ivy League New Englander with a reserved and wooden demeanour; he was very different from the polished performer who had occupied the post before him and patently lacked the warmth Reagan had brought to his dealings with party staff and officials. Bush listened to the briefings on the RNC's redistricting campaign but offered little advice or encouragement.

'The guy's a cold fish,' Mike told Pete. 'With Reagan, you felt he was interested in what you were doing, even if he didn't always understand what it was. With Bush, you kind of feel he understands all the issues but doesn't want you to know what he's thinking. It's unsettling and I don't like it.'

The 1989 Easter vigil in Shepherdstown was one of the best attended in the five years it had been running; Mike's new position had given him a status in Washington society that made people keen to know him. The late-March weather was warm and the music spilled into the garden for much of the night. After Mass on Easter Sunday those guests who had stayed the course played pool or lounged on the grass outside. Ben Kronfeld, who had split up with Mark O'Connor and was there on his own, stretched out on a blanket on the concrete cover of the old well behind the house. He dozed peacefully for an hour or so, then woke and stretched. As he rolled over sleepily onto his stomach, he was horrified to see a snake staring him in the face, black, four or five inches in diameter and around five feet long. He ran inside to tell Mike about it, and Mike winced. The snakes came with the house, he said, a slithering, unsettling presence in the cellar beneath – more than once he had climbed into bed to find one curled up waiting for him between the sheets.

FIFTEEN

1989–91

The four years of the Bush presidency were more restrained than those of the Reagan era: fewer Hollywood stars came and went at the White House and the balls and parties were less extravagant. But as chief counsel Mike was invited to receptions and dinners, and he revelled in the feeling that he was there by right, that his admission to the inner circle was the result of his own qualities and efforts. He regretted that he was unable to take Pete to social events connected with his job – it irked him that Pete could not see at first hand the success he was making of his life – but he accepted it and Pete did too. They had been together for eight years now and had promised to have no secrets.

For the most part, Mike's work was going well. The Bandemer decision had given him the ammunition the RNC needed to bring suits in states around the country, and there was a sense their efforts were tilting the electoral map in the Republicans' direction. But the key case – the one with most at stake – was California, and as the months went by and the RNC lost in the district court, the signs were becoming increasingly discouraging. Mike and his team were convinced the Democrats' gerrymandering was so outrageous and so manifestly contrary to the constitution that the Supreme Court would surely strike it down. They celebrated when they succeeded in getting the case referred, but were shocked when the Court threw it out without comment.

On the evening the decision was announced, Mike came home in a state of nervous agitation.

'God, I can't believe it,' he said as soon as he came through the door. 'Justice has not had a good day today.'

He was angry and on edge; Pete recognized the telltale signs.

'Is it the California thing, Mike? I heard on the radio that it got turned down. It sounds a little unfair to—'

'Unfair? It's a goddam scandal! The Democrats upped their majority from one to eleven seats by redrawing those district lines, and the court has just turned a blind eye! And what *really* gets me is that I heard nothing at all from Bush's guys when we were winning cases for them and now suddenly, as soon as we lose, I get this pissy message saying, "How come we lost?" and making out like we did it on purpose or something.'

Mike was pacing up and down and looked ready to strike at anyone or anything that got in his way. Pete had seen him like this before. He knew it was a portent of blackness and rage but he tried to contain it.

'Hey, Mike, how about we take a time out? We're not going to fix this thing tonight, and if we sit and fret it'll just seem worse than it is. Let's get a cab and drive up to Glen Echo or somewhere by the river. We could eat at the Old Angler's and share a bottle of red.'

Mike dismissed that. 'I can't relax, Pete. This thing's got me too wound up, and anyway I need to . . .'

A frown flitted over Mike's face, followed by a look that hovered somewhere between cunning and guilt. 'Let's go to the Eagle,' he said. 'I'll put on my biker gear. We don't have to do anything, OK? You can sit with me and we can get drunk . . . Or I can. It's what I need right now.'

He was justifying the idea to Pete, and maybe to himself. The prospect of the dark grimy bar with its sexual charge and promise of delicious guilt made him feel light-headed.

Pete hated leather bars and hated the thought of what went on in their upstairs rooms and private cubicles, but he could see Mike was stressed and uptight, and he figured that if he didn't agree, Mike would go on his own.

'OK, Mike, let's do it. But we go, and then we come home, right? We both have work in the morning.'

Mike nodded and went through to the bedroom. They had a closet each, and at the back of his Mike kept a large black case, buckled shut. He lifted it onto the bed.

When he returned, he was wearing tight black leather pants and a leather vest with studs and chains over a bare chest.

The Eagle Bar on New York Avenue near Mount Vernon Square did not seem busy. The large downstairs room had a dozen customers, most of them dressed like Mike, cans of beer in their hands, listening to very loud country music on the sound system. They glowered at the new arrivals with a show of stagey aggression. Pete, in his smart jacket and chinos, felt out of place. Mike sat him down at a corner table and ordered some nachos and pizza slices. After an hour and a few drinks, Mike's fearsome eruption of nervous anxiety had transmuted into fast-talking excitement. One of his feet tapped rapidly on the floor and his fingers drummed on the table.

'OK, let's go upstairs now,' he mumbled with his eyes fixed on the tablecloth. 'Let's go, OK?'

Pete stared at him.

'I thought we were just coming for a drink, Mike. I thought we said we weren't going to do anything.'

'Well, maybe *you* said that,' Mike hissed. 'What's the point of coming here if we don't go upstairs?'

Pete sighed and stood up.

The upstairs room was much smaller, warm and dark, the air fetid with testosterone. The men crowded in there were from the leather and kink crowd, many of them hairy and tattooed, wearing Levi's and metal-studded biker jackets with coloured bandannas. In a corner a group of four or five guys wearing only the briefest of leather jockstraps and military-style leather caps were making out, feeling each other's bodies. The atmosphere was hostile. Pete began to say he felt uncomfortable, that he would like to leave, but Mike motioned him to be quiet.

On a small raised dais a pale, slim man in a fluorescent thong was tied to a wall and two burly guys in black executioner masks were pouring molten candle wax onto his naked body; another was whipping him with a leather cat-o'-nine-tails. It was crowded, dark and hot.

Pete began to feel faint. He took Mike's arm. 'I need to go, Mike. Will you come now – please?'

But Mike pushed him away. 'You go if you like. I'm staying.'

'But you'll be home soon, Mike, won't you? Remember what we said.'

Mike grunted but did not turn to look – did not even notice – as Pete slipped out down the stairs.

In their elegant apartment Pete lay awake. Around six he heard Mike come in and go straight to the bathroom. He pulled on his robe and went through. When Mike emerged, he was dressed for work and wearing sunglasses.

'Thank God you're back, Mike. I've been so worried.'

Pete went to give him a hug, but Mike winced and pushed him away. As he left, Mike pulled up his shirt collar, but Pete caught a glimpse of the bruises on his neck.

SIXTEEN

1991–2

In the months that followed, Mike seemed to unravel. He would get home from work, make a show of casual normality for an hour, then slip out for the rest of the evening while Pete was in the shower, leaving a non-committal note taped to the fridge. It was the same sly, evasive behaviour that had destroyed his relationship with Mark, but he simply couldn't make himself stop – you might as well have asked an alcoholic why he couldn't stop drinking. Mike's addiction was secrecy and the rush of being in the wrong – of proving he was the flawed being he always knew he was. He drank heavily and was picked up twice for driving while drunk. He awoke from stupors steeped in self-loathing, comforted not by the thought of redemption and recovery but by the promise of another secret, guilty evening to come.

Pete tried pleading with him and Mike promised to change, but nothing happened. Pete opened the chest in Mike's closet and found it full of sadomasochistic pornography, bondage magazines and pictures of leather and rubber sex. This was not the usual gay porn but stories of torture and cruelty, men roped or tied in slings, then abused and violated. Pete was at loss, and finally called Susan Kavanagh and asked if they could meet.

'Susan, Mike's in a bad way, and it's not something that's easy for me to speak about.' He glanced around the bar. 'It's to do with how he's behaving . . .'

Susan nodded, 'It's OK, Pete. It's not the first time.'

'Yeah, I know. It's that whole disappearing thing again, like when he split up from Mark O'Connor, but I think it's even worse this time. He's spending so much time in leather bars and I never know where he is or who he's with. The kind of thing he gets up to, Susan – it's a whole different level, and it's not a level I'm happy accepting. It's not about being gay; it's about being *depraved* . . .'

'And what does he say when you tackle him about it?' Susan asked.

'That's the problem: he won't say anything – I find things out by chance . . . like the money that goes missing from the bank account or the stuff he leaves lying around. I found another drinking while driving citation that he'd never told me about and it looks like he was thrown in jail this time, because the release form that got him out of there . . . I noticed the signature on it was Bobby Burchfield, Susan – George Bush's personal lawyer, the guy who's running the Bush re-election campaign. The White House sent Bobby Burchfield to get Mike out of jail!'

'So the big boys know?' Susan mused. 'Isn't that enough to get him worried – to make him do something about it?'

Pete shook his head.

'He bought a book on being an alcoholic and how to deal with it, but he's never opened it. And when he comes back from his lost weekends, I find drugs in his pockets. I can hardly recognize the guy I fell in love with any more: it's like he wants to throw himself into the dirt . . . because he *hates* himself so much.'

'Well, you know, that thought crossed my mind,' Susan said. 'I know he depends pretty badly on what people think about him. When he got fired from NIMLO, he was so down on himself it was like his whole world had collapsed. He doesn't look it, but I think he's fragile, Pete. It only takes a little knock – some withdrawal of love – for him to fall apart.'

Pete frowned.

'It's just all happened so fast. It's like he's had all those years of conforming and repressing his identity, then suddenly he can't do it any more and there's this huge explosion . . . like he's just letting go of everything all at once.' He thought for a moment and picked up the thought that Susan had begun. 'It's like he's always lived this compartmentalized life where he has to deny his sexuality at work and then defend his work to his friends . . . And he was able to cope with all that as long as things were going well, as long as he was being promoted and praised, but as soon as something went wrong – when he thought the White House didn't love him enough – that's when it all collapsed.'

Susan took Pete's hand.

'I know it's hard for you, Pete. I know you love him . . . and he loves you too – I'm sure of that. It seems to me the only thing you can do is just keep on being there for him. If you keep loving him, if you can be the constant in his life when the rest of the world turns against him, I'm sure you can make the difference.'

Pete stayed constant. Through all the lost nights and lost weekends he refused to answer excess with anger. He stayed kind and solicitous when Mike was surly and dismissive, and eventually his devotion worked the miracle. In the spring of 1992 Mike came back from the blackness and into the light of the love that had always been there for him. The Easter vigil at Shepherdstown that year was a special one.

'This is my welcome home party,' Mike announced to the guests. It was midnight and he was standing glass in hand.

'This is a celebration of Easter, of friendship and of love'– a cheer rose around the table – 'and for me it's a personal celebration . . . a celebration of the man who—' His breath caught in his throat as his gaze settled on Pete. 'I'd like to propose a toast to Pete Nilsson, the man I love – the man who saved me from myself.'

'Thank you,' he whispered into Pete's ear, then, turning to the guests around the table, 'This is a poem by a man who meant a lot to me as a child . . . and it's for the man who means the most to me as an adult.

Wine comes in at the mouth
And love comes in at the eye;
That's all we shall know for truth
Before we grow old and die.
I lift the glass to my mouth,
I look at you, and I sigh.'

In church the following morning Mike took Pete's hand as the priest offered the Peace of Christ and did not let go until the Mass was over. When the guests had left on Sunday evening he lay in bed with his lover and whispered in his ear, 'I love you so much, Pete. I've been selfish and unkind but you never let me down, even when I was trying to hurt you. Now I want to be with you forever. I want to grow old with you, and if you're with me I won't be scared or lonely any more. When old age comes we'll welcome it together. You've rescued me, and now we can live forever.'

In the early summer Mike fell ill with pneumonia. The doctors said it was a strange time of year to get it, but maybe there was a bug going round and Mike had just been unlucky.

SEVENTEEN

1992–3

Fate has a curious way of crossing – or nearly crossing – the paths of those whose lives it will one day bring together. I remember the Republican convention of 1992 quite clearly. Arriving in Houston on 16 August, I had the strong presentiment that George Bush and his party were in trouble. I had come from the Democrats' convention in New York, where Bill Clinton had been acclaimed in an eruption of rock music and misty evocations of JFK's Camelot, and walked into a Houston Astrodome packed with tight-lipped sour-faced men in cheap suits with walkie-talkies and badges proclaiming GOD, FAMILY, AMERICA. Bush had been riding high – the Soviet Union had collapsed and US forces had freed Kuwait – but now the country had slid into recession, and Clinton kept saying, 'It's the economy, stupid.'

Michael Hess had arrived in Houston a week earlier. This was his third convention representing the RNC and by now he had figured out most of the pitfalls – and most of the ways to have fun. Pete had come down for a couple of days on a business trip and they spent the evening before the convention in a restaurant with other gay men who worked for the party. They spoke of the gloomy political outlook and how Bush had been forced to make a sharp turn to the right by the powerful conservative lobby.

'And guess who's been nominated as the keynote speaker?' Mike said. 'It's your friend and mine, Patrick J. Buchanan. It'll be a good time for you guys to get out of the hall and go find somewhere to get drunk!'

'And what about you, Mike?' Pete asked. 'Do you have to be up on the podium while he speaks?'

'Uh-uh.' Mike smiled. 'The minute he starts I'll be heading out of there. I'll come back once he's finished – I need to be there for the president – then it'll be time to hit the beer and drown a few sorrows.'

Pat Buchanan did not disappoint. His speech was a bullying, tub-thumping assault on liberals, radicals and destroyers of American family values, and the theme running through it was that homosexuality was bringing the country to its knees.

'So we stand against the amoral idea that gay and lesbian couples should have the same standing in law as married men and women. We stand in favour of the right of communities to control the raw sewage of pornography that pollutes our popular culture. We stand for right to life and voluntary prayer in public schools. My friends, this election is about much more than who gets what. It is about who we are, what we believe in and what we stand for as Americans. There is a war going on in our country . . . a cultural war . . . a struggle for the soul of America!'

The cheers from the floor shook the Astrodome, but the party was torn. Mary Fisher, adopted daughter of a wealthy Republican fundraiser, took to the podium on the penultimate night to reveal that she was HIV positive and to make an impassioned plea on behalf of all AIDS victims.

'I ask the Republican Party to lift the shroud of silence which has been draped over the issue of HIV and AIDS! I bear a message of challenge . . . I want your attention, not your applause! The reality of AIDS is brutally clear. Two hundred thousand Americans are dead or dying; a million more are infected. And I represent an AIDS community whose members have been reluctantly drafted from every segment of American society . . . Though I am white and a mother and contracted this disease in marriage and enjoy the warm support of my family, I am one with the lonely gay man sheltering a flickering candle from the cold wind of his family's rejection . . .'

There was a smattering of applause in the hall, but the effect of Mary Fisher's words was to highlight the Republicans' failure to act on AIDS and the party's ingrained homophobia. In the November election George Bush was defeated by Bill Clinton, and on 20 January 1993 the Grand Old Party vacated the White House for the first time in twelve years.

In the spring the pneumonia came back. This time Mike recognized the symptoms and went at once to see his doctor, but after two weeks on antibiotics he was still coughing and running a 104-degree fever. Out in Shepherdstown for the weekend, Pete put him to bed and sat with him as shaking chills gripped his body and pain stabbed his chest with every breath. On Sunday morning, when Mike's skin had turned a dusky purple, Pete dressed him and drove the fifteen miles to City Hospital in Martinsburg.

The medics who examined Mike were assiduous: they ordered a chest X-ray and blood tests and nodded when the results came through.

'Well, Mr Hess, it's as classic a case of lobar pneumonia as ever I saw. Your white blood cells are all over the place – you got a high count of neutrophils and a real low count of lymphocytes, and that means you got yourself a humdinger of a virus there.'

Mike smiled wanly. Pete spoke for him.

'He's hardly ever been sick in his life, Doctor; hardly even a cold. This is all a shock. Will you need to keep him here for long? He has FEHB insurance from his job with the Republican Party.'

'Well, good, that's fine and dandy. And we'll definitely do our best for a Republican.' The doctor's laugh was inscrutable.

Mike was in hospital in Martinsburg for five days, attached to a drip as he slowly recovered. On the third day Pete broached the subject that was in both of their minds.

'Mike, I'm not saying this to upset you – and it's probably nothing – but have you thought maybe this could be . . . AIDS related?'

Mike did not respond immediately.

'I don't think so,' he said at last, making himself believe it. 'I had the test last time and it was negative, and now the doctors have done all these new tests . . . I'm pretty sure it's just pneumonia.'

Pete let the matter drop. That evening, alone in the house in Shepherdstown, the thought occurred to him that Martinsburg, and West Virginia as a whole, probably had little experience of AIDS and maybe the medics did not automatically test for it, but then he put the thought out of his head.

Susan Kavanagh came to visit. She leaned over and kissed Mike's unshaven cheek. Her lips felt so smooth and cold – *like an ice cube,* he thought, on his feverish skin.

'You know, Mike,' Susan said, 'you got us all a bit worried there. Pete says you're getting better, but I . . . I have to say you still don't look too good.'

'Yeah, I know,' he said with an effort. 'I don't feel too good, either. But they've promised to get me back on my feet and out of here . . . and I need to get back to work. I'm kind of worried what they'll all be thinking . . .'

Susan guessed from the tone of his voice what was concerning him.

'What do you mean, Mike? What should they be thinking?'

'Well, let me ask you: if you worked where I work and somebody got sick with pneumonia a year ago and now they're out sick with pneumonia again in the hospital, what would you think?'

Mike watched her. She was weighing something up, her eyes on his.

'I would think they had AIDS,' she said at last.

Mike sought for a last straw to grasp.

'OK, but you're from New York, right? And you guys have seen so much of this AIDS stuff that maybe you just jump to conclusions.'

Before she could reply, he had turned away to adjust the flowers she had placed at his bedside.

Mike was released from hospital and returned to his work at the RNC. With the Republicans out of the White House the mood was less ebullient, but there was a lot of work still to be done on redistricting litigation across the nation. The defeat in California had been a setback, but other suits in other states were hitting the courts and the party was winning enough of them to keep alive the target of a Republican House in 1994.

The defeat of Bush and Quayle had shaken the leadership, and the Republican National Committee called for a complete rethink of the party's platform. There was something of a backlash against the conservatives who had hijacked the Houston convention and whose bulging-eyed intolerance was blamed for sending moderate Republican voters running to the Democrats. Pat Buchanan, Jerry Falwell and Pat Robertson found themselves temporarily out of favour; Gerry Hauer and Bill Bennett lost much of their influence. As chief counsel, Mike had his say in the RNC's policy debates and argued for greater flexibility on social issues, but his thoughts were elsewhere.

He still had a racking cough that gave him no peace, and at the end of May asked Pete if he would come with him to see a pulmonary specialist. They held hands surreptitiously as they sat in the waiting room.

When he had sounded Mike's chest and listened to the description of his symptoms, the doctor said he would send him for a lung X-ray. As he was filling in a form on his desk, and without looking up, he said, 'Are there any other tests you would like me to carry out at the same time?'

Mike coughed and cleared his throat. 'Oh, yeah. I guess you should also do an AIDS test . . . If you don't mind.'

He was struck by the calmness of his voice – he had just requested a pronouncement on his own life or death in a tone so offhand he might have been asking for a pound of apples. As the doctor wrote another line on his form, Mike felt Pete squeezing his hand under the table and returned the pressure with a rush of gratitude.

The doctor had said they could expect the results by the end of the week. The days became a zone in which thought seemed suspended: they would start to say something and stop in mid-sentence – whatever they said, whatever they decided, might soon have to be recast, rethought and possibly countermanded by the news that would soon be with them.

On the Friday morning they parted with a careful show of normality.

At work Mike had three cases to review for his report to the Federal Election Commission, but he couldn't focus. At eleven he started to call the clinic a couple of times but hung up as soon as it rang. The third time, the nurse answered. When Mike asked for his test results there was a pause, then: 'Hello, Mr Hess. Yes, we have your results. Are you free to come down to the clinic this afternoon? There are a few things the doctor would like to go through with you.'

During an afternoon meeting that Pete was attending but hardly managing to follow, his secretary slipped him a note to say he had a call waiting.

'It's bad news.' Mike's voice on the end of the line was expressionless. 'Can you come get me? I'm at the apartment.'

EIGHTEEN

1993

It took a half-hour for Pete to extricate himself from the meeting. He drove to their apartment building, where Mike was in the lobby with cases packed for the weekend.

They did not embrace.

Pete slid back behind the wheel and Mike climbed into the passenger seat.

Shock and anger, fear and resentment vied with love and pity in the cramped space of the car.

Pete turned the key.

'Mike . . .'

'Yeah, what?'

'Mike, how could you—'

'How could I *what*?'

The words were spat out hard.

Pete reached to put his hand on Mike's knee, but it was pushed away. He hit the accelerator and headed for the GW Parkway.

'Tell me what he said, Mike.'

'What do you mean? He said I got AIDS, that's what.'

Pete hit the horn and the guy in front looked round.

'Just like that? On the phone?'

'No, I went to see him. Then I went back to the office. Then I couldn't stay there, so I went back to the apartment.'

For some reason the ordering of the facts seemed suddenly important. They were circling round the big questions, playing for time with the little details.

'And did he say . . . how bad it is?'

Pete sensed the futility of the question. Mike threw up his hands, furious, terrified.

'Fuck, Pete! Of course it's bad. It's the fucking end, OK? The fucking end of everything!'

Mike was breathing in short sobs that racked his body. Pete felt tears beneath the anger and the same frightened cocktail of emotions inside himself. He wanted to comfort him, slap him, kiss him.

'So where did it come from, Mike?'

The question arose from fear. If Mike was infected then *he* must be infected too, but Mike didn't seem to get it. His response stemmed from terror, the egotism of the condemned man.

'Well, you must have given it to me, Pete!'

The words were unjust and shocking, but also an acknowledgment that Pete was a sharer in this terrible thing.

The car in front braked and they screeched to a halt an inch from its fender.

'God, Mike, this is madness,' Pete said. 'You know I didn't give it to you . . . But if you've got it, then so have I, that's for sure.'

'Yeah,' Mike half whispered. 'That's what I was thinking.'

Suddenly, tears were streaming down Mike's face and Pete felt them in his eyes too. He couldn't wipe them away because his hands were on the wheel, and because he couldn't wipe them away he couldn't see to drive. Through his tears he heard himself say, 'Well, at least it means we don't have to get old . . .' And he gave a little laugh, as if there were some silver lining after all.

Mike's reply was heart-wrenching. 'But I always *wanted* to get old,' he sobbed. 'I wanted to grow old with *you*.'

The weekend at the house in Shepherdstown was etched with grief and exhaustion. Pete feared he too was facing death but would have to wait until Monday for the test that would confirm his fate. By

Sunday morning he was resigned: he was going to die.

Mike was able to think more calmly and apologized for his behaviour.

'I was going crazy,' he said as they ate their breakfast on the back porch of the house. The horses were grazing in the field that sloped down to the river. 'I never should have said those things – accused you. Whatever else is true or untrue, we're in this together and there needs to be no resentments to drive us apart.'

Life was divided now into the before and after: before, when death had been a figure of speech beyond the horizon, and after, when death was a reality, a certainty that coloured thought and action.

'I feel calm right now,' Pete murmured. 'I have moments when I forget what has happened and it's like things are normal again.'

'Yes,' Mike said. 'As if life will carry on just how it was. But then . . . the awful, dreadful knowledge that it *won't* carry on. That it'll never be the same. It's like being in hell.'

They went for a walk through the fields and found themselves on the bank of the Potomac. Pete sat on a rock at the water's edge and waited for Mike to join him, but Mike paced along the shore, walked away, then turned suddenly towards him.

'I don't know where I got it, Pete. You asked me where I got it, but I don't know and that's the truth.'

Mike had lost the serenity that had surfaced at breakfast; now he was tormented again and angry.

'That's the most terrible thing. I don't know where this came from and I don't know why it's happened to me. It's so fucking unfair! I never did anything that millions of other people didn't do. So why me? Why am I the one that gets it when they don't?'

Pete said nothing. Mike tried to sting him into a response.

'This is the 1990s, for fuck's sake; it's not the eighties when everyone got infected. It's like we dodged the bullet in the bad times and now suddenly this comes along!'

Pete gazed at the distress in his lover's face and felt resentment swell beneath his pity. If Mike didn't know where he got infected, Pete had a pretty good idea. For a moment he wanted to ask, 'What about all the nights you went out cruising and never asked who you were going with? What about the lost weekends you got so drunk or stoned you couldn't remember where you'd been?' But he said nothing. Mike was consumed by the furious envy of the condemned man for those who still have hope. At their backs the torrent of the Potomac roared in its eternal inexorable rush to the sea.

NINETEEN

Pete opened the envelope, glanced at the paper and thrust it immediately back inside. He found it hard to say what he felt – relief, yes, but guilt too, disappointment almost, as if this were a failure, a rejected audition, the abandonment of a quest on which his partner would now embark without him.

Mike was silent when Pete told him his test was negative.

He lay on the couch in their apartment and stared at the ceiling.

'I'm glad,' he whispered at last. 'I'm glad you will live. I'm glad I've been spared the guilt of making you share this with me.'

They went together to the Infectious Diseases Department of GW Hospital. Mike registered with the AIDS support service. He remembered the days he had spent waiting for David Carlin to die and thought how different things were when you were the one waiting for death. The specialist was in his mid-thirties, with rimless glasses and a tic that made it look like he was winking.

'Well, Mr Hess,' he said with a wink, 'your numbers are not great. Your CD4 count is 200, which is exactly the threshold of full-blown AIDS. Now that of course is merely a snapshot of where you are today, so we'll need to monitor your blood counts over the coming months to see if they are falling, falling rapidly or remaining steady. Do you have an idea how long you have been HIV positive?

It would help us determine how aggressively the virus is behaving.'

Mike shrugged and said he honestly did not know.

'No matter.' The doctor winked. 'We'll put you on AZT as a matter of urgency. It's expensive, but I see you have FEHB cover, so that should be OK. Now, lifestyle. You're an educated man so I guess I don't need to labour the point, but in your condition you are highly infectious. There must be no unprotected sex and you must take the greatest of care with bodily fluids. The other side of the coin is that your own immune system is badly weakened and you will be prone to infections that a man of your age would normally resist – your bouts of pneumonia were almost certainly the first of them.'

In most spheres of life Mike was confident in the way he dealt with people, but the medical profession cowed him. Pete had noticed this before and knew there were things Mike should be asking.

'There are a couple of questions that I have, if it's OK?' Pete said. 'First of all, can you say how long the infection might have been there? And also what effect is the AZT likely to have in a case like this?'

The doctor put his hand to his face as if the stop the tic in his eye.

'To your first question, I cannot say with any precision. The virus could have been in incubation for many months or even years and is only now making its presence felt. As for AZT, it's been around since 1987 and there's no doubt it has slowed the advance of AIDS in patients in the early stages. Unfortunately, there has been research this year in England which concludes the drug is not effective in delaying full-blown AIDS. In this instance, Mr Hess, your T-cell count is already very low and I'm not certain AZT will—'

'In that case,' Pete said quietly, 'I think you need to tell us what the prospects are . . .'

'Well, that of course is a question for the patient himself to pose. Mr Hess?'

The doctor looked to Mike, who nodded silently.

'Then I'm afraid the news is not great. In my experience, patients with your level of T-cells have survived for approximately a year, although with AZT it can be closer to two.'

In the weeks following his diagnosis Mike could barely sleep. In the semi-conscious borderlands, his thoughts rushed down dark, narrow streets, one dead end after another, always seeking the one that would lead him to the light. But there was blackness everywhere. Finally, he dreamt of sunshine and nuns' white habits brushing softly past him. There was a half-opened door in his dream, a chink in the gloom, and Mike put his hand on the door handle. He sensed it was one of those old manual locks that could be flicked open with little effort. His hand was on it, beginning to lift, beginning to imagine the light beyond.

In the office he covered up the thoughts that never left him and concentrated on the work in hand. One day when he reached for the DC phone directory to look up the number of a political lobbyist, it fell open at the page that listed international travel agents.

Mike thought about telling Mary he was going to Ireland, but in the end he decided against it. Very few people knew about his illness – only Pete, Susan and the doctors – and if he invited Mary to come with him, he would have to explain more than he wanted to at the moment. Pete told him it was a great idea. It would give him something to focus on, and at the very least they could have two weeks' holiday together in a place that would take their minds off their troubles at home. In the weeks before they left, Pete found himself having to temper Mike's exhilarated expectation, certainty almost, that *this time* he would find his mother. He asked him how he would feel if he failed again, but Mike was not listening. There was something desperate in his search now.

For Mike, in the shadow of the unknown, the reunion with his mother seemed the key to unlocking the sorrow and the pain, a last chance to find the answers to the puzzle of his life. *Because if I don't find out now*, he told himself, *I never will. And I have to find out who I am before I am no more.*

TWENTY

August 1993

They arrived in Roscrea in early August and took a room in the old manor house that stands a mile down the road from Sean Ross Abbey. The place was owned by two sisters in their eighties whose family had lived there for a century but was heirless now. Grace Darcy was the older of the two, blind and dependent on her sister Ellen to guide her, but with a strange serenity about her and an unnatural ability to read people's voices. Over breakfast on the first morning the sisters asked why they had come to Ireland. Mike explained the story of his birth and adoption, and Grace's face grew serious.

'We've had orphans staying here before,' she said. 'And we have seen the sorrow they go through. Sometimes it is not a good idea to search for your mother; sometimes it turns out badly.'

Mike and Pete looked at each other, and Mike felt a chill skitter over the skin on his neck.

'What . . . do you mean?' he asked.

Grace shook her head.

'Sometimes it turns out badly.'

Mike wanted Pete with him when he went to the abbey, and Pete wanted to see where Mike had spent his first years in the world. It was after eleven when they parked their hire car on the gravelled drive and the sun was already high in the sky. Mike knocked on the door of the old house and it was opened immediately by a pretty young nun with green eyes and freckles, who greeted them with a smile. When Mike said what he had come for, she looked puzzled.

'Oh now, it's been twenty years or more since we had any orphans here, and I'm not sure how much we can help you. What did you say your name was again?'

'Michael Hess, but I was born Anthony Lee; that's the name that would appear in your records, my real name.'

Mike smiled encouragingly at the girl. 'May we come inside, please?'

She stood back from the doorway to let them through.

'I have come all the way from America and I am not leaving here without finding my mother,' he said gently but deliberately. 'May I please speak with Mother Barbara?'

The young nun gave him a look of sympathy.

'I'm so sorry,' she said. 'Mother Barbara died three years ago, in 1990 – July the twentieth, it was. She's buried in the nuns' cemetery just over the path there; you can see her grave on the way out.'

Mike had not expected this. Why had he not thought? Of course, she was an old woman! Why had he not checked before he came all this way on an errand that now looked doomed to failure? But then another name surfaced, a name he had glimpsed only once, when he had surreptitiously opened Doc's letter to the Notre Dame Admissions office a quarter-century ago.

'Sister Hildegarde!' he exclaimed. 'Sister Hildegarde is the woman who brokered my adoption papers.' Then, with a look of foreboding, '*She's* not dead, is she?'

The young nun laughed. 'Indeed she is not. Sister Hildegarde is eighty-six years old, so she is, but, God be praised, she's still with us. Will I go and ask if she can see you?'

Mike felt like hugging her. 'Yes, Sister, please go ask her. I'd be so grateful.'

Mike and Pete sat in the parlour and waited. They drank the nuns' tea and ate the nuns' biscuits, and the ormolu clock above the fireplace ticked off a half-hour, then another. When eventually footsteps sounded in the hall and the door creaked open, the nun who shuffled in on slippered feet was tiny and frail. Even if he had been capable of recalling their last meeting forty years earlier, Mike would not have recognized her: the vigorous despot who had struck fear into the hearts of fallen women had shrunk to an ethereal old lady with white hair tucked beneath her blue linen wimple and a thick woollen cardigan over her long habit despite the heat of the August day. The two men leapt to their feet, but Sister Hildegarde waved her hand for them to be seated.

'There's no need for any of that here.' Her voice was thin and breathy but to Mike it seemed full of warmth and humanity; he felt drawn to her.

'Oh, Sister, thank you so much for agreeing to see us,' he said. 'I can't tell you how much this means to me.'

'Then I take it you are Anthony?' Sister Hildegarde shook Mike's hand and turned to smile at Pete. 'I think, if you don't mind, Anthony and I should have this conversation alone. There is such a lot of emotion on these occasions and we must be sensitive to the feelings of our children. Our children are our most important priority in everything we do.'

Pete rose to his feet.

'Of course. I completely understand. I think I'll go take a look at your gardens, if you don't mind.' He rested a hand lightly on Mike's shoulder for a second, then left the room.

'It's so comforting to know that you were here when I was born,' Mike said as he pulled up a chair for Sister Hildegarde at the plain wooden table. 'I'm sure you must have been a great help to my mother and all the other girls who came to you.'

The nun gave him a glance, as if trying to discern any hint of mockery in his voice.

'Well, you know, the girls did not stay with us long, but we did our best for them.'

Mike felt a sudden surge of excitement. She was not going to refuse to talk with him; there was not going to be a repeat of the sterile confrontation he had had with Mother Barbara.

'So how long was my mother here, Sister?' Mike asked. 'It's a question that has always haunted me – whether she cared for me or whether she just abandoned me . . .'

Sister Hildegarde gazed at the man beside her, wondering if she could place him among all the children she had dealt with and eventually deciding that, yes, he must be the boy she had taken to Shannon with the little girl the adopters tried to send back as a defective. She remembered his mother too, the pretty young thing from Newcastle West with the slight cast in her eye, always cooing and fussing over her baby and panicking whenever he got sick.

'Well, she may have been here just for a little while,' she said at length. 'That was the way of things back in those days, but it's impossible to be certain.'

'Oh, OK. That's . . . I had kind of hoped . . . But anyway, what I really wanted to ask is, do you have any records of my mother . . . anything that could help me?'

Sister Hildegarde gave him a look of sympathy.

'Unfortunately, Anthony, I simply cannot remember your mother,' she said. 'We had so many of them going through here in those days. Your mother was most likely given up to us by her parents on the streets of Dublin or somewhere.'

The anonymity of that 'or somewhere' was a blow. Mike felt suddenly weary and cheated. Sister Hildegarde pulled an envelope out of her bag.

'Well, I do have one thing I can let you have.'

Mike looked up.

'This is your birth certificate. It has your birth listed as 5 July 1952 and your mother's name as Philomena Lee.'

Mike took the piece of paper and turned it over in his hands. He saw his birth had been registered on 11 July by an Eileen Finnegan, whom he took to be one of the nuns, but a black line had been drawn through the spaces 'Father's Name and Address' and 'Father's Profession', and the form contained no other information.

'Thank you, Sister,' he said. 'This is lovely to have, but actually

I already knew my mother's name. Don't you have anything else that might help me find her?'

Sister Hildegarde smiled and shook her head.

'No, I'm afraid this is all.'

She glanced up at a portrait of Christ on the wall, and for the first time Mike sensed the nun might not be telling the whole truth.

'Sister,' he said slowly, 'I have been diagnosed with . . . an illness, and I have been given just two years to live. Now I hope you can understand this – there is one thing I want above all others, one thing I *need* to do before I die, and that is to find my mother. So I beg you, please, to heed the request of a dying man; I beg you to have mercy on my suffering.'

'I'm so sorry, Anthony. I would like to help you, but the truth is, the records are gone.'

Mike sensed a flicker of the same intransigence he had met in Mother Barbara – a closing down in the nun's eyes, a withdrawal of goodwill – and he hastened to soften it.

'Sister, please believe me. I'm not interested in anything but the present – where my mother is *now*. I think we should forget the past and whatever things went on back then. That's all over now. But can't you tell me, for the love of God, where did my birth mother go when she left here?'

'As I say' – Sister Hildegarde frowned – 'I have looked through our files – that is why I kept you waiting just now – and I have found nothing. I am so sorry.'

'But, Sister, if we know my mother's name is Philomena Lee, surely you must have some record of where she went?'

Sister Hildegarde seemed to grow impatient. 'Many of our records were destroyed in a fire. You could possibly try the Irish Passport Office, but I can help you no further.'

'Well, what about the money?' Mike was desperate now and desperation kindled anger. 'What about the money you took from the Americans who came here looking for babies? The money you took from my parents? Is there no record of all the graft and corruption that went on over that?'

Sister Hildegarde stood up. Mike stood up hastily with her, clutching his head.

'No, don't go, Sister. I'm sorry. It's just . . . I'm just very overwrought about everything that's happening to me.'

The nun hesitated and sat down again.

'Let me ask you one thing,' Mike said quietly. 'A favour. When I die, and I am going to die soon, the greatest regret I shall take to my grave is that I never knew the woman who gave me birth. I was never able to tell her about the life I had or ask her about her feelings for me. But if I cannot find her in life, perhaps I can find her in death . . .'

Mike paused as a tear rose to his eye and slowly subsided.

'Sister, what I want to ask you is . . . will you allow me to be buried in Sean Ross Abbey?' He blew his nose. 'Because I have always had the feeling my mother is trying to find me in the same way I have been trying to find her. And if she is looking for me, the place she will come is right here.'

He thought for a moment, trying to picture the future, the time when it would be too late.

'But if you would let me be buried here, she might find my grave. It might give her comfort . . . and, who knows? Maybe one day she can use the information on my headstone to discover what I did with my life. Do not refuse me this favour, Sister . . . please.'

Sister Hildegarde's reply, when it came, was slow and deliberate.

'Our graveyard is crowded. There is little space left for anyone other than the sisters, who have their plots reserved. But I can see it means a great deal to you, Anthony, so if you are willing to make a donation to the abbey – and we would need to discuss the size of that donation – then I believe something may be possible . . .'

When Mike emerged from the convent, he saw Pete sitting in the sun on the far side of the lawn. He watched him for a while, thinking how handsome, how very *good* he looked. Mike walked over and, without a word, sat down beside him, slipped his arm round his waist and laid his head on his shoulder.

That evening over dinner their landladies asked how they had got on. Mike told them what Sister Hildegarde had said about trying to find his records but that they had disappeared.

Grace snorted. 'The records are not there because *she* destroyed them! She burned them all as soon as the scandals started, may God forgive her. I will never forget the smell of that bonfire – it was the smell of those babies' souls rising up to heaven. She burned their records and she burned their hope.'

Her sister Ellen nodded. 'It's true. Four years ago, in 1989, people started talking about how the nuns had coerced those young women into giving away their babies – how they made mothers sign terrible pledges that they would never seek to contact their children or try to find out what happened to them, how they were so brazen that they even forged some of the signatures and how they took stacks of money from the Americans who bought the babies off them. They may have called them donations but they were cash payments – for babies that weren't theirs to sell! We who live here have always known about these things. Hildegarde McNulty burned those records because she was scared people would find out what they did.'

Mike and Pete returned to the convent the following morning but were told Sister Hildegarde was sick in bed. For the next two days they travelled the local area searching phone books and visiting churches and cemeteries. They combed every row of graves looking for family tombs with the name Lee, but they did not travel the seventy miles down the N7 to Newcastle West. Had they done so, they would have found not only the Lee family grave but Mike's uncle Jack, who had bounced him on his knee forty years earlier and spent the rest of his life regretting that he did not pick him up and run off with him, still living in the same council house in Connolly's Terrace.

On the final day of their stay they walked through the grounds of Sean Ross Abbey and sat together in the ruins of the ancient monastery beside the old graveyard. The place was deserted, the white maypole shorn of its ribbons; the only sound was the desultory humming of bees in the summer heat and the faint rustle of sycamore branches in the breeze.

For an hour they lay there in silence. The tranquillity of the garden seemed to calm Mike's spirit, and when he spoke he sounded brighter than he had for many weeks.

'Pete? Did you notice anything about the way people look over here?'

Pete sat up.

'How do you mean?'

'I keep seeing guys in the street and thinking they look just like me. Haven't you noticed?'

Pete laughed. 'If all the guys in the street looked like you, I'd be in heaven! But yeah, I guess I do know what you mean – dark brows, black hair and stuff.'

'Exactly. Sometimes I look at these people and it's like looking at myself. There's something reassuring about it – like these people are my people and this has always been their home. It's where they belong, and it feels like I do too.'

Pete mulled over Mike's words and then said, 'Why we don't we just pack everything in and come retire over here? We could buy a little farm and just forget everything and be ourselves. What do you think?'

Mike smiled.

'I think you are a lovely man, Pete Nilsson. Thank you so much for caring about me. Retiring to Ireland would be a dream, but it's not going to happen now, is it?'

Mike watched as the bees flew from flower to flower, carrying pollen in the endless round. The world would continue to turn. Leaves would fall and grow anew. He leaned over to Pete and took his hand.

'We'll never come to live here; it's too late for that. But when I die, that's when I want to come back. This is where I want to be buried, right here in this graveyard in the shadow of the old monastery. Will you remember that when the time comes? Will you do that for me?'

TWENTY-ONE

1993–5

When they returned to Washington, Mike slept better at night, the bad dreams came less frequently and when they did, they seemed less intense. He didn't tell Pete what he had agreed with Sister Hildegarde, but Pete saw her letter lying on the coffee table.

16 August 1993

Dear Michael,

Just a short note to thank you for your very generous donation – I only discovered the cheques after you had gone.

I was delighted that you called to see me. It is always nice to see old friends and you know you will always be welcome here at Sean Ross.

God bless you.

Sister Hildegarde

Over the next year Mike threw himself into his work. Practising the law became his emotional outlet: its certainties reassured him and his successes helped him forget his private Calvary. The 1994 midterms were the target the party had set for capturing the House and Mike was determined to see it through. He might not leave much of a legacy, he told himself, but so much of his life had been invested in the Republican cause that capturing Congress would leave something tangible he could put his name to.

For twelve months his health stayed steady. The doctor at GW Hospital winked every time he read out Mike's blood results and discovered his T-cell numbers still hovering round 200. In the fall of 1994 he offered his congratulations. 'Mr Hess, you have just become one of my longest-surviving full-blown AIDS patients not to suffer any serious reverses. Your blood counts have held steady so that means the AZT is working, and you have avoided all the noxious side effects I have seen in other cases.'

On 8 November 1994, with a fifty-four-seat swing, the Republicans gained control of the House of Representatives for the first time in forty years. Many long-serving Democrats who had previously relied on gerrymandered districts suddenly found themselves out of office, while not a single Republican incumbent lost his or her seat.

In the RNC building on First Street in the shadow of the Capitol champagne corks popped on election night and celebrations continued the next day. Mike's speech was one of quiet satisfaction.

'For the first time ever,' he told his team of lawyers, 'we have created an electoral system in which the number of seats won by each party reflects honestly and fairly its share of the popular vote. Because of your efforts' – he waved his arm to take in the whole of the room – 'we have done away with much of the gerrymandering that distorted previous elections stretching back thirty or forty years. Tonight brings not only a change in control of Congress, but a change in the way politics are done in this country. The media are talking of a Republican revolution' – cheers rang out – 'but what they don't say is that that revolution was made possible by the efforts of dedicated people like all of you, like the late Roger Allan Moore and like Mark Braden, the man who held this job before me.'

There was respectful applause and a voice called out from the back of the room, 'But *you* made it happen, boss. You're the man who did it!'

Republican euphoria lasted until the new Congress convened in January. Mike was on a high that Christmas and New Year, congratulated and feted by the party leadership. On 4 January the populist Newt Gingrich took over as House speaker and immediately launched the Republicans' guerrilla war against President Bill Clinton. GOP control of both the Senate and the House gave the party unprecedented scope to sabotage some of the liberal measures Clinton had tried to introduce, including universal healthcare and tighter gun control, and it led to the resurgence of the conservative religious right. Suddenly, Falwell, Buchanan and Robertson were back, and the campaign against abortion, women's rights and same-sex marriage was centre stage again.

During January Mike received letters and emails from Republican friends congratulating him on helping to engineer the party's revival, and from gay friends expressing their horror at his role in helping the conservatives regain power. By the end of the month, he was coming home from work looking harassed and exhausted.

'What have I done, Pete?' he said. 'I've been so stupid – devoting my life to this goddam party. I can't tell you how despicable they are. I closed my eyes to it for so long. I must have been blind . . . or dazzled by the glitz and power, because I just never focused on what they're really about.'

Pete stood behind him and put his hands on Mike's shoulders. 'What's the matter, Mike?' he asked, massaging his neck. 'What's got you so wound up? Isn't there something we can do about it?'

'It's this anti-gay bill that Jesse Helms is introducing on behalf of the party. It's so fanatical that even the "Moral Morons" are having second thoughts. It establishes the right of federal agencies and employers to discriminate against gay men: anyone employed by the federal government can be fired simply for being gay.'

Pete took Mike's hand and stroked it gently.

'That's terrible. But it's not much worse than the stuff they've been doing for years, is it? And it won't affect us, so why get so agitated about it?'

But Mike *was* agitated. From his pocket he produced a printout of an email bearing that afternoon's date. Pete scanned it with growing unease.

> To Michael Hess.
>
> This is to inform you that if the Helms Bill goes through Congress, you will be the first to suffer its consequences. You have aided and abetted this party of bigots; you have stood by as they let gay Americans die and invoked the curse of God on them. Now it will be your turn to feel their wrath when the media discover the Republicans' chief counsel is gay himself – then let's see who gets fired.
>
> Sincerely, a friend.

In the middle of February Mike fell sick. It began with a slight fever one evening; the next morning he still felt bad. In the bathroom he looked in the mirror and it was there – so innocuous he could easily have missed it – a pale reddish purple, an inch above his right nipple. When he touched it, it felt tender and a little raised like a bruise. He ran his fingers over his stomach and neck, turned to examine his back, raised his arms and saw that two other lesions had appeared in the soft flesh of his armpit.

Mike showered and dressed slowly. When he emerged he told Pete he was feeling much better. As he left he called out, 'I'll be late home, but don't worry – I'll be OK.'

That evening when Mike came in from work, Pete met him at the door and hugged him. 'Did you see the doctor?' he asked.

Mike's face was buried in Pete's right shoulder; they held each other close and their eyes did not meet. It was easier that way for both of them, easier to say things that were important and difficult and fraught with the spectre of separation.

'Yes, I did. The numbers have dropped. I've got lesions now. It's most likely Kaposi's. They're going to do a scan, but I think it's the endgame.'

The flatness of Mike's voice, the quiet enumeration of the fatal symptoms lent the moment an illusion of calm. Then they began to cry, still locked in the embrace that gave them hope and strength. Their sobs were almost apologetic. Weeping undermined the old pretence that nothing had changed and life would continue; it acknowledged a loss that could no longer be postponed.

Their relationship felt the strain. They were no longer equal partners. There was resentment from Mike – the resentment of the sick for the healthy – though he kept it veiled, and there was anxiety from Pete. They were affectionate, kissed and hugged, but sex was proscribed and its absence cast a pall. They stayed loyal to each other, though, and Pete, sensing things were coming to a close, tried to do what he could for Mike while there still was time.

'Do you want to go back to Ireland again?'

Mike thought for a moment and shook his head. 'There's no point, Pete. It's too late to go chasing dreams.'

Every week brought bad news. Mike's T-cell count dipped alarmingly, then recovered and plunged again to new lows. After twelve months of remarkable good health his condition was deteriorating fast. He coughed and lost weight; his body was marked with discoloured patches where lesions bloomed and faded; his fingernails were turning black; his face had taken on the gaunt, sallow look that was the badge of membership in the brotherhood of AIDS. The lower he sank, the higher the mountain of his medication became: by the spring of 1995 he was taking so many pills he needed a chart to keep track of them.

The doctors at GW Hospital offered him counselling but he told them he didn't want it. When Pete tried to persuade him, he lashed out: 'Counselling's for losers. If I'm going to get through this, I'll do it on my own.'

They had not discussed Mike's death, and Pete suspected he was being offered a cue.

'*If* you get through it, Mike?'

But Mike drew back. 'Oh, if, if, if – it's all ifs. There's no point even talking about it. I'll keep taking the medication, so there can be no excuses, but I don't think there's much anyone can do for me now.'

When Mike thought about how he was responding to what was happening to him, he felt – hoped – there was courage in his resignation, not cowardice. He sensed Pete wanted him to keep trying, keep fighting, but he was very tired. Death's presence imposed a calm, lucid logic. He had tried to explain this to Pete, but Pete just wanted him to keep on living. As the cherry blossom unfurled along the Mall and the Capitol glowed pink in the spring sunshine, it seemed that all that remained was for them to say goodbye.

Then cruel hope returned.

Reports of a new generation of drugs had been circulating in the medical press since the turn of the year. All the articles Mike read stressed they were only at a developmental stage and would not be ready for months or even years so the letter he got in the middle of March threw him into a panic. Having struggled to accept that he would die, he found it almost impossible to adjust to the thought that he now might live.

The scheme was a double-blind randomized placebo-controlled study of 1,200 patients with advanced AIDS – not even the doctors would know who got the new antiretrovirals and who got the sugar pills – and the letter stressed that all who signed up for it would have to accept these conditions. Mike looked through the terms of the proposal, carefully set out in cautious legalese with clauses and sub-clauses neatly arrayed, and put it away in his desk. For the next week he was restless, disturbed that he found certainty easier to deal with than hope.

The following Monday he went for a full-day appointment at the hospital. When he came back, he threw open his shirt with a triumphant 'Ta-rah!' and displayed the shunt that had been inserted in his chest – a thin white plastic catheter emerging from his breast above the nipple with three transparent couplings attached to it. The sight of the thing stitched into Mike's flesh made Pete feel queasy, but Mike was jubilant.

'I signed up, Pete! I didn't tell you I was going to. They've asked me to test out this new treatment. Maybe you won't be getting rid of me quite as soon as you thought!'

Mike launched into an explanation of how the new drugs would provide a cocktail of protease and reverse transcriptase inhibitors known as highly active antiretroviral therapy, or HAART, that would reduce the viral load in the body and help normalize his red and white cell counts. He had spent so much time researching the advances in AIDS treatments that he knew almost as much as the doctors did, and he seemed convinced the new drugs were lifesavers.

Pete listened to his explanations, asked a few questions and said what marvellous news it was that he had been selected for the trial. 'But Mike,' he said, 'it's only going to work if you get the real drugs and not the placebos. Don't you think just taking pot luck is too much of a lottery when it's a matter of life and death?'

Mike looked at him blankly.

'What's the alternative? I signed the form agreeing to the conditions of the thing. And anyway, even the doctors don't know which is which.'

TWENTY-TWO

1995

In March Mike phoned Mary to invite her to the house in Shepherds-town for Easter. He had been on the new drug therapy for a couple of weeks, and even though his physical condition was not improving, the thought that something was being done gave him a psychological boost, which in turn lent him the strength to talk.

As soon as Mary heard his voice she knew something was wrong. Mike sounded excited and nervous, repeating that she *must* come see him, already making arrangements for her trip, reading out flight times, insisting that he would pay the airfare.

Mary had something to tell him too: she had recently split up with Nathan's father, but now she had a new man in her life. She was very much in love with George and wanted him to meet her brother.

'Sure, you should bring him along,' Mike said. 'The more the merrier. I'm so happy for you.'

Easter fell in the middle of April. On the Thursday before, Mary and George flew from Tampa to Washington National and Pete came to the airport. Mary had hoped Mike might be there too, but Pete said he couldn't make it. On the drive out to West Virginia Mary sat up front, chatted about life and probed gently, but Pete's answer to all her questions was, 'You'll need to ask Mike.'

He came to the front porch to greet them. When she saw him,

she bit her lip. He was thin and stooped; his old bowling jacket hung loose on his emaciated frame. Mary wanted to cry. She composed herself and gave him a hug.

'It's good to see you, Bro. Are you OK?'

Mike struggled to smile and Mary saw tears in his eyes. He fought them back and extended a hand to George.

'Come on in, guys. You'll be needing a coffee and I've got some raspberry jam for you to try – won me first prize at the Shepherdstown fair. Of course, it was only me and Mrs Van Rooen who entered . . .'

Mike fussed over his visitors and listened to Mary's stories about Nathan and about Doc who had a new lady friend he was thinking of moving in with. But Mary was his focus – he kept looking at her and smiling, and when he brought in the drinks he sat down beside her and ran his fingers through her hair.

'You know, Sis,' he said, 'when we were kids I never thought I'd grow up to have a sister with so many beautiful blonde curls!'

Mary laughed, for the first time since they arrived.

'That's the wonder of peroxide, Mikey! Gets rid of grey hair in a trice. Looks like yours has stayed black and beautiful, though.'

Mike put his hand up to his head and ran it over his cropped scalp as if he were scared of discovering something unexpected and dreadful, then suddenly broke into a dazzling smile.

'Listen, guys,' he announced. 'I want to say something. Don't mind me, George; it's just I haven't seen this one in quite a while. I want to say how pleased I am, how happy it makes me . . . to have you here.' He swallowed. 'I've been thinking a lot about when we were kids growing up together, you and me, and I want you to know how much joy those memories hold. I want you to know how much I owe you for all those years and how much I appreciate you being there for me. You'll think I'm being sappy – maybe I am – but what I want to say is . . . how much I love you, Sis.'

Mike looked at the ceiling; Mary pulled out her handkerchief and ran out to the porch.

A minute later he went out to join her. 'Hey, Sis, I didn't want to make you cry . . .'

Mary looked at him, half smiling through her tears. Behind the mask of the invalid, behind the sunken eyes and sallow cheeks, she could see the Mike from long ago now – the caring child who had been buried under life's hard rind. Life might have made him harsh – bitter perhaps – but underneath was the same, wondering little boy.

'Oh, Mikey.' She sniffed. 'It's so beautiful what you said; it just made me so happy . . . and . . . and so sad.'

Mike took her arm. They leaned on the rail of the porch together, looking out over the peaceful green fields.

'You know, things have been tough,' Mike said. 'I've been kinda sick . . . In fact I've been real sick, Mary. It's AIDS.'

Mary began to weep. 'Oh Mikey, I knew it. I just *knew* things weren't right. I could tell right off. Mikey, poor, *poor* Mikey . . .'

But Mike gripped her arm and shook his head.

'No, wait, Sis. That's not the end of it. There's good news; that's what I got you here to tell you. They've come up with these new drugs and I've been chosen to try them, so there's hope . . . And, you know, I just have a feeling that I'm going to make it – you know how you get those feelings? And how usually they're never wrong?'

Mary squeezed his hand and forced herself to smile, but she couldn't say a word.

Over the next few days she saw how much Mike had changed; saw how much he had slowed down. He shuffled now where he used to bound about, and kept having to sit to catch his breath. He no longer ran the kitchen with his old dictatorial zeal – Pete had taken over cooking duties – and he spent a lot of time on the couch snuggled up with his dogs, Cashel and Finn McCool.

But for all his pain Mike stayed upbeat: he showed Mary the port stitched into his chest and gave her a tour of his medication, kept in a medical cooler in the hall. They sat on the porch, like they had when they were kids in Rockford, and talked. They laughed at old memories and wondered what their classmates from Boylan might think about little Mikey Hess and his rise to power and influence in the White House. Mary said how proud she was of her brother, and for a moment the cloud that hung over them seemed to disperse, but not for long.

'Mikey,' Mary asked, 'did you tell anyone – I mean, like Doc or the boys – that you've been sick?'

Mike shook his head.

'So I guess you don't want me to say anything, right? And Mikey, did you ever tell any of them that you're gay?'

Mike shrugged. 'You know, I don't see the point. None of them could care a dime about that . . . or about me. Maybe I'll call James and talk to him some day – he's the one who might listen.'

The conversation turned again and again to Ireland, and Mike told Mary about his last trip. 'It's the greatest regret I'll have,' he said, 'not finding my mom. I guess she could be dead or she's gone off and found a new life, but something tells me no; something tells me she's alive and hasn't forgotten me. You know, Mary, you should go find your mom while you still can: it's the one thing that can make all the difference to your life.'

Having come all the way to Washington, Mary and George wanted to make the most of their trip so rented a car and went off touring for a couple of weeks. When they came back to Shepherdstown on their way down to Florida, Mary thought Mike was worse.

Pete agreed. 'I don't think the drugs are working,' he said. 'I think he's been unlucky and they put him on the placebo instead of the real thing. But when I try and tell him to pull strings and get himself on the real medication, he just says he doesn't want to argue with the doctors. And the saddest thing is he thinks he's getting better.'

In the weeks after Mary's visit Mike was visited by all the plagues he had so remarkably avoided for the first twelve months. He had constant headaches now, dizziness and nausea. His fingernails were so black it looked like he was wearing polish; the muscles in his arms and in his legs had wasted to airy thinness; he had recurring liver problems and his hair was beginning to fall out. Pete felt Mike was disappearing in front of his eyes: one day he would simply melt into nothingness.

At first Mike had struggled never to miss a day of work: the obsessive thought that the party would discover he had AIDS and he would lose his job never left him, and he frequently went to the office when he should have been home in bed. By early summer he had given up the pretence. He had to spend more and more time in hospital – three days here, four days there – during which he would gather enough strength to be discharged, then begin the next slow decline that would bring him back through the same doors to the same ward and oftentimes the same bed.

His fear of what his colleagues would think of his increasing absences proved unfounded. Far from firing him, the RNC sent messages of support and encouragement. There were other gay men in the committee, like Finance Director Jay Banning and Mark Clacton in the redistricting team, who were especially helpful in taking over Mike's workload, but straight co-workers too – men and women – were quick to send him their sympathy. They couldn't fail to know he had AIDS, but they never wavered in their support. As he lay in GW Hospital with drips in his arms and machines monitoring his organs, Mike marvelled at the humanity of the individuals who made up the Republican leadership – and at the inhumanity of the policies that emerged from it. These were good people, yet few if any of them spoke out against the politics that shamed the name of their party.

By July Mike was spending more time off work than in his office. He was scheduled to attend a three-day planning meeting in Philadelphia for the following year's convention, but the morning he was due to travel felt tired and nauseous. Pete told him to stay home, but Mike insisted on going. He might not live to see the convention, but he was determined to make a contribution to it – it would be like extending his life.

Mike's wasted body wasn't up to it. On the first morning he collapsed in the meeting room and was taken in a limo to catch the train home. At Union Station in Washington he staggered from the carriage, his body bent under the weight of his bag, and waved to

Pete. As he watched Pete's face crumple, he fought back a tear. When Pete drove him to GW Hospital, he felt in his heart that they were making the trip for the last time. But hooked up to the drips he seemed to rally, and after twenty-four hours he was able to sit up and talk to the nurses. He thought the guy in the next bed looked familiar. They exchanged glances and Mike saw a similar glint of recognition in the other man's eyes.

'Hi,' Mike managed. 'We've met somewhere before, right? Michael Hess.'

'Oh my God, Michael Hess! We met at the party in Old Town Alexandria. It's me, Rudy Kellerman. I wouldn't have recognized you in a million years, you look so bad!'

Mike summoned up a picture of the small, chubby guy with an overbite who had harangued him about the administration's AIDS policies the night he was appointed deputy counsel.

'Well, you're not looking too great yourself,' Mike countered. 'The only positive thing I can say is you've slimmed down pretty good since I last saw you.'

'I sure have,' Rudy said mirthlessly. 'It's a programme called slimming to death and it looks like we're both on it.'

Silence descended as each man stirred memories of mutual resentment that refused to recede, even in the awfulness of their shared situation.

'Wanna read this magazine?' Rudy said eventually. 'Got a pretty good article in it about one of your guys – Arthur Finkelstein. You know him?'

Mike said of course he did; Finkelstein was one of the Republicans' leading strategists, working with senators on the conservative right like Jesse Helms and Don Nickles.

'Well, it seems the guy's gay!' Rudy announced. 'Been living with his lover and two adopted kids up in a mansion in Massachusetts for the past twenty years – all the time he's been churning out that homophobic bile you guys use to bash the queers!'

Mike scanned the copy of *Boston Magazine*. The article was a crude exercise in outing, listing the voting record of the senators Finkelstein had advised. All had opposed Clinton's anti gay-discrimination bill; all had voted against equal marriage rights for homosexuals; all had supported the Helms amendment on federal employees.

'So tell me, Michael,' Rudy was saying. 'How can a guy like Finkelstein sleep at night? Does he hate himself so much for being gay that he takes out his self-loathing on the rest of us? Did he join the Republicans because that gives him the platform he needs to flagellate the homo he despises in himself?'

Mike shifted in bed.

'Look,' he said. 'I don't know what Finkelstein thinks. And I can't speak for the party.'

'But you can speak for yourself, can't you?' Rudy snorted. 'Or were you just following orders like those Nazis at Nuremberg? It's *your* fault we're here dying, Michael; it's *you* who've condemned us to death, along with millions of others, because *your* party dismissed AIDS as a righteous punishment on the gays. How does it make you feel to know the drugs that could cure us are just around the corner – maybe just months away – but they'll be months *too late* for us because the goddam Republicans wouldn't start spending on a cure until it was too late!'

The argument went back and forth. Mike found the conversation enervating and distasteful. He hated Rudy's hectoring tone; there was no escape from his accusations and his glare. When Pete came to take him home Mike breathed a sigh of relief. He sat and stared straight ahead as the DC suburbs merged into the lush green woodlands on the far side of the Potomac.

'Pete?' he said. 'I think we need to go see the lawyers. Are you OK to come with me?'

TWENTY-THREE

1995

Doris White had been Mike and Pete's attorney for years. She liked 'the boys', as she called them, and she was shocked by the change she saw in Mike.

'Why, Michael!' she said, hurrying to bring him a chair and watching in horror as he lowered his emaciated body into it. 'Are you all right, dear? What can I get you? Coffee? Something to eat? You surely look like you could use it.'

Mike smiled.

'Thank you for being kind, but I don't think coffee's going to help me now. I've come to ask if you'll help me draw up my will.'

Doris went to fetch some files from a cabinet, came back to her desk and looked Mike in the eye.

'I surely will help you, Michael; it's not a difficult thing.' She hesitated. 'But first I want to . . . I'd like to say I'm very sorry . . . to see you this way. I've always considered you guys . . . Well, I'm fond of you. You don't . . . deserve this.' She coughed. 'Oh my, I'm so sorry. Now tell me, who are the beneficiaries you have in mind?'

Mike ran through his estate. The house in West Virginia and its ten acres of land he left in its entirety to 'Peter J. Nilsson, friend, unmarried'. Pete also got the proceeds of his life insurance policies, his personal effects, jewellery, silverware, furniture, pictures, books, objets d'art, automobiles and all other tangible personal property.

'Mary Harris, sister' got 90 per cent of his residual estate and all his US Savings Bonds. The other 10 per cent, he said, had to go to a place in Ireland, and he spelled out the name and address: 'Sean Ross Abbey of Roscrea, County Tipperary.'

By the time he had dealt with all the legal questions, Mike was exhausted.

'I see you have left nothing to your father, Dr Hess, or to your brothers,' Doris said. 'That is your call, of course, but I just need to check those are the arrangements you want.'

Mike was slouched in his chair now, white and frail.

'Doris,' he said, 'those are the arrangements. Maybe we should add another clause to avoid doubt. Can you put in, "I have intentionally not made provision for my father and brothers and any of their lineal descendants in this Will"? That should make things clear.'

Doris asked if he had any other questions before she sent the documents to be typed.

'Just one thing,' Mike replied. 'I'm kind of worried Doc will try and get me shipped off to be buried in the Hess family plot in Iowa, and that's something I don't want to happen. Pete knows my wishes about my final resting place, but I'm worried Doc will argue parental rights – that he'll try and contest it. Is there some legal way of making sure the right thing happens to me – when I'm gone?'

The conformed copies of Michael A. Hess's Last Will and Testament arrived in the mail a week later. Doris White's covering letter was a little apologetic.

> We have looked into the state of the law in the District of Columbia regarding the control of the disposition of one's remains. Unfortunately, there is no statute or other law protecting one's right to determine how one's remains are treated. Your father, as heir at law, would indeed have the power to determine how to dispose of your remains. As a practical matter, however, prearrangement, including

prepayment of costs, often helps to ensure that your preference will be honored. Once prearrangements are in place and
costs are paid, family members are often unwilling to finance
the additional costs to change the disposition arrangements.
Thus, we recommend that you make prearrangements at this
time and prepay the costs in full. If you do not have other
connections, you might try DeVol Funeral Home at 2222
Wisconsin Avenue, N.W., Washington, DC. Arrangements can
be made through them for West Virginia also.

If we can help in any other way, please do not hesitate to
call.

With kindest regards,

Sincerely,

Doris White

Mike sat in silence after reading Doris's letter. Pete was at the breakfast table making a pretence of reading the *Post*, but Mike knew he
was waiting for him to speak.

'Well, that's it, Pete. This paper here says you get my worldly
goods.' He sighed and smiled. 'And my heart says you get my love
forever.' Mike felt tears sting his eyes; his throat tightened. 'I'm sorry
we could never get married – what a wedding we could have had! We
could have invited everyone out to the house – then you would have
had an anniversary to remember and celebrate.'

Pete came to sit on the sofa. Mike could barely lift his arm to
take his hand.

'The letter's about remains. Here, you take it and read it. But
what will remain of *me*, do you think? Of the real me?'

Pete kissed him on the cheek.

'*You'll* remain, Mike. You'll remain with me. I'll always miss you,
and I'll always love you.'

'Thank you.' Mike's voice trembled. 'I'll miss you' – the strange-
ness of the idea prompted an involuntary smile – 'but I won't miss
myself. Because the truth is I never knew *who* I was. I'm looking
back on my life because of this' – he motioned to the document

lying on his knee – 'and it just feels like I never found anywhere I could fit.'

Pete made to object, but Mike shook his head.

'I've always been an orphan. I never had any ties in this world, and when I wanted to find some the nuns turned me away. Then I tried to build an identity, but I got it all wrong. The party gave me somewhere I felt I could belong, but Rudy's right – I had to sell out to get it. And most of all I wanted the love and solace of being with you, Pete; but I ruined it by doing . . . this.' He gestured weakly to his wasted body. 'I love you, Pete. I always loved you, but I blew it, and it's death that puts an end to love.'

The last week Mike spent at home in Shepherdstown was hard. He listened to music, started drinking in the mornings and spent the afternoons calling friends. Frequently he called them back the following morning to apologize for the rage, the despair or the self-pity of the previous day's call.

In the evenings Pete came home to find Mike stretched out on the couch. He offered his hand; Mike sometimes took it and sometimes not. It seemed pointless to ask, 'Are you OK?' but Pete asked anyway. If Mike was willing to be comforted, he smiled and asked how Pete's day had been. But more often he was not open to sympathy, pulling a bitter face and turning to the wall. Pete knew not to insist on talking; he found other paths – subtle detours, tender subterfuges – that would allow him admission to Mike's inner world. Sometimes he simply went to the kitchen and prepared the ingredients for their favourite dishes – a bouillabaisse or saddle of veal with ginger and spring onions. The power of the aromas – the sharp sea-tinted tang of the bubbling fish, the enveloping warmth of the slow-cooking meat – wakened memories in Mike that roused him. He lifted himself from the sofa and shuffled through to the kitchen in his thick felt slippers. Silently he would put his hand on Pete's shoulder – a signal of truce, a signal that now he wished for the comfort he had rejected.

On Monday 7 August, in the middle of the afternoon, Mike fell and lay helpless on the wooden floor of the living room for over an hour before he could drag himself to the phone. Pete immediately drove out to the house and together they took the familiar trip into DC, along the Parkway, over Key Bridge and down K Street to the ER entrance of George Washington Hospital. The specialist who had been treating Mike grimaced at his condition. He was taken to a private room in the monitoring unit and remained there for the next six days. By Sunday morning, 13 August, his condition had improved a little and he was transferred to a regular ward. The move seemed to lift his spirits and he talked optimistically about a vacation in Italy. Pete went home for a few hours, but in the afternoon the hospital called to say Mike had crashed and Pete should get back as quick as he could. He found Mike semi-conscious and on life support in the intensive care unit. The doctor said they had had to resuscitate him with oxygen and were uncertain about his outlook. When Pete squeezed his hand, Mike responded. He could nod or shake his head, but he could no longer talk.

Pete called Mary in Florida and she made the last flight that day up to Washington. She asked Mike if he wanted her to tell Doc and the boys what was happening, but he shook his head, his eyes bright with fevered determination. She asked him again and his response was unmistakably negative.

For the next twenty-four hours Mike hovered in a limbo of unknowing. Then late on Monday night alarms sounded on the monitoring equipment by his bed and the emergency resuscitation team came running. When the panic was over, a doctor told Pete and Mary he had slipped into a coma and asked if they wanted to consider switching off life support. For the rest of the night they discussed it by his bedside. Mike had made a living will asking not to be kept alive, but for Mary the situation brought back sad memories of the decision they had taken with Marge. Pete agreed and the machines were left to grumble and bubble.

Early on Tuesday morning Pete mentioned Mike's dying wish to be buried in Sean Ross Abbey, and Mary said he had told her the exact same thing.

'Look,' Pete muttered, rubbing his face. 'Sorry for being practical at such an emotional time, but we need to discuss arrangements. I got a bunch of stuff . . .'

He handed her a booklet he'd picked up from the Irish embassy and pointed out the section about transferring human remains: 'Documentary evidence of the cause of death must accompany the coffin . . . and in the case of death from an infectious disease the Chief Medical Officers have special powers to dispose of the remains.'

Early on the morning of Tuesday 15 August, after thirty-six hours at Mike's bedside, Mary and Pete went to the cafeteria for coffee. They returned at 11.30 to find Mike's bed empty and the doctor writing up his notes. Mike had suffered a series of cardiac arrests. He had died at 11.10 a.m.

TWENTY-FOUR

1956–89
Thursday 22 November 1956

The waves were tossing the boat with a roar that seemed to rise out of the darkening depths of the heaving water.

The girl pulled her raincoat tight around her neck and ducked into the warmth of the bar. The place scared her with its smell of stale beer and the men singing and shouting all night, but it was nine hours from Liverpool to Dublin and she had to shelter somewhere. The storm had overtaken them around midnight, with the wind and rain driving across the Irish Sea, and the SS *Munster* was rolling in the swell. The girl felt nauseous and lonely. She had on a thin cotton frock under a translucent pakamac with the hood pulled down over her jet-black hair. In her hand she clutched a bag with her passport and ticket and a bunch of photographs. When they made port in Dublin she said a Hail Mary.

The Irish customs officers, instructed to question girls travelling alone on Irish passports, picked her out as the passengers disembarked.

'So were you *over there* for an abortion, then?' the senior officer asked. 'Did you go and kill your child?'

But she shook her head. The other customs man was young and not above flirting. 'So, what is it? Been gallivanting over in Liverpool, have you?'

The girl stayed tight-lipped.

'Well, you'll have to tell me – I can't guess.'

She looked at him with accusing eyes.

'I've come back here to *look* for my baby.'

At Sean Ross Abbey Mother Barbara was dismissive. She remembered the girl well enough and had always suspected she was a trouble-maker.

'I have no idea what you want from us,' she said. 'You gave away your child and the Church found a home for him. The Church acts on its duty of charity; sinners like you should be grateful.'

'Oh yes, I know,' the girl said. She was twenty-three now and out of Sean Ross for ten months, but she felt the same panic and dread. 'I *am* grateful, very grateful . . . I just wondered if you would tell me where he's gone, so I can—'

'Listen to me, girl,' Mother Barbara cut in. 'You seem to have forgotten what you promised. You signed a pledge in the eyes of God to relinquish your child. You promised you would *never* to try to see him or make any claim to him. Do you not remember that? Because we have everything written down in our records, you know.'

'But Mother Superior,' Philomena said, 'I *tried* . . . I tried to forget him, but I couldn't. As the Lord's my witness, he's been in my thoughts every hour of every day since he drove away from here in the back of that car and I was sent to England. On the ferry last night when the storm struck us, I could see his little face in the clouds every time the lightning flashed, and he was calling out to me, so he was!'

'Oh, don't talk nonsense, girl.' Mother Barbara's patience was wearing thin. 'Your child is miles away from here and he can no more speak to you than the man in the moon.'

'But he did, Reverend Mother. He called out to me and I heard him. He's missing me and he wants his mammy back. A mother can tell . . . And I need to know he's all right – that he's safe where he is, and not sad. I can never be at peace until I know.'

But Mother Barbara had no time for the feelings of sinners.

'You can find no peace because your sin weighs upon you. Your sin will be with you always and you must make amends for it. Pray to God that He will forgive you, for I cannot.'

Philomena bowed her head. Her sin *was* with her and it soured her life. Because of it she felt her confidence drain away. She wanted the interview to be over now, before Mother Barbara made things even worse. But the nun had not finished.

'You must forget your child, for he is the product of sin, and above all you must never speak of him to anyone.The fires of hell await sinners like you, and if you go talking about your baby to other people you will burn in them forever. You have not spoken of your sin, have you? Or of what was done with your child?'

Philomena had spoken to no one.

Her joy and her shame were buried deep within her. Because of them her existence had been changed forever; because of them she was taking the night boat back to England now, condemned to live in a foreign place.

After Anthony left Roscrea in December 1955, Philomena had cried for two weeks. To get her off their hands, the sisters had put her on the ferry from Dublin, and on 14 January 1956 she had begun work in their school for delinquent boys outside Liverpool.

The Sisters of the Sacred Hearts of Jesus and Mary had run the Ormskirk Approved School for decades. Generations of sinful girls from Ireland had worked there, caring for the lads and repaying their debt to God. Philomena hated it; she pitied the boys and sympathized with their fate, but at the first opportunity she left.

In January 1958 she applied to train as a nurse and was accepted by a psychiatric hospital in the town of St Albans just north of London. She worked with disturbed patients at Hill End Hospital and came to recognize the terrible impact mental trauma can have. The more she learned about the men and women in her care, the more she understood the mental cruelty she herself had been subjected to. Every day she thought of her lost child and every night she saw him in her dreams. For a dozen years, first in Liverpool and then in St Albans, she lived with her pain and loss. She had a drawer full of memories – the tiny black and white photos from Sister Annunciata's Box Brownie; a child's first pair of shoes, black leather with a little chrome buckle that was loose from wear; a lock of jet-black hair that she treasured like a holy relic.

In the 1960s she worried Anthony might be in Vietnam fighting for the country that had taken him from her; in times of economic hardship she worried he might be in jail or on skid row. But it was the absence of knowledge, the absence of certainty that haunted her most – if she knew nothing it meant he could be anything or anywhere, and the thought was immensely disturbing.

Philomena married a young male nurse by the name of John Libberton and had two children, Kevin and Jane, but she never told her new family her secret – Mother Barbara's warnings of hellfire were still too vivid. She did not stop thinking and planning, though, and in September 1977 she went back to Roscrea.

Philomena did not know why she chose that month of that year – she had no inkling that Anthony, now Michael, had been there just three weeks earlier – but when she sat in the nuns' parlour with Mother Barbara she sensed something strange about the way the woman spoke to her. It was not that she was any more helpful – the mother superior still refused to speak about the fate of Philomena's child – but she was quieter now, less categorical in her opinions and more hesitant in condemning the sins she had denounced so fiercely in the past. They parted with a sense that something had shifted between them, that they had become linked, not by friendship or understanding, but by a mutual interest and a shared need for forgiveness.

Philomena saw Mother Barbara for the last time in 1989. She had divorced John five years before and was now married to Philip Gibson. She was in her mid-fifties, no longer the naive young girl who had been bullied and coerced by the nuns, and Mother Barbara was an old woman with less than a year to live. The conversation was strained. Philomena wanted to ask, 'If my son had been here looking for me, you would tell me, wouldn't you?' but she did not, and the nun volunteered nothing. In her eighties, crippled by arthritis, her eyes filled with rheumy tears as they drank tea and spoke about the past, the fire had gone from Mother Barbara – she appeared sad and resigned. Philomena wondered if she regretted never having children of her own and the thought made her feel sorry for her. A couple of times Mother Barbara seemed close to apologizing for what had happened, but each time something held her back. It was only later that Philomena learned questions were starting to be asked about the Church's role in the baby trade with America – and that, perhaps, was why she had hesitated.

Philomena returned to England convinced this had been her last visit to Roscrea.

Epilogue

Pete Nilsson's speech at Michael Hess's funeral service,
St Peter's parish church, Washington DC, 21 August 1995

I have spent the last few days trying to understand Michael's passing. I'm not sure I've succeeded because deep down I know Michael did not want to go ... He had so much he still wanted to do ... For someone who looked forward to achieving so much more in life, how do you justify his passing? The answer is simply – you can't. Michael left us before his time and fought hard all the way. He wanted to go on living until the very end. Keeping his illness to himself was his way of focusing on life and not giving in to death. When he finally went, he went very quickly. One of the great mysteries of death is where does all this knowledge and intensity go when someone closes their eyes for the last time? I hope it has gone to each of us in some way. I know that I am a different person for having known Michael over the past fifteen years – a better person. It is with that comfort that I say goodbye to him now, knowing that – through us – he will live on. Many of you who have shared a drink with Michael know that he liked to quote a toast from Yeats, and I'd like to end by making that toast to Michael:

> *Wine comes in at the mouth*
> *And love comes in at the eye;*
> *That's all we shall know for truth*
> *Until we grow old and die.*
> *I lift the glass to my mouth,*
> *I look at you, and I sigh.*

When Jane Libberton came to meet me at the British Library that New Year of 2004, she brought with her the snaps of Anthony that Sister Annunciata had been caring enough to take all those years before. She told me everything she had gleaned from her mother – the name of her lost brother; that he was born on 5 July 1952; that he had been taken to America by an unknown woman; that he had blue eyes and black hair.

We agreed that we did not have much to go on. The name of Anthony Lee would not help us – he would almost certainly have taken the name of his new family – and Philomena's experience of seeking information from the nuns at Sean Ross did not bode well. I was close to concluding the whole thing was a wild goose chase. I was about to tell Jane I wasn't interested, but I didn't.

Philomena's family had grown over the years. Every time a grand-child or great-grandchild was born – especially when she found Jane pregnant and a single mother at the age of seventeen – she had been desperate to tell her children they had a brother in America. Philomena's own brother Jack had told their sisters Kaye and Mary about the little fellow from Sean Ross Abbey and they had all urged her to tell her family, but the hold of the Church was abiding and cruel and Philomena kept her secret for fifty years.

Jane had often noticed her mother got sentimental just before Christmas. She would start talking about her childhood and the bad old days with tears in her eyes, and Jane had never understood the reason for it. In 2003 she found out. On 18 December Philomena had a couple of glasses of sherry and, fuelled by alcohol and long-repressed emotions, told her children of her secret disgrace. She told them this was the anniversary of the day their brother had been taken away from her; that he was living in America now and would be fifty-one years old.

As Philomena talked, Jane had gone to the drawer in her mother's sideboard and pulled out the black and white photographs of the little boy she had always been told was a distant cousin somewhere in rural Ireland. Philomena had said, 'That's him.'

The three of us travelled to Sean Ross Abbey in the spring of 2004. The nuns were lovely. None of them had been there in the 1950s: Mother Barbara and Sister Hildegarde were dead – we photographed their graves in the carefully tended nuns' cemetery – and the convent records showed that brave young Sister Annunciata, Mary Kelly of the Limerick Kellys, had not lived to see her thirtieth birthday but had died in England soon after her transfer to London in 1955. The current mother superior was a friendly, educated woman from the outskirts of Liverpool who had devoted her life to the care of disadvantaged and disabled people, making Sean Ross a haven for youngsters with cerebral palsy and other debilitating conditions. The nuns were evidently used to enquiries from former inmates of the mother-and-baby home: when we explained the purpose of our visit, they began a practised routine involving tea and cakes in the parlour, the viewing of albums of old photographs and seemingly genuine expressions of sympathy for those who had suffered.

'We can't take away your pain,' the mother superior said, 'but we can walk through it with you hand in hand.'

We visited the chapel where Philomena and Annunciata had sung in the choir, and the corridor where Philomena was beaten by the angry nun. The girls' dormitories and the children's nurseries were still there, but the French windows were broken and the long rooms were empty and abandoned – birds had made their nests in the beams and the parquet floors were littered with chunks of plaster. The laundries where Philomena had toiled to wash away the stain of her sins were gone, flattened to make way for disabled housing. The remains of the medieval monastery still stood, three ruined walls covered in ivy with an oak tree growing within them, but the mother superior told us the council had warned they were dangerously unstable and the order would have to find the money to underpin them, money the nuns did not have. On a patch of bright green grass by the old Georgian convent house a white maypole stood ribbonless in front of a tall alabaster angel.

We thanked the nuns for letting us see the place and raised again the purpose of our visit: would they be kind enough to show us the adoption records of Anthony Lee? The mother superior said she would love to help, but any records that still remained had been sent to a centralized office at a convent in Cork which now dealt with archives from all the old orphanages. She gave us the name of the place and the nun who ran it, and we left. On the way out I took photographs of the convent and of the three very different graveyards – the one for the nuns, the recently tidied field where the mothers and babies were interred and the ancient burial ground in the shadow of the ruined monastery.

Back in England, Philomena phoned the number the nuns had provided. It was for the Sacred Heart Adoption Society in the Bessboro Convent in Cork, and her call was answered by the head of the agency, Sister Sarto Harney. Sister Sarto promised to look in the records. Her letter, a couple of weeks later, contained no new information.

Dear Mrs Gibson,

You were admitted to Roscrea on 6 May 1952 and discharged on 14 January 1956. Anthony was born on 5 July 1952 at 7 p.m., breech delivery, weight 7 lb 10 oz., a full-term baby. Anthony was discharged for US adoption on 18 December 1955.

Letters to the Irish Adoption Board brought equally negative results – they had no record of any Anthony Lee – and a prompt but disappointing reply came back from the Foreign Ministry.

Dear Mrs Gibson,

I can confirm that this Department had papers in connection with the issue of a passport for Anthony Lee so that he could travel to the United States for adoption. The file, 345/96/755, access to which is restricted, as with all similar files, is now in the custody of the National Archives. I am mindful of the restrictions on access to certain information which arise from the constitutional right to privacy and the requirements of the National Archives Act, 1986.

I enclose herewith a copy of the sworn statement that you made on 27 June 1955, surrendering Anthony Lee to the Superioress of Sean Ross Abbey and authorizing her to make him available for adoption.

You may wish to contact the Sacred Heart Adoption Society in Cork, where the records of Sean Ross Abbey are now kept.

Our search had run into the sand. Confidentiality and restricted access were constant official themes. The Irish Foreign Ministry referred us to the Sacred Heart Adoption Society and the Sacred Heart Adoption Society referred us to the Foreign Ministry.

But an unexpected breakthrough gave us new hope.

Shortly after the disappointing news from the Foreign Ministry, the photographs of our visit to Sean Ross Abbey came back from being printed. Jane and I pored over the pictures of the convent, the derelict nurseries and the graveyards in the convent grounds. We saw the crosses marking the graves of Mother Barbara and Sister Hildegarde in the nuns' cemetery with their dates of death neatly recorded, and we saw the sad memorials to dead babies and dead mothers, erected after the orphanage had closed by parents and relatives. A stone tablet read, 'This garden is dedicated to the babies and infants who died in Sean Ross Abbey and are buried here. May they from their place in Heaven pray for us who loved them on earth.' The burial ground had no marked graves, but around its edges small plaques had begun to appear to dead children – 'Martin: 29.10.1945 to 28.12.1945'; 'Daughter, our memories of you will never grow old; they are locked in our hearts in letters of gold' – and to young mothers who died in childbirth – 'Josephine Dillon, aged 28 years. RIP'; 'Mary J. Lawlor, aged 14½ years. RIP'. Among the memorials, one caught our eye: 'In loving memory of

Anthony: If tears could build a stairway, / And memories a lane, / We could walk the way to Heaven / And take you back again.' The name jumped out, but this Anthony was a baby who had died at birth.

Jane picked up a photo for a last look. It showed a new and rather shiny gravestone that was neither in the nuns' cemetery nor the field of mothers and babies. This one was in the shadow of the ruined walls of the ancient monastery, amid old headstones overgrown with grass and covered in moss. The name on the inscription was unfamiliar to us, but Jane spotted something: the birth date was the same as that of Philomena's son Anthony – 5 July 1952. The photograph was blurred and it took two enlargements and a magnifying glass to read the carved silver lettering on the black marble background.

Michael A. Hess.
A Man of Two Nations and Many Talents.
Born July 5, 1952, Sean Ross Abbey, Roscrea.
Died August 15, 1995, Washington DC, USA.

It was the only gravestone in the whole of the abbey that did not belong to a nun or a mother or child who had died there. It could be that another baby had been born on the same day but now there was the terrible possibility that Philomena's search had brought her to Anthony only to discover he was forever beyond her reach.

We renewed contact with the Church archivists. An enquiry to the Sacred Heart Adoption Society brought a polite letter from Sister Sarto: it did not confirm that Anthony Lee was one and the same as Michael Hess, but it did make the offer of a personal conversation with Philomena. When the phone rang a week later, she was in an agony of uncertainty.

Sister Sarto's first words raised her hopes: 'Mrs Gibson, I have news for you about Anthony.' Then she asked, 'Do you have anyone with you?' Philomena confirmed she was not alone and sat down. 'Mrs Gibson,' Sister Sarto said, 'I'm so sorry, but your son is no longer alive . . .'

Philomena wept. She was distraught. She blamed herself for not speaking about Anthony earlier, while he might still have been found. It was hard to know what to say to a mother who has lost her child not once but twice.

'You mustn't blame yourself,' I said a little lamely. 'It's not your fault.'

But she did blame herself.

'If only, Martin, if only. I curse myself every time I think of it. If only I'd mentioned it all those years ago, maybe he wouldn't . . . But it was so ingrained down deep in my heart that I mustn't tell anybody. We were browbeaten; it was such a sin. Then I thought we'd found him, but now he's gone forever! Oh Lord, it makes my heart ache! All those years I used to worry about him and I wanted to speak about him. I'm sure there are lots of women to this very day – they're the same as me; they haven't said anything. All the time I was thinking *Lord, I wish I knew* . . . It was a secret I kept all my life, but I've never stopped praying for him, praying for Anthony, and maybe now he's up there in heaven . . .'

Philomena spent the weeks after the discovery of her son's death planning to visit his grave. She went in the summer of 2004 and had a Mass said on his birthday. She gave the nuns money to put flowers by his headstone and engaged a local gardener to plant a tree in his memory. It calmed her. She seemed more resigned to the second loss of her child, even if consumed with regrets. We spoke about continuing the hunt for Michael Hess, as we now knew him, and eventually she said yes, she did want us to keep looking.

We knew Michael's name and we knew his birth date. We did not know where he had lived in the US or what sort of work he had been engaged in, but something stirred my memory. I had been the BBC's Washington correspondent from 1991 to 1995 at the end of George Bush Senior's presidency, and I recalled that I had come across a senior White House official named Michael Hess, but this was well over a decade before, and most of my Republican contacts had left or retired.

While I worked on the White House connection, we followed our last Irish lead, the marble headstone in the shadow of the ruined monastery. Roscrea is not a big town and there is only one stone-mason. We wrote to ask if he would tell us who had brought Michael Hess to be buried in the place of his birth.

We were still waiting for his reply when I heard back from Jill Holtzman Vogel in Washington. Jill was a recently elected Republican state senator in Virginia, having previously served as George Bush Junior's counsel in the contentious Florida recount that swung the 2000 election. In an email in January 2005 she confirmed that Anthony Lee, the little Irish orphan, had grown up to become Michael Hess, chief counsel of the Republican National Committee.

> I did not know Michael personally, but I joined the RNC Counsel's Office in 1997 and Michael's legacy was still very fresh. They talked about him all the time. He was clearly loved and respected by the people there and he was part of a lot of office lore. I am really touched by your effort to help Michael's mother. I will forward your contact information to the people that I know were close to him and I hope they will be able to assist you. Jill.

I forwarded Jill's email to Jane and got an immediate reply.

> Dear Martin
>
> Thank you so much for passing on the email from Jill Holtzman Vogel. You have no idea how much it pleased my mum to hear such nice things about Anthony. Although she shed a few tears, I think it makes her feel a bit better to know that he was so obviously liked by people who knew or knew of him. Any little piece of information is just so precious to her and it would be so good if we can find out even more. The months since we heard about his death have been hard, and I think hearing some positive things about him really does help her. Jane.

On Jill's recommendation I flew to Washington and spoke with many of Michael Hess's professional colleagues in the Republican Party, including the current leaders of the Republican National Committee. I spoke to the RNC secretaries who had worked with him, and all were effusive.

'He was a lovely man; he was very gentle,' said Nancy Hibbs, who first met Michael when she was a twenty-three-year-old administrative assistant. 'I remember when I met him I thought he was one of the most attractive men I'd ever seen. He was adorable. I was very young, but he was a very, really nice guy and such a gentleman. He had a stressful job, but he never was unkind to anybody. Held a door for a lady, you know . . . please and thank you; never ordered anybody around. Used to bring all the girls roses from his house in the country. We work with a lot of people who – especially then, when I was younger – people who were very brusque with young people, but he never was.'

Mark Braden, initially Michael's boss at the RNC, spoke about the importance of his redistricting work for the party.

'He was a brilliant lawyer. We are all the children of his litigation, our litigation back in the early and mid-eighties. Redistricting was a big deal. We took a lot of political heat over that . . . but Michael was the developer of all the theories and arguments. Without them . . . the Republicans would not have been able to win a majority in 1994. They would not have got the majority they got . . . so his legacy lives on. He was one of my closest friends. It was a tragedy when he died.'

After a week in Washington I felt I understood the public side of Michael Hess, but the private man eluded me. His sexuality remained cloaked. Nancy Hibbs at the Republican National Committee made it clearer.

'We all knew he was gay. But nobody talked about it because, as you can imagine, the Republican Party . . . It was a different time then. And he was so handsome – that beautiful black hair and piercing eyes – so of course all the girls were like, Oh, what a darn shame!'

Eventually a Washington contact told me, 'You must talk to Pete Nilsson,' and that same evening at the Watergate Hotel I found a message from my wife: the Roscrea stonemason said the man who ordered the monument for Michael's grave was – Pete Nilsson. I found Pete's contact details with little trouble, but he was out of town and would not be back before my return to London. I left him a message and he called me in England: he had heard about my research and was willing to talk to me.

Philomena, Jane and I met Pete Nilsson at my house in London in April 2005.

The information Pete provided at that and several subsequent interviews, together with the introductions he provided to other people in Michael's life, made the writing of this book possible. But more than that, it gave Philomena the cathartic reassurance that her actions had not blighted her son's life – that he had never stopped loving his birth mother, and had never stopped seeking for her.

Pete brought photographs and mementos of Michael, and Philomena and Jane soaked up every image. They wanted every detail Pete could give them, every success Michael had known. Philomena marvelled at the standard of life he and Pete had enjoyed.

'He had a good life, didn't he? I could have never given him all of that,' she said. 'I couldn't have given him that, Peter.'

Philomena was unconcerned that her child had been gay. She embraced Pete almost as a substitute son. Michael had been *hers*, with *her* black hair and *her* musical talent. She urged Pete to tell her that Doc and Marge had been kind parents; she was delighted to hear that Michael and Mary had stayed so close and that they had considered themselves brother and sister for life – the thought seemed to comfort her. But there was also shock and anger when Pete said that Michael had lived his whole life not knowing if she had abandoned him at birth or if she had been with him in the convent.

The idea that the mothers had given up their babies right after they were born was one the nuns seemed deliberately to have fostered, perhaps out of shame that they had kept the girls working as virtual prisoners for three years and more. Mother Barbara and Sister Hildegarde had deliberately misled Michael and Mary when they visited the convent. The lies seared Philomena. 'How could they tell him I abandoned him! How could they do that! I never wanted to give him away – never!'

Pete spoke of his visit to Roscrea with Mike in 1993, and Philomena was outraged that the nuns had not told them her family lived just down the road. But she was consoled that Michael had never given up his search for her.

'Oh now, that is what I always felt. I felt he wanted to find me . . . that he must have wanted to find me. And that is why I wondered so often if he came, you know. Somehow there must have been something, because all my life I have sensed it and all my life I have never, ever forgotten him. I have prayed for him every day. I was sure one day I would find him.'

Pete told her of the day they sat in the ruins of the old abbey and of Michael's wish to be brought back to be buried in Ireland. She wept when Pete spoke of his death and the funeral service the Republican Party arranged for him in the shadow of the Capitol. Pete had the order of service from the Mass and showed her the names of the Republican luminaries who attended; he told her of the personal phone call from Nancy Reagan on behalf of herself and the former president and of the moving eulogies from Mark Braden and Robert Hampden. Pete listed the pall-bearers who carried Michael's body from the church and he told Philomena how 'Danny Boy' was played as the coffin, draped in the flag that had flown over the Capitol, went slowly down the aisle. He spoke of the extravagant 'Irish' wake that was held for Mike and the sympathy of the Republican officials who attended an overwhelmingly gay occasion.

But he also told Philomena that Doc Hess and two of his sons had come to Washington for the funeral Mass. There Doc announced that he intended to take possession of Michael's estate, his insurance money, his share of the apartment in town and the house in West Virginia. Pete had had to show him Mike's will in which everything had been left to him. There were arguments too over where Mike would be buried. Doc tried to have his body taken to Iowa, and Pete brought in their lawyer to stop him. In the course of their dealings Pete came to realize that Doc and his sons had never known that

Michael was gay; now they were discovering that he had died of AIDS. The conversations were difficult. Doc and his boys were unfriendly and dismissive towards Pete. They left Washington without saying goodbye and never contacted him again.

Philomena asked how Pete had managed to get Michael buried in Roscrea, and Pete told the whole story. Mike's body had been cremated at the Metropolitan Crematory in Alexandria, Virginia, and Pete had written to ask the mother superior of Sean Ross Abbey if she would agree to his dying wish.

> Dear Sister Christina,
>
> It is with sadness that I write this letter . . . Although Michael lived a very happy and successful life in the United States, his last wish was to have his ashes returned to the place of his birth . . . Michael's emotional connection to the Abbey ran deep and I would not feel true to his wishes by burying him anywhere else. Michael asked that a donation be made to the Abbey in his name.
>
> > Throughout his life he held his Irish roots very close to his heart. I know he will only truly be able to rest in peace if he returns to the Abbey . . .

Pete explained that the deal had been brokered by an Irish priest called Father Leonard: 'I'd met Father Leonard socially when he'd been to the States. He was one of those Irish priests who were the core strength of the Irish Church. I said, "I really want to get Michael buried at Roscrea in the grounds, but they don't have it open for burials." I said, "See what you can do. I'm ready to donate a big chunk. Tell them I'll send them a cheque and see if we can make it work." He called me back the next day.'

The burial took place on 9 May 1996 and Father Leonard officiated. Pete produced a copy of the priest's funeral oration: 'We are about to lay to rest the mortal remains of Michael Hess . . . Michael set out from this place in 1955. After a very successful life and career

in the United States, he has returned to the land of his forebears . . .
He is now at peace.'

All paths in the search for Philomena's lost child had led back to
Roscrea and the convent where his story began.

After speaking to Pete Nilsson, I talked to the other significant people
in Michael's life, including Robert Hampden, Susan Kavanagh, Ben
Kronfeld, Mark Braden, John Clarkson and Mark O'Connor, who
later emailed me: 'Martin, one final thought I should share is that
while we were young and frivolous back then, and not so serious
about relationships, Michael was my first love, with all the intensity
that implies. I miss him very much.'

Susan told me Michael's death had left her bereft. 'When I think
of Michael, I try not to focus on all the end stuff, which is very sad.
When I think about him I just think of how much fun we had. It was
always, 'What are we going to do? Are we going to do this or are we
going to do that?' I just remember everything was an event; he always
made things special. And I think, God, life has gotten so boring
without him.'

Most importantly, Pete put me in touch with Mary, Michael's
sister in life if not in blood. She lives in Florida near her grandchildren and looks back on her odyssey with the little boy from Roscrea
with an awareness of how different things could have been. If Anthony
Lee had not tugged at the heart of Marge Hess that day in August
1955, Mary would have flown alone on the night flight from Shannon
to America; she would have been alone with her new family that
Christmas in St Louis, and she would have faced the rest of her life
without the support of her closest friend. She has been back to Roscrea
herself; she has taken her new husband there; and she is talking of
following Mike's example and searching for her own birth mother.
She lives in the certitude that she will one day be reunited with her
brother.

'Michael was my confidant and I was his all through our lives. I
have missed him so much these past years since he's been gone . . .

When I was in Roscrea I was talking with the mother superior and I told her, "Really, you know when I die I would like to be brought over and buried here. Is it going to be a problem for me to be buried next to my brother?" Because when Michael was buried there nobody had opened a grave in a hundred years so they had to get special permission to do that. Now, she told me that if I wanted to be buried at Roscrea then I could be buried where the nuns are buried; she said I could be buried in that graveyard, you know, and I kind of thought about it and that would be OK, but I would rather be next to my brother.'

Philomena goes regularly to Roscrea and I have stood with her at her son's graveside. It is over fifty years since she last talked to him in life, but she talks to him now.

'Thank God you are home again in Ireland, son. You're here where I can visit you now . . . But you came here and no one told you anything. No one told you I was looking for you and I loved you, my son. How different it all would have been . . .'

The quest to find Anthony has come to an end, but there is one final thread. On behalf of Philomena, I spoke to the archivists of the Irish government and the Limerick post office in search of a tall dark civil servant named John McInerney. He was in his early twenties when he met Philomena Lee at the Limerick Carnival on the Ennis Road in October 1951. Some lines of enquiry have emerged and are being pursued, but that, as they say, is a story for another occasion.